THE COLLECTED WORKS

OF

C. G. JUNG

VOLUME 9, PART I

EDITORS

†SIR HERBERT READ

MICHAEL FORDHAM, F.R.C.PSYCH., HON. F.B.PS.S.

GERHARD ADLER, PH.D.

WILLIAM MCGUIRE, *executive editor*

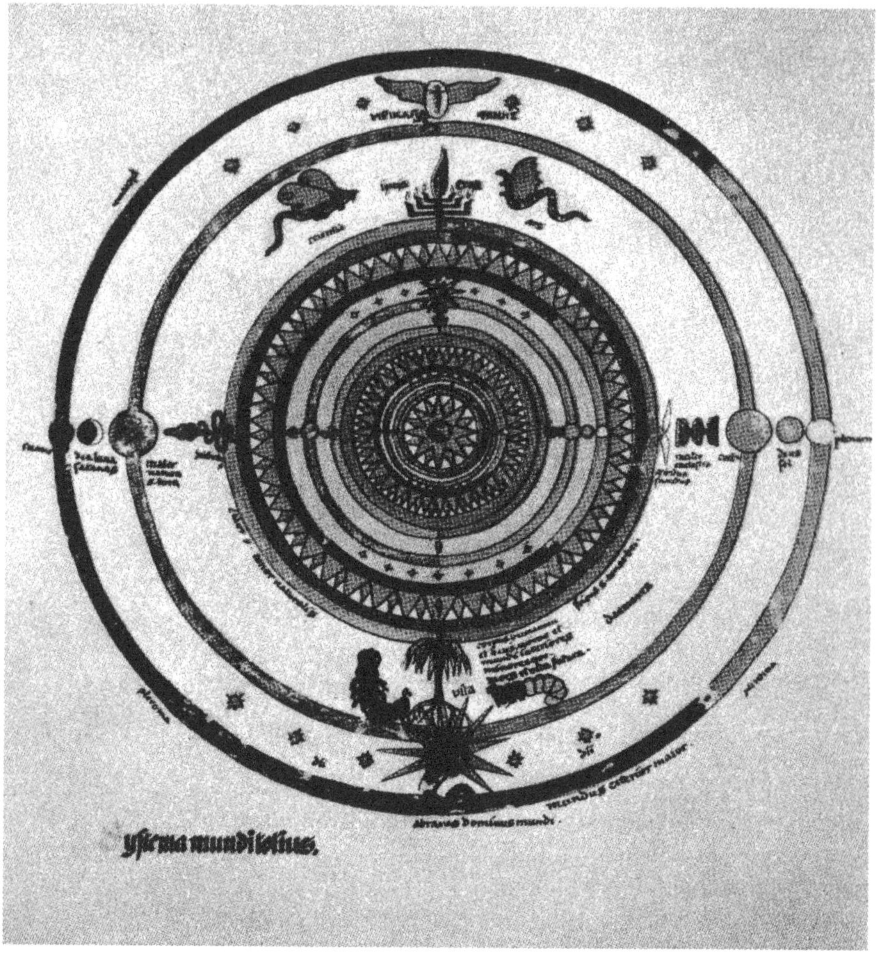

Mandala of a Modern Man

THE ARCHETYPES AND THE COLLECTIVE UNCONSCIOUS

SECOND EDITION

C. G. JUNG

TRANSLATED BY R. F. C. HULL

Routledge
Taylor & Francis Group
LONDON AND NEW YORK

FIRST PUBLISHED IN ENGLAND IN 1959
BY ROUTLEDGE & KEGAN PAUL LTD

Second Edition 1968

THIS EDITION PUBLISHED 2014 BY ROUTLEDGE
27 CHURCH ROAD, HOVE, EAST SUSSEX BN3 2FA
711 THIRD AVENUE, NEW YORK, NY 10017, USA

FIRST PUBLISHED IN PAPERBACK BY
ROUTLEDGE IN 1991

Routledge is an imprint of the Taylor & Francis Group, an Informa business

THIS EDITION IS BEING PUBLISHED IN THE UNITED KINGDOM BY ROUTLEDGE, AND BY PRINCETON UNIVERSITY PRESS, IN THE UNITED STATES OF AMERICA, UNDER THE SPONSORSHIP OF BOLLINGEN FOUNDATION. THE PRESENT VOLUME IS NUMBER 9 OF THE COLLECTED WORKS AND WAS THE EIGHTH TO APPEAR. IT IS IN TWO PARTS, PUBLISHED SEPARATELY, THIS BEING PART 1.

ISBN: 978-1-032-60114-4 (hbk)

EDITORIAL NOTE

The concept of archetypes and its correlate, that of the collective unconscious, are among the better known theories developed by Professor Jung. Their origins may be traced to his earliest publication, "On the Psychology and Pathology of So-called Occult Phenomena" (1902),* in which he described the fantasies of an hysterical medium. Intimations of the concepts can be found in many of his subsequent writings, and gradually tentative statements crystallized and were reformulated until a stable core of theory was established.

Part I of Volume 9 consists of essays—written from 1933 onward—describing and elaborating the two concepts. The volume is introduced by three essays establishing the theoretical basis, followed by others describing specific archetypes. The relation of these to the process of individuation is defined in essays in the last section.

Part II of the volume, entitled *Aion* and published separately, is devoted to a long monograph on the symbolism of the self as revealed in the "Christian aeon." Together the two parts give the nucleus of Jung's work on the theory and meaning of archetypes in relation to the psyche as a whole.

*

While the illustrations that accompany the last two papers are the same subjects published with the Swiss versions in *Gestaltungen des Unbewussten,* they have now been rephotographed and improved in presentation. It has been possible to give the entire pictorial series illustrating "A Study in the Process of Individuation" in colour and to add seven additional pictures, which were

* In *Psychiatric Studies,* vol. 1 of the *Coll. Works.*

chosen by the author from those in his possession (par. 616). Several of the illustrations for "Concerning Mandala Symbolism," also, are now given in colour. Grateful acknowledgment is made to Mrs. Aniela Jaffé and to Mrs. Margaret Schevill-Link for their kind assistance in connection with the pictures. The frontispiece was published in the Swiss magazine *Du* (April 1955), with the brief article by Professor Jung on mandalas which is given in the appendix. This "Mandala of a Modern Man" was painted in 1916.

EDITORIAL NOTE TO THE SECOND EDITION

Bibliographical citations and entries have been revised in the light of subsequent publications in the *Collected Works* and essential corrections have been made. Jung's acknowledgment in his *Memories, Dreams, Reflections* of having painted the mandala illustrated in the frontispiece, and four other mandalas in this volume, is explained on page 355, n. 1.

TRANSLATOR'S NOTE

Grateful acknowledgment is made to those whose translations have been consulted: Mr. W. S. Dell, for help derived from his translations of two papers: "Archetypes of the Collective Unconscious" and "The Meaning of Individuation" (here entitled "Conscious, Unconscious, and Individuation"), both published in *The Integration of the Personality;* Mrs. Cary F. Baynes and Miss Ximena de Angulo, for permission to use, virtually unchanged, long portions of their translations of "Psychological Aspects of the Mother Archetype" and "Concerning Rebirth," issued in *Spring* (New York), 1943 and 1944; and to Miss Hildegard Nagel, for reference to her translation of "The Psychology of the Trickster-Figure," in *Spring,* 1955.

TABLE OF CONTENTS

LIST OF ILLUSTRATIONS

I

ARCHETYPES OF THE COLLECTIVE UNCONSCIOUS

THE CONCEPT OF THE COLLECTIVE UNCONSCIOUS

CONCERNING THE ARCHETYPES, WITH SPECIAL REFERENCE TO THE ANIMA CONCEPT

ARCHETYPES OF THE COLLECTIVE UNCONSCIOUS[1]

1 The hypothesis of a collective unconscious belongs to the class of ideas that people at first find strange but soon come to possess and use as familiar conceptions. This has been the case with the concept of the unconscious in general. After the philosophical idea of the unconscious, in the form presented chiefly by Carus and von Hartmann, had gone down under the overwhelming wave of materialism and empiricism, leaving hardly a ripple behind it, it gradually reappeared in the scientific domain of medical psychology.

2 At first the concept of the unconscious was limited to denoting the state of repressed or forgotten contents. Even with Freud, who makes the unconscious—at least metaphorically—take the stage as the acting subject, it is really nothing but the gathering place of forgotten and repressed contents, and has a functional significance thanks only to these. For Freud, accordingly, the unconscious is of an exclusively personal nature,[2] although he was aware of its archaic and mythological thought-forms.

3 A more or less superficial layer of the unconscious is undoubtedly personal. I call it the *personal unconscious*. But this personal unconscious rests upon a deeper layer, which does not derive from personal experience and is not a personal acquisition but is inborn. This deeper layer I call the *collective unconscious*. I have chosen the term "collective" because this part of the unconscious is not individual but universal; in contrast to

1 [First published in the *Eranos-Jahrbuch 1934*, and later revised and published in *Von den Wurzeln des Bewusstseins* (Zurich, 1954), from which version the present translation is made. The translation of the original version, by Stanley Dell, in *The Integration of the Personality* (New York, 1939; London, 1940), has been freely consulted.—EDITORS.]

2 In his later works Freud differentiated the basic view mentioned here. He called the instinctual psyche the "id," and his "super-ego" denotes the collective consciousness, of which the individual is partly conscious and partly unconscious (because it is repressed).

the personal psyche, it has contents and modes of behaviour that are more or less the same everywhere and in all individuals. It is, in other words, identical in all men and thus constitutes a common psychic substrate of a suprapersonal nature which is present in every one of us.

4 Psychic existence can be recognized only by the presence of contents that are *capable of consciousness.* We can therefore speak of an unconscious only in so far as we are able to demonstrate its contents. The contents of the personal unconscious are chiefly the *feeling-toned complexes,* as they are called; they constitute the personal and private side of psychic life. The contents of the collective unconscious, on the other hand, are known as *archetypes.*

5 The term "archetype" occurs as early as Philo Judaeus,[3] with reference to the *Imago Dei* (God-image) in man. It can also be found in Irenaeus, who says: "The creator of the world did not fashion these things directly from himself but copied them from archetypes outside himself." [4] In the *Corpus Hermeticum,*[5] God is called τὸ ἀρχέτυπον φῶς (archetypal light). The term occurs several times in Dionysius the Areopagite, as for instance in *De caelesti hierarchia,* II, 4: "immaterial Archetypes," [6] and in *De divinis nominibus,* I, 6: "Archetypal stone." [7] The term "archetype" is not found in St. Augustine, but the idea of it is. Thus in *De diversis quaestionibus LXXXIII* he speaks of *"ideae principales,* 'which are themselves not formed . . . but are contained in the divine understanding.' " [8] "Archetype" is an explanatory paraphrase of the Platonic εἶδος. For our purposes this term is apposite and helpful, because it tells us that so far as the col-

[3] *De opificio mundi,* I, 69. Cf. Colson/Whitaker trans., I, p. 55.

[4] *Adversus haereses* II, 7, 5: "Mundi fabricator non a semetipso fecit haec, sed de alienis archetypis transtulit." (Cf. Roberts/Rambaut trans., I, p. 139.)

[5] Scott, *Hermetica,* I, p. 140.

[6] In Migne, *P.G.,* vol. 3, col. 144.

[7] Ibid., col. 595. Cf. *The Divine Names* (trans. by Rolt), pp. 62, 72.

[8] Migne, *P.L.,* vol. 40, col. 30. "Archetype" is used in the same way by the alchemists, as in the "Tractatus aureus" of Hermes Trismegistus (*Theatrum chemicum,* IV, 1613, p. 718): "As God [contains] all the treasure of his godhead . . . hidden in himself as in an archetype [*in se tanquam archetypo absconditum*] . . . in like manner Saturn carries the similitudes of metallic bodies hiddenly in himself." In the "Tractatus de igne et sale" of Vigenerus (*Theatr. chem.,* VI, 1661, p. 3), the world is "ad archetypi sui similitudinem factus" (made after the likeness of its archetype) and is therefore called the "magnus homo" (the "homo maximus" of Swedenborg).

lective unconscious contents are concerned we are dealing with archaic or—I would say—primordial types, that is, with universal images that have existed since the remotest times. The term "représentations collectives," used by Lévy-Bruhl to denote the symbolic figures in the primitive view of the world, could easily be applied to unconscious contents as well, since it means practically the same thing. Primitive tribal lore is concerned with archetypes that have been modified in a special way. They are no longer contents of the unconscious, but have already been changed into conscious formulae taught according to tradition, generally in the form of esoteric teaching. This last is a typical means of expression for the transmission of collective contents originally derived from the unconscious.

6 Another well-known expression of the archetypes is myth and fairytale. But here too we are dealing with forms that have received a specific stamp and have been handed down through long periods of time. The term "archetype" thus applies only indirectly to the "représentations collectives," since it designates only those psychic contents which have not yet been submitted to conscious elaboration and are therefore an immediate datum of psychic experience. In this sense there is a considerable difference between the archetype and the historical formula that has evolved. Especially on the higher levels of esoteric teaching the archetypes appear in a form that reveals quite unmistakably the critical and evaluating influence of conscious elaboration. Their immediate manifestation, as we encounter it in dreams and visions, is much more individual, less understandable, and more naïve than in myths, for example. The archetype is essentially an unconscious content that is altered by becoming conscious and by being perceived, and it takes its colour from the individual consciousness in which it happens to appear.[9]

7 What the word "archetype" means in the nominal sense is clear enough, then, from its relations with myth, esoteric teaching, and fairytale. But if we try to establish what an archetype is *psychologically,* the matter becomes more complicated. So far mythologists have always helped themselves out with solar,

[9] One must, for the sake of accuracy, distinguish between "archetype" and "archetypal ideas." The archetype as such is a hypothetical and irrepresentable model, something like the "pattern of behaviour" in biology. Cf. "On the Nature of the Psyche," sec. 7.

lunar, meteorological, vegetal, and other ideas of the kind. The fact that myths are first and foremost psychic phenomena that reveal the nature of the soul is something they have absolutely refused to see until now. Primitive man is not much interested in objective explanations of the obvious, but he has an imperative need—or rather, his unconscious psyche has an irresistible urge—to assimilate all outer sense experiences to inner, psychic events. It is not enough for the primitive to see the sun rise and set; this external observation must at the same time be a psychic happening: the sun in its course must represent the fate of a god or hero who, in the last analysis, dwells nowhere except in the soul of man. All the mythologized processes of nature, such as summer and winter, the phases of the moon, the rainy seasons, and so forth, are in no sense allegories [10] of these objective occurrences; rather they are symbolic expressions of the inner, unconscious drama of the psyche which becomes accessible to man's consciousness by way of projection—that is, mirrored in the events of nature. The projection is so fundamental that it has taken several thousand years of civilization to detach it in some measure from its outer object. In the case of astrology, for instance, this age-old "scientia intuitiva" came to be branded as rank heresy because man had not yet succeeded in making the psychological description of character independent of the stars. Even today, people who still believe in astrology fall almost without exception for the old superstitious assumption of the influence of the stars. And yet anyone who can calculate a horoscope should know that, since the days of Hipparchus of Alexandria, the spring-point has been fixed at 0° Aries, and that the zodiac on which every horoscope is based is therefore quite arbitrary, the spring-point having gradually advanced, since then, into the first degrees of Pisces, owing to the precession of the equinoxes.

8 Primitive man impresses us so strongly with his subjectivity that we should really have guessed long ago that myths refer to something psychic. His knowledge of nature is essentially the language and outer dress of an unconscious psychic process. But the very fact that this process is unconscious gives us the reason

[10] An allegory is a paraphrase of a conscious content, whereas a symbol is the best possible expression for an unconscious content whose nature can only be guessed, because it is still unknown.

why man has thought of everything except the psyche in his attempts to explain myths. He simply didn't know that the psyche contains all the images that have ever given rise to myths, and that our unconscious is an acting and suffering subject with an inner drama which primitive man rediscovers, by means of analogy, in the processes of nature both great and small.[11]

9 "The stars of thine own fate lie in thy breast,"[12] says Seni to Wallenstein—a dictum that should satisfy all astrologers if we knew even a little about the secrets of the heart. But for this, so far, men have had little understanding. Nor would I dare to assert that things are any better today.

10 Tribal lore is always sacred and dangerous. All esoteric teachings seek to apprehend the unseen happenings in the psyche, and all claim supreme authority for themselves. What is true of primitive lore is true in even higher degree of the ruling world religions. They contain a revealed knowledge that was originally hidden, and they set forth the secrets of the soul in glorious images. Their temples and their sacred writings proclaim in image and word the doctrine hallowed from of old, making it accessible to every believing heart, every sensitive vision, every farthest range of thought. Indeed, we are compelled to say that the more beautiful, the more sublime, the more comprehensive the image that has evolved and been handed down by tradition, the further removed it is from individual experience. We can just feel our way into it and sense something of it, but the original experience has been lost.

11 Why is psychology the youngest of the empirical sciences? Why have we not long since discovered the unconscious and raised up its treasure-house of eternal images? Simply because we had a religious formula for everything psychic—and one that is far more beautiful and comprehensive than immediate experience. Though the Christian view of the world has paled for many people, the symbolic treasure-rooms of the East are still full of marvels that can nourish for a long time to come the passion for show and new clothes. What is more, these images—be they Christian or Buddhist or what you will—are lovely,

11 Cf. my papers on the divine child and the Kore in the present volume, and Kerényi's complementary essays in *Essays on* [or *Introduction to*] *a Science of Mythology*. 12 [Schiller, *Piccolomini*, II, 6.—EDITORS.]

mysterious, richly intuitive. Naturally, the more familiar we are with them the more does constant usage polish them smooth, so that what remains is only banal superficiality and meaningless paradox. The mystery of the Virgin Birth, or the homoousia of the Son with the Father, or the Trinity which is nevertheless not a triad—these no longer lend wings to any philosophical fancy. They have stiffened into mere objects of belief. So it is not surprising if the religious need, the believing mind, and the philosophical speculations of the educated European are attracted by the symbols of the East—those grandiose conceptions of divinity in India and the abysms of Taoist philosophy in China—just as once before the heart and mind of the men of antiquity were gripped by Christian ideas. There are many Europeans who began by surrendering completely to the influence of the Christian symbol until they landed themselves in a Kierkegaardian neurosis, or whose relation to God, owing to the progressive impoverishment of symbolism, developed into an unbearably sophisticated I-You relationship—only to fall victims in their turn to the magic and novelty of Eastern symbols. This surrender is not necessarily a defeat; rather it proves the receptiveness and vitality of the religious sense. We can observe much the same thing in the educated Oriental, who not infrequently feels drawn to the Christian symbol or to the science that is so unsuited to the Oriental mind, and even develops an enviable understanding of them. That people should succumb to these eternal images is entirely normal, in fact it is what these images are for. They are meant to attract, to convince, to fascinate, and to overpower. They are created out of the primal stuff of revelation and reflect the ever-unique experience of divinity. That is why they always give man a premonition of the divine while at the same time safeguarding him from immediate experience of it. Thanks to the labours of the human spirit over the centuries, these images have become embedded in a comprehensive system of thought that ascribes an order to the world, and are at the same time represented by a mighty, farspread, and venerable institution called the Church.

12 I can best illustrate my meaning by taking as an example the Swiss mystic and hermit, Brother Nicholas of Flüe,[13] who has recently been canonized. Probably his most important re-

[13] Cf. my "Brother Klaus."

ligious experience was the so-called Trinity Vision, which preoccupied him to such an extent that he painted it, or had it painted, on the wall of his cell. The painting is still preserved in the parish church at Sachseln. It is a mandala divided into six parts, and in the centre is the crowned countenance of God. Now we know that Brother Klaus investigated the nature of his vision with the help of an illustrated devotional booklet by a German mystic, and that he struggled to get his original experience into a form he could understand. He occupied himself with it for years. This is what I call the "elaboration" of the symbol. His reflections on the nature of the vision, influenced as they were by the mystic diagrams he used as a guiding thread, inevitably led him to the conclusion that he must have gazed upon the Holy Trinity itself—the *summum bonum,* eternal love. This is borne out by the "expurgated" version now in Sachseln.

13 The original experience, however, was entirely different. In his ecstasy there was revealed to Brother Klaus a sight so terrible that his own countenance was changed by it—so much so, indeed, that people were terrified and felt afraid of him. What he had seen was a vision of the utmost intensity. Woelflin,[14] our oldest source, writes as follows:

> All who came to him were filled with terror at the first glance. As to the cause of this, he himself used to say that he had seen a piercing light resembling a human face. At the sight of it he feared that his heart would burst into little pieces. Therefore, overcome with terror, he instantly turned his face away and fell to the ground. And that was the reason why his face was now terrible to others.

14 This vision has rightly been compared[15] with the one in Revelation 1 : 13ff., that strange apocalyptic Christ-image, which for sheer gruesomeness and singularity is surpassed only by the monstrous seven-eyed lamb with seven horns (Rev. 5 : 6f.). It is certainly very difficult to see what is the relationship between this figure and the Christ of the gospels. Hence Brother Klaus's vision was interpreted in a quite definite way by the earliest sources. In 1508, the humanist Karl Bovillus (Charles de Bouelles) wrote to a friend:

14 Heinrich Woelflin, also called by the Latin form Lupulus, born 1470, humanist and director of Latin studies at Bern. Cited in Fritz Blanke, *Bruder Klaus von Flüe,* pp. 92f.

15 Ibid., p. 94.

I wish to tell you of a vision which appeared to him in the sky, on a night when the stars were shining and he stood in prayer and contemplation. He saw the head of a human figure with a terrifying face, full of wrath and threats.[16]

15 This interpretation agrees perfectly with the modern amplification furnished by Revelation 1 : 13.[17] Nor should we forget Brother Klaus's other visions, for instance, of Christ in the bearskin, of God the Father and God the Mother, and of himself as the Son. They exhibit features which are very undogmatic indeed.

16 Traditionally this great vision was brought into connection with the Trinity picture in the church at Sachseln, and so, likewise, was the wheel symbolism in the so-called "Pilgrim's Tract." [18] Brother Klaus, we are told, showed the picture of the wheel to a visiting pilgrim. Evidently this picture had preoccupied him for some time. Blanke is of the opinion that, contrary to tradition, there is no connection between the vision and the Trinity picture.[19] This scepticism seems to me to go too far. There must have been some reason for Brother Klaus's interest in the wheel. Visions like the one he had often cause mental confusion and disintegration (witness the heart bursting "into little pieces"). We know from experience that the protective circle, the mandala, is the traditional antidote for chaotic states of mind. It is therefore only too clear why Brother Klaus was fascinated by the symbol of the wheel. The interpretation of the terrifying vision as an experience of God need not be so wide of the mark either. The connection between the great vision and the Trinity picture, and of both with the wheel-symbol, therefore seems to me very probable on psychological grounds.

16 *Ein gesichte Bruder Clausen ynn Schweytz und seine deutunge* (Wittemberg, 1528), p. 5. Cited in Alban Stoeckli, O. M. Cap., *Die Visionen des seligen Bruder Klaus,* p. 34.

17 M. B. Lavaud, O.P. (*Vie Profonde de Nicolas de Flue*) gives just as apt a parallel with a text from the *Horologium sapientiae* of Henry Suso, where the apocalyptic Christ appears as an infuriated and wrathful avenger, very much in contrast to the Jesus who preached the Sermon on the Mount. [Cf. Suso, *Little Book of Eternal Wisdom,* Clark trans., pp. 77–78.—EDITORS.]

18 *Ein nutzlicher und loblicher Tractat von Bruder Claus und einem Bilger* (1488).

19 Blanke, pp. 95ff.

17 This vision, undoubtedly fearful and highly perturbing, which burst like a volcano upon his religious view of the world, without any dogmatic prelude and without exegetical commentary, naturally needed a long labour of assimilation in order to fit it into the total structure of the psyche and thus restore the disturbed psychic balance. Brother Klaus came to terms with his experience on the basis of dogma, then firm as a rock; and the dogma proved its powers of assimilation by turning something horribly alive into the beautiful abstraction of the Trinity idea. But the reconciliation might have taken place on a quite different basis provided by the vision itself and its unearthly actuality—much to the disadvantage of the Christian conception of God and no doubt to the still greater disadvantage of Brother Klaus himself, who would then have become not a saint but a heretic (if not a lunatic) and would probably have ended his life at the stake.

18 This example demonstrates the use of the dogmatic symbol: it formulates a tremendous and dangerously decisive psychic experience, fittingly called an "experience of the Divine," in a way that is tolerable to our human understanding, without either limiting the scope of the experience or doing damage to its overwhelming significance. The vision of divine wrath, which we also meet in Jakob Böhme, ill accords with the God of the New Testament, the loving Father in heaven, and for this reason it might easily have become the source of an inner conflict. That would have been quite in keeping with the spirit of the age—the end of the fifteenth century, the time of Nicholas Cusanus, whose formula of the "complexio oppositorum" actually anticipated the schism that was imminent. Not long afterwards the Yahwistic conception of God went through a series of rebirths in Protestantism. Yahweh is a God-concept that contains the opposites in a still undivided state.

19 Brother Klaus put himself outside the beaten track of convention and habit by leaving his home and family, living alone for years, and gazing deep into the dark mirror, so that the wondrous and terrible boon of original experience befell him. In this situation the dogmatic image of divinity that had been developed over the centuries worked like a healing draught. It helped him to assimilate the fatal incursion of an archetypal image and so escape being torn asunder. Angelus Silesius was

not so fortunate; the inner conflict tore him to pieces, because in his day the stability of the Church that dogma guarantees was already shattered.

20 Jakob Böhme, too, knew a God of the "Wrath-fire," a real *Deus absconditus.* He was able to bridge the profound and agonizing contradiction on the one hand by means of the Christian formula of Father and Son and embody it speculatively in his view of the world—which, though Gnostic, was in all essential points Christian. Otherwise he would have become a dualist. On the other hand it was undoubtedly alchemy, long brewing the union of opposites in secret, that came to his aid. Nevertheless the opposition has left obvious traces in the mandala appended to his *XL Questions concerning the Soule,*[20] showing the nature of the divinity. The mandala is divided into a dark and a light half, and the semicircles that are drawn round them, instead of joining up to form a ring, are turned back to back.[21]

21 Dogma takes the place of the collective unconscious by formulating its contents on a grand scale. The Catholic way of life is completely unaware of psychological problems in this sense. Almost the entire life of the collective unconscious has been channelled into the dogmatic archetypal ideas and flows along like a well-controlled stream in the symbolism of creed and ritual. It manifests itself in the inwardness of the Catholic psyche. The collective unconscious, as we understand it today, was never a matter of "psychology," for before the Christian Church existed there were the antique mysteries, and these reach back into the grey mists of neolithic prehistory. Mankind has never lacked powerful images to lend magical aid against all the uncanny things that live in the depths of the psyche. Always the figures of the unconscious were expressed in protecting and healing images and in this way were expelled from the psyche into cosmic space.

22 The iconoclasm of the Reformation, however, quite literally made a breach in the protective wall of sacred images, and since then one image after another has crumbled away. They became dubious, for they conflicted with awakening reason. Besides, people had long since forgotten what they meant. Or had they really forgotten? Could it be that men had never really known what they meant, and that only in recent times did it occur to

20 London, 1647.

21 Cf. my "Study in the Process of Individuation," infra.

the Protestant part of mankind that actually we haven't the remotest conception of what is meant by the Virgin Birth, the divinity of Christ, and the complexities of the Trinity? It almost seems as if these images had just lived, and as if their living existence had simply been accepted without question and without reflection, much as everyone decorates Christmas trees or hides Easter eggs without ever knowing what these customs mean. The fact is that archetypal images are so packed with meaning in themselves that people never think of asking what they really do mean. That the gods die from time to time is due to man's sudden discovery that they do not mean anything, that they are made by human hands, useless idols of wood and stone. In reality, however, he has merely discovered that up till then he has never thought about his images at all. And when he starts thinking about them, he does so with the help of what he calls "reason"—which in point of fact is nothing more than the sum-total of all his prejudices and myopic views.

23 The history of Protestantism has been one of chronic iconoclasm. One wall after another fell. And the work of destruction was not too difficult once the authority of the Church had been shattered. We all know how, in large things as in small, in general as well as in particular, piece after piece collapsed, and how the alarming poverty of symbols that is now the condition of our life came about. With that the power of the Church has vanished too—a fortress robbed of its bastions and casemates, a house whose walls have been plucked away, exposed to all the winds of the world and to all dangers.

24 Although this is, properly speaking, a lamentable collapse that offends our sense of history, the disintegration of Protestantism into nearly four hundred denominations is yet a sure sign that the restlessness continues. The Protestant is cast out into a state of defencelessness that might well make the natural man shudder. His enlightened consciousness, of course, refuses to take cognizance of this fact, and is quietly looking elsewhere for what has been lost to Europe. We seek the effective images, the thought-forms that satisfy the restlessness of heart and mind, and we find the treasures of the East.

25 There is no objection to this, in and for itself. Nobody forced the Romans to import Asiatic cults in bulk. If Christianity had really been—as so often described—"alien" to the Germanic

tribes, they could easily have rejected it when the prestige of the Roman legions began to wane. But Christianity had come to stay, because it fits in with the existing archetypal pattern. In the course of the centuries, however, it turned into something its founder might well have wondered at had he lived to see it; and the Christianity of Negroes and other dark-skinned converts is certainly an occasion for historical reflections. Why, then, should the West not assimilate Eastern forms? The Romans too went to Eleusis, Samothrace, and Egypt in order to get themselves initiated. In Egypt there even seems to have been a regular tourist trade in this commodity.

26 The gods of Greece and Rome perished from the same disease as did our Christian symbols: people discovered then, as today, that they had no thoughts whatever on the subject. On the other hand, the gods of the strangers still had unexhausted mana. Their names were weird and incomprehensible and their deeds portentously dark—something altogether different from the hackneyed *chronique scandaleuse* of Olympus. At least one couldn't understand the Asiatic symbols, and for this reason they were not banal like the conventional gods. The fact that people accepted the new as unthinkingly as they had rejected the old did not become a problem at that time.

27 Is it becoming a problem today? Shall we be able to put on, like a new suit of clothes, ready-made symbols grown on foreign soil, saturated with foreign blood, spoken in a foreign tongue, nourished by a foreign culture, interwoven with foreign history, and so resemble a beggar who wraps himself in kingly raiment, a king who disguises himself as a beggar? No doubt this is possible. Or is there something in ourselves that commands us to go in for no mummeries, but perhaps even to sew our garment ourselves?

28 I am convinced that the growing impoverishment of symbols has a meaning. It is a development that has an inner consistency. Everything that we have not thought about, and that has therefore been deprived of a meaningful connection with our developing consciousness, has got lost. If we now try to cover our nakedness with the gorgeous trappings of the East, as the theosophists do, we would be playing our own history false. A man does not sink down to beggary only to pose afterwards as an Indian potentate. It seems to me that it would be far better

stoutly to avow our spiritual poverty, our symbol-lessness, instead of feigning a legacy to which we are not the legitimate heirs at all. We are, surely, the rightful heirs of Christian symbolism, but somehow we have squandered this heritage. We have let the house our fathers built fall into decay, and now we try to break into Oriental palaces that our fathers never knew. Anyone who has lost the historical symbols and cannot be satisfied with substitutes is certainly in a very difficult position today: before him there yawns the void, and he turns away from it in horror. What is worse, the vacuum gets filled with absurd political and social ideas, which one and all are distinguished by their spiritual bleakness. But if he cannot get along with these pedantic dogmatisms, he sees himself forced to be serious for once with his alleged trust in God, though it usually turns out that his fear of things going wrong if he did so is even more persuasive. This fear is far from unjustified, for where God is closest the danger seems greatest. It is dangerous to avow spiritual poverty, for the poor man has desires, and whoever has desires calls down some fatality on himself. A Swiss proverb puts it drastically: "Behind every rich man stands a devil, and behind every poor man two."

29 Just as in Christianity the vow of worldly poverty turned the mind away from the riches of this earth, so spiritual poverty seeks to renounce the false riches of the spirit in order to withdraw not only from the sorry remnants—which today call themselves the Protestant church—of a great past, but also from all the allurements of the odorous East; in order, finally, to dwell with itself alone, where, in the cold light of consciousness, the blank barrenness of the world reaches to the very stars.

30 We have inherited this poverty from our fathers. I well remember the confirmation lessons I received at the hands of my own father. The catechism bored me unspeakably. One day I was turning over the pages of my little book, in the hope of finding something interesting, when my eye fell on the paragraphs about the Trinity. This interested me at once, and I waited impatiently for the lessons to get to that section. But when the longed-for lesson arrived, my father said: "We'll skip this bit; I can't make head or tail of it myself." With that my last hope was laid in the grave. I admired my father's honesty,

but this did not alter the fact that from then on all talk of religion bored me to death.

31 Our intellect has achieved the most tremendous things, but in the meantime our spiritual dwelling has fallen into disrepair. We are absolutely convinced that even with the aid of the latest and largest reflecting telescope, now being built in America, men will discover behind the farthest nebulae no fiery empyrean; and we know that our eyes will wander despairingly through the dead emptiness of interstellar space. Nor is it any better when mathematical physics reveals to us the world of the infinitely small. In the end we dig up the wisdom of all ages and peoples, only to find that everything most dear and precious to us has already been said in the most superb language. Like greedy children we stretch out our hands and think that, if only we could grasp it, we would possess it too. But what we possess is no longer valid, and our hands grow weary from the grasping, for riches lie everywhere, as far as the eye can reach. All these possessions turn to water, and more than one sorcerer's apprentice has been drowned in the waters called up by himself—if he did not first succumb to the saving delusion that *this* wisdom was good and *that* was bad. It is from these adepts that there come those terrifying invalids who think they have a prophetic mission. For the artificial sundering of true and false wisdom creates a tension in the psyche, and from this there arises a loneliness and a craving like that of the morphine addict, who always hopes to find companions in his vice.

32 When our natural inheritance has been dissipated, then the spirit too, as Heraclitus says, has descended from its fiery heights. But when spirit becomes heavy it turns to water, and with Luciferian presumption the intellect usurps the seat where once the spirit was enthroned. The spirit may legitimately claim the *patria potestas* over the soul; not so the earth-born intellect, which is man's sword or hammer, and not a creator of spiritual worlds, a father of the soul. Hence Ludwig Klages [22] and Max Scheler [23] were moderate enough in their attempts to rehabilitate the spirit, for both were children of an age in which the spirit was no longer up above but down below, no longer fire but water.

22 [Cf. *Der Geist als Widersacher der Seele.*]

23 [Cf., e.g., *Die Stellung des Menschen im Kosmos.*—EDITORS.]

Therefore the way of the soul in search of its lost father—like Sophia seeking Bythos—leads to the water, to the dark mirror that reposes at its bottom. Whoever has elected for the state of spiritual poverty, the true heritage of Protestantism carried to its logical conclusion, goes the way of the soul that leads to the water. This water is no figure of speech, but a living symbol of the dark psyche. I can best illustrate this by a concrete example, one out of many:

A Protestant theologian often dreamed the same dream: *He stood on a mountain slope with a deep valley below, and in it a dark lake. He knew in the dream that something had always prevented him from approaching the lake. This time he resolved to go to the water. As he approached the shore, everything grew dark and uncanny, and a gust of wind suddenly rushed over the face of the water. He was seized by a panic fear, and awoke.*

This dream shows us the natural symbolism. The dreamer descends into his own depths, and the way leads him to the mysterious water. And now there occurs the miracle of the pool of Bethesda: an angel comes down and touches the water, endowing it with healing power. In the dream it is the wind, the pneuma, which bloweth where it listeth. Man's descent to the water is needed in order to evoke the miracle of its coming to life. But the breath of the spirit rushing over the dark water is uncanny, like everything whose cause we do not know—since it is not ourselves. It hints at an unseen presence, a numen to which neither human expectations nor the machinations of the will have given life. It lives of itself, and a shudder runs through the man who thought that "spirit" was merely what he believes, what he makes himself, what is said in books, or what people talk about. But when it happens spontaneously it is a spookish thing, and primitive fear seizes the naïve mind. The elders of the Elgonyi tribe in Kenya gave me exactly the same description of the nocturnal god whom they call the "maker of fear." "He comes to you," they said, "like a cold gust of wind, and you shudder, or he goes whistling round in the tall grass"—an African Pan who glides among the reeds in the haunted noontide hour, playing on his pipes and frightening the shepherds.

Thus, in the dream, the breath of the pneuma frightened another pastor, a shepherd of the flock, who in the darkness of the night trod the reed-grown shore in the deep valley of the psyche. Yes, that erstwhile fiery spirit has made a descent to the realm of nature, to the trees and rocks and the waters of the psyche, like the old man in Nietzsche's *Zarathustra,* who, wearied of humankind, withdrew into the forest to growl with the bears in honour of the Creator.

37 We must surely go the way of the waters, which always tend downward, if we would raise up the treasure, the precious heritage of the father. In the Gnostic hymn to the soul,[24] the son is sent forth by his parents to seek the pearl that fell from the King's crown. It lies at the bottom of a deep well, guarded by a dragon, in the land of the Egyptians—that land of fleshpots and drunkenness with all its material and spiritual riches. The son and heir sets out to fetch the jewel, but forgets himself and his task in the orgies of Egyptian worldliness, until a letter from his father reminds him what his duty is. He then sets out for the water and plunges into the dark depths of the well, where he finds the pearl on the bottom, and in the end offers it to the highest divinity.

38 This hymn, ascribed to Bardesanes, dates from an age that resembled ours in more than one respect. Mankind looked and waited, and it was a *fish*—"levatus de profundo" (drawn from the deep)[25]—that became the symbol of the saviour, the bringer of healing.

39 As I wrote these lines, I received a letter from Vancouver, from a person unknown to me. The writer is puzzled by his dreams, which are always about water: "Almost every time I dream it is about water: *either I am having a bath, or the water-closet is overflowing, or a pipe is bursting, or my home has drifted down to the water's edge, or I see an acquaintance about to sink into water, or I am trying to get out of water, or I am having a bath and the tub is about to overflow,*" etc.

40 Water is the commonest symbol for the unconscious. The lake in the valley is the unconscious, which lies, as it were, underneath consciousness, so that it is often referred to as the "subconscious," usually with the pejorative connotation of an inferior consciousness. Water is the "valley spirit," the water dragon of Tao, whose nature resembles water—a *yang* embraced in the *yin.* Psychologically, therefore, water means spirit that

24 James, *Apocryphal New Testament,* pp. 411–15.

25 Augustine, *Confessions,* Lib. XIII, cap. XXI.

has become unconscious. So the dream of the theologian is quite right in telling him that down by the water he could experience the working of the living spirit like a miracle of healing in the pool of Bethesda. The descent into the depths always seems to precede the ascent. Thus another theologian [26] dreamed that *he saw on a mountain a kind of Castle of the Grail. He went along a road that seemed to lead straight to the foot of the mountain and up it. But as he drew nearer he discovered to his great disappointment that a chasm separated him from the mountain, a deep, darksome gorge with underworldly water rushing along the bottom. A steep path led downwards and toilsomely climbed up again on the other side. But the prospect looked uninviting,* and the dreamer awoke. Here again the dreamer, thirsting for the shining heights, had first to descend into the dark depths, and this proves to be the indispensable condition for climbing any higher. The prudent man avoids the danger lurking in these depths, but he also throws away the good which a bold but imprudent venture might bring.

41 The statement made by the dream meets with violent resistance from the conscious mind, which knows "spirit" only as something to be found in the heights. "Spirit" always seems to come from above, while from below comes everything that is sordid and worthless. For people who think in this way, spirit means highest freedom, a soaring over the depths, deliverance from the prison of the chthonic world, and hence a refuge for all those timorous souls who do not want to become anything different. But water is earthy and tangible, it is also the fluid of the instinct-driven body, blood and the flowing of blood, the odour of the beast, carnality heavy with passion. The unconscious is the psyche that reaches down from the daylight of mentally and morally lucid consciousness into the nervous system that for ages has been known as the "sympathetic." This does not govern perception and muscular activity like the cerebrospinal system, and thus control the environment; but, though functioning without sense-organs, it maintains the balance of life and, through the mysterious paths of sympathetic

[26] The fact that it was another theologian who dreamed this dream is not so surprising, since priests and clergymen have a professional interest in the motif of "ascent." They have to speak of it so often that the question naturally arises as to what they are doing about their own spiritual ascent.

excitation, not only gives us knowledge of the innermost life of other beings but also has an inner effect upon them. In this sense it is an extremely collective system, the operative basis of all *participation mystique,* whereas the cerebrospinal function reaches its high point in separating off the specific qualities of the ego, and only apprehends surfaces and externals—always through the medium of space. It experiences everything as an outside, whereas the sympathetic system experiences everything as an inside.

42 The unconscious is commonly regarded as a sort of incapsulated fragment of our most personal and intimate life—something like what the Bible calls the "heart" and considers the source of all evil thoughts. In the chambers of the heart dwell the wicked blood-spirits, swift anger and sensual weakness. This is how the unconscious looks when seen from the conscious side. But consciousness appears to be essentially an affair of the cerebrum, which sees everything separately and in isolation, and therefore sees the unconscious in this way too, regarding it outright as *my* unconscious. Hence it is generally believed that anyone who descends into the unconscious gets into a suffocating atmosphere of egocentric subjectivity, and in this blind alley is exposed to the attack of all the ferocious beasts which the caverns of the psychic underworld are supposed to harbour.

43 True, whoever looks into the mirror of the water will see first of all his own face. Whoever goes to himself risks a confrontation with himself. The mirror does not flatter, it faithfully shows whatever looks into it; namely, the face we never show to the world because we cover it with the *persona,* the mask of the actor. But the mirror lies behind the mask and shows the true face.

44 This confrontation is the first test of courage on the inner way, a test sufficient to frighten off most people, for the meeting with ourselves belongs to the more unpleasant things that can be avoided so long as we can project everything negative into the environment. But if we are able to see our own shadow and can bear knowing about it, then a small part of the problem has already been solved: we have at least brought up the personal unconscious. The shadow is a living part of the personality and therefore wants to live with it in some form. It cannot be argued out of existence or rationalized into harmlessness. This problem

is exceedingly difficult, because it not only challenges the whole man, but reminds him at the same time of his helplessness and ineffectuality. Strong natures—or should one rather call them weak?—do not like to be reminded of this, but prefer to think of themselves as heroes who are beyond good and evil, and to cut the Gordian knot instead of untying it. Nevertheless, the account has to be settled sooner or later. In the end one has to admit that there are problems which one simply cannot solve on one's own resources. Such an admission has the advantage of being honest, truthful, and in accord with reality, and this prepares the ground for a compensatory reaction from the collective unconscious: you are now more inclined to give heed to a helpful idea or intuition, or to notice thoughts which had not been allowed to voice themselves before. Perhaps you will pay attention to the dreams that visit you at such moments, or will reflect on certain inner and outer occurrences that take place just at this time. If you have an attitude of this kind, then the helpful powers slumbering in the deeper strata of man's nature can come awake and intervene, for helplessness and weakness are the eternal experience and the eternal problem of mankind. To this problem there is also an eternal answer, otherwise it would have been all up with humanity long ago. When you have done everything that could possibly be done, the only thing that remains is what you could still do if only you knew it. But how much do we know of ourselves? Precious little, to judge by experience. Hence there is still a great deal of room left for the unconscious. Prayer, as we know, calls for a very similar attitude and therefore has much the same effect.

45 The necessary and needful reaction from the collective unconscious expresses itself in archetypally formed ideas. The meeting with oneself is, at first, the meeting with one's own shadow. The shadow is a tight passage, a narrow door, whose painful constriction no one is spared who goes down to the deep well. But one must learn to know oneself in order to know who one is. For what comes after the door is, surprisingly enough, a boundless expanse full of unprecedented uncertainty, with apparently no inside and no outside, no above and no below, no here and no there, no mine and no thine, no good and no bad. It is the world of water, where all life floats in suspension; where the realm of the sympathetic system, the soul of everything

living, begins; where I am indivisibly this *and* that; where I experience the other in myself and the other-than-myself experiences me.

46 No, the collective unconscious is anything but an incapsulated personal system; it is sheer objectivity, as wide as the world and open to all the world. There I am the object of every subject, in complete reversal of my ordinary consciousness, where I am always the subject that has an object. There I am utterly one with the world, so much a part of it that I forget all too easily who I really am. "Lost in oneself" is a good way of describing this state. But this self is the world, if only a consciousness could see it. That is why we must know who we are.

47 The unconscious no sooner touches us than we *are* it—we become unconscious of ourselves. That is the age-old danger, instinctively known and feared by primitive man, who himself stands so very close to this pleroma. His consciousness is still uncertain, wobbling on its feet. It is still childish, having just emerged from the primal waters. A wave of the unconscious may easily roll over it, and then he forgets who he was and does things that are strange to him. Hence primitives are afraid of uncontrolled emotions, because consciousness breaks down under them and gives way to possession. All man's strivings have therefore been directed towards the consolidation of consciousness. This was the purpose of rite and dogma; they were dams and walls to keep back the dangers of the unconscious, the "perils of the soul." Primitive rites consist accordingly in the exorcizing of spirits, the lifting of spells, the averting of the evil omen, propitiation, purification, and the production by sympathetic magic of helpful occurrences.

48 It is these barriers, erected in primitive times, that later became the foundations of the Church. It is also these barriers that collapse when the symbols become weak with age. Then the waters rise and boundless catastrophes break over mankind. The religious leader of the Taos pueblo, known as the Loco Tenente Gobernador, once said to me: "The Americans should stop meddling with our religion, for when it dies and we can no longer help the sun our Father to cross the sky, the Americans and the whole world will learn something in ten years' time, for then the sun won't rise any more." In other words, night will

fall, the light of consciousness is extinguished, and the dark sea of the unconscious breaks in.

49 Whether primitive or not, mankind always stands on the brink of actions it performs itself but does not control. The whole world wants peace and the whole world prepares for war, to take but one example. Mankind is powerless against mankind, and the gods, as ever, show it the ways of fate. Today we call the gods "factors," which comes from *facere,* 'to make.' The makers stand behind the wings of the world-theatre. It is so in great things as in small. In the realm of consciousness we are our own masters; we seem to be the "factors" themselves. But if we step through the door of the shadow we discover with terror that we are the objects of unseen factors. To know this is decidedly unpleasant, for nothing is more disillusioning than the discovery of our own inadequacy. It can even give rise to primitive panic, because, instead of being believed in, the anxiously guarded supremacy of consciousness—which is in truth one of the secrets of human success—is questioned in the most dangerous way. But since ignorance is no guarantee of security, and in fact only makes our insecurity still worse, it is probably better despite our fear to know where the danger lies. To ask the right question is already half the solution of a problem. At any rate we then know that the greatest danger threatening us comes from the unpredictability of the psyche's reactions. Discerning persons have realized for some time that external historical conditions, of whatever kind, are only occasions, jumping-off grounds, for the real dangers that threaten our lives. These are the present politico-social delusional systems. We should not regard them causally, as necessary consequences of external conditions, but as decisions precipitated by the collective unconscious.

50 This is a new problem. All ages before us have believed in gods in some form or other. Only an unparalleled impoverishment of symbolism could enable us to rediscover the gods as psychic factors, that is, as archetypes of the unconscious. No doubt this discovery is hardly credible at present. To be convinced, we need to have the experience pictured in the dream of the theologian, for only then do we experience the self-activity of the spirit moving over the waters. Since the stars have fallen from heaven and our highest symbols have paled, a secret life holds sway in the unconscious. That is why we have a psychology

today, and why we speak of the unconscious. All this would be quite superfluous in an age or culture that possessed symbols. Symbols are spirit from above, and under those conditions the spirit is above too. Therefore it would be a foolish and senseless undertaking for such people to wish to experience or investigate an unconscious that contains nothing but the silent, undisturbed sway of nature. Our unconscious, on the other hand, hides living water, spirit that has become nature, and that is why it is disturbed. Heaven has become for us the cosmic space of the physicists, and the divine empyrean a fair memory of things that once were. But "the heart glows," and a secret unrest gnaws at the roots of our being. In the words of the *Völuspa* we may ask:

> What murmurs Wotan over Mimir's head?
> Already the spring boils . . .

51 Our concern with the unconscious has become a vital question for us—a question of spiritual being or non-being. All those who have had an experience like that mentioned in the dream know that the treasure lies in the depths of the water and will try to salvage it. As they must never forget who they are, they must on no account imperil their consciousness. They will keep their standpoint firmly anchored to the earth, and will thus—to preserve the metaphor—become fishers who catch with hook and net what swims in the water. There may be consummate fools who do not understand what fishermen do, but the latter will not mistake the timeless meaning of their action, for the symbol of their craft is many centuries older than the still unfaded story of the Grail. But not every man is a fisherman. Sometimes this figure remains arrested at an early, instinctive level, and then it is an otter, as we know from Oskar Schmitz's fairytales.[27]

52 Whoever looks into the water sees his own image, but behind it living creatures soon loom up; fishes, presumably, harmless dwellers of the deep—harmless, if only the lake were not haunted. They are water-beings of a peculiar sort. Sometimes a nixie gets into the fisherman's net, a female, half-human fish.[28]

27 [The "Fischottermärchen" in *Märchen aus dem Unbewussten*, pp. 14ff., 43ff.—EDITORS.]

28 Cf. Paracelsus, *De vita longa* (1562), and my commentary in "Paracelsus as a Spiritual Phenomenon" [concerning Melusina, pars. 179f., 215ff.].

Nixies are entrancing creatures:

> Half drew she him,
> Half sank he down
> And nevermore was seen.

53 The nixie is an even more instinctive version of a magical feminine being whom I call the *anima*. She can also be a siren, *melusina* (mermaid),[29] wood-nymph, Grace, or Erlking's daughter, or a lamia or succubus, who infatuates young men and sucks the life out of them. Moralizing critics will say that these figures are projections of soulful emotional states and are nothing but worthless fantasies. One must admit that there is a certain amount of truth in this. But is it the whole truth? Is the nixie really nothing but a product of moral laxity? Were there not such beings long ago, in an age when dawning human consciousness was still wholly bound to nature? Surely there were spirits of forest, field, and stream long before the question of moral conscience ever existed. What is more, these beings were as much dreaded as adored, so that their rather peculiar erotic charms were only one of their characteristics. Man's consciousness was then far simpler, and his possession of it absurdly small. An unlimited amount of what we now feel to be an integral part of our psychic being disports itself merrily for the primitive in projections ranging far and wide.

54 The word "projection" is not really appropriate, for nothing has been cast out of the psyche; rather, the psyche has attained its present complexity by a series of acts of introjection. Its complexity has increased in proportion to the despiritualization of nature. An alluring nixie from the dim bygone is today called an "erotic fantasy," and she may complicate our psychic life in a most painful way. She comes upon us just as a nixie might; she sits on top of us like a succubus; she changes into all sorts of shapes like a witch, and in general displays an unbearable independence that does not seem at all proper in a psychic

29 Cf. the picture of the adept in *Liber mutus* (1677) (fig. 13 in *The Practice of Psychotherapy*, p. 320). He is fishing, and has caught a nixie. His *soror mystica*, however, catches birds in her net, symbolizing the animus. The idea of the anima often turns up in the literature of the 16th and 17th cent., for instance in Richardus Vitus, Aldrovandus, and the commentator of the *Tractatus aureus*. Cf. "The Enigma of Bologna" in my *Mysterium Coniunctionis*, pars. 51ff.

content. Occasionally she causes states of fascination that rival the best bewitchment, or unleashes terrors in us not to be outdone by any manifestation of the devil. She is a mischievous being who crosses our path in numerous transformations and disguises, playing all kinds of tricks on us, causing happy and unhappy delusions, depressions and ecstasies, outbursts of affect, etc. Even in a state of reasonable introjection the nixie has not laid aside her roguery. The witch has not ceased to mix her vile potions of love and death; her magic poison has been refined into intrigue and self-deception, unseen though none the less dangerous for that.

55 But how do we dare to call this elfin being the "anima"? Anima means soul and should designate something very wonderful and immortal. Yet this was not always so. We should not forget that this kind of soul is a dogmatic conception whose purpose it is to pin down and capture something uncannily alive and active. The German word *Seele* is closely related, via the Gothic form *saiwalô,* to the Greek word αἰόλος, which means 'quick-moving,' 'changeful of hue,' 'twinkling,' something like a butterfly—ψυχή in Greek—which reels drunkenly from flower to flower and lives on honey and love. In Gnostic typology the ἄνθρωπος ψυχικός, 'psychic man,' is inferior to the πνευματικός, 'spiritual man,' and finally there are wicked souls who must roast in hell for all eternity. Even the quite innocent soul of the unbaptized newborn babe is deprived of the contemplation of God. Among primitives, the soul is the magic breath of life (hence the term "anima"), or a flame. An uncanonical saying of our Lord's aptly declares: "Whoso is near unto me is near to the fire." For Heraclitus the soul at the highest level is fiery and dry, because ψυχή as such is closely akin to "cool breath"—ψύχειν means 'to breathe,' 'to blow'; ψυχρός and ψῦχος mean 'cold,' 'chill,' 'damp.'

56 Being that has soul is living being. Soul is the living thing in man, that which lives of itself and causes life. Therefore God breathed into Adam a living breath, that he might live. With her cunning play of illusions the soul lures into life the inertness of matter that does not want to live. She makes us believe incredible things, that life may be lived. She is full of snares and traps, in order that man should fall, should reach the earth, entangle himself there, and stay caught, so that life should be

lived; as Eve in the garden of Eden could not rest content until she had convinced Adam of the goodness of the forbidden apple. Were it not for the leaping and twinkling of the soul, man would rot away in his greatest passion, idleness.[30] A certain kind of reasonableness is its advocate, and a certain kind of morality adds its blessing. But to have soul is the whole venture of life, for soul is a life-giving daemon who plays his elfin game above and below human existence, for which reason—in the realm of dogma—he is threatened and propitiated with superhuman punishments and blessings that go far beyond the possible deserts of human beings. Heaven and hell are the fates meted out to the soul and not to civilized man, who in his nakedness and timidity would have no idea of what to do with himself in a heavenly Jerusalem.

57 The anima is not the soul in the dogmatic sense, not an *anima rationalis,* which is a philosophical conception, but a natural archetype that satisfactorily sums up all the statements of the unconscious, of the primitive mind, of the history of language and religion. It is a "factor" in the proper sense of the word. Man cannot make it; on the contrary, it is always the *a priori* element in his moods, reactions, impulses, and whatever else is spontaneous in psychic life. It is something that lives of itself, that makes us live; it is a life behind consciousness that cannot be completely integrated with it, but from which, on the contrary, consciousness arises. For, in the last analysis, psychic life is for the greater part an unconscious life that surrounds consciousness on all sides—a notion that is sufficiently obvious when one considers how much unconscious preparation is needed, for instance, to register a sense-impression.

58 Although it seems as if the whole of our unconscious psychic life could be ascribed to the anima, she is yet only one archetype among many. Therefore, she is not characteristic of the unconscious in its entirety. She is only one of its aspects. This is shown by the very fact of her femininity. What is not-I, not masculine, is most probably feminine, and because the not-I is felt as not belonging to me and therefore as outside me, the anima-image is usually projected upon women. Either sex is inhabited by the opposite sex up to a point, for, biologically speaking, it is simply the greater number of masculine genes that tips the scales in

30 La Rochefoucauld, Pensées DLX. Quoted in *Symbols of Transformation,* p. 174.

favour of masculinity. The smaller number of feminine genes seems to form a feminine character, which usually remains unconscious because of its subordinate position.

59 With the archetype of the anima we enter the realm of the gods, or rather, the realm that metaphysics has reserved for itself. Everything the anima touches becomes numinous—unconditional, dangerous, taboo, magical. She is the serpent in the paradise of the harmless man with good resolutions and still better intentions. She affords the most convincing reasons for not prying into the unconscious, an occupation that would break down our moral inhibitions and unleash forces that had better been left unconscious and undisturbed. As usual, there is something in what the anima says; for life in itself is not good only, it is also bad. Because the anima wants life, she wants both good and bad. These categories do not exist in the elfin realm. Bodily life as well as psychic life have the impudence to get along much better without conventional morality, and they often remain the healthier for it.

60 The anima believes in the *καλὸν κἀγαθόν*, the 'beautiful and the good,' a primitive conception that antedates the discovery of the conflict between aesthetics and morals. It took more than a thousand years of Christian differentiation to make it clear that the good is not always the beautiful and the beautiful not necessarily good. The paradox of this marriage of ideas troubled the ancients as little as it does the primitives. The anima is conservative and clings in the most exasperating fashion to the ways of earlier humanity. She likes to appear in historic dress, with a predilection for Greece and Egypt. In this connection we would mention the classic anima stories of Rider Haggard and Pierre Benoît. The Renaissance dream known as the *Ipnerotomachia* of Poliphilo,[31] and Goethe's *Faust,* likewise reach deep into antiquity in order to find "le vrai mot" for the situation. Poliphilo conjured up Queen Venus; Goethe, Helen of Troy. Aniela Jaffé [32] has sketched a lively picture of the anima in the age of Biedermeier and the Romantics. If you want to know what happens when the anima appears in modern society, I can warmly recommend John Erskine's *Private Life of Helen of*

31 Cf. *The Dream of Poliphilo,* ed. by Linda Fierz-David. [For Haggard and Benoît, see the bibliography.—EDITORS.]

32 "Bilder und Symbole aus E. T. A. Hoffmanns Märchen 'Der Goldne Topf.' "

Troy. She is not a shallow creation, for the breath of eternity lies over everything that is really alive. The anima lives beyond all categories, and can therefore dispense with blame as well as with praise. Since the beginning of time man, with his wholesome animal instinct, has been engaged in combat with his soul and its daemonism. If the soul were uniformly dark it would be a simple matter. Unfortunately this is not so, for the anima can appear also as an angel of light, a psychopomp who points the way to the highest meaning, as we know from *Faust*.

61 If the encounter with the shadow is the "apprentice-piece" in the individual's development, then that with the anima is the "master-piece." The relation with the anima is again a test of courage, an ordeal by fire for the spiritual and moral forces of man. We should never forget that in dealing with the anima we are dealing with psychic facts which have never been in man's possession before, since they were always found "outside" his psychic territory, so to speak, in the form of projections. For the son, the anima is hidden in the dominating power of the mother, and sometimes she leaves him with a sentimental attachment that lasts throughout life and seriously impairs the fate of the adult. On the other hand, she may spur him on to the highest flights. To the men of antiquity the anima appeared as a goddess or a witch, while for medieval man the goddess was replaced by the Queen of Heaven and Mother Church. The desymbolized world of the Protestant produced first an unhealthy sentimentality and then a sharpening of the moral conflict, which, because it was so unbearable, led logically to Nietzsche's "beyond good and evil." In centres of civilization this state shows itself in the increasing insecurity of marriage. The American divorce rate has been reached, if not exceeded, in many European countries, which proves that the anima projects herself by preference on the opposite sex, thus giving rise to magically complicated relationships. This fact, largely because of its pathological consequences, has led to the growth of modern psychology, which in its Freudian form cherishes the belief that the essential cause of all disturbances is sexuality—a view that only exacerbates the already existing conflict.[33] There is a confusion here between cause and effect. The sexual disturbance is by no means the cause of neurotic difficulties, but is, like these, one of the patho-

33 I have expounded my views at some length in "Psychology of the Transference."

logical effects of a maladaptation of consciousness, as when consciousness is faced with situations and tasks to which it is not equal. Such a person simply does not understand how the world has altered, and what his attitude would have to be in order to adapt to it.

62 In dealing with the shadow or anima it is not sufficient just to know about these concepts and to reflect on them. Nor can we ever experience their content by feeling our way into them or by appropriating other people's feelings. It is no use at all to learn a list of archetypes by heart. Archetypes are complexes of experience that come upon us like fate, and their effects are felt in our most personal life. The anima no longer crosses our path as a goddess, but, it may be, as an intimately personal misadventure, or perhaps as our best venture. When, for instance, a highly esteemed professor in his seventies abandons his family and runs off with a young red-headed actress, we know that the gods have claimed another victim. This is how daemonic power reveals itself to us. Until not so long ago it would have been an easy matter to do away with the young woman as a witch.

63 In my experience there are very many people of intelligence and education who have no trouble in grasping the idea of the anima and her relative autonomy, and can also understand the phenomenology of the animus in women. Psychologists have more difficulties to overcome in this respect, probably because they are under no compulsion to grapple with the complex facts peculiar to the psychology of the unconscious. If they are doctors as well, their somato-psychological thinking gets in the way, with its assumption that psychological processes can be expressed in intellectual, biological, or physiological terms. Psychology, however, is neither biology nor physiology nor any other science than just this knowledge of the psyche.

64 The picture I have drawn of the anima so far is not complete. Although she may be the chaotic urge to life, something strangely meaningful clings to her, a secret knowledge or hidden wisdom, which contrasts most curiously with her irrational elfin nature. Here I would like to refer again to the authors already cited. Rider Haggard calls She "Wisdom's Daughter"; Benoît's Queen of Atlantis has an excellent library that even contains a lost book of Plato. Helen of Troy, in her reincarnation, is

rescued from a Tyrian brothel by the wise Simon Magus and accompanies him on his travels. I purposely refrained from mentioning this thoroughly characteristic aspect of the anima earlier, because the first encounter with her usually leads one to infer anything rather than wisdom.[34] This aspect appears only to the person who gets to grips with her seriously. Only then, when this hard task has been faced,[35] does he come to realize more and more that behind all her cruel sporting with human fate there lies something like a hidden purpose which seems to reflect a superior knowledge of life's laws. It is just the most unexpected, the most terrifyingly chaotic things which reveal a deeper meaning. And the more this meaning is recognized, the more the anima loses her impetuous and compulsive character. Gradually breakwaters are built against the surging of chaos, and the meaningful divides itself from the meaningless. When sense and nonsense are no longer identical, the force of chaos is weakened by their subtraction; sense is then endued with the force of meaning, and nonsense with the force of meaninglessness. In this way a new cosmos arises. This is not a new discovery in the realm of medical psychology, but the age-old truth that out of the richness of a man's experience there comes a teaching which the father can pass on to the son.[36]

65 In elfin nature wisdom and folly appear as one and the same; and they *are* one and the same as long as they are acted out by the anima. Life is crazy and meaningful at once. And when we do not laugh over the one aspect and speculate about the other, life is exceedingly drab, and everything is reduced to the littlest scale. There is then little sense and little nonsense either. When you come to think about it, nothing has any meaning, for when there was nobody to think, there was nobody to interpret what happened. Interpretations are only for those who don't understand; it is only the things we don't understand that have any meaning. Man woke up in a world he did not understand, and that is why he tries to interpret it.

34 I am referring here to literary examples that are generally accessible and not to clinical material. These are quite sufficient for our purpose.

35 I.e., coming to terms with the contents of the collective unconscious in general. This is *the* great task of the integration process.

36 A good example is the little book by Gustav Schmaltz, *Östliche Weisheit und Westliche Psychotherapie.*

66 Thus the anima and life itself are meaningless in so far as they offer no interpretation. Yet they have a nature that can be interpreted, for in all chaos there is a cosmos, in all disorder a secret order, in all caprice a fixed law, for everything that works is grounded on its opposite. It takes man's discriminating understanding, which breaks everything down into antinomial judgments, to recognize this. Once he comes to grips with the anima, her chaotic capriciousness will give him cause to suspect a secret order, to sense a plan, a meaning, a purpose over and above her nature, or even—we might almost be tempted to say—to "postulate" such a thing, though this would not be in accord with the truth. For in actual reality we do not have at our command any power of cool reflection, nor does any science or philosophy help us, and the traditional teachings of religion do so only to a limited degree. We are caught and entangled in aimless experience, and the judging intellect with its categories proves itself powerless. Human interpretation fails, for a turbulent life-situation has arisen that refuses to fit any of the traditional meanings assigned to it. It is a moment of collapse. We sink into a final depth—Apuleius calls it "a kind of voluntary death." It is a surrender of our own powers, not artificially willed but forced upon us by nature; not a voluntary submission and humiliation decked in moral garb but an utter and unmistakable defeat crowned with the panic fear of demoralization. Only when all props and crutches are broken, and no cover from the rear offers even the slightest hope of security, does it become possible for us to experience an archetype that up till then had lain hidden behind the meaningful nonsense played out by the anima. This is the *archetype of meaning,* just as the anima is the *archetype of life itself.*

67 It always seems to us as if meaning—compared with life—were the younger event, because we assume, with some justification, that we assign it of ourselves, and because we believe, equally rightly no doubt, that the great world can get along without being interpreted. But how do we assign meaning? From what source, in the last analysis, do we derive meaning? The forms we use for assigning meaning are historical categories that reach back into the mists of time—a fact we do not take sufficiently into account. Interpretations make use of certain linguistic matrices that are themselves derived from primordial

images. From whatever side we approach this question, everywhere we find ourselves confronted with the history of language, with images and motifs that lead straight back to the primitive wonder-world.

68 Take, for instance, the word "idea." It goes back to the εἶδος concept of Plato, and the eternal ideas are primordial images stored up ἐν ὑπερουρανίῳ τόπῳ (in a supracelestial place) as eternal, transcendent forms. The eye of the seer perceives them as "imagines et lares," or as images in dreams and revelatory visions. Or let us take the concept of energy, which is an interpretation of physical events. In earlier times it was the secret fire of the alchemists, or phlogiston, or the heat-force inherent in matter, like the "primal warmth" of the Stoics, or the Heraclitean πῦρ ἀεὶ ζῶον (ever-living fire), which borders on the primitive notion of an all-pervading vital force, a power of growth and magic healing that is generally called *mana.*

69 I will not go on needlessly giving examples. It is sufficient to know that there is not a single important idea or view that does not possess historical antecedents. Ultimately they are all founded on primordial archetypal forms whose concreteness dates from a time when consciousness did not *think,* but only *perceived.* "Thoughts" were objects of inner perception, not thought at all, but sensed as external phenomena—seen or heard, so to speak. Thought was essentially revelation, not invented but forced upon us or bringing conviction through its immediacy and actuality. Thinking of this kind precedes the primitive ego-consciousness, and the latter is more its object than its subject. But we ourselves have not yet climbed the last peak of consciousness, so we also have a pre-existent thinking, of which we are not aware so long as we are supported by traditional symbols—or, to put it in the language of dreams, so long as the father or the king is not dead.

70 I would like to give you an example of how the unconscious "thinks" and paves the way for solutions. It is the case of a young theological student, whom I did not know personally. He was in great straits because of his religious beliefs, and about this time he dreamed the following dream: [37]

[37] I have already used this dream in "The Phenomenology of the Spirit in Fairytales," par. 398, infra, and in "Psychology and Education," pp. 117ff., as an example of a "big" dream, without commenting on it more closely.

71 *He was standing in the presence of a handsome old man dressed entirely in* black. *He knew it was the* white *magician. This personage had just addressed him at considerable length, but the dreamer could no longer remember what it was about. He had only retained the closing words: "And for this we need the help of the* black *magician." At that moment the door opened and in came another old man exactly like the first, except that he was dressed in* white. *He said to the white magician, "I need your advice," but threw a sidelong, questioning look at the dreamer, whereupon the white magician answered: "You can speak freely, he is an innocent." The black magician then began to relate his story. He had come from a distant land where something extraordinary had happened. The country was ruled by an old king who felt his death near. He—the king—had sought out a tomb for himself. For there were in that land a great number of tombs from ancient times, and the king had chosen the finest for himself. According to legend, a virgin had been buried in it. The king caused the tomb to be opened, in order to get it ready for use. But when the bones it contained were exposed to the light of day, they suddenly took on life and changed into a black horse, which at once fled into the desert and there vanished. The black magician had heard of this story and immediately set forth in pursuit of the horse. After a journey of many days, always on the tracks of the horse, he came to the desert and crossed to the other side, where the grasslands began again. There he met the horse grazing, and there also he came upon the find on whose account he now needed the advice of the white magician. For he had found the lost* keys of paradise, *and he did not know what to do with them.* At this exciting moment the dreamer awoke.

72 In the light of our earlier remarks the meaning of the dream is not hard to guess: the old king is the ruling symbol that wants to go to its eternal rest, and in the very place where similar "dominants" lie buried. His choice falls, fittingly enough, on the grave of anima, who lies in the death trance of a Sleeping Beauty so long as the king is alive—that is, so long as a valid principle (Prince or *princeps*) regulates and expresses life. But when the king draws to his end,[38] she comes to life again and changes into a black horse, which in Plato's parable stands for

[38] Cf. the motif of the "old king" in alchemy. *Psychology and Alchemy*, pars. 434ff.

the unruliness of the passions. Anyone who follows this horse comes into the desert, into a wild land remote from men—an image of spiritual and moral isolation. But there lie the keys of paradise.

73 Now what is paradise? Clearly, the Garden of Eden with its two-faced tree of life and knowledge and its four streams. In the Christian version it is also the heavenly city of the Apocalypse, which, like the Garden of Eden, is conceived as a mandala. But the mandala is a symbol of individuation. So it is the *black* magician who finds the keys to the solution of the problems of belief weighing on the dreamer, the keys that open the way of individuation. The contrast between desert and paradise therefore signifies isolation as contrasted with individuation, or the becoming of the self.

74 This part of the dream is a remarkable paraphrase of the Oxyrhynchus sayings of Jesus,[39] in which the way to the kingdom of heaven is pointed out by animals, and where we find the admonition: "Therefore know yourselves, for you are the city, and the city is the kingdom." It is also a paraphrase of the serpent of paradise who persuaded our first parents to sin, and who finally leads to the redemption of mankind through the Son of God. As we know, this causal nexus gave rise to the Ophitic identification of the serpent with the Σωτήρ (Saviour). The black horse and the black magician are half-evil elements whose relativity with respect to good is hinted at in the exchange of garments. The two magicians are, indeed, two aspects of the *wise old man,* the superior master and teacher, the archetype of the spirit, who symbolizes the pre-existent meaning hidden in the chaos of life. He is the father of the soul, and yet the soul, in some miraculous manner, is also his virgin mother, for which reason he was called by the alchemists the "first son of the mother." The black magician and the black horse correspond to the descent into darkness in the dreams mentioned earlier.

75 What an unbearably hard lesson for a young student of theology! Fortunately he was not in the least aware that the father of all prophets had spoken to him in the dream and placed a great secret almost within his grasp. One marvels at the inappropriateness of such occurrences. Why this prodigality? But I have to admit that we do not know how this dream

39 Cf. James, *The Apocryphal New Testament,* pp. 27f.

affected the student in the long run, and I must emphasize that to me, at least, the dream had a very great deal to say. It was not allowed to get lost, even though the dreamer did not understand it.

76 The old man in this dream is obviously trying to show how good and evil function together, presumably as an answer to the still unresolved moral conflict in the Christian psyche. With this peculiar relativization of opposites we find ourselves approaching nearer to the ideas of the East, to the *nirdvandva* of Hindu philosophy, the freedom from opposites, which is shown as a possible way of solving the conflict through reconciliation. How perilously fraught with meaning this Eastern relativity of good and evil is, can be seen from the Indian aphoristic question: "Who takes longer to reach perfection, the man who loves God, or the man who hates him?" And the answer is: "He who loves God takes seven reincarnations to reach perfection, and he who hates God takes only three, for he who hates God will think of him more than he who loves him." Freedom from opposites presupposes their functional equivalence, and this offends our Christian feelings. Nonetheless, as our dream example shows, the balanced co-operation of moral opposites is a natural truth which has been recognized just as naturally by the East. The clearest example of this is to be found in Taoist philosophy. But in the Christian tradition, too, there are various sayings that come very close to this standpoint. I need only remind you of the parable of the unjust steward.

77 Our dream is by no means unique in this respect, for the tendency to relativize opposites is a notable peculiarity of the unconscious One must immediately add, however, that this is true only in cases of exaggerated moral sensibility; in other cases the unconscious can insist just as inexorably on the irreconcilability of the opposites. As a rule, the standpoint of the unconscious is relative to the conscious attitude. We can probably say, therefore, that our dream presupposes the specific beliefs and doubts of a theological consciousness of Protestant persuasion. This limits the statement of the dream to a definite set of problems. But even with this paring down of its validity the dream clearly demonstrates the superiority of its standpoint. Fittingly enough, it expresses its meaning in the opinion and voice of a wise magician, who goes back in direct line to the figure of the

medicine man in primitive society. He is, like the anima, an immortal daemon that pierces the chaotic darknesses of brute life with the light of meaning. He is the enlightener, the master and teacher, a psychopomp whose personification even Nietzsche, that breaker of tablets, could not escape—for he had called up his reincarnation in Zarathustra, the lofty spirit of an almost Homeric age, as the carrier and mouthpiece of his own "Dionysian" enlightenment and ecstasy. For him God was dead, but the driving daemon of wisdom became as it were his bodily double. He himself says:

> Then one was changed to two
> And Zarathustra passed me by.

78 Zarathustra is more for Nietzsche than a poetic figure; he is an involuntary confession, a testament. Nietzsche too had lost his way in the darknesses of a life that turned its back upon God and Christianity, and that is why there came to him the revealer and enlightener, the speaking fountainhead of his soul. Here is the source of the hieratic language of *Zarathustra,* for that is the style of this archetype.

79 Modern man, in experiencing this archetype, comes to know that most ancient form of thinking as an autonomous activity whose object he is. Hermes Trismegistus or the Thoth of Hermetic literature, Orpheus, the Poimandres (shepherd of men) and his near relation the Poimen of Hermes,[40] are other formulations of the same experience. If the name "Lucifer" were not prejudicial, it would be a very suitable one for this archetype. But I have been content to call it the *archetype of the wise old man,* or *of meaning.* Like all archetypes it has a positive and a negative aspect, though I don't want to enter into this here. The reader will find a detailed exposition of the two-facedness of the wise old man in "The Phenomenology of the Spirit in Fairytales."

80 The three archetypes so far discussed—the shadow, the anima, and the wise old man—are of a kind that can be directly experienced in personified form. In the foregoing I tried to indicate the general psychological conditions in which such an experience arises. But what I conveyed were only abstract

40 Reitzenstein interprets the "Shepherd" of Hermas as a Christian rejoinder to the Poimandres writings.

generalizations. One could, or rather should, really give a description of the process as it occurs in immediate experience. In the course of this process the archetypes appear as active personalities in dreams and fantasies. But the process itself involves another class of archetypes which one could call the *archetypes of transformation.* They are not personalities, but are typical situations, places, ways and means, that symbolize the kind of transformation in question. Like the personalities, these archetypes are true and genuine symbols that cannot be exhaustively interpreted, either as signs or as allegories. They are genuine symbols precisely because they are ambiguous, full of half-glimpsed meanings, and in the last resort inexhaustible. The ground principles, the *ἀρχαί,* of the unconscious are indescribable because of their wealth of reference, although in themselves recognizable. The discriminating intellect naturally keeps on trying to establish their singleness of meaning and thus misses the essential point; for what we can above all establish as the one thing consistent with their nature is their *manifold meaning,* their almost limitless wealth of reference, which makes any unilateral formulation impossible. Besides this, they are in principle paradoxical, just as for the alchemists the spirit was conceived as "senex et iuvenis simul"—an old man and a youth at once.

81 If one wants to form a picture of the symbolic process, the series of pictures found in alchemy are good examples, though the symbols they contain are for the most part traditional despite their often obscure origin and significance. An excellent Eastern example is the Tantric *chakra* system,[41] or the mystical nerve system of Chinese yoga.[42] It also seems as if the set of pictures in the Tarot cards were distantly descended from the archetypes of transformation, a view that has been confirmed for me in a very enlightening lecture by Professor Bernoulli.[43]

82 The symbolic process is an experience *in images and of images.* Its development usually shows an enantiodromian structure like the text of the *I Ching,* and so presents a rhythm of negative and positive, loss and gain, dark and light. Its beginning is almost invariably characterized by one's getting stuck

41 Arthur Avalon, *The Serpent Power.*

42 Erwin Rousselle, "Spiritual Guidance in Contemporary Taoism."

43 R. Bernoulli, "Zur Symbolik geometrischer Figuren und Zahlen," pp. 397ff.

in a blind alley or in some impossible situation; and its goal is, broadly speaking, illumination or higher consciousness, by means of which the initial situation is overcome on a higher level. As regards the time factor, the process may be compressed into a single dream or into a short moment of experience, or it may extend over months and years, depending on the nature of the initial situation, the person involved in the process, and the goal to be reached. The wealth of symbols naturally varies enormously from case to case. Although everything is experienced in image form, i.e., symbolically, it is by no means a question of fictitious dangers but of very real risks upon which the fate of a whole life may depend. The chief danger is that of succumbing to the fascinating influence of the archetypes, and this is most likely to happen when the archetypal images are not made conscious. If there is already a predisposition to psychosis, it may even happen that the archetypal figures, which are endowed with a certain autonomy anyway on account of their natural numinosity, will escape from conscious control altogether and become completely independent, thus producing the phenomena of possession. In the case of an anima-possession, for instance, the patient will want to change himself into a woman through self-castration, or he is afraid that something of the sort will be done to him by force. The best-known example of this is Schreber's *Memoirs of My Nervous Illness*. Patients often discover a whole anima mythology with numerous archaic motifs. A case of this kind was published some time ago by Nelken.[44] Another patient has described his experiences himself and commented on them in a book.[45] I mention these examples because there are still people who think that the archetypes are subjective chimeras of my own brain.

83 The things that come to light brutally in insanity remain hidden in the background in neurosis, but they continue to influence consciousness nonetheless. When, therefore, the analysis penetrates the background of conscious phenomena, it discovers the same archetypal figures that activate the deliriums of psychotics. Finally, there is any amount of literary and historical evidence to prove that in the case of these archetypes we are dealing with normal types of fantasy that occur practically

44 "Analytische Beobachtungen über Phantasien eines Schizophrenen," pp. 504ff.

45 John Custance, *Wisdom, Madness, and Folly.*

everywhere and not with the monstrous products of insanity. The pathological element does not lie in the existence of these ideas, but in the dissociation of consciousness that can no longer control the unconscious. In all cases of dissociation it is therefore necessary to integrate the unconscious into consciousness. This is a synthetic process which I have termed the "individuation process."

84 As a matter of fact, this process follows the natural course of life—a life in which the individual becomes what he always was. Because man has consciousness, a development of this kind does not run very smoothly; often it is varied and disturbed, because consciousness deviates again and again from its archetypal, instinctual foundation and finds itself in opposition to it. There then arises the need for a synthesis of the two positions. This amounts to psychotherapy even on the primitive level, where it takes the form of restitution ceremonies. As examples I would mention the identification of the Australian aborigines with their ancestors in the *alcheringa* period, identification with the "sons of the sun" among the Pueblos of Taos, the Helios apotheosis in the Isis mysteries, and so on. Accordingly, the therapeutic method of complex psychology consists on the one hand in making as fully conscious as possible the constellated unconscious contents, and on the other hand in synthetizing them with consciousness through the act of recognition. Since, however, civilized man possesses a high degree of dissociability and makes continual use of it in order to avoid every possible risk, it is by no means a foregone conclusion that recognition will be followed by the appropriate action. On the contrary, we have to reckon with the singular ineffectiveness of recognition and must therefore insist on a meaningful application of it. Recognition by itself does not as a rule do this, nor does it imply, as such, any moral strength. In these cases it becomes very clear how much the cure of neurosis is a moral problem.

85 As the archetypes, like all numinous contents, are relatively autonomous, they cannot be integrated simply by rational means, but require a dialectical procedure, a real coming to terms with them, often conducted by the patient in dialogue form, so that, without knowing it, he puts into effect the alchemical definition of the *meditatio*: "an inner colloquy with

one's good angel." [46] Usually the process runs a dramatic course, with many ups and downs. It expresses itself in, or is accompanied by, dream symbols that are related to the "représentations collectives," which in the form of mythological motifs have portrayed psychic processes of transformation since the earliest times.[47]

86 In the short space of a lecture I must content myself with giving only a few examples of archetypes. I have chosen the ones that play the chief part in an analysis of the masculine psyche, and have tried to give you some idea of the transformation process in which they appear. Since this lecture was first published, the figures of the shadow, anima, and wise old man, together with the corresponding figures of the feminine unconscious, have been dealt with in greater detail in my contributions to the symbolism of the self,[48] and the individuation process in its relation to alchemical symbolism has also been subjected to closer investigation.[49]

46 Ruland, *Lexicon alchemiae* (1612).

47 Cf. *Symbols of Transformation.*

48 *Aion,* Part II of this volume.

49 *Psychology and Alchemy.*

THE CONCEPT OF THE COLLECTIVE UNCONSCIOUS[1]

87 Probably none of my empirical concepts has met with so much misunderstanding as the idea of the collective unconscious. In what follows I shall try to give (1) a definition of the concept, (2) a description of what it means for psychology, (3) an explanation of the method of proof, and (4) an example.

1. *Definition*

88 The collective unconscious is a part of the psyche which can be negatively distinguished from a personal unconscious by the fact that it does not, like the latter, owe its existence to personal experience and consequently is not a personal acquisition. While the personal unconscious is made up essentially of contents which have at one time been conscious but which have disappeared from consciousness through having been forgotten or repressed, the contents of the collective unconscious have never been in consciousness, and therefore have never been individually acquired, but owe their existence exclusively to heredity. Whereas the personal unconscious consists for the most part of *complexes,* the content of the collective unconscious is made up essentially of *archetypes.*

89 The concept of the archetype, which is an indispensable correlate of the idea of the collective unconscious, indicates the existence of definite forms in the psyche which seem to be present always and everywhere. Mythological research calls them "motifs"; in the psychology of primitives they correspond to Lévy-Bruhl's concept of "représentations collectives," and in the field of comparative religion they have been defined by

1 [Originally given as a lecture to the Abernethian Society at St. Bartholomew's Hospital, London, on Oct. 19, 1936, and published in the Hospital's *Journal,* XLIV (1936/37), 46–49, 64–66. The present version has been slightly revised by the author and edited in terminology.—EDITORS.]

Hubert and Mauss as "categories of the imagination." Adolf Bastian long ago called them "elementary" or "primordial thoughts." From these references it should be clear enough that my idea of the archetype—literally a pre-existent form—does not stand alone but is something that is recognized and named in other fields of knowledge.

90 My thesis, then, is as follows: In addition to our immediate consciousness, which is of a thoroughly personal nature and which we believe to be the only empirical psyche (even if we tack on the personal unconscious as an appendix), there exists a second psychic system of a collective, universal, and impersonal nature which is identical in all individuals. This collective unconscious does not develop individually but is inherited. It consists of pre-existent forms, the archetypes, which can only become conscious secondarily and which give definite form to certain psychic contents.

2. *The Psychological Meaning of the Collective Unconscious*

91 Medical psychology, growing as it did out of professional practice, insists on the *personal* nature of the psyche. By this I mean the views of Freud and Adler. It is a *psychology of the person,* and its aetiological or causal factors are regarded almost wholly as personal in nature. Nonetheless, even this psychology is based on certain general biological factors, for instance on the sexual instinct or on the urge for self-assertion, which are by no means merely personal peculiarities. It is forced to do this because it lays claim to being an explanatory science. Neither of these views would deny the existence of *a priori* instincts common to man and animals alike, or that they have a significant influence on personal psychology. Yet instincts are impersonal, universally distributed, hereditary factors of a dynamic or motivating character, which very often fail so completely to reach consciousness that modern psychotherapy is faced with the task of helping the patient to become conscious of them. Moreover, the instincts are not vague and indefinite by nature, but are specifically formed motive forces which, long before there is any consciousness, and in spite of any degree of consciousness later on, pursue their inherent goals. Consequently they form very close analogies to the archetypes, so

close, in fact, that there is good reason for supposing that the archetypes are the unconscious images of the instincts themselves, in other words, that they are *patterns of instinctual behaviour.*

92 The hypothesis of the collective unconscious is, therefore, no more daring than to assume there are instincts. One admits readily that human activity is influenced to a high degree by instincts, quite apart from the rational motivations of the conscious mind. So if the assertion is made that our imagination, perception, and thinking are likewise influenced by inborn and universally present formal elements, it seems to me that a normally functioning intelligence can discover in this idea just as much or just as little mysticism as in the theory of instincts. Although this reproach of mysticism has frequently been levelled at my concept, I must emphasize yet again that the concept of the collective unconscious is neither a speculative nor a philosophical but an empirical matter. The question is simply this: are there or are there not unconscious, universal forms of this kind? If they exist, then there is a region of the psyche which one can call the collective unconscious. It is true that the diagnosis of the collective unconscious is not always an easy task. It is not sufficient to point out the often obviously archetypal nature of unconscious products, for these can just as well be derived from acquisitions through language and education. Cryptomnesia should also be ruled out, which it is almost impossible to do in certain cases. In spite of all these difficulties, there remain enough individual instances showing the autochthonous revival of mythological motifs to put the matter beyond any reasonable doubt. But if such an unconscious exists at all, psychological explanation must take account of it and submit certain alleged personal aetiologies to sharper criticism.

93 What I mean can perhaps best be made clear by a concrete example. You have probably read Freud's discussion[2] of a certain picture by Leonardo da Vinci: St. Anne with the Virgin Mary and the Christ-child. Freud interprets this remarkable picture in terms of the fact that Leonardo himself had two mothers. This causality is personal. We shall not linger over the fact that this picture is far from unique, nor over the minor

[2] *Leonardo da Vinci and a Memory of His Childhood,* sec. IV.

inaccuracy that St. Anne happens to be the grandmother of Christ and not, as required by Freud's interpretation, the mother, but shall simply point out that interwoven with the apparently personal psychology there is an impersonal motif well known to us from other fields. This is the motif of the *dual mother,* an archetype to be found in many variants in the field of mythology and comparative religion and forming the basis of numerous "représentations collectives." I might mention, for instance, the motif of the *dual descent,* that is, descent from human and divine parents, as in the case of Heracles, who received immortality through being unwittingly adopted by Hera. What was a myth in Greece was actually a ritual in Egypt: Pharaoh was both human and divine by nature. In the birth chambers of the Egyptian temples Pharaoh's second, divine conception and birth is depicted on the walls; he is "twice-born." It is an idea that underlies all rebirth mysteries, Christianity included. Christ himself is "twice-born": through his baptism in the Jordan he was regenerated and reborn from water and spirit. Consequently, in the Roman liturgy the font is designated the "uterus ecclesiae," and, as you can read in the Roman missal, it is called this even today, in the "benediction of the font" on Holy Saturday before Easter. Further, according to an early Christan-Gnostic idea, the spirit which appeared in the form of a dove was interpreted as Sophia-Sapientia—Wisdom and the Mother of Christ. Thanks to this motif of the dual birth, children today, instead of having good and evil fairies who magically "adopt" them at birth with blessings or curses, are given sponsors—a "godfather" and a "godmother."

94 The idea of a second birth is found at all times and in all places. In the earliest beginnings of medicine it was a magical means of healing; in many religions it is the central mystical experience; it is the key idea in medieval, occult philosophy, and, last but not least, it is an infantile fantasy occurring in numberless children, large and small, who believe that their parents are not their real parents but merely foster-parents to whom they were handed over. Benvenuto Cellini also had this idea, as he himself relates in his autobiography.

95 Now it is absolutely out of the question that all the individuals who believe in a dual descent have in reality always had

two mothers, or conversely that those few who shared Leonardo's fate have infected the rest of humanity with their complex. Rather, one cannot avoid the assumption that the universal occurrence of the dual-birth motif together with the fantasy of the two mothers answers an omnipresent human need which is reflected in these motifs. If Leonardo da Vinci did in fact portray his two mothers in St. Anne and Mary—which I doubt—he nonetheless was only expressing something which countless millions of people before and after him have believed. The vulture symbol (which Freud also discusses in the work mentioned) makes this view all the more plausible. With some justification he quotes as the source of the symbol the *Hieroglyphica* of Horapollo,[3] a book much in use in Leonardo's time. There you read that vultures are female only and symbolize the mother. They conceive through the wind (*pneuma*). This word took on the meaning of "spirit" chiefly under the influence of Christianity. Even in the account of the miracle at Pentecost the pneuma still has the double meaning of wind and spirit. This fact, in my opinion, points without doubt to Mary, who, a virgin by nature, conceived through the pneuma, like a vulture. Furthermore, according to Horapollo, the vulture also symbolizes Athene, who sprang, unbegotten, directly from the head of Zeus, was a virgin, and knew only spiritual motherhood. All this is really an allusion to Mary and the rebirth motif. There is not a shadow of evidence that Leonardo meant anything else by his picture. Even if it is correct to assume that he identified himself with the Christ-child, he was in all probability representing the mythological dual-mother motif and by no means his own personal prehistory. And what about all the other artists who painted the same theme? Surely not all of them had two mothers?

96 Let us now transpose Leonardo's case to the field of the neuroses, and assume that a patient with a mother complex is suffering from the delusion that the cause of his neurosis lies in his having really had two mothers. The personal interpretation would have to admit that he is right—and yet it would be quite wrong. For in reality the cause of his neurosis would lie in the reactivation of the dual-mother archetype,

[3] [Cf. the trans. by George Boas, pp. 63ff., and Freud, *Leonardo*, sec. II.—EDITORS.]

quite regardless of whether he had one mother or two mothers, because, as we have seen, this archetype functions individually and historically without any reference to the relatively rare occurrence of dual motherhood.

97 In such a case, it is of course tempting to presuppose so simple and personal a cause, yet the hypothesis is not only inexact but totally false. It is admittedly difficult to understand how a dual-mother motif—unknown to a physician trained only in medicine—could have so great a determining power as to produce the effect of a traumatic condition. But if we consider the tremendous powers that lie hidden in the mythological and religious sphere in man, the aetiological significance of the archetype appears less fantastic. In numerous cases of neurosis the cause of the disturbance lies in the very fact that the psychic life of the patient lacks the co-operation of these motive forces. Nevertheless a purely personalistic psychology, by reducing everything to personal causes, tries its level best to deny the existence of archetypal motifs and even seeks to destroy them by personal analysis. I consider this a rather dangerous procedure which cannot be justified medically. Today you can judge better than you could twenty years ago the nature of the forces involved. Can we not see how a whole nation is reviving an archaic symbol, yes, even archaic religious forms, and how this mass emotion is influencing and revolutionizing the life of the individual in a catastrophic manner? The man of the past is alive in us today to a degree undreamt of before the war, and in the last analysis what is the fate of great nations but a summation of the psychic changes in individuals?

98 So far as a neurosis is really only a private affair, having its roots exclusively in personal causes, archetypes play no role at all. But if it is a question of a general incompatibility or an otherwise injurious condition productive of neuroses in relatively large numbers of individuals, then we must assume the presence of constellated archetypes. Since neuroses are in most cases not just private concerns, but *social* phenomena, we must assume that archetypes are constellated in these cases too. The archetype corresponding to the situation is activated, and as a result those explosive and dangerous forces hidden in the archetype come into action, frequently with unpredictable

consequences. There is no lunacy people under the domination of an archetype will not fall a prey to. If thirty years ago anyone had dared to predict that our psychological development was tending towards a revival of the medieval persecutions of the Jews, that Europe would again tremble before the Roman fasces and the tramp of legions, that people would once more give the Roman salute, as two thousand years ago, and that instead of the Christian Cross an archaic swastika would lure onward millions of warriors ready for death—why, that man would have been hooted at as a mystical fool. And today? Surprising as it may seem, all this absurdity is a horrible reality. Private life, private aetiologies, and private neuroses have become almost a fiction in the world of today. The man of the past who lived in a world of archaic "représentations collectives" has risen again into very visible and painfully real life, and this not only in a few unbalanced individuals but in many millions of people.

99 There are as many archetypes as there are typical situations in life. Endless repetition has engraved these experiences into our psychic constitution, not in the form of images filled with content, but at first only as *forms without content,* representing merely the possibility of a certain type of perception and action. When a situation occurs which corresponds to a given archetype, that archetype becomes activated and a compulsiveness appears, which, like an instinctual drive, gains its way against all reason and will, or else produces a conflict of pathological dimensions, that is to say, a neurosis.

3. *Method of Proof*

100 We must now turn to the question of how the existence of archetypes can be proved. Since archetypes are supposed to produce certain psychic forms, we must discuss how and where one can get hold of the material demonstrating these forms. The main source, then, is *dreams,* which have the advantage of being involuntary, spontaneous products of the unconscious psyche and are therefore pure products of nature not falsified by any conscious purpose. By questioning the individual one can ascertain which of the motifs appearing in the dream are known to him. From those which are unknown to him we must

naturally exclude all motifs which *might* be known to him, as for instance—to revert to the case of Leonardo—the vulture symbol. We are not sure whether Leonardo took this symbol from Horapollo or not, although it would have been perfectly possible for an educated person of that time, because in those days artists were distinguished for their wide knowledge of the humanities. Therefore, although the bird motif is an archetype par excellence, its existence in Leonardo's fantasy would still prove nothing. Consequently, we must look for motifs which could not possibly be known to the dreamer and yet behave functionally in his dream in such a manner as to coincide with the functioning of the archetype known from historical sources.

101 Another source for the material we need is to be found in "active imagination." By this I mean a sequence of fantasies produced by deliberate concentration. I have found that the existence of unrealized, unconscious fantasies increases the frequency and intensity of dreams, and that when these fantasies are made conscious the dreams change their character and become weaker and less frequent. From this I have drawn the conclusion that dreams often contain fantasies which "want" to become conscious. The sources of dreams are often repressed instincts which have a natural tendency to influence the conscious mind. In cases of this sort, the patient is simply given the task of contemplating any one fragment of fantasy that seems significant to him—a chance idea, perhaps, or something he has become conscious of in a dream—until its context becomes visible, that is to say, the relevant associative material in which it is embedded. It is not a question of the "free association" recommended by Freud for the purpose of dream-analysis, but of elaborating the fantasy by observing the further fantasy material that adds itself to the fragment in a natural manner.

102 This is not the place to enter upon a technical discussion of the method. Suffice it to say that the resultant sequence of fantasies relieves the unconscious and produces material rich in archetypal images and associations. Obviously, this is a method that can only be used in certain carefully selected cases. The method is not entirely without danger, because it may carry the patient too far away from reality. A warning against thoughtless application is therefore in place.

103 Finally, very interesting sources of archetypal material are to be found in the delusions of paranoiacs, the fantasies observed in trance-states, and the dreams of early childhood, from the third to the fifth year. Such material is available in profusion, but it is valueless unless one can adduce convincing mythological parallels. It does not, of course, suffice simply to connect a dream about a snake with the mythological occurrence of snakes, for who is to guarantee that the functional meaning of the snake in the dream is the same as in the mythological setting? In order to draw a valid parallel, it is necessary to know the functional meaning of the individual symbol, and then to find out whether the apparently parallel mythological symbol has a similar context and therefore the same functional meaning. Establishing such facts not only requires lengthy and wearisome researches, but is also an ungrateful subject for demonstration. As the symbols must not be torn out of their context, one has to launch forth into exhaustive descriptions, personal as well as symbological, and this is practically impossible in the framework of a lecture. I have repeatedly tried it at the risk of sending one half of my audience to sleep.

4. *An Example*

104 I am choosing as an example a case which, though already published, I use again because its brevity makes it peculiarly suitable for illustration. Moreover, I can add certain remarks which were omitted in the previous publication.[4]

105 About 1906 I came across a very curious delusion in a paranoid schizophrenic who had been interned for many years. The patient had suffered since his youth and was incurable. He had been educated at a State school and been employed as a clerk in an office. He had no special gifts, and I myself knew nothing of mythology or archaeology in those days, so the situation was not in any way suspect. One day I found the patient standing at the window, wagging his head and blinking into the sun. He told me to do the same, for then I would see something very interesting. When I asked him what he saw, he was aston-

[4] *Wandlungen und Symbole der Libido* (orig. 1912). [Trans. as *Psychology of the Unconscious,* 1916. Cf. the revised edition, *Symbols of Transformation,* pars. 149ff., 223.—EDITORS.]

ished that I could see nothing, and said: "Surely you see the sun's penis—when I move my head to and fro, it moves too, and that is where the wind comes from." Naturally I did not understand this strange idea in the least, but I made a note of it. Then about four years later, during my mythological studies, I came upon a book by the late Albrecht Dieterich,[5] the well-known philologist, which threw light on this fantasy. The work, published in 1910, deals with a Greek papyrus in the Bibliothèque Nationale, Paris. Dieterich believed he had discovered a Mithraic ritual in one part of the text. The text is undoubtedly a religious prescription for carrying out certain incantations in which Mithras is named. It comes from the Alexandrian school of mysticism and shows affinities with certain passages in the Leiden papyri and the *Corpus Hermeticum*. In Dieterich's text we read the following directions:

> Draw breath from the rays, draw in three times as strongly as you can and you will feel yourself raised up and walking towards the height, and you will seem to be in the middle of the aerial region. . . . The path of the visible gods will appear through the disc of the sun, who is God my father. Likewise the so-called tube, the origin of the ministering wind. For you will see hanging down from the disc of the sun something that looks like a tube. And towards the regions westward it is as though there were an infinite east wind. But if the other wind should prevail towards the regions of the east, you will in like manner see the vision veering in that direction.[6]

106 It is obviously the author's intention to enable the reader to experience the vision which he had, or which at least he believes in. The reader is to be initiated into the inner religious experience either of the author, or—what seems more likely—of one of those mystic communities of which Philo Judaeus gives contemporary accounts. The fire- or sun-god here invoked is a figure which has close historical parallels, for instance with the Christ-figure of the Apocalypse. It is therefore a "représentation collective," as are also the ritual actions described, such as the imitating of animal noises, etc. The vision is embedded in a

[5] *Eine Mithrasliturgie*. [As the author subsequently learned, the 1910 edition was actually the second, there having been a first edition in 1903. The patient had, however, been committed some years before 1903.—EDITORS.]

[6] Ibid., pp. 6ff.

religious context of a distinctly ecstatic nature and describes a kind of initiation into mystic experience of the Deity.

107 Our patient was about ten years older than I. In his megalomania, he thought he was God and Christ in one person. His attitude towards me was patronizing; he liked me probably because I was the only person with any sympathy for his abstruse ideas. His delusions were mainly religious, and when he invited me to blink into the sun like he did and waggle my head he obviously wanted to let me share his vision. He played the role of the mystic sage and I was the neophyte. He felt he was the sun-god himself, creating the wind by wagging his head to and fro. The ritual transformation into the Deity is attested by Apuleius in the Isis mysteries, and moreover in the form of a Helios apotheosis. The meaning of the "ministering wind" is probably the same as the procreative pneuma, which streams from the sun-god into the soul and fructifies it. The association of sun and wind frequently occurs in ancient symbolism.

108 It must now be shown that this is not a purely chance coincidence of two isolated cases. We must therefore show that the idea of a wind-tube connected with God or the sun exists independently of these two testimonies and that it occurs at other times and in other places. Now there are, as a matter of fact, medieval paintings that depict the fructification of Mary with a tube or hose-pipe coming down from the throne of God and passing into her body, and we can see the dove or the Christ-child flying down it. The dove represents the fructifying agent, the wind of the Holy Ghost.

109 Now it is quite out of the question that the patient could have had any knowledge whatever of a Greek papyrus published four years later, and it is in the highest degree unlikely that his vision had anything to do with the rare medieval representations of the Conception, even if through some incredibly improbable chance he had ever seen a copy of such a painting. The patient was certified in his early twenties. He had never travelled. And there is no such picture in the public art gallery in Zurich, his native town.

110 I mention this case not in order to prove that the vision is an archetype but only to show you my method of procedure in the simplest possible form. If we had only such cases, the task of investigation would be relatively easy, but in reality the proof

is much more complicated. First of all, certain symbols have to be isolated clearly enough to be recognizable as typical phenomena, not just matters of chance. This is done by examining a series of dreams, say a few hundred, for typical figures, and by observing their development in the series. The same method can be applied to the products of active imagination. In this way it is possible to establish certain continuities or modulations of one and the same figure. You can select any figure which gives the impression of being an archetype by its behaviour in the series of dreams or visions. If the material at one's disposal has been well observed and is sufficiently ample, one can discover interesting facts about the variations undergone by a single type. Not only the type itself but its variants too can be substantiated by evidence from comparative mythology and ethnology. I have described the method of investigation elsewhere [7] and have also furnished the necessary case material.

[7] *Psychology and Alchemy*, Part II.

CONCERNING THE ARCHETYPES, WITH SPECIAL REFERENCE TO THE ANIMA CONCEPT[1]

111 Although modern man appears to believe that the non-empirical approach to psychology is a thing of the past, his general attitude remains very much the same as it was before, when psychology was identified with some theory about the psyche. In academic circles, a drastic revolution in methodology, initiated by Fechner[2] and Wundt,[3] was needed in order to make clear to the scientific world that psychology was a field of experience and not a philosophical theory. To the increasing materialism of the late nineteenth century, however, it meant nothing that there had once been an "experimental psychology,"[4] to which we owe many descriptions that are still valuable today. I have only to mention Dr. Justinus Kerner's *Seherin von Prevorst*.[5] All "romantic" descriptions in psychology were anathema to the new developments in scientific method. The exaggerated expectations of this experimental laboratory science were reflected in Fechner's "psychophysics," and its results today take the form of "psychological tests" and a general shifting of the scientific standpoint in favour of phenomenology.

112 Nevertheless, it cannot be maintained that the phenomenological point of view has made much headway. Theory still plays far too great a role, instead of being included in phenomenology as it should. Even Freud, whose empirical attitude is beyond doubt, coupled his theory as a *sine qua non* with his

1 [Originally published as "Über den Archetypus mit besonderer Berücksichtigung des Animabegriffes" in the *Zentralblatt für Psychotherapie und ihre Grenzgebiete* (Leipzig), IX (1936) : 5, 259–75. Revised and republished in *Von den Wurzeln des Bewusstseins* (Zurich, 1954), from which version the present translation is made. —Editors.]

2 *Elemente der Psychophysik* (1860).

3 *Principles of Physiological Psychology* (orig. 1874) .

4 Cf. G. H. von Schubert's compilation, *Altes und Neues aus dem Gebiet der innern Seelenkunde* (1825–44).

5 First published 1829. Trans. as *The Seeress of Prevorst* (1859).

method, as if psychic phenomena had to be viewed in a certain light in order to mean something. All the same, it was Freud who cleared the ground for the investigation of complex phenomena, at least in the field of neurosis. But the ground he cleared extended only so far as certain basic physiological concepts permitted, so that it looked almost as if psychology were an offshoot of the physiology of the instincts. This limitation of psychology was very welcome to the materialistic outlook of that time, nearly fifty years ago, and, despite our altered view of the world, it still is in large measure today. It gives us not only the advantage of a "delimited field of work," but also an excellent excuse not to bother with what goes on in a wider world.

113 Thus it was overlooked by the whole of medical psychology that a psychology of the neuroses, such as Freud's, is left hanging in mid air if it lacks knowledge of a general phenomenology. It was also overlooked that in the field of the neuroses Pierre Janet, even before Freud, had begun to build up a descriptive methodology [6] without loading it with too many theoretical and philosophical assumptions. Biographical descriptions of psychic phenomena, going beyond the strictly medical field, were represented chiefly by the work of the philosopher Théodore Flournoy, of Geneva, in his account of the psychology of an unusual personality.[7] This was followed by the first attempt at synthesis: William James's *Varieties of Religious Experience* (1902). I owe it mainly to these two investigators that I learnt to understand the nature of psychic disturbances within the setting of the human psyche as a whole. I myself did experimental work for several years, but, through my intensive studies of the neuroses and psychoses, I had to admit that, however desirable quantitative definitions may be, it is impossible to do without qualitatively descriptive methods. Medical psychology has recognized that the salient facts are extraordinarily complex and can be grasped only through descriptions based on case material. But this method presupposes freedom from theoretical prejudice. Every science is descriptive at the point where it can no longer proceed experimentally, without on that account ceasing to be

6 *L'Automatisme psychologique* (1889); *The Mental State of Hystericals* (orig., 1893); *Névroses et idées fixes* (1898).

7 *From India to the Planet Mars* (orig., 1900), and "Nouvelles Observations sur un cas de somnambulisme avec glossolalie."

scientific. But an experimental science makes itself impossible when it delimits its field of work in accordance with theoretical concepts. The psyche does not come to an end where some physiological assumption or other stops. In other words, in each individual case that we observe scientifically, we have to consider the manifestations of the psyche in their totality.

114 These reflections are essential when discussing an empirical concept like that of the anima. As against the constantly reiterated prejudice that this is a theoretical invention or—worse still—sheer mythology, I must emphasize that the concept of the anima is a purely empirical concept, whose sole purpose is to give a name to a group of related or analogous psychic phenomena. The concept does no more and means no more than, shall we say, the concept "arthropods," which includes all animals with articulated body and limbs and so gives a name to this phenomenological group. The prejudice I have mentioned stems, regrettable though this is, from ignorance. My critics are not acquainted with the phenomena in question, for these lie mostly outside the pale of merely medical knowledge, in a realm of universal human experience. But the psyche, which the medical man has to do with, does not worry about the limitations of his knowledge; it manifests a life of its own and reacts to influences coming from every field of human experience. Its nature shows itself not merely in the personal sphere, or in the instinctual or social, but in phenomena of world-wide distribution. So if we want to understand the psyche, we have to include the whole world. For practical reasons we can, indeed must, delimit our fields of work, but this should be done only with the conscious recognition of limitation. The more complex the phenomena which we have to do with in practical treatment, the wider must be our frame of reference and the greater the corresponding knowledge.

115 Anyone, therefore, who does not know the universal distribution and significance of the *syzygy* motif in the psychology of primitives,[8] in mythology, in comparative religion, and in the history of literature, can hardly claim to say anything about the concept of the anima. His knowledge of the psychology of the neuroses may give him some idea of it, but it is only a knowl-

[8] I am thinking especially of shamanism with its idea of the "celestial wife" (Eliade, *Shamanism*, pp. 76–81).

edge of its general phenomenology that could open his eyes to the real meaning of what he encounters in individual cases, often in pathologically distorted form.

116 Although common prejudice still believes that the sole essential basis of our knowledge is given exclusively from outside, and that "nihil est in intellectu quod non antea fuerit in sensu," it nevertheless remains true that the thoroughly respectable atomic theory of Leucippus and Democritus was not based on any observations of atomic fission but on a "mythological" conception of smallest particles, which, as the smallest animated parts, the soul-atoms, are known even to the still palaeolithic inhabitants of central Australia.[9] How much "soul" is projected into the unknown in the world of external appearances is, of course, familiar to anyone acquainted with the natural science and natural philosophy of the ancients. It is, in fact, so much that we are absolutely incapable of saying how the world is constituted in itself—and always shall be, since we are obliged to convert physical events into psychic processes as soon as we want to say anything about knowledge. But who can guarantee that this conversion produces anything like an adequate "objective" picture of the world? That could only be if the physical event were also a psychic one. But a great distance still seems to separate us from such an assertion. Till then, we must for better or worse content ourselves with the assumption that the psyche supplies those images and forms which alone make knowledge of objects possible.

117 These forms are generally supposed to be transmitted by tradition, so that we speak of "atoms" today because we have heard, directly or indirectly, of the atomic theory of Democritus. But where did Democritus, or whoever first spoke of minimal constitutive elements, hear of atoms? This notion had its origin in archetypal ideas, that is, in primordial images which were never reflections of physical events but are spontaneous products of the psychic factor. Despite the materialistic tendency to understand the psyche as a mere reflection or imprint of physical and chemical processes, there is not a single proof of this hypothesis. Quite the contrary, innumerable facts prove that the

9 Spencer and Gillen, *The Northern Tribes of Central Australia,* pp. 331 and elsewhere. Also Crawley, *The Idea of the Soul,* pp. 87f.

psyche translates physical processes into sequences of images which have hardly any recognizable connection with the objective process. The materialistic hypothesis is much too bold and flies in the face of experience with almost metaphysical presumption. The only thing that can be established with certainty, in the present state of our knowledge, is our ignorance of the nature of the psyche. There is thus no ground at all for regarding the psyche as something secondary or as an epiphenomenon; on the contrary, there is every reason to regard it, at least hypothetically, as a factor *sui generis,* and to go on doing so until it has been sufficiently proved that psychic processes can be fabricated in a retort. We have laughed at the claims of the alchemists to be able to manufacture a *lapis philosophorum* consisting of body, soul, and spirit, as impossible, hence we should stop dragging along with us the logical consequence of this medieval assumption, namely the materialistic prejudice regarding the psyche, as though it were a proven fact.

118 It will not be so easy to reduce complex psychic facts to a chemical formula. Hence the psychic factor must, *ex hypothesi,* be regarded for the present as an autonomous reality of enigmatic character, primarily because, judging from all we know, it appears to be *essentially different* from physicochemical processes. Even if we do not ultimately know what its substantiality is, this is equally true of physical objects and of matter in general. So if we regard the psyche as an independent factor, we must logically conclude that there is a psychic life which is not subject to the caprices of our will. If, then, those qualities of elusiveness, superficiality, shadowiness, and indeed of futility attach to anything psychic, this is primarily true of the subjective psychic, i.e., the contents of consciousness, but not of the objective psychic, the unconscious, which is an *a priori* conditioning factor of consciousness and its contents. From the unconscious there emanate determining influences which, independently of tradition, guarantee in every single individual a similarity and even a sameness of experience, and also of the way it is represented imaginatively. One of the main proofs of this is the almost universal parallelism between mythological motifs, which, on account of their quality as primordial images, I have called *archetypes.*

119 One of these archetypes, which is of paramount practical importance for the psychotherapist, I have named the anima. This Latin expression is meant to connote something that should not be confused with any dogmatic Christian idea of the soul or with any of the previous philosophical conceptions of it. If one wishes to form anything like a concrete conception of what this term covers, one would do better to go back to a classical author like Macrobius,[10] or to classical Chinese philosophy,[11] where the anima (*p'o* or *kuei*) is regarded as the feminine and chthonic part of the soul. A parallel of this kind always runs the risk of metaphysical concretism, which I do my best to avoid, though any attempt at graphic description is bound to succumb to it up to a point. For we are dealing here not with an abstract concept but with an empirical one, and the form in which it appears necessarily clings to it, so that it cannot be described at all except in terms of its specific phenomenology.

120 Unperturbed by the philosophical pros and cons of the age, a scientific psychology must regard those transcendental intuitions that sprang from the human mind in all ages as *projections,* that is, as psychic contents that were extrapolated in metaphysical space and hypostatized.[12] We encounter the anima historically above all in the divine syzygies, the male-female pairs of deities. These reach down, on the one side, into the obscurities of primitive mythology,[13] and up, on the other, into the philosophical speculations of Gnosticism [14] and of classical Chinese philosophy, where the cosmogonic pair of concepts are designated *yang* (masculine) and *yin* (feminine).[15] We can safely assert that these syzygies are as universal as the existence of man and woman. From this fact we may reasonably conclude that man's imagination is bound by this motif, so that he was largely

10 *Commentary on the Dream of Scipio.*

11 Cf. my "Commentary on *The Secret of the Golden Flower,*" pars. 57ff., and Chantepie de la Saussaye, *Lehrbuch der Religionsgeschichte,* I, p. 71.

12 This standpoint derives from Kant's theory of knowledge and has nothing to do with materialism.

13 Winthuis, *Das Zweigeschlechterwesen bei den Zentralaustraliern und anderen Völkern.*

14 Especially in the system of the Valentinians. Cf. Irenaeus, *Adversus haereses.*

15 Cf. *The I Ching or Book of Changes.* [Also Needham, *Science and Civilization in China,* II, pp. 273f.—EDITORS.]

compelled to project it again and again, at all times and in all places.[16]

121 Now, as we know from psychotherapeutic experience, projection is an unconscious, automatic process whereby a content that is unconscious to the subject transfers itself to an object, so that it seems to belong to that object. The projection ceases the moment it becomes conscious, that is to say when it is seen as belonging to the subject.[17] Thus the polytheistic heaven of the ancients owes its depotentiation not least to the view first propounded by Euhemeros,[18] who maintained that the gods were nothing but reflections of human character. It is indeed easy to show that the divine pair is simply an idealization of the parents or of some other human couple, which for some reason appeared in heaven. This assumption would be simple enough if projection were not an unconscious process but were a conscious intention. It would generally be supposed that one's own parents are the best known of all individuals, the ones of which the subject is most conscious. But precisely for this reason they could not be projected, because projection always contains something of which the subject is not conscious and which seems not to belong to him. The image of the parents is the very one that could be projected least, because it is too conscious.

122 In reality, however, it is just the parental imagos that seem to be projected most frequently, a fact so obvious that one could almost draw the conclusion that it is precisely the conscious contents which are projected. This can be seen most plainly in cases of transference, where it is perfectly clear to the patient that the father-imago (or even the mother-imago) is projected on to the analyst and he even sees through the incest-fantasies bound up with them, without, however, being freed from the reactive effect of his projection, i.e., from the transference. In other

16 Hermetic alchemical philosophy from the 14th to the 17th cents. provides a wealth of instructive examples. For our purposes, a glimpse into Michael Maier's *Symbola aureae mensae* (1617) would suffice.

17 There are of course cases where, in spite of the patient's seemingly sufficient insight, the reactive effect of the projection does not cease, and the expected liberation does not take place. I have often observed that in such cases meaningful but unconscious contents are still bound up with the projection carrier. It is these contents that keep up the effect of the projection, although it has apparently been seen through.

18 Fl. *c.* 300 B.C. Cf. Block, *Euhémère: son livre et sa doctrine.*

words, he behaves exactly as if he had not seen through his projection at all. Experience shows that projection is never conscious: projections are always there first and are recognized afterwards. We must therefore assume that, over and above the incest-fantasy, highly emotional contents are still bound up with the parental imagos and need to be made conscious. They are obviously more difficult to make conscious than the incest-fantasies, which are supposed to have been repressed through violent resistance and to be unconscious for that reason. Supposing this view is correct, we are driven to the conclusion that besides the incest-fantasy there must be contents which are repressed through a still greater resistance. Since it is difficult to imagine anything more repellent than incest, we find ourselves rather at a loss to answer this question.

123 If we let practical experience speak, it tells us that, apart from the incest-fantasy, religious ideas are associated with the parental imagos. I do not need to cite historical proofs of this, as they are known to all. But what about the alleged objectionableness of religious associations?

124 Someone once observed that in ordinary society it is more embarrassing to talk about God at table than to tell a risqué story. Indeed, for many people it is more bearable to admit their sexual fantasies than to be forced to confess that their analyst is a saviour, for the former are biologically legitimate, whereas the latter instance is definitely pathological, and this is something we greatly fear. It seems to me, however, that we make too much of "resistance." The phenomena in question can be explained just as easily by lack of imagination and reflectiveness, which makes the act of conscious realization so difficult for the patient. He may perhaps have no particular resistance to religious ideas, only the thought has never occurred to him that he could seriously regard his analyst as a God or saviour. Mere reason alone is sufficient to protect him from such illusions. But he is less slow to assume that his analyst thinks himself one. When one is dogmatic oneself, it is notoriously easy to take other people for prophets and founders of religions.

125 Now religious ideas, as history shows, are charged with an extremely suggestive, emotional power. Among them I naturally reckon all *représentations collectives,* everything that we learn from the history of religion, and anything that has an "-ism"

attached to it. The latter is only a modern variant of the denominational religions. A man may be convinced in all good faith that he has no religious ideas, but no one can fall so far away from humanity that he no longer has any dominating *représentation collective*. His very materialism, atheism, communism, socialism, liberalism, intellectualism, existentialism, or what not, testifies against his innocence. Somewhere or other, overtly or covertly, he is possessed by a supraordinate idea.

126 The psychologist knows how much religious ideas have to do with the parental imagos. History has preserved overwhelming evidence of this, quite apart from modern medical findings, which have even led certain people to suppose that the relationship to the parents is the real origin of religious ideas. This hypothesis is based on very poor knowledge of the facts. In the first place, one should not simply translate the family psychology of modern man into a context of primitive conditions, where things are so very different; secondly, one should beware of ill-considered tribal-father and primal-horde fantasies; thirdly and most importantly, one should have the most accurate knowledge of the phenomenology of religious experience, which is a subject in itself. Psychological investigations in this field have so far not fulfilled any of these three conditions.

127 The only thing we know positively from psychological experience is that theistic ideas are associated with the parental imagos, and that our patients are mostly unconscious of them. If the corresponding projections cannot be withdrawn through insight, then we have every reason to suspect the presence of emotional contents of a religious nature, regardless of the rationalistic resistance of the patient.

128 So far as we have any information about man, we know that he has always and everywhere been under the influence of dominating ideas. Any one who alleges that he is not can immediately be suspected of having exchanged a known form of belief for a variant which is less known both to himself and to others. Instead of theism he is a devotee of atheism, instead of Dionysus he favours the more modern Mithras, and instead of heaven he seeks paradise on earth.

129 A man without a dominating *représentation collective* would be a thoroughly abnormal phenomenon. But such a person ex-

ists only in the fantasies of isolated individuals who are deluded about themselves. They are mistaken not only about the existence of religious ideas, but also and more especially about their intensity. The archetype behind a religious idea has, like every instinct, its specific energy, which it does not lose even if the conscious mind ignores it. Just as it can be assumed with the greatest probability that every man possesses all the average human functions and qualities, so we may expect the presence of normal religious factors, the archetypes, and this expectation does not prove fallacious. Any one who succeeds in putting off the mantle of faith can do so only because another lies close to hand. No one can escape the prejudice of being human.

130 The *représentations collectives* have a dominating power, so it is not surprising that they are repressed with the most intense resistance. When repressed, they do not hide behind any trifling thing but behind ideas and figures that have already become problematical for other reasons, and intensify and complicate their dubious nature. For instance, everything that we would like, in infantile fashion, to attribute to our parents or blame them for is blown up to fantastic proportions from this secret source, and for this reason it remains an open question how much of the ill-reputed incest-fantasy is to be taken seriously. Behind the parental pair, or pair of lovers, lie contents of extreme tension which are not apperceived in consciousness and can therefore become perceptible only through projection. That projections of this kind do actually occur and are not just traditional opinions is attested by historical documents. These show that syzygies were projected which were in complete contradiction to the traditional beliefs, and that they were often experienced in the form of a vision.[19]

131 One of the most instructive examples in this respect is the vision of the recently canonized Nicholas of Flüe, a Swiss mystic of the fifteenth century, of whose visions we possess reports by

19 This is not to overlook the fact that there is probably a far greater number of visions which agree with the dogma. Nevertheless, they are not spontaneous and autonomous projections in the strict sense but are *visualizations of conscious contents,* evoked through prayer, autosuggestion, and heterosuggestion. Most spiritual exercises have this effect, and so do the prescribed meditation practices of the East. In any thorough investigation of such visions it would have to be ascertained, among other things, what the actual vision was and how far dogmatic elaboration contributed to its form.

his contemporaries.[20] In the visions that marked his initiation into the state of adoption by God, God appeared in dual form, once as a majestic *father* and once as a majestic *mother*. This representation could not be more unorthodox, since the Church had eliminated the feminine element from the Trinity a thousand years earlier as heretical. Brother Klaus was a simple unlettered peasant who doubtless had received none but the approved Church teaching, and was certainly not acquainted with the Gnostic interpretation of the Holy Ghost as the feminine and motherly Sophia.[21] His so-called Trinity Vision is at the same time a perfect example of the intensity of projected contents. Brother Klaus's psychological situation was eminently suited to a projection of this kind, for his conscious idea of God was so little in accord with the unconscious content that the latter had to appear in the form of an alien and shattering experience. We must conclude from this that it was not the traditional idea of God but, on the contrary, an "heretical" image [22] that realized itself in visionary form; an archetypal interpretation which came to life again spontaneously, independently of tradition. It was the archetype of the divine pair, the syzygy.

132 There is a very similar case in the visions of Guillaume de Digulleville,[23] which are described in *Le Pèlerinage de l'âme*. He saw God in the highest heaven as the King on a shining round throne, and beside him sat the Queen of Heaven on a throne of brown crystal. For a monk of the Cistercian Order, which as we know is distinguished for its severity, this vision is exceedingly heretical. So here again the condition for projection is fulfilled.

133 Another impressive account of the syzygy vision can be found in the work of Edward Maitland, who wrote the biography of

20 Cf. Stoeckli, *Die Visionen des seligen Bruder Klaus*, and Blanke, *Bruder Klaus von Flüe*.

21 The peculiar love-story of this youngest Aeon can be found in Irenaeus, *Adv. haer.*, I, 2, 2ff. (Roberts/Rambaut trans., I, pp. 7ff.)

22 Cf. my "Brother Klaus."

23 Guillaume wrote three *Pèlerinages* in the manner of the Divine Comedy, but independently of Dante, between 1330 and 1350. He was Prior of the Cistercian monastery at Châlis, in Normandy. Cf. Delacotte, *Guillaume de Digulleville: Trois Romans-poèmes du XIVe siècle*. [Also cf. *Psychology and Alchemy*, pars. 315ff. —EDITORS.]

Anna Kingsford. There he describes in detail his own experience of God, which, like that of Brother Klaus, consisted in a vision of light. He says: "This was . . . God as the Lord, proving by His duality that God is Substance as well as Force, Love as well as Will, feminine as well as masculine, Mother as well as Father." [24]

134 These few examples may suffice to characterize the experience of projection and those features of it which are independent of tradition. We can hardly get round the hypothesis that an emotionally charged content is lying ready in the unconscious and springs into projection at a certain moment. This content is the syzygy motif, and it expresses the fact that a masculine element is always paired with a feminine one. The wide distribution and extraordinary emotionality of this motif prove that it is a fundamental psychic factor of great practical importance, no matter whether the individual psychotherapist or psychologist understands where and in what way it influences his special field of work. Microbes, as we know, played their dangerous role long before they were discovered.

135 As I have said, it is natural to suspect the parental pair in all syzygies. The feminine part, the mother, corresponds to the anima. But since, for the reasons discussed above, consciousness of the object prevents its projection, there is nothing for it but to assume that parents are also the least known of all human beings, and consequently that an unconscious reflection of the parental pair exists which is as unlike them, as utterly alien and incommensurable, as a man compared with a god. It would be conceivable, and has as we know been asserted, that the unconscious reflection is none other than the image of father and mother that was acquired in early childhood, overvalued, and later repressed on account of the incest-fantasy associated with it. This hypothesis presupposes that the image was once *conscious,* otherwise it could not have been "repressed." It also presupposes that the act of moral repression has itself become unconscious, for otherwise the act would remain preserved in

24 *Anna Kingsford: Her Life, Letters, Diary, and Work,* I, pp. 130. Maitland's vision is similar in form and meaning to the one in the Poimandres (Scott, *Hermetica,* I, Libellus I, pp. 114ff.), where the spiritual light is described as "male-female." I do not know whether Maitland was acquainted with the Poimandres; probably not.

consciousness together with the memory of the repressive moral reaction, from which the nature of the thing repressed could easily be recognized. I do not want to enlarge on these misgivings, but would merely like to emphasize that there is general agreement on one point: that the parental imago comes into existence not in the pre-puberal period or at a time when consciousness is more or less developed, but in the initial stages between the first and fourth year, when consciousness does not show any real continuity and is characterized by a kind of island-like discontinuity. The ego-relationship that is required for continuity of consciousness is present only in part, so that a large proportion of psychic life at this stage runs on in a state which can only be described as relatively unconscious. At all events it is a state which would give the impression of a somnambulistic, dream, or twilight state if observed in an adult. These states, as we know from the observation of small children, are always characterized by an apperception of reality filled with fantasies. The fantasy-images outweigh the influence of sensory stimuli and mould them into conformity with a *pre-existing psychic image.*

136 It is in my view a great mistake to suppose that the psyche of a new-born child is a *tabula rasa* in the sense that there is absolutely nothing in it. In so far as the child is born with a differentiated brain that is predetermined by heredity and therefore individualized, it meets sensory stimuli coming from outside not with *any* aptitudes, but with *specific* ones, and this necessarily results in a particular, individual choice and pattern of apperception. These aptitudes can be shown to be inherited instincts and preformed patterns, the latter being the *a priori* and formal conditions of apperception that are based on instinct. Their presence gives the world of the child and the dreamer its anthropomorphic stamp. They are the archetypes, which direct all fantasy activity into its appointed paths and in this way produce, in the fantasy-images of children's dreams as well as in the delusions of schizophrenia, astonishing mythological parallels such as can also be found, though in lesser degree, in the dreams of normal persons and neurotics. It is not, therefore, a question of inherited *ideas* but of inherited *possibilities* of ideas. Nor are they individual acquisitions but, in the main,

common to all, as can be seen from the universal occurrence of the archetypes.[25]

137 Just as the archetypes occur on the ethnological level as myths, so also they are found in every individual, and their effect is always strongest, that is, they anthropomorphize reality most, where consciousness is weakest and most restricted, and where fantasy can overrun the facts of the outer world. This condition is undoubtedly present in the child during the first years of its life. It therefore seems to me more probable that the archetypal form of the divine syzygy first covers up and assimilates the image of the real parents until, with increasing consciousness, the real figures of the parents are perceived—often to the child's disappointment. Nobody knows better than the psychotherapist that the mythologizing of the parents is often pursued far into adulthood and is given up only with the greatest resistance.

138 I remember a case that was presented to me as the victim of a high-grade mother and castration complex, which had still not been overcome in spite of psychoanalysis. Without any hint from me, the man had made some drawings which showed the mother first as a superhuman being, and then as a figure of woe, with bloody mutilations. I was especially struck by the fact that a castration had obviously been performed on the mother, for in front of her gory genitals lay the cut-off male sexual organs. The drawings clearly represented a diminishing climax: first the mother was a divine hermaphrodite, who then, through the son's disappointing experience of reality, was robbed of its androgynous, Platonic perfection and changed into the woeful figure of an ordinary old woman. Thus from the very beginning, from the son's earliest childhood, the mother was assimilated to the archetypal idea of the syzygy, or conjunction of male and female, and for this reason appeared perfect and super-

25 Hubert and Mauss (*Mélanges d'histoire des religions,* preface, p. xxix) call these *a priori* thought-forms "categories," presumably with reference to Kant: "They exist ordinarily as habits which govern consciousness, but are themselves unconscious." The authors conjecture that the primordial images are conditioned by language. This conjecture may be correct in certain cases, but in general it is contradicted by the fact that a great many archetypal images and associations are brought to light by dream psychology and psychopathology which would be absolutely incommunicable through language.

human.[26] The latter quality invariably attaches to the archetype and explains why the archetype appears strange and as if not belonging to consciousness, and also why, if the subject identifies with it, it often causes a devastating change of personality, generally in the form of megalomania or its opposite.

139 The son's disappointment effected a castration of the hermaphroditic mother: this was the patient's so-called castration complex. He had tumbled down from his childhood Olympus and was no longer the son-hero of a divine mother. His so-called fear of castration was fear of real life, which refused to come up to his erstwhile childish expectations, and everywhere lacked that mythological meaning which he still dimly remembered from his earliest youth. His life was, in the truest sense of the word, "godless." And that, for him—though he did not realize it—meant a dire loss of hope and energy. He thought of himself as "castrated," which is a very plausible neurotic misunderstanding—so plausible that it could even be turned into a theory of neurosis.

140 Because people have always feared that the connection with the instinctive, archetypal stage of consciousness might get lost in the course of life, the custom has long since been adopted of giving the new-born child, in addition to his bodily parents, two godparents, a "godfather" and a "godmother," who are supposed to be responsible for the spiritual welfare of their godchild. They represent the pair of gods who appear at its birth, thus illustrating the "dual birth" motif.[27]

26 Conforming to the bisexual Original Man in Plato, *Symposium*, XIV, and to the hermaphroditic Primal Beings in general.

27 The "dual birth" refers to the motif, well known from hero mythology, which makes the hero descend from divine as well as from human parents. In most mysteries and religions it plays an important role as a baptism or rebirth motif. It was this motif that misled Freud in his study of Leonardo da Vinci. Without taking account of the fact that Leonardo was by no means the only artist to paint the motif of St. Anne, Mary, and the Christ-child, Freud tried to reduce Anne and Mary, the grandmother and mother, to the mother and stepmother of Leonardo; in other words, to assimilate the painting to his theory. But did the other painters all have stepmothers?! What prompted Freud to this violent interpretation was obviously the fantasy of dual descent suggested by Leonardo's biography. This fantasy covered up the inconvenient reality that St. Anne was the grandmother, and prevented Freud from inquiring into the biographies of other artists who also painted St. Anne. The "religious inhibition of thought" mentioned on p. 79 (1957 edn.) proved true of the author himself. Similarly, the incest theory on

141 The anima image, which lends the mother such superhuman glamour in the eyes of the son, gradually becomes tarnished by commonplace reality and sinks back into the unconscious, but without in any way losing its original tension and instinctivity. It is ready to spring out and project itself at the first opportunity, the moment a woman makes an impression that is out of the ordinary. We then have Goethe's experience with Frau von Stein, and its repercussions in the figures of Mignon and Gretchen, all over again. In the case of Gretchen, Goethe also showed us the whole underlying "metaphysic." The love life of a man reveals the psychology of this archetype in the form either of boundless fascination, overvaluation, and infatuation, or of misogyny in all its gradations and variants, none of which can be explained by the real nature of the "object" in question, but only by a transference of the mother complex. The complex, however, was caused in the first place by the assimilation of the mother (in itself a normal and ubiquitous phenomenon) to the pre-existent, feminine side of an archetypal "male-female" pair of opposites, and secondly by an abnormal delay in detaching from the primordial image of the mother. Actually, nobody can stand the total loss of the archetype. When that happens, it gives rise to that frightful "discontent in our culture," where nobody feels at home because a "father" and "mother" are missing. Everyone knows the provisions that religion has always made in this respect. Unfortunately there are very many people who thoughtlessly go on asking whether these provisions are "true," when it is really a question of a psychological need. Nothing is achieved by explaining them away rationalistically.

142 When projected, the anima always has a feminine form with definite characteristics. This empirical finding does not mean

which he lays so much stress is based on another archetype, the well-known incest motif frequently met with in hero myths. It is logically derived from the original hermaphrodite type, which seems to go far back into prehistory. Whenever a psychological theory is forcibly applied, we have reason to suspect that an archetypal fantasy-image is trying to distort reality, thus bearing out Freud's own idea of the "religious inhibition of thought." But to explain the genesis of archetypes by means of the incest theory is about as useful as ladling water from one kettle into another kettle standing beside it, which is connected with the first by a pipe. You cannot explain one archetype by another; that is, it is impossible to say where the archetype comes from, because there is no Archimedean point outside the *a priori* conditions it represents.

that the archetype is constituted like that *in itself*. The male-female syzygy is only one among the possible pairs of opposites, albeit the most important one in practice and the commonest. It has numerous connections with other pairs which do not display any sex differences at all and can therefore be put into the sexual category only by main force. These connections, with their manifold shades of meaning, are found more particularly in Kundalini yoga,[28] in Gnosticism,[29] and above all in alchemical philosophy,[30] quite apart from the spontaneous fantasy-products in neurotic and psychotic case material. When one carefully considers this accumulation of data, it begins to seem probable that an archetype in its quiescent, unprojected state has no exactly determinable form but is in itself an indefinite structure which can assume definite forms only in projection.

143 This seems to contradict the concept of a "type." If I am not mistaken, it not only seems but actually *is* a contradiction. Empirically speaking, we are dealing all the time with "types," definite forms that can be named and distinguished. But as soon as you divest these types of the phenomenology presented by the case material, and try to examine them in relation to other archetypal forms, they branch out into such far-reaching ramifications in the history of symbols that one comes to the conclusion that the basic psychic elements are infinitely varied and ever changing, so as utterly to defy our powers of imagination. The empiricist must therefore content himself with a theoretical "as if." In this respect he is no worse off than the atomic physicist, even though his method is not based on quantitative measurement but is a morphologically descriptive one.

144 The anima is a factor of the utmost importance in the psychology of a man wherever emotions and affects are at work. She intensifies, exaggerates, falsifies, and mythologizes all emotional relations with his work and with other people of both sexes. The resultant fantasies and entanglements are all her doing. When the anima is strongly constellated, she softens the man's character and makes him touchy, irritable, moody, jealous, vain, and unadjusted. He is then in a state of "discontent" and spreads

28 Cf. Avalon, *The Serpent Power; Shrī-Chakra-Sambhara Tantra;* Woodroffe, *Shakti and Shakta.*

29 Schultz, *Dokumente der Gnosis,* especially the lists in Irenaeus, *Adversus haereses.*

30 Cf. *Psychology and Alchemy.*

discontent all around him. Sometimes the man's relationship to the woman who has caught his anima accounts for the existence of this syndrome.

145 The anima, as I have remarked elsewhere,[31] has not escaped the attentions of the poets. There are excellent descriptions of her, which at the same time tell us about the symbolic context in which the archetype is usually embedded. I give first place to Rider Haggard's novels *She, The Return of She,* and *Wisdom's Daughter,* and Benoît's *L'Atlantide.* Benoît was accused of plagiarizing Rider Haggard, because the two accounts are disconcertingly alike. But it seems he was able to acquit himself of this charge. Spitteler's *Prometheus* contains some very subtle observations, too, and his novel *Imago* gives an admirable description of projection.

146 The question of *therapy* is a problem that cannot be disposed of in a few words. It was not my intention to deal with it here, but I would like to outline my point of view. Younger people, who have not yet reached the middle of life (around the age of 35), can bear even the total loss of the anima without injury. The important thing at this stage is for a man to be a man. The growing youth must be able to free himself from the anima fascination of his mother. There are exceptions, notably artists, where the problem often takes a different turn; also homosexuality, which is usually characterized by identity with the anima. In view of the recognized frequency of this phenomenon, its interpretation as a pathological perversion is very dubious. The psychological findings show that it is rather a matter of incomplete detachment from the hermaphroditic archetype, coupled with a distinct resistance to identify with the role of a one-sided sexual being. Such a disposition should not be adjudged negative in all circumstances, in so far as it preserves the archetype of the Original Man, which a one-sided sexual being has, up to a point, lost.

147 After the middle of life, however, permanent loss of the anima means a diminution of vitality, of flexibility, and of human kindness. The result, as a rule, is premature rigidity, crustiness, stereotypy, fanatical one-sidedness, obstinacy, pedantry, or else resignation, weariness, sloppiness, irresponsibility, and finally a childish *ramollissement* with a tendency to alcohol. After

31 Cf. the first paper in this volume.

middle life, therefore, the connection with the archetypal sphere of experience should if possible be re-established.[32]

32 The most important problems for therapy are discussed in my essay "The Relations between the Ego and the Unconscious" and also in the "Psychology of the Transference." For the mythological aspects of the anima, the reader is referred to another paper in this volume, "The Psychological Aspects of the Kore."

II

PSYCHOLOGICAL ASPECTS OF THE MOTHER ARCHETYPE

[First published as a lecture, "Die psychologischen Aspekte des Mutterarchetypus," in *Eranos-Jahrbuch 1938*. Later revised and published in *Von den Wurzeln des Bewusstseins* (Zurich, 1954). The present translation is of the latter, but it is also based partially on a translation of the 1938 version by Cary F. Baynes and Ximena de Angulo, privately issued in *Spring* (New York), 1943.—EDITORS.]

1. ON THE CONCEPT OF THE ARCHETYPE

148 The concept of the Great Mother belongs to the field of comparative religion and embraces widely varying types of mother-goddess. The concept itself is of no immediate concern to psychology, because the image of a Great Mother in this form is rarely encountered in practice, and then only under very special conditions. The symbol is obviously a derivative of the *mother archetype.* If we venture to investigate the background of the Great Mother image from the standpoint of psychology, then the mother archetype, as the more inclusive of the two, must form the basis of our discussion. Though lengthy discussion of the *concept* of an archetype is hardly necessary at this stage, some preliminary remarks of a general nature may not be out of place.

149 In former times, despite some dissenting opinion and the influence of Aristotle, it was not too difficult to understand Plato's conception of the Idea as supraordinate and pre-existent to all phenomena. "Archetype," far from being a modern term, was already in use before the time of St. Augustine, and was synonymous with "Idea" in the Platonic usage. When the *Corpus Hermeticum,* which probably dates from the third century, describes God as τὸ ἀρχέτυπον φῶς, the 'archetypal light,' it expresses the idea that he is the prototype of all light; that is to say, pre-existent and supraordinate to the phenomenon "light." Were I a philosopher, I should continue in this Platonic strain and say: Somewhere, in "a place beyond the skies," there is a prototype or primordial image of the mother that is pre-existent and supraordinate to all phenomena in which the "maternal," in the broadest sense of the term, is manifest. But I am an empiricist, not a philosopher; I cannot let myself presuppose that my peculiar temperament, my own attitude to intellectual problems, is universally valid. Apparently this is an assumption in which only the philosopher may indulge, who always takes it for granted that his own disposition and attitude are universal,

and will not recognize the fact, if he can avoid it, that his "personal equation" conditions his philosophy. As an empiricist, I must point out that there is a temperament which regards ideas as real entities and not merely as *nomina*. It so happens—by the merest accident, one might say—that for the past two hundred years we have been living in an age in which it has become unpopular or even unintelligible to suppose that ideas could be anything but *nomina*. Anyone who continues to think as Plato did must pay for his anachronism by seeing the "supracelestial," i.e., metaphysical, essence of the Idea relegated to the unverifiable realm of faith and superstition, or charitably left to the poet. Once again, in the age-old controversy over universals, the nominalistic standpoint has triumphed over the realistic, and the Idea has evaporated into a mere *flatus vocis*. This change was accompanied—and, indeed, to a considerable degree caused—by the marked rise of empiricism, the advantages of which were only too obvious to the intellect. Since that time the Idea is no longer something *a priori*, but is secondary and derived. Naturally, the new nominalism promptly claimed universal validity for itself in spite of the fact that it, too, is based on a definite and limited thesis coloured by temperament. This thesis runs as follows: we accept as valid anything that comes from outside and can be verified. The ideal instance is verification by experiment. The antithesis is: we accept as valid anything that comes from inside and cannot be verified. The hopelessness of this position is obvious. Greek natural philosophy with its interest in matter, together with Aristotelian reasoning, has achieved a belated but overwhelming victory over Plato.

150 Yet every victory contains the germ of future defeat. In our own day signs foreshadowing a change of attitude are rapidly increasing. Significantly enough, it is Kant's doctrine of categories, more than anything else, that destroys in embryo every attempt to revive metaphysics in the old sense of the word, but at the same time paves the way for a rebirth of the Platonic spirit. If it be true that there can be no metaphysics transcending human reason, it is no less true that there can be no empirical knowledge that is not already caught and limited by the *a priori* structure of cognition. During the century and a half that have elapsed since the appearance of the *Critique of Pure Reason*, the conviction has gradually gained ground that thinking, under-

standing, and reasoning cannot be regarded as independent processes subject only to the eternal laws of logic, but that they are *psychic functions* co-ordinated with the personality and subordinate to it. We no longer ask, "Has this or that been seen, heard, handled, weighed, counted, thought, and found to be logical?" We ask instead, "*Who* saw, heard, or thought?" Beginning with "the personal equation" in the observation and measurement of minimal processes, this critical attitude has gone on to the creation of an empirical psychology such as no time before ours has known. Today we are convinced that in all fields of knowledge psychological premises exist which exert a decisive influence upon the choice of material, the method of investigation, the nature of the conclusions, and the formulation of hypotheses and theories. We have even come to believe that Kant's personality was a decisive conditioning factor of his *Critique of Pure Reason*. Not only our philosophers, but our own predilections in philosophy, and even what we are fond of calling our "best" truths are affected, if not dangerously undermined, by this recognition of a personal premise. All creative freedom, we cry out, is taken away from us! What? Can it be possible that a man only thinks or says or does what he himself *is*?

151 Provided that we do not again exaggerate and so fall a victim to unrestrained "psychologizing," it seems to me that the critical standpoint here defined is inescapable. It constitutes the essence, origin, and method of modern psychology. There *is* an *a priori* factor in all human activities, namely the inborn, preconscious and unconscious individual structure of the psyche. The preconscious psyche—for example, that of a new-born infant—is not an empty vessel into which, under favourable conditions, practically anything can be poured. On the contrary, it is a tremendously complicated, sharply defined individual entity which appears indeterminate to us only because we cannot see it directly. But the moment the first visible manifestations of psychic life begin to appear, one would have to be blind not to recognize their individual character, that is, the unique personality behind them. It is hardly possible to suppose that all these details come into being only at the moment in which they appear. When it is a case of morbid predispositions already present in the parents, we infer hereditary transmission through

the germ-plasm; it would not occur to us to regard epilepsy in the child of an epileptic mother as an unaccountable mutation. Again, we explain by heredity the gifts and talents which can be traced back through whole generations. We explain in the same way the reappearance of complicated instinctive actions in animals that have never set eyes on their parents and therefore could not possibly have been "taught" by them.

152 Nowadays we have to start with the hypothesis that, so far as predisposition is concerned, there is no essential difference between man and all other creatures. Like every animal, he possesses a preformed psyche which breeds true to his species and which, on closer examination, reveals distinct features traceable to family antecedents. We have not the slightest reason to suppose that there are certain human activities or functions that could be exempted from this rule. We are unable to form any idea of what those dispositions or aptitudes are which make instinctive actions in animals possible. And it is just as impossible for us to know the nature of the preconscious psychic disposition that enables a child to react in a human manner. We can only suppose that his behaviour results from patterns of functioning, which I have described as *images*. The term "image" is intended to express not only the form of the activity taking place, but the typical situation in which the activity is released.[1] These images are "primordial" images in so far as they are peculiar to whole species, and if they ever "originated" their origin must have coincided at least with the beginning of the species. They are the "human quality" of the human being, the specifically human form his activities take. This specific form is hereditary and is already present in the germ-plasm. The idea that it is not inherited but comes into being in every child anew would be just as preposterous as the primitive belief that the sun which rises in the morning is a different sun from that which set the evening before.

153 Since everything psychic is preformed, this must also be true of the individual functions, especially those which derive directly from the unconscious predisposition. The most important of these is creative fantasy. In the products of fantasy the primordial images are made visible, and it is here that the concept of the archetype finds its specific application. I do not claim to

1 Cf. my "Instinct and the Unconscious," par. 277.

have been the first to point out this fact. The honour belongs to Plato. The first investigator in the field of ethnology to draw attention to the widespread occurrence of certain "elementary ideas" was Adolf Bastian. Two later investigators, Hubert and Mauss,[2] followers of Dürkheim, speak of "categories" of the imagination. And it was no less an authority than Hermann Usener [3] who first recognized unconscious preformation under the guise of "unconscious thinking." If I have any share in these discoveries, it consists in my having shown that archetypes are not disseminated only by tradition, language, and migration, but that they can rearise spontaneously, at any time, at any place, and without any outside influence.

154 The far-reaching implications of this statement must not be overlooked. For it means that there are present in every psyche forms which are unconscious but nonetheless active—living dispositions, ideas in the Platonic sense, that preform and continually influence our thoughts and feelings and actions.

155 Again and again I encounter the mistaken notion that an archetype is determined in regard to its content, in other words that it is a kind of unconscious idea (if such an expression be admissible). It is necessary to point out once more that archetypes are not determined as regards their content, but only as regards their form and then only to a very limited degree. A primordial image is determined as to its content only when it has become conscious and is therefore filled out with the material of conscious experience. Its form, however, as I have explained elsewhere, might perhaps be compared to the axial system of a crystal, which, as it were, preforms the crystalline structure in the mother liquid, although it has no material existence of its own. This first appears according to the specific way in which the ions and molecules aggregate. The archetype in itself is empty and purely formal, nothing but a *facultas praeformandi,* a possibility of representation which is given *a priori.* The representations themselves are not inherited, only the forms, and in that respect they correspond in every way to the instincts, which are also determined in form only. The existence of the instincts can no more be proved than the existence of the archetypes, so long as they do not manifest them-

2 [Cf. the previous paper, "Concerning the Archetypes," par. 137, n. 25.—EDITORS.]
3 Usener, *Das Weihnachtsfest,* p. 3.

selves concretely. With regard to the definiteness of the form, our comparison with the crystal is illuminating inasmuch as the axial system determines only the stereometric structure but not the concrete form of the individual crystal. This may be either large or small, and it may vary endlessly by reason of the different size of its planes or by the growing together of two crystals. The only thing that remains constant is the axial system, or rather, the invariable geometric proportions underlying it. The same is true of the archetype. In principle, it can be named and has an invariable nucleus of meaning—but always only in principle, never as regards its concrete manifestation. In the same way, the specific appearance of the mother-image at any given time cannot be deduced from the mother archetype alone, but depends on innumerable other factors.

2. THE MOTHER ARCHETYPE

156 Like any other archetype, the mother archetype appears under an almost infinite variety of aspects. I mention here only some of the more characteristic. First in importance are the personal mother and grandmother, stepmother and mother-in-law; then any woman with whom a relationship exists—for example, a nurse or governess or perhaps a remote ancestress. Then there are what might be termed mothers in a figurative sense. To this category belongs the goddess, and especially the Mother of God, the Virgin, and Sophia. Mythology offers many variations of the mother archetype, as for instance the mother who reappears as the maiden in the myth of Demeter and Kore; or the mother who is also the beloved, as in the Cybele-Attis myth. Other symbols of the mother in a figurative sense appear in things representing the goal of our longing for redemption, such as Paradise, the Kingdom of God, the Heavenly Jerusalem. Many things arousing devotion or feelings of awe, as for instance the Church, university, city or country, heaven, earth, the woods, the sea or any still waters, matter even, the underworld and the moon, can be mother-symbols. The archetype is often associated with things and places standing for fertility and fruitfulness: the cornucopia, a ploughed field, a garden. It can be attached to a rock, a cave, a tree, a spring, a deep well, or to various vessels such as the baptismal font, or to vessel-shaped flowers like the rose or the lotus. Because of the protection it implies, the magic circle or mandala can be a form of mother archetype. Hollow objects such as ovens and cooking vessels are associated with the mother archetype, and, of course, the uterus, *yoni,* and anything of a like shape. Added to this list there are many animals, such as the cow, hare, and helpful animals in general.

157 All these symbols can have a positive, favourable meaning or a negative, evil meaning. An ambivalent aspect is seen in the goddesses of fate (Moira, Graeae, Norns). Evil symbols are the

witch, the dragon (or any devouring and entwining animal, such as a large fish or a serpent), the grave, the sarcophagus, deep water, death, nightmares and bogies (Empusa, Lilith, etc.). This list is not, of course, complete; it presents only the most important features of the mother archetype.

158 The qualities associated with it are maternal solicitude and sympathy; the magic authority of the female; the wisdom and spiritual exaltation that transcend reason; any helpful instinct or impulse; all that is benign, all that cherishes and sustains, that fosters growth and fertility. The place of magic transformation and rebirth, together with the underworld and its inhabitants, are presided over by the mother. On the negative side the mother archetype may connote anything secret, hidden, dark; the abyss, the world of the dead, anything that devours, seduces, and poisons, that is terrifying and inescapable like fate. All these attributes of the mother archetype have been fully described and documented in my book *Symbols of Transformation*. There I formulated the ambivalence of these attributes as "the loving and the terrible mother." Perhaps the historical example of the dual nature of the mother most familiar to us is the Virgin Mary, who is not only the Lord's mother, but also, according to the medieval allegories, his cross. In India, "the loving and terrible mother" is the paradoxical Kali. Sankhya philosophy has elaborated the mother archetype into the concept of *prakṛti* (matter) and assigned to it the three *gunas* or fundamental attributes: *sattva, rajas, tamas:* goodness, passion, and darkness.[1] These are three essential aspects of the mother: her cherishing and nourishing goodness, her orgiastic emotionality, and her Stygian depths. The special feature of the philosophical myth, which shows Prakṛti dancing before Purusha in order to remind him of "discriminating knowledge," does not belong to the mother archetype but to the archetype of the anima, which in a man's psychology invariably appears, at first, mingled with the mother-image.

159 Although the figure of the mother as it appears in folklore is more or less universal, this image changes markedly when it appears in the individual psyche. In treating patients one is at

1 This is the etymological meaning of the three *gunas*. See Weckerling, *Anandaraya-makhi: Das Glück des Lebens*, pp. 21ff., and Garbe, *Die Samkhya Philosophie*, pp. 272ff. [Cf. also Zimmer, *Philosophies of India*, index, s.v.—Editors.]

first impressed, and indeed arrested, by the apparent significance of the personal mother. This figure of the personal mother looms so large in all personalistic psychologies that, as we know, they never got beyond it, even in theory, to other important aetiological factors. My own view differs from that of other medico-psychological theories principally in that I attribute to the personal mother only a limited aetiological significance. That is to say, all those influences which the literature describes as being exerted on the children do not come from the mother herself, but rather from the archetype projected upon her, which gives her a mythological background and invests her with authority and numinosity.[2] The aetiological and traumatic effects produced by the mother must be divided into two groups: (1) those corresponding to traits of character or attitudes actually present in the mother, and (2) those referring to traits which the mother only seems to possess, the reality being composed of more or less fantastic (i.e., archetypal) projections on the part of the child. Freud himself had already seen that the real aetiology of neuroses does not lie in traumatic effects, as he at first suspected, but in a peculiar development of infantile fantasy. This is not to deny that such a development can be traced back to disturbing influences emanating from the mother. I myself make it a rule to look first for the cause of infantile neuroses in the mother, as I know from experience that a child is much more likely to develop normally than neurotically, and that in the great majority of cases definite causes of disturbances can be found in the parents, especially in the mother. The contents of the child's abnormal fantasies can be referred to the personal mother only in part, since they often contain clear and unmistakable allusions which could not possibly have reference to human beings. This is especially true where definitely mythological products are concerned, as is frequently the case in infantile phobias where the mother may appear as a wild beast, a witch, a spectre, an ogre, a hermaphrodite, and so on. It must be borne in mind, however, that such fantasies are not always of unmistakably mythological origin, and even if they are, they may not always be rooted in the unconscious archetype but may have been occasioned by fairytales or accidental remarks. A

2 American psychology can supply us with any amount of examples. A blistering but instructive lampoon on this subject is Philip Wylie's *Generation of Vipers.*

thorough investigation is therefore indicated in each case. For practical reasons, such an investigation cannot be made so readily with children as with adults, who almost invariably transfer their fantasies to the physician during treatment—or, to be more precise, the fantasies are projected upon him automatically.

160 When that happens, nothing is gained by brushing them aside as ridiculous, for archetypes are among the inalienable assets of every psyche. They form the "treasure in the realm of shadowy thoughts" of which Kant spoke, and of which we have ample evidence in the countless treasure motifs of mythology. An archetype is in no sense just an annoying prejudice; it becomes so only when it is in the wrong place. In themselves, archetypal images are among the highest values of the human psyche; they have peopled the heavens of all races from time immemorial. To discard them as valueless would be a distinct loss. Our task is not, therefore, to deny the archetype, but to dissolve the projections, in order to restore their contents to the individual who has involuntarily lost them by projecting them outside himself.

3. THE MOTHER-COMPLEX

161 The mother archetype forms the foundation of the so-called mother-complex. It is an open question whether a mother-complex can develop without the mother having taken part in its formation as a demonstrable causal factor. My own experience leads me to believe that the mother always plays an active part in the origin of the disturbance, especially in infantile neuroses or in neuroses whose aetiology undoubtedly dates back to early childhood. In any event, the child's instincts are disturbed, and this constellates archetypes which, in their turn, produce fantasies that come between the child and its mother as an alien and often frightening element. Thus, if the children of an over-anxious mother regularly dream that she is a terrifying animal or a witch, these experiences point to a split in the child's psyche that predisposes it to a neurosis.

I. THE MOTHER-COMPLEX OF THE SON

162 The effects of the mother-complex differ according to whether it appears in a son or a daughter. Typical effects on the son are homosexuality and Don Juanism, and sometimes also impotence.[1] In homosexuality, the son's entire heterosexuality is tied to the mother in an unconscious form; in Don Juanism, he unconsciously seeks his mother in every woman he meets. The effects of a mother-complex on the son may be seen in the ideology of the Cybele and Attis type: self-castration, madness, and early death. Because of the difference in sex, a son's mother-complex does not appear in pure form. This is the reason why in every masculine mother-complex, side by side with the mother archetype, a significant role is played by the image of the man's sexual counterpart, the anima. The mother is the first feminine being with whom the man-to-be comes in contact, and

1 But the father-complex also plays a considerable part here.

she cannot help playing, overtly or covertly, consciously or unconsciously, upon the son's masculinity, just as the son in his turn grows increasingly aware of his mother's femininity, or unconsciously responds to it by instinct. In the case of the son, therefore, the simple relationships of identity or of resistance and differentiation are continually cut across by erotic attraction or repulsion, which complicates matters very considerably. I do not mean to say that for this reason the mother-complex of a son ought to be regarded as more serious than that of a daughter. The investigation of these complex psychic phenomena is still in the pioneer stage. Comparisons will not become feasible until we have some statistics at our disposal, and of these, so far, there is no sign.

163 Only in the daughter is the mother-complex clear and uncomplicated. Here we have to do either with an overdevelopment of feminine instincts indirectly caused by the mother, or with a weakening of them to the point of complete extinction. In the first case, the preponderance of instinct makes the daughter unconscious of her own personality; in the latter, the instincts are projected upon the mother. For the present we must content ourselves with the statement that in the daughter a mother-complex either unduly stimulates or else inhibits the feminine instinct, and that in the son it injures the masculine instinct through an unnatural sexualization.

164 Since a "mother-complex" is a concept borrowed from psychopathology, it is always associated with the idea of injury and illness. But if we take the concept out of its narrow psychopathological setting and give it a wider connotation, we can see that it has positive effects as well. Thus a man with a mother-complex may have a finely differentiated Eros [2] instead of, or in addition to, homosexuality. (Something of this sort is suggested by Plato in his *Symposium*.) This gives him a great capacity for friendship, which often creates ties of astonishing tenderness between men and may even rescue friendship between the sexes from the limbo of the impossible. He may have good taste and an aesthetic sense which are fostered by the presence of a feminine streak. Then he may be supremely gifted as a teacher because of his almost feminine insight and tact. He is likely to have a feeling for history, and to be conservative in the best

[2] [Cf. *Two Essays on Analytical Psychology*, pars. 16ff.—EDITORS.]

sense and cherish the values of the past. Often he is endowed with a wealth of religious feelings, which help to bring the *ecclesia spiritualis* into reality; and a spiritual receptivity which makes him responsive to revelation.

165 In the same way, what in its negative aspect is Don Juanism can appear positively as bold and resolute manliness; ambitious striving after the highest goals; opposition to all stupidity, narrow-mindedness, injustice, and laziness; willingness to make sacrifices for what is regarded as right, sometimes bordering on heroism; perseverance, inflexibility and toughness of will; a curiosity that does not shrink even from the riddles of the universe; and finally, a revolutionary spirit which strives to put a new face upon the world.

166 All these possibilities are reflected in the mythological motifs enumerated earlier as different aspects of the mother archetype. As I have already dealt with the mother-complex of the son, including the anima complication, elsewhere, and my present theme is the archetype of the mother, in the following discussion I shall relegate masculine psychology to the background.

II. THE MOTHER-COMPLEX OF THE DAUGHTER [3]

167 (a) *Hypertrophy of the Maternal Element.*—We have noted that in the daughter the mother-complex leads either to a hypertrophy of the feminine side or to its atrophy. The exaggeration of the feminine side means an intensification of all female instincts, above all the maternal instinct. The negative aspect is seen in the woman whose only goal is childbirth. To her the husband is obviously of secondary importance; he is first and foremost the instrument of procreation, and she regards him merely as an object to be looked after, along with children, poor relations, cats, dogs, and household furniture. Even her own

3 In the present section I propose to present a series of different "types" of mother-complex; in formulating them, I am drawing on my own therapeutic experiences. "Types" are not individual cases, neither are they freely invented schemata into which all individual cases have to be fitted. "Types" are ideal instances, or pictures of the average run of experience, with which no single individual can be identified. People whose experience is confined to books or psychological laboratories can form no proper idea of the cumulative experience of a practising psychologist.

personality is of secondary importance; she often remains entirely unconscious of it, for her life is lived in and through others, in more or less complete identification with all the objects of her care. First she gives birth to the children, and from then on she clings to them, for without them she has no existence whatsoever. Like Demeter, she compels the gods by her stubborn persistence to grant her the right of possession over her daughter. Her Eros develops exclusively as a maternal relationship while remaining unconscious as a personal one. An unconscious Eros always expresses itself as will to power.[4] Women of this type, though continually "living for others," are, as a matter of fact, unable to make any real sacrifice. Driven by ruthless will to power and a fanatical insistence on their own maternal rights, they often succeed in annihilating not only their own personality but also the personal lives of their children. The less conscious such a mother is of her own personality, the greater and the more violent is her unconscious will to power. For many such women Baubo rather than Demeter would be the appropriate symbol. The mind is not cultivated for its own sake but usually remains in its original condition, altogether primitive, unrelated, and ruthless, but also as true, and sometimes as profound, as Nature herself.[5] She herself does not know this and is therefore unable to appreciate the wittiness of her mind or to marvel philosophically at its profundity; like as not she will immediately forget what she has said.

168 (b) *Overdevelopment of Eros.*—It by no means follows that the complex induced in a daughter by such a mother must necessarily result in hypertrophy of the maternal instinct. Quite the contrary, this instinct may be wiped out altogether. As a substitute, an overdeveloped Eros results, and this almost invariably leads to an unconscious incestuous relationship with the father.[6] The intensified Eros places an abnormal emphasis on the personality of others. Jealousy of the mother and the desire to outdo her become the leitmotifs of subsequent undertakings, which

4 This statement is based on the repeated experience that, where love is lacking, power fills the vacuum.

5 In my English seminars [privately distributed] I have called this the "natural mind."

6 Here the initiative comes from the daughter. In other cases the father's psychology is responsible; his projection of the anima arouses an incestuous fixation in the daughter.

are often disastrous. A woman of this type loves romantic and sensational episodes for their own sake, and is interested in married men, less for themselves than for the fact that they are married and so give her an opportunity to wreck a marriage, that being the whole point of her manoeuvre. Once the goal is attained, her interest evaporates for lack of any maternal instinct, and then it will be someone else's turn.[7] This type is noted for its remarkable unconsciousness. Such women really seem to be utterly blind to what they are doing,[8] which is anything but advantageous either for themselves or for their victims. I need hardly point out that for men with a passive Eros this type offers an excellent hook for anima projections.

169 (c) *Identity with the Mother.*—If a mother-complex in a woman does not produce an overdeveloped Eros, it leads to identification with the mother and to paralysis of the daughter's feminine initiative. A complete projection of her personality on to the mother then takes place, owing to the fact that she is unconscious both of her maternal instinct and of her Eros. Everything which reminds her of motherhood, responsibility, personal relationships, and erotic demands arouses feelings of inferiority and compels her to run away—to her mother, naturally, who lives to perfection everything that seems unattainable to her daughter. As a sort of superwoman (admired involuntarily by the daughter), the mother lives out for her beforehand all that the girl might have lived for herself. She is content to cling to her mother in selfless devotion, while at the same time unconsciously striving, almost against her will, to tyrannize over her, naturally under the mask of complete loyalty and devotion. The daughter leads a shadow-existence, often visibly sucked dry by her mother, and she prolongs her mother's life by a sort of continuous blood transfusion. These bloodless maidens are by no means immune to marriage. On the contrary, despite their shadowiness and passivity, they command a high price on the marriage market. First, they are so empty that a man is free to impute to them anything he fancies. In addition, they are so unconscious that the unconscious puts out countless invisible

7 Herein lies the difference between this type of complex and the feminine father-complex related to it, where the "father" is mothered and coddled.

8 This does not mean that they are unconscious of the *facts*. It is only their *meaning* that escapes them.

feelers, veritable octopus-tentacles, that suck up all masculine projections; and this pleases men enormously. All that feminine indefiniteness is the longed-for counterpart of male decisiveness and single-mindedness, which can be satisfactorily achieved only if a man can get rid of everything doubtful, ambiguous, vague, and muddled by projecting it upon some charming example of feminine innocence.[9] Because of the woman's characteristic passivity, and the feelings of inferiority which make her continually play the injured innocent, the man finds himself cast in an attractive role: he has the privilege of putting up with the familiar feminine foibles with real superiority, and yet with forbearance, like a true knight. (Fortunately, he remains ignorant of the fact that these deficiencies consist largely of his own projections.) The girl's notorious helplessness is a special attraction. She is so much an appendage of her mother that she can only flutter confusedly when a man approaches. She just doesn't know a thing. She is so inexperienced, so terribly in need of help, that even the gentlest swain becomes a daring abductor who brutally robs a loving mother of her daughter. Such a marvellous opportunity to pass himself off as a gay Lothario does not occur every day and therefore acts as a strong incentive. This was how Pluto abducted Persephone from the inconsolable Demeter. But, by a decree of the gods, he had to surrender his wife every year to his mother-in-law for the summer season. (The attentive reader will note that such legends do not come about by chance!)

170 (d) *Resistance to the Mother.*—These three extreme types are linked together by many intermediate stages, of which I shall mention only one important example. In the particular intermediate type I have in mind, the problem is less an overdevelopment or an inhibition of the feminine instincts than an overwhelming resistance to maternal supremacy, often to the exclusion of all else. It is the supreme example of the negative mother-complex. The motto of this type is: Anything, so long as it is not like Mother! On one hand we have a fascination which never reaches the point of identification; on the other, an intensification of Eros which exhausts itself in jealous resist-

[9] This type of woman has an oddly disarming effect on her husband, but only until he discovers that the person he has married and who shares his nuptial bed is his mother-in-law.

ance. This kind of daughter knows what she does *not* want, but is usually completely at sea as to what she would choose as her own fate. All her instincts are concentrated on the mother in the negative form of resistance and are therefore of no use to her in building her own life. Should she get as far as marrying, either the marriage will be used for the sole purpose of escaping from her mother, or else a diabolical fate will present her with a husband who shares all the essential traits of her mother's character. All instinctive processes meet with unexpected difficulties; either sexuality does not function properly, or the children are unwanted, or maternal duties seem unbearable, or the demands of marital life are responded to with impatience and irritation. This is quite natural, since none of it has anything to do with the realities of life when stubborn resistance to the power of the mother in every form has come to be life's dominating aim. In such cases one can often see the attributes of the mother archetype demonstrated in every detail. For example, the mother as representative of the family (or clan) causes either violent resistances or complete indifference to anything that comes under the head of family, community, society, convention, and the like. Resistance to the mother as *uterus* often manifests itself in menstrual disturbances, failure of conception, abhorrence of pregnancy, hemorrhages and excessive vomiting during pregnancy, miscarriages, and so on. The mother as *materia,* 'matter,' may be at the back of these women's impatience with objects, their clumsy handling of tools and crockery and bad taste in clothes.

171 Again, resistance to the mother can sometimes result in a spontaneous development of intellect for the purpose of creating a sphere of interest in which the mother has no place. This development springs from the daughter's own needs and not at all for the sake of a man whom she would like to impress or dazzle by a semblance of intellectual comradeship. Its real purpose is to break the mother's power by intellectual criticism and superior knowledge, so as to enumerate to her all her stupidities, mistakes in logic, and educational shortcomings. Intellectual development is often accompanied by the emergence of masculine traits in general.

4. POSITIVE ASPECTS OF THE MOTHER-COMPLEX

1. THE MOTHER

172 The positive aspect of the first type of complex, namely the overdevelopment of the maternal instinct, is identical with that well-known image of the mother which has been glorified in all ages and all tongues. This is the mother-love which is one of the most moving and unforgettable memories of our lives, the mysterious root of all growth and change; the love that means homecoming, shelter, and the long silence from which everything begins and in which everything ends. Intimately known and yet strange like Nature, lovingly tender and yet cruel like fate, joyous and untiring giver of life—*mater dolorosa* and mute implacable portal that closes upon the dead. Mother is mother-love, *my* experience and *my* secret. Why risk saying too much, too much that is false and inadequate and beside the point, about that human being who was our mother, the accidental carrier of that great experience which includes herself and myself and all mankind, and indeed the whole of created nature, the experience of life whose children we are? The attempt to say these things has always been made, and probably always will be; but a sensitive person cannot in all fairness load that enormous burden of meaning, responsibility, duty, heaven and hell, on to the shoulders of one frail and fallible human being—so deserving of love, indulgence, understanding, and forgiveness—who was our mother. He knows that the mother carries for us that inborn image of the *mater natura* and *mater spiritualis,* of the totality of life of which we are a small and helpless part. Nor should we hesitate for one moment to relieve the human mother of this appalling burden, for our own sakes as well as hers. It is just this massive weight of meaning that ties us to the mother and chains her to her child, to the physical and mental

detriment of both. A mother-complex is not got rid of by blindly reducing the mother to human proportions. Besides that we run the risk of dissolving the experience "Mother" into atoms, thus destroying something supremely valuable and throwing away the golden key which a good fairy laid in our cradle. That is why mankind has always instinctively added the pre-existent divine pair to the personal parents—the "god"-father and "god"-mother of the newborn child—so that, from sheer unconsciousness or shortsighted rationalism, he should never forget himself so far as to invest his own parents with divinity.

173 The archetype is really far less a scientific problem than an urgent question of psychic hygiene. Even if all proofs of the existence of archetypes were lacking, and all the clever people in the world succeeded in convincing us that such a thing could not possibly exist, we would have to invent them forthwith in order to keep our highest and most important values from disappearing into the unconscious. For when these fall into the unconscious the whole elemental force of the original experience is lost. What then appears in its place is fixation on the mother-imago; and when this has been sufficiently rationalized and "corrected," we are tied fast to human reason and condemned from then on to believe exclusively in what is rational. That is a virtue and an advantage on the one hand, but on the other a limitation and impoverishment, for it brings us nearer to the bleakness of doctrinairism and "enlightenment." This Déesse Raison emits a deceptive light which illuminates only what we know already, but spreads a darkness over all those things which it would be most needful for us to know and become conscious of. The more independent "reason" pretends to be, the more it turns into sheer intellectuality which puts doctrine in the place of reality and shows us man not as he is but how it wants him to be.

174 Whether he understands them or not, man must remain conscious of the world of the archetypes, because in it he is still a part of Nature and is connected with his own roots. A view of the world or a social order that cuts him off from the primordial images of life not only is no culture at all but, in increasing degree, is a prison or a stable. If the primordial images remain conscious in some form or other, the energy that belongs to

them can flow freely into man. But when it is no longer possible to maintain contact with them, then the tremendous sum of energy stored up in these images, which is also the source of the fascination underlying the infantile parental complex, falls back into the unconscious. The unconscious then becomes charged with a force that acts as an irresistible *vis a tergo* to whatever view or idea or tendency our intellect may choose to dangle enticingly before our desiring eyes. In this way man is delivered over to his conscious side, and reason becomes the arbiter of right and wrong, of good and evil. I am far from wishing to belittle the divine gift of reason, man's highest faculty. But in the role of absolute tyrant it has no meaning—no more than light would have in a world where its counterpart, darkness, was absent. Man would do well to heed the wise counsel of the mother and obey the inexorable law of nature which sets limits to every being. He ought never to forget that the world exists only because opposing forces are held in equilibrium. So, too, the rational is counterbalanced by the irrational, and what is planned and purposed by what *is*.

175 This excursion into the realm of generalities was unavoidable, because the mother is the first world of the child and the last world of the adult. We are all wrapped as her children in the mantle of this great Isis. But let us now return to the different types of feminine mother-complex. It may seem strange that I am devoting so much more time to the mother-complex in woman than to its counterpart in man. The reason for this has already been mentioned: in a man, the mother-complex is never "pure," it is always mixed with the anima archetype, and the consequence is that a man's statements about the mother are always emotionally prejudiced in the sense of showing "animosity." Only in women is it possible to examine the effects of the mother archetype without admixture of animosity, and even this has prospects of success only when no compensating animus has developed.

II. THE OVERDEVELOPED EROS

176 I drew a very unfavourable picture of this type as we encounter it in the field of psychopathology. But this type, uninviting

as it appears, also has positive aspects which society could ill afford to do without. Indeed, behind what is possibly the worst effect of this attitude, the unscrupulous wrecking of marriages, we can see an extremely significant and purposeful arrangement of nature. This type often develops in reaction to a mother who is wholly a thrall of nature, purely instinctive and therefore all-devouring. Such a mother is an anachronism, a throw-back to a primitive state of matriarchy where the man leads an insipid existence as a mere procreator and serf of the soil. The reactive intensification of the daughter's Eros is aimed at some man who ought to be rescued from the preponderance of the female-maternal element in his life. A woman of this type instinctively intervenes when provoked by the unconsciousness of the marriage partner. She will disturb that comfortable ease so dangerous to the personality of a man but frequently regarded by him as marital faithfulness. This complacency leads to blank unconsciousness of his own personality and to those supposedly ideal marriages where he is nothing but Dad and she is nothing but Mom, and they even call each other that. This is a slippery path that can easily degrade marriage to the level of a mere breeding-pen.

177 A woman of this type directs the burning ray of her Eros upon a man whose life is stifled by maternal solicitude, and by doing so she arouses a moral conflict. Yet without this there can be no consciousness of personality. "But why on earth," you may ask, "should it be necessary for man to achieve, by hook or by crook, a higher level of consciousness?" This is truly the crucial question, and I do not find the answer easy. Instead of a real answer I can only make a confession of faith: I believe that, after thousands and millions of years, someone had to realize that this wonderful world of mountains and oceans, suns and moons, galaxies and nebulae, plants and animals, *exists*. From a low hill in the Athi plains of East Africa I once watched the vast herds of wild animals grazing in soundless stillness, as they had done from time immemorial, touched only by the breath of a primeval world. I felt then as if I were the first man, the first creature, to know that all this *is*. The entire world round me was still in its primeval state; it did not know that it *was*. And then, in that one moment in which I came to know, the world sprang into being; without that moment it would never have

been. All Nature seeks this goal and finds it fulfilled in man, but only in the most highly developed and most fully conscious man. Every advance, even the smallest, along this path of conscious realization adds that much to the world.

178 There is no consciousness without discrimination of opposites. This is the paternal principle, the Logos, which eternally struggles to extricate itself from the primal warmth and primal darkness of the maternal womb; in a word, from unconsciousness. Divine curiosity yearns to be born and does not shrink from conflict, suffering, or sin. Unconsciousness is the primal sin, evil itself, for the Logos. Therefore its first creative act of liberation is matricide, and the spirit that dared all heights and all depths must, as Synesius says, suffer the divine punishment, enchainment on the rocks of the Caucasus. Nothing can exist without its opposite; the two were one in the beginning and will be one again in the end. Consciousness can only exist through continual recognition of the unconscious, just as everything that lives must pass through many deaths.

179 The stirring up of conflict is a Luciferian virtue in the true sense of the word. Conflict engenders fire, the fire of affects and emotions, and like every other fire it has two aspects, that of combustion and that of creating light. On the one hand, emotion is the alchemical fire whose warmth brings everything into existence and whose heat burns all superfluities to ashes (*omnes superfluitates comburit*). But on the other hand, emotion is the moment when steel meets flint and a spark is struck forth, for emotion is the chief source of consciousness. There is no change from darkness to light or from inertia to movement without emotion.

180 The woman whose fate it is to be a disturbing element is not solely destructive, except in pathological cases. Normally the disturber is herself caught in the disturbance; the worker of change is herself changed, and the glare of the fire she ignites both illuminates and enlightens all the victims of the entanglement. What seemed a senseless upheaval becomes a process of purification:

> So that all that is vain
> Might dwindle and wane.[1]

[1] *Faust*, Part II, Act 5.

181 If a woman of this type remains unconscious of the meaning of her function, if she does not know that she is

> Part of that power which would
> Ever work evil but engenders good,[2]

she will herself perish by the sword she brings. But consciousness transforms her into a deliverer and redeemer.

III. THE "NOTHING-BUT" DAUGHTER

182 The woman of the third type, who is so identified with the mother that her own instincts are paralysed through projection, need not on that account remain a hopeless nonentity forever. On the contrary, if she is at all normal, there is a good chance of the empty vessel being filled by a potent anima projection. Indeed, the fate of such a woman depends on this eventuality; she can never find herself at all, not even approximately, without a man's help; she has to be literally abducted or stolen from her mother. Moreover, she must play the role mapped out for her for a long time and with great effort, until she actually comes to loathe it. In this way she may perhaps discover who she really is. Such women may become devoted and self-sacrificing wives of husbands whose whole existence turns on their identification with a profession or a great talent, but who, for the rest, are unconscious and remain so. Since they are nothing but masks themselves, the wife, too, must be able to play the accompanying part with a semblance of naturalness. But these women sometimes have valuable gifts which remained undeveloped only because they were entirely unconscious of their own personality. They may project the gift or talent upon a husband who lacks it himself, and then we have the spectacle of a totally insignificant man who seemed to have no chance whatsoever suddenly soaring as if on a magic carpet to the highest summits of achievement. *Cherchez la femme,* and you have the secret of his success. These women remind me—if I may be forgiven the impolite comparison—of hefty great bitches who turn tail before the smallest cur simply because he is a terrible male and it never occurs to them to bite him.

2 Ibid., Part I, Act 1.

183 Finally, it should be remarked that *emptiness* is a great feminine secret. It is something absolutely alien to man; the chasm, the unplumbed depths, the *yin*. The pitifulness of this vacuous nonentity goes to his heart (I speak here as a man), and one is tempted to say that this constitutes the whole "mystery" of woman. Such a female is fate itself. A man may say what he likes about it; be for it or against it, or both at once; in the end he falls, absurdly happy, into this pit, or, if he doesn't, he has missed and bungled his only chance of making a man of himself. In the first case one cannot disprove his foolish good luck to him, and in the second one cannot make his misfortune seem plausible. "The Mothers, the Mothers, how eerily it sounds!"[3] With this sigh, which seals the capitulation of the male as he approaches the realm of the Mothers, we will turn to the fourth type.

IV. THE NEGATIVE MOTHER-COMPLEX

184 As a pathological phenomenon this type is an unpleasant, exacting, and anything but satisfactory partner for her husband, since she rebels in every fibre of her being against everything that springs from natural soil. However, there is no reason why increasing experience of life should not teach her a thing or two, so that for a start she gives up fighting the mother in the personal and restricted sense. But even at her best she will remain hostile to all that is dark, unclear, and ambiguous, and will cultivate and emphasize everything certain and clear and reasonable. Excelling her more feminine sister in her objectivity and coolness of judgment, she may become the friend, sister, and competent adviser of her husband. Her own masculine aspirations make it possible for her to have a human understanding of the individuality of her husband quite transcending the realm of the erotic. The woman with this type of mother-complex probably has the best chance of all to make her marriage an outstanding success during the second half of life. But this is true only if she succeeds in overcoming the hell of "nothing but femininity," the chaos of the maternal womb, which is her greatest danger because of her negative complex. As we know, a com-

[3] Ibid., Part II, Act 1.

plex can be really overcome only if it is lived out to the full. In other words, if we are to develop further we have to draw to us and drink down to the very dregs what, because of our complexes, we have held at a distance.

185 This type started out in the world with averted face, like Lot's wife looking back on Sodom and Gomorrah. And all the while the world and life pass by her like a dream—an annoying source of illusions, disappointments, and irritations, all of which are due solely to the fact that she cannot bring herself to look straight ahead for once. Because of her merely unconscious, reactive attitude toward reality, her life actually becomes dominated by what she fought hardest against—the exclusively maternal feminine aspect. But if she should later turn her face, she will see the world for the first time, so to speak, in the light of maturity, and see it embellished with all the colours and enchanting wonders of youth, and sometimes even of childhood. It is a vision that brings knowledge and discovery of truth, the indispensable prerequisite for consciousness. A part of life was lost, but the meaning of life has been salvaged for her.

186 The woman who fights against her father still has the possibility of leading an instinctive, feminine existence, because she rejects only what is alien to her. But when she fights against the mother she may, at the risk of injury to her instincts, attain to greater consciousness, because in repudiating the mother she repudiates all that is obscure, instinctive, ambiguous, and unconscious in her own nature. Thanks to her lucidity, objectivity, and masculinity, a woman of this type is frequently found in important positions in which her tardily discovered maternal quality, guided by a cool intelligence, exerts a most beneficial influence. This rare combination of womanliness and masculine understanding proves valuable in the realm of intimate relationships as well as in practical matters. As the spiritual guide and adviser of a man, such a woman, unknown to the world, may play a highly influential part. Owing to her qualities, the masculine mind finds this type easier to understand than women with other forms of mother-complex, and for this reason men often favour her with the projection of positive mother-complexes. The excessively feminine woman terrifies men who have a mother-complex characterized by great sensitivity. But this woman is not frightening to a man, because she builds bridges

for the masculine mind over which he can safely guide his feelings to the opposite shore. Her clarity of understanding inspires him with confidence, a factor not to be underrated and one that is absent from the relationship between a man and a woman much more often than one might think. The man's Eros does not lead upward only but downward into that uncanny dark world of Hecate and Kali, which is a horror to any intellectual man. The understanding possessed by this type of woman will be a guiding star to him in the darkness and seemingly unending mazes of life.

5. CONCLUSION

187 From what has been said it should be clear that in the last analysis all the statements of mythology on this subject as well as the observed effects of the mother-complex, when stripped of their confusing detail, point to the unconscious as their place of origin. How else could it have occurred to man to divide the cosmos, on the analogy of day and night, summer and winter, into a bright day-world and a dark night-world peopled with fabulous monsters, unless he had the prototype of such a division in himself, in the polarity between the conscious and the invisible and unknowable unconscious? Primitive man's perception of objects is conditioned only partly by the objective behaviour of the things themselves, whereas a much greater part is often played by intrapsychic facts which are not related to the external objects except by way of projection.[1] This is due to the simple fact that the primitive has not yet experienced that ascetic discipline of mind known to us as the critique of knowledge. To him the world is a more or less fluid phenomenon within the stream of his own fantasy, where subject and object are undifferentiated and in a state of mutual interpenetration. "All that is outside, also is inside," we could say with Goethe. But this "inside," which modern rationalism is so eager to derive from "outside," has an *a priori* structure of its own that antedates all conscious experience. It is quite impossible to conceive how "experience" in the widest sense, or, for that matter, anything psychic, could originate exclusively in the outside world. The psyche is part of the inmost mystery of life, and it has its own peculiar structure and form like every other organism. Whether this psychic structure and its elements, the archetypes, ever "originated" at all is a metaphysical question and therefore unanswerable. The structure is something given, the precondition that is found to be present in every case. And this is the *mother*, the matrix—the form into which all experience is

1 [Cf. above, "Archetypes of the Collective Unconscious," par. 7.—EDITORS.]

poured. The *father,* on the other hand, represents the *dynamism* of the archetype, for the archetype consists of both—form and energy.

188 The carrier of the archetype is in the first place the personal mother, because the child lives at first in complete participation with her, in a state of unconscious identity. She is the psychic as well as the physical precondition of the child. With the awakening of ego-consciousness the participation gradually weakens, and consciousness begins to enter into opposition to the unconscious, its own precondition. This leads to differentiation of the ego from the mother, whose personal peculiarities gradually become more distinct. All the fabulous and mysterious qualities attaching to her image begin to fall away and are transferred to the person closest to her, for instance the grandmother. As the mother of the mother, she is "greater" than the latter; she is in truth the "grand" or "Great Mother." Not infrequently she assumes the attributes of wisdom as well as those of a witch. For the further the archetype recedes from consciousness and the clearer the latter becomes, the more distinctly does the archetype assume mythological features. The transition from mother to grandmother means that the archetype is elevated to a higher rank. This is clearly demonstrated in a notion held by the Bataks. The funeral sacrifice in honour of a dead father is modest, consisting of ordinary food. But if the son has a son of his own, then the father has become a grandfather and has consequently attained a more dignified status in the Beyond, and very important offerings are made to him.[2]

189 As the distance between conscious and unconscious increases, the grandmother's more exalted rank transforms her into a "Great Mother," and it frequently happens that the opposites contained in this image split apart. We then get a good fairy and a wicked fairy, or a benevolent goddess and one who is malevolent and dangerous. In Western antiquity and especially in Eastern cultures the opposites often remain united in the same figure, though this paradox does not disturb the primitive mind in the least. The legends about the gods are as full of contradictions as are their moral characters. In the West, the paradoxical behaviour and moral ambivalence of the gods scandalized people even in antiquity and gave rise to criticism that led

2 Warnecke, *Die Religion der Batak.*

finally to a devaluation of the Olympians on the one hand and to their philosophical interpretation on the other. The clearest expression of this is the Christian reformation of the Jewish concept of the Deity: the morally ambiguous Yahweh became an exclusively good God, while everything evil was united in the devil. It seems as if the development of the feeling function in Western man forced a choice on him which led to the moral splitting of the divinity into two halves. In the East the predominantly intuitive intellectual attitude left no room for feeling values, and the gods—Kali is a case in point—could retain their original paradoxical morality undisturbed. Thus Kali is representative of the East and the Madonna of the West. The latter has entirely lost the shadow that still distantly followed her in the allegories of the Middle Ages. It was relegated to the hell of popular imagination, where it now leads an insignificant existence as the devil's grandmother.[3] Thanks to the development of feeling-values, the splendour of the "light" god has been enhanced beyond measure, but the darkness supposedly represented by the devil has localized itself in man. This strange development was precipitated chiefly by the fact that Christianity, terrified of Manichaean dualism, strove to preserve its monotheism by main force. But since the reality of darkness and evil could not be denied, there was no alternative but to make man responsible for it. Even the devil was largely, if not entirely, abolished, with the result that this metaphysical figure, who at one time was an integral part of the Deity, was introjected into man, who thereupon became the real carrier of the *mysterium iniquitatis:* "omne bonum a Deo, omne malum ab homine." In recent times this development has suffered a diabolical reverse, and the wolf in sheep's clothing now goes about whispering in our ear that evil is really nothing but a misunderstanding of good and an effective instrument of progress. We think that the world of darkness has thus been abolished for good and all, and nobody realizes what a poisoning this is of man's soul. In this way he turns himself into the devil, for the devil is half of the archetype whose irresistible power makes even unbelievers ejaculate "Oh God!" on every suitable and unsuitable occasion. If one can possibly avoid it, one ought never to identify with an archetype, for, as psychopathology

3 [A familiar figure of speech in German.—EDITORS.]

and certain contemporary events show, the consequences are terrifying.

190 Western man has sunk to such a low level spiritually that he even has to deny the apotheosis of untamed and untameable psychic power—the divinity itself—so that, after swallowing evil, he may possess himself of the good as well. If you read Nietzsche's *Zarathustra* with attention and psychological understanding, you will see that he has described with rare consistency and with the passion of a truly religious person the psychology of the "Superman" for whom God is dead, and who is himself burst asunder because he tried to imprison the divine paradox within the narrow framework of the mortal man. Goethe has wisely said: "What terror then shall seize the Superman!"—and was rewarded with a supercilious smile from the Philistines. His glorification of the Mother who is great enough to include in herself both the Queen of Heaven and Maria Aegyptiaca is supreme wisdom and profoundly significant for anyone willing to reflect upon it. But what can one expect in an age when the official spokesmen of Christianity publicly announce their inability to understand the foundations of religious experience! I extract the following sentence from an article by a Protestant theologian: "We understand ourselves—whether naturalistically or idealistically—to be *homogeneous creatures who are not so peculiarly divided that alien forces can intervene in our inner life,* as the New Testament supposes."[4] (Italics mine.) The author is evidently unacquainted with the fact that science demonstrated the lability and dissociability of consciousness more than half a century ago and proved it by experiment. Our conscious intentions are continually disturbed and thwarted, to a greater or lesser degree, by unconscious intrusions whose causes are at first strange to us. The psyche is far from being a homogeneous unit—on the contrary, it is a boiling cauldron of contradictory impulses, inhibitions, and affects, and for many people the conflict between them is so insupportable that they even wish for the deliverance preached by theologians. Deliverance from what? Obviously, from a highly questionable psychic state. The unity of consciousness or of the so-called personality is not a reality at all but a desideratum. I still have a vivid memory of a certain philosopher who also raved about this unity and

[4] Buri, "Theologie und Philosophie," p. 117. [Quoting Rudolf Bultmann.—Eds.]

used to consult me about his neurosis: he was obsessed by the idea that he was suffering from cancer. I do not know how many specialists he had consulted already, and how many X-ray pictures he had had made. They all assured him that he had no cancer. He himself told me: "I know I have no cancer, but I still could have one." Who is responsible for this "imaginary" idea? He certainly did not make it himself; it was forced on him by an "alien" power. There is little to choose between this state and that of the man possessed in the New Testament. Now whether you believe in a demon of the air or in a factor in the unconscious that plays diabolical tricks on you is all one to me. The fact that man's imagined unity is menaced by alien powers remains the same in either case. Theologians would do better to take account for once of these psychological facts than to go on "demythologizing" them with rationalistic explanations that are a hundred years behind the times.

*

191 I have tried in the foregoing to give a survey of the psychic phenomena that may be attributed to the predominance of the mother-image. Although I have not always drawn attention to them, my reader will presumably have had no difficulty in recognizing those features which characterize the Great Mother mythologically, even when they appear under the guise of personalistic psychology. When we ask patients who are particularly influenced by the mother-image to express in words or pictures what "Mother" means to them—be it positive or negative—we invariably get symbolical figures which must be regarded as direct analogies of the mythological mother-image. These analogies take us into a field that still requires a great deal more work of elucidation. At any rate, I personally do not feel able to say anything definitive about it. If, nevertheless, I venture to offer a few suggestions, they should be regarded as altogether provisional and tentative.

192 Above all, I should like to point out that the mother-image in a man's psychology is entirely different in character from a woman's. For a woman, the mother typifies her own conscious life as conditioned by her sex. But for a man the mother typifies something alien, which he has yet to experience and which is filled with the imagery latent in the unconscious. For this

reason, if for no other, the mother-image of a man is essentially different from a woman's. The mother has from the outset a decidedly symbolical significance for a man, which probably accounts for his strong tendency to idealize her. Idealization is a hidden apotropaism; one idealizes whenever there is a secret fear to be exorcized. What is feared is the unconscious and its magical influence.[5]

193 Whereas for a man the mother is *ipso facto* symbolical, for a woman she becomes a symbol only in the course of her psychological development. Experience reveals the striking fact that the Urania type of mother-image predominates in masculine psychology, whereas in a woman the chthonic type, or Earth Mother, is the most frequent. During the manifest phase of the archetype an almost complete identification takes place. A woman can identify directly with the Earth Mother, but a man cannot (except in psychotic cases). As mythology shows, one of the peculiarities of the Great Mother is that she frequently appears paired with her male counterpart. Accordingly the man identifies with the son-lover on whom the grace of Sophia has descended, with a *puer aeternus* or a *filius sapientiae*. But the companion of the chthonic mother is the exact opposite: an ithyphallic Hermes (the Egyptian Bes) or a lingam. In India this symbol is of the highest spiritual significance, and in the West Hermes is one of the most contradictory figures of Hellenistic syncretism, which was the source of extremely important spiritual developments in Western civilization. He is also the god of revelation, and in the unofficial nature philosophy of the early Middle Ages he is nothing less than the world-creating Nous itself. This mystery has perhaps found its finest expression in the words of the *Tabula smaragdina:* "omne superius sicut inferius" (as it is above, so it is below).

194 It is a psychological fact that as soon as we touch on these identifications we enter the realm of the syzygies, the paired opposites, where the One is never separated from the Other, its antithesis. It is a field of personal experience which leads directly to the experience of individuation, the attainment of the self. A vast number of symbols for this process could be mustered from the medieval literature of the West and even more

5 Obviously a daughter can idealize her mother too, but for this special circumstances are needed, whereas in a man idealization is almost the normal thing.

from the storehouses of Oriental wisdom, but in this matter words and ideas count for little. Indeed, they may become dangerous bypaths and false trails. In this still very obscure field of psychological experience, where we are in direct contact, so to speak, with the archetype, its psychic power is felt in full force. This realm is so entirely one of immediate experience that it cannot be captured by any formula, but can only be hinted at to one who already knows. He will need no explanations to understand what was the tension of opposites expressed by Apuleius in his magnificent prayer to the Queen of Heaven, when he associates "heavenly Venus" with "Proserpina, who strikest terror with midnight ululations": [6] it was the terrifying paradox of the primordial mother-image.

*

195 When, in 1938, I originally wrote this paper, I naturally did not know that twelve years later the Christian version of the mother archetype would be elevated to the rank of a dogmatic truth. The Christian "Queen of Heaven" has, obviously, shed all her Olympian qualities except for her brightness, goodness, and eternality; and even her human body, the thing most prone to gross material corruption, has put on an ethereal incorruptibility. The richly varied allegories of the Mother of God have nevertheless retained some connection with her pagan prefigurations in Isis (Io) and Semele. Not only are Isis and the Horus-child iconological exemplars, but the ascension of Semele, the originally mortal mother of Dionysus, likewise anticipates the Assumption of the Blessed Virgin. Further, this son of Semele is a dying and resurgent god and the youngest of the Olympians. Semele herself seems to have been an earth-goddess, just as the Virgin Mary is the earth from which Christ was born. This being so, the question naturally arises for the psychologist: what has become of the characteristic relation of the mother-image to the earth, darkness, the abysmal side of the bodily man with his animal passions and instinctual nature, and to "matter" in general? The declaration of the dogma comes at a time when the achievements of science and technology, combined with a rationalistic and materialistic view of the world, threaten

6 "Nocturnis ululatibus horrenda Proserpina." Cf. *Symbols of Transformation*, par. 148.

the spiritual and psychic heritage of man with instant annihilation. Humanity is arming itself, in dread and fascinated horror, for a stupendous crime. Circumstances might easily arise when the hydrogen bomb would have to be used and the unthinkably frightful deed became unavoidable in legitimate self-defence. In striking contrast to this disastrous turn of events, the Mother of God is now enthroned in heaven; indeed, her Assumption has actually been interpreted as a deliberate counterstroke to the materialistic doctrinairism that provoked the chthonic powers into revolt. Just as Christ's appearance in his own day created a real devil and adversary of God out of what was originally a son of God dwelling in heaven, so now, conversely, a heavenly figure has split off from her original chthonic realm and taken up a counter-position to the titanic forces of the earth and the underworld that have been unleashed. In the same way that the Mother of God was divested of all the essential qualities of materiality, matter became completely de-souled, and this at a time when physics is pushing forward to insights which, if they do not exactly "de-materialize" matter, at least endue it with properties of its own and make its relation to the psyche a problem that can no longer be shelved. For just as the tremendous advancement of science led at first to a premature dethronement of mind and to an equally ill-considered deification of matter, so it is this same urge for scientific knowledge that is now attempting to bridge the huge gulf that has opened out between the two *Weltanschauungen*. The psychologist inclines to see in the dogma of the Assumption a symbol which, in a sense, anticipates this whole development. For him the relationship to the earth and to matter is one of the inalienable qualities of the mother archetype. So that when a figure that is conditioned by this archetype is represented as having been taken up into heaven, the realm of the spirit, this indicates a union of earth and heaven, or of matter and spirit. The approach of natural science will almost certainly be from the other direction: it will see in matter itself the equivalent of spirit, but this "spirit" will appear divested of all, or at any rate most, of its known qualities, just as earthly matter was stripped of its specific characteristics when it staged its entry into heaven. Nevertheless, the way will gradually be cleared for a union of the two principles.

196 Understood concretely, the Assumption is the absolute opposite of materialism. Taken in this sense, it is a counterstroke that does nothing to diminish the tension between the opposites, but drives it to extremes.

197 Understood symbolically, however, the Assumption of the body is a recognition and acknowledgment of matter, which in the last resort was identified with evil only because of an overwhelmingly "pneumatic" tendency in man. In themselves, spirit and matter are neutral, or rather, "utriusque capax"—that is, capable of what man calls good or evil. Although as names they are exceedingly relative, underlying them are very real opposites that are part of the energic structure of the physical and of the psychic world, and without them no existence of any kind could be established. There is no position without its negation. In spite or just because of their extreme opposition, neither can exist without the other. It is exactly as formulated in classical Chinese philosophy: *yang* (the light, warm, dry, masculine principle) contains within it the seed of *yin* (the dark, cold, moist, feminine principle), and vice versa. Matter therefore would contain the seed of spirit and spirit the seed of matter. The long-known "synchronistic" phenomena that have now been statistically confirmed by Rhine's experiments [7] point, to all appearances, in this direction. The "psychization" of matter puts the absolute immateriality of spirit in question, since this would then have to be accorded a kind of substantiality. The dogma of the Assumption, proclaimed in an age suffering from the greatest political schism history has ever known, is a compensating symptom that reflects the strivings of science for a uniform world-picture. In a certain sense, both developments were anticipated by alchemy in the *hieros gamos* of opposites, but only in symbolic form. Nevertheless, the symbol has the great advantage of being able to unite heterogeneous or even incommensurable factors in a *single* image. With the decline of alchemy the symbolical unity of spirit and matter fell apart, with the result that modern man finds himself uprooted and alienated in a de-souled world.

198 The alchemist saw the union of opposites under the symbol of the tree, and it is therefore not surprising that the unconscious of present-day man, who no longer feels at home in his

7 Cf. my "Synchronicity: An Acausal Connecting Principle."

world and can base his existence neither on the past that is no more nor on the future that is yet to be, should hark back to the symbol of the cosmic tree rooted in this world and growing up to heaven—the tree that is also man. In the history of symbols this tree is described as the way of life itself, a growing into that which eternally is and does not change; which springs from the union of opposites and, by its eternal presence, also makes that union possible. It seems as if it were only through an experience of symbolic reality that man, vainly seeking his own "existence" and making a philosophy out of it, can find his way back to a world in which he is no longer a stranger.

III

CONCERNING REBIRTH

This paper represents the substance of a lecture which I delivered on the spur of the moment at the Eranos meeting in 1939. In putting it into written form I have made use of the stenographic notes which were taken at the meeting. Certain portions had to be omitted, chiefly because the requirements of a printed text are different from those of the spoken word. However, so far as possible, I have carried out my original intention of summing up the content of my lecture on the theme of rebirth, and have also endeavoured to reproduce my analysis of the Eighteenth Sura of the Koran as an example of a rebirth mystery. I have added some references to source material, which the reader may welcome. My summary does not purport to be more than a survey of a field of knowledge which can only be treated very superficially in the framework of a lecture.—C. G. J.

[First published as a lecture, "Die verschiedenen Aspekte der Wiedergeburt," in *Eranos-Jahrbuch 1939* (Zurich, 1940). Revised and expanded as "Über Wiedergeburt," *Gestaltungen des Unbewussten* (Zurich, 1950), from which the present translation is made.—EDITORS.]

1. FORMS OF REBIRTH

199 The concept of rebirth is not always used in the same sense. Since this concept has various aspects, it may be useful to review its different meanings. The five different forms which I am going to enumerate could probably be added to if one were to go into greater detail, but I venture to think that my definitions cover at least the cardinal meanings. In the first part of my exposition, I give a brief summary of the different forms of rebirth, while the second part presents its various psychological aspects. In the third part, I give an example of a rebirth mystery from the Koran.

200 1. *Metempsychosis.* The first of the five aspects of rebirth to which I should like to draw attention is that of metempsychosis, or transmigration of souls. According to this view, one's life is prolonged in time by passing through different bodily existences; or, from another point of view, it is a life-sequence interrupted by different reincarnations. Even in Buddhism, where this doctrine is of particular importance—the Buddha himself experienced a very long sequence of such rebirths—it is by no means certain whether continuity of personality is guaranteed or not: there may be only a continuity of *karma.* The Buddha's disciples put this question to him during his lifetime, but he never made any definite statement as to whether there is or is not a continuity of personality.[1]

201 2. *Reincarnation.* This concept of rebirth necessarily implies the continuity of personality. Here the human personality is regarded as continuous and accessible to memory, so that, when one is incarnated or born, one is able, at least potentially, to remember that one has lived through previous existences and that these existences were one's own, i.e., that they had the same ego-form as the present life. As a rule, reincarnation means rebirth in a human body.

[1] Cf. the *Samyutta-Nikaya (Book of the Kindred Sayings),* Part II: The Nidana Book, pp. 150f.

202 3. *Resurrection.* This means a re-establishment of human existence after death. A new element enters here: that of the change, transmutation, or transformation of one's being. The change may be either essential, in the sense that the resurrected being is a different one; or nonessential, in the sense that only the general conditions of existence have changed, as when one finds oneself in a different place or in a body which is differently constituted. It may be a carnal body, as in the Christian assumption that this body will be resurrected. On a higher level, the process is no longer understood in a gross material sense; it is assumed that the resurrection of the dead is the raising up of the *corpus glorificationis,* the "subtle body," in the state of incorruptibility.

203 4. *Rebirth (renovatio).* The fourth form concerns rebirth in the strict sense; that is to say, rebirth within the span of individual life. The English word *rebirth* is the exact equivalent of the German *Wiedergeburt,* but the French language seems to lack a term having the peculiar meaning of "rebirth." This word has a special flavour; its whole atmosphere suggests the idea of *renovatio,* renewal, or even of improvement brought about by magical means. Rebirth may be a renewal without any change of being, inasmuch as the personality which is renewed is not changed in its essential nature, but only its functions, or parts of the personality, are subjected to healing, strengthening, or improvement. Thus even bodily ills may be healed through rebirth ceremonies.

204 Another aspect of this fourth form is essential transformation, i.e., total rebirth of the individual. Here the renewal implies a change of his essential nature, and may be called a transmutation. As examples we may mention the transformation of a mortal into an immortal being, of a corporeal into a spiritual being, and of a human into a divine being. Well-known prototypes of this change are the transfiguration and ascension of Christ, and the assumption of the Mother of God into heaven after her death, together with her body. Similar conceptions are to be found in Part II of Goethe's *Faust*; for instance, the transformation of Faust into the boy and then into Doctor Marianus.

205 5. *Participation in the process of transformation.* The fifth and last form is indirect rebirth. Here the transformation is

brought about not directly, by passing through death and rebirth oneself, but indirectly, by participating in a process of transformation which is conceived of as taking place outside the individual. In other words, one has to witness, or take part in, some rite of transformation. This rite may be a ceremony such as the Mass, where there is a transformation of substances. Through his presence at the rite the individual participates in divine grace. Similar transformations of the Deity are to be found in the pagan mysteries; there too the initiate sharing the experience is vouchsafed the gift of grace, as we know from the Eleusinian mysteries. A case in point is the confession of the initiate in the Eleusinian mysteries, who praises the grace conferred through the certainty of immortality.[2]

2 Cf. the Homeric Hymn to Demeter, verses 480–82: "Blessed is he among men who has seen these mysteries; but he who is uninitiate and has no part in them, never has lot of like good things once he is dead, down in the darkness and gloom." (Trans. by Evelyn-White, *Hesiod, the Homeric Hymns and Homerica*, p. 323.) And in an Eleusinian epitaph we read:

> "Truly the blessed gods have proclaimed a most beautiful secret:
> Death comes not as a curse, but as a blessing to men."

2. THE PSYCHOLOGY OF REBIRTH

206 Rebirth is not a process that we can in any way observe. We can neither measure nor weigh nor photograph it. It is entirely beyond sense perception. We have to do here with a purely *psychic* reality, which is transmitted to us only indirectly through personal statements. One speaks of rebirth; one professes rebirth; one is filled with rebirth. This we accept as sufficiently real. We are not concerned here with the question: is rebirth a tangible process of some sort? We have to be content with its psychic reality. I hasten to add that I am not alluding to the vulgar notion that anything "psychic" is either nothing at all or at best even more tenuous than a gas. Quite the contrary; I am of the opinion that the psyche is the most tremendous fact of human life. Indeed, it is the mother of all human facts; of civilization and of its destroyer, war. All this is at first psychic and invisible. So long as it is "merely" psychic it cannot be experienced by the senses, but is nonetheless indisputably real. The mere fact that people talk about rebirth, and that there is such a concept at all, means that a store of psychic experiences designated by that term must actually exist. What these experiences are like we can only infer from the statements that have been made about them. So, if we want to find out what rebirth really is, we must turn to history in order to ascertain what "rebirth" has been understood to mean.

207 Rebirth is an affirmation that must be counted among the primordial affirmations of mankind. These primordial affirmations are based on what I call archetypes. In view of the fact that all affirmations relating to the sphere of the suprasensual are, in the last analysis, invariably determined by archetypes, it is not surprising that a concurrence of affirmations concerning rebirth can be found among the most widely differing peoples. There must be psychic events underlying these affirmations which it is the business of psychology to discuss—without entering into all the metaphysical and philosophical assumptions regarding their

significance. In order to obtain a general view of their phenomenology, it is necessary to sketch the whole field of transformation experiences in sharper outline. Two main groups of experience may be distinguished: that of the transcendence of life, and that of one's own transformation.

I. EXPERIENCE OF THE TRANSCENDENCE OF LIFE

208 a. *Experiences induced by ritual.* By the "transcendence of life" I mean those aforementioned experiences of the initiate who takes part in a sacred rite which reveals to him the perpetual continuation of life through transformation and renewal. In these mystery-dramas the transcendence of life, as distinct from its momentary concrete manifestations, is usually represented by the fateful transformations—death and rebirth—of a god or a godlike hero. The initiate may either be a mere witness of the divine drama or take part in it or be moved by it, or he may see himself identified through the ritual action with the god. In this case, what really matters is that an objective substance or form of life is ritually transformed through some process going on independently, while the initiate is influenced, impressed, "consecrated," or granted "divine grace" on the mere ground of his presence or participation. The transformation process takes place not within him but outside him, although he may become involved in it. The initiate who ritually enacts the slaying, dismemberment, and scattering of Osiris, and afterwards his resurrection in the green wheat, experiences in this way the permanence and continuity of life, which outlasts all changes of form and, phoenix-like, continually rises anew from its own ashes. This participation in the ritual event gives rise, among other effects, to that hope of immortality which is characteristic of the Eleusinian mysteries.[1]

209 A living example of the mystery drama representing the permanence as well as the transformation of life is the Mass. If we observe the congregation during this sacred rite we note all degrees of participation, from mere indifferent attendance to the profoundest emotion. The groups of men standing about

1 [Cf. infra, "The Psychology of the Kore," and Kerényi's companion essays in *Essays on a Science of Mythology*.—EDITORS.]

near the exit, who are obviously engaged in every sort of worldly conversation, crossing themselves and genuflecting in a purely mechanical way—even they, despite their inattention, participate in the sacral action by their mere presence in this place where grace abounds. The Mass is an extramundane and extratemporal act in which Christ is sacrificed and then resurrected in the transformed substances; and this rite of his sacrificial death is not a repetition of the historical event but the original, unique, and eternal act. The experience of the Mass is therefore a participation in the transcendence of life, which overcomes all bounds of space and time. It is a moment of eternity in time.[2]

210 b. *Immediate Experiences.* All that the mystery drama represents and brings about in the spectator may also occur in the form of a spontaneous, ecstatic, or visionary experience, without any ritual. Nietzsche's Noontide Vision is a classic example of this kind.[3] Nietzsche, as we know, substitutes for the Christian mystery the myth of Dionysus-Zagreus, who was dismembered and came to life again. His experience has the character of a Dionysian nature myth: the Deity appears in the garb of Nature, as classical antiquity saw it,[4] and the moment of eternity is the noonday hour, sacred to Pan: "Hath time flown away? Do I not fall? Have I not fallen—hark!—into the well of eternity?" Even the "golden ring," the "ring of return," appears to him as a promise of resurrection and life.[5] It is just as if Nietzsche had been present at a performance of the mysteries.

211 Many mystic experiences have a similar character: they represent an action in which the spectator becomes involved though his nature is not necessarily changed. In the same way, the most beautiful and impressive dreams often have no lasting or transformative effect on the dreamer. He may be impressed by them, but he does not necessarily see any problem in them. The event then naturally remains "outside," like a ritual action performed by others. These more aesthetic forms of experience must be carefully distinguished from those which indubitably involve a change of one's nature.

2 Cf. my "Transformation Symbolism in the Mass."
3 *Thus Spake Zarathustra*, trans. by Common, pp. 315ff.
4 Ibid.: "An old, bent and gnarled tree, hung with grapes."
5 Horneffer, *Nietzsches Lehre von der ewigen Wiederkehr.*

II. SUBJECTIVE TRANSFORMATION

212 Transformations of personality are by no means rare occurrences. Indeed, they play a considerable role in psychopathology, although they are rather different from the mystical experiences just discussed, which are not easily accessible to psychological investigation. However, the phenomena we are now about to examine belong to a sphere quite familiar to psychology.

213 a. *Diminution of personality.* An example of the alteration of personality in the sense of diminution is furnished by what is known in primitive psychology as "loss of soul." The peculiar condition covered by this term is accounted for in the mind of the primitive by the supposition that a soul has gone off, just like a dog that runs away from his master overnight. It is then the task of the medicine-man to fetch the fugitive back. Often the loss occurs suddenly and manifests itself in a general malaise. The phenomenon is closely connected with the nature of primitive consciousness, which lacks the firm coherence of our own. We have control of our will power, but the primitive has not. Complicated exercises are needed if he is to pull himself together for any activity that is conscious and intentional and not just emotional and instinctive. Our consciousness is safer and more dependable in this respect; but occasionally something similar can happen to civilized man, only he does not describe it as "loss of soul" but as an "abaissement du niveau mental," Janet's apt term for this phenomenon.[6] It is a slackening of the tensity of consciousness, which might be compared to a low barometric reading, presaging bad weather. The tonus has given way, and this is felt subjectively as listlessness, moroseness, and depression. One no longer has any wish or courage to face the tasks of the day. One feels like lead, because no part of one's body seems willing to move, and this is due to the fact that one no longer has any disposable energy.[7] This well-known phenomenon corresponds to the primitive's loss of soul. The listlessness and paralysis of will can go so far that the whole personality falls apart, so to speak, and consciousness loses its

6 *Les Névroses*, p. 358.

7 The *gana* phenomena described by Count Keyserling (*South-American Meditations*, pp. 161ff.) come into this category.

unity; the individual parts of the personality make themselves independent and thus escape from the control of the conscious mind, as in the case of anaesthetic areas or systematic amnesias. The latter are well known as hysterical "loss of function" phenomena. This medical term is analogous to the primitive loss of soul.

214 *Abaissement du niveau mental* can be the result of physical and mental fatigue, bodily illness, violent emotions, and shock, of which the last has a particularly deleterious effect on one's self-assurance. The *abaissement* always has a restrictive influence on the personality as a whole. It reduces one's self-confidence and the spirit of enterprise, and, as a result of increasing egocentricity, narrows the mental horizon. In the end it may lead to the development of an essentially negative personality, which means that a falsification of the original personality has supervened.

215 b. *Enlargement of personality.* The personality is seldom, in the beginning, what it will be later on. For this reason the possibility of enlarging it exists, at least during the first half of life. The enlargement may be effected through an accretion from without, by new vital contents finding their way into the personality from outside and being assimilated. In this way a considerable increase of personality may be experienced. We therefore tend to assume that this increase comes *only* from without, thus justifying the prejudice that one becomes a personality by stuffing into oneself as much as possible from outside. But the more assiduously we follow this recipe, and the more stubbornly we believe that all increase has to come from without, the greater becomes our inner poverty. Therefore, if some great idea takes hold of us from outside, we must understand that it takes hold of us only because something in us responds to it and goes out to meet it. Richness of mind consists in mental receptivity, not in the accumulation of possessions. What comes to us from outside, and, for that matter, everything that rises up from within, can only be made our own if we are capable of an inner amplitude equal to that of the incoming content. Real increase of personality means consciousness of an enlargement that flows from inner sources. Without psychic depth we can never be adequately related to the magnitude of our object. It has therefore been said quite truly that a man grows with the

greatness of his task. But he must have within himself the capacity to grow; otherwise even the most difficult task is of no benefit to him. More likely he will be shattered by it.

216 A classic example of enlargement is Nietzsche's encounter with Zarathustra, which made of the critic and aphorist a tragic poet and prophet. Another example is St. Paul, who, on his way to Damascus, was suddenly confronted by Christ. True though it may be that this Christ of St. Paul's would hardly have been possible without the historical Jesus, the apparition of Christ came to St. Paul not from the historical Jesus but from the depths of his own unconscious.

217 When a summit of life is reached, when the bud unfolds and from the lesser the greater emerges, then, as Nietzsche says, "One becomes Two," and the greater figure, which one always was but which remained invisible, appears to the lesser personality with the force of a revelation. He who is truly and hopelessly little will always drag the revelation of the greater down to the level of his littleness, and will never understand that the day of judgment for his littleness has dawned. But the man who is inwardly great will know that the long expected friend of his soul, the immortal one, has now really come, "to lead captivity captive"; [8] that is, to seize hold of him by whom this immortal had always been confined and held prisoner, and to make his life flow into that greater life—a moment of deadliest peril! Nietzsche's prophetic vision of the Tightrope Walker [9] reveals the awful danger that lies in having a "tightrope-walking" attitude towards an event to which St. Paul gave the most exalted name he could find.

218 Christ himself is the perfect symbol of the hidden immortal within the mortal man.[10] Ordinarily this problem is symbolized by a dual motif such as the Dioscuri, one of whom is mortal and the other immortal. An Indian parallel is the parable of the two friends:

> Behold, upon the selfsame tree,
> Two birds, fast-bound companions, sit.

8 Ephesians 4 : 8.

9 "Thy soul will be dead even sooner than thy body." *Thus Spake Zarathustra,* p. 74.

10 Cf. "A Psychological Approach to the Dogma of the Trinity," pars. 226ff.

This one enjoys the ripened fruit,
The other looks, but does not eat.

On such a tree my spirit crouched,
Deluded by its powerlessness,
Till seeing with joy how great its Lord,
It found from sorrow swift release. . . .[11]

219 Another notable parallel is the Islamic legend of the meeting of Moses and Khidr,[12] to which I shall return later on. Naturally the transformation of personality in this enlarging sense does not occur only in the form of such highly significant experiences. There is no lack of more trivial instances, a list of which could easily be compiled from the clinical history of neurotic patients. Indeed, any case where the recognition of a greater personality seems to burst an iron ring round the heart must be included in this category.[13]

220 c. *Change of internal structure.* We now come to changes of personality which imply neither enlargement nor diminution but a structural alteration. One of the most important forms is the phenomenon of possession: some content, an idea or a part of the personality, obtains mastery of the individual for one reason or another. The contents which thus take possession appear as peculiar convictions, idiosyncrasies, stubborn plans, and so forth. As a rule, they are not open to correction. One has to be an especially good friend of the possessed person and willing to put up with almost anything if one is to attempt to deal with such a condition. I am not prepared to lay down any hard and fast line of demarcation between possession and paranoia. Possession can be formulated as identity of the ego-personality with a complex.[14]

221 A common instance of this is identity with the persona, which is the individual's system of adaptation to, or the manner he assumes in dealing with, the world. Every calling or profes-

11 Shvetashvatara Upanishad 4, 6ff. (Trans. based on Hume, *The Thirteen Principal Upanishads*, pp. 403ff.).

12 Koran, 18th Sura.

13 I have discussed one such case of a widening of the personality in my inaugural dissertation, "On the Psychology and Pathology of So-called Occult Phenomena."

14 For the Church's view of possession see de Tonquédec, *Les Maladies nerveuses ou mentales et les manifestations diaboliques;* also "A Psychological Approach to the Dogma of the Trinity," p. 163, n. 15.

sion, for example, has its own characteristic persona. It is easy to study these things nowadays, when the photographs of public personalities so frequently appear in the press. A certain kind of behaviour is forced on them by the world, and professional people endeavour to come up to these expectations. Only, the danger is that they become identical with their personas—the professor with his text-book, the tenor with his voice. Then the damage is done; henceforth he lives exclusively against the background of his own biography. For by that time it is written: ". . . then he went to such and such a place and said this or that," etc. The garment of Deianeira has grown fast to his skin, and a desperate decision like that of Heracles is needed if he is to tear this Nessus shirt from his body and step into the consuming fire of the flame of immortality, in order to transform himself into what he really is. One could say, with a little exaggeration, that the persona is that which in reality one is not, but which oneself as well as others think one is.[15] In any case the temptation to be what one seems to be is great, because the persona is usually rewarded in cash.

222 There are still other factors which may take possession of the individual, one of the most important being the so-called "inferior function." This is not the place to enter into a detailed discussion of this problem; [16] I should only like to point out that the inferior function is practically identical with the dark side of the human personality. The darkness which clings to every personality is the door into the unconscious and the gateway of dreams, from which those two twilight figures, the shadow and the anima, step into our nightly visions or, remaining invisible, take possession of our ego-consciousness. A man who is possessed by his shadow is always standing in his own light and falling into his own traps. Whenever possible, he prefers to make an unfavourable impression on others. In the long run luck is always against him, because he is living below his own level and at best only attains what does not suit him. And if there is no doorstep for him to stumble over, he manufactures one for himself and then fondly believes he has done something useful.

15 In this connection, Schopenhauer's "The Wisdom of Life: Aphorisms" (*Essays from the Parerga and Paralipomena*) could be read with profit.

16 This important problem is discussed in detail in Ch. II of *Psychological Types*.

223 Possession caused by the anima or animus presents a different picture. Above all, this transformation of personality gives prominence to those traits which are characteristic of the opposite sex; in man the feminine traits, and in woman the masculine. In the state of possession both figures lose their charm and their values; they retain them only when they are turned away from the world, in the introverted state, when they serve as bridges to the unconscious. Turned towards the world, the anima is fickle, capricious, moody, uncontrolled and emotional, sometimes gifted with daemonic intuitions, ruthless, malicious, untruthful, bitchy, double-faced, and mystical.[17] The animus is obstinate, harping on principles, laying down the law, dogmatic, world-reforming, theoretic, word-mongering, argumentative, and domineering.[18] Both alike have bad taste: the anima surrounds herself with inferior people, and the animus lets himself be taken in by second-rate thinking.

224 Another form of structural change concerns certain unusual observations about which I speak only with the utmost reserve. I refer to states of possession in which the possession is caused by something that could perhaps most fitly be described as an "ancestral soul," by which I mean the soul of some definite forebear. For all practical purposes, such cases may be regarded as striking instances of identification with deceased persons. (Naturally, the phenomena of identity only occur after the "ancestor's" death.) My attention was first drawn to such possibilities by Léon Daudet's confused but ingenious book *L'Hérédo*. Daudet supposes that, in the structure of the personality, there are ancestral elements which under certain conditions may suddenly come to the fore. The individual is then precipitately thrust into an ancestral role. Now we know that ancestral roles play a very important part in primitive psychology. Not only are ancestral spirits supposed to be reincarnated in children, but an attempt is made to implant them into

17 Cf. the apt description of the anima in Aldrovandus, *Dendrologiae libri duo* (1668, p. 211): "She appeared both very soft and very hard at the same time, and while for some two thousand years she had made a show of inconstant looks like a Proteus, she bedevilled the love of Lucius Agatho Priscus, then a citizen of Bologna, with anxious cares and sorrows, which assuredly were conjured up from chaos, or from what Plato calls Agathonian confusion." There is a similar description in Fierz-David, *The Dream of Poliphilo*, pp. 189ff.

18 Cf. Emma Jung, "On the Nature of the Animus."

the child by naming him after an ancestor. So, too, primitives try to change themselves back into their ancestors by means of certain rites. I would mention especially the Australian conception of the *alcheringamijina*,[19] ancestral souls, half man and half animal, whose reactivation through religious rites is of the greatest functional significance for the life of the tribe. Ideas of this sort, dating back to the Stone Age, were widely diffused, as may be seen from numerous other traces that can be found elsewhere. It is therefore not improbable that these primordial forms of experience may recur even today as cases of identification with ancestral souls, and I believe I have seen such cases.

225 d. *Identification with a group.* We shall now discuss another form of transformation experience which I would call identification with a group. More accurately speaking, it is the identification of an individual with a number of people who, as a group, have a collective experience of transformation. This special psychological situation must not be confused with participation in a transformation rite, which, though performed before an audience, does not in any way depend upon group identity or necessarily give rise to it. To experience transformation in a group and to experience it in oneself are two totally different things. If any considerable group of persons are united and identified with one another by a particular frame of mind, the resultant transformation experience bears only a very remote resemblance to the experience of individual transformation. A group experience takes place on a lower level of consciousness than the experience of an individual. This is due to the fact that, when many people gather together to share one common emotion, the total psyche emerging from the group is below the level of the individual psyche. If it is a very large group, the collective psyche will be more like the psyche of an animal, which is the reason why the ethical attitude of large organizations is always doubtful. The psychology of a large crowd inevitably sinks to the level of mob psychology.[20] If, therefore, I have a so-called collective experience as a member of a group, it takes place on a lower level of consciousness than if I had the experience by myself alone. That is why this group experience is very much more frequent than an individual experience of transformation. It is also much easier to achieve,

19 Cf. Lévy-Bruhl, *La Mythologie primitive.*

20 Le Bon, *The Crowd.*

because the presence of so many people together exerts great suggestive force. The individual in a crowd easily becomes the victim of his own suggestibility. It is only necessary for something to happen, for instance a proposal backed by the whole crowd, and we too are all for it, even if the proposal is immoral. In the crowd one feels no responsibility, but also no fear.

226 Thus identification with the group is a simple and easy path to follow, but the group experience goes no deeper than the level of one's own mind in that state. It does work a change in you, but the change does not last. On the contrary, you must have continual recourse to mass intoxication in order to consolidate the experience and your belief in it. But as soon as you are removed from the crowd, you are a different person again and unable to reproduce the previous state of mind. The mass is swayed by *participation mystique,* which is nothing other than an unconscious identity. Supposing, for example, you go to the theatre: glance meets glance, everybody observes everybody else, so that all those who are present are caught up in an invisible web of mutual unconscious relationship. If this condition increases, one literally feels borne along by the universal wave of identity with others. It may be a pleasant feeling—one sheep among ten thousand! Again, if I feel that this crowd is a great and wonderful unity, I am a hero, exalted along with the group. When I am myself again, I discover that I am Mr. So-and-So, and that I live in such and such a street, on the third floor. I also find that the whole affair was really most delightful, and I hope it will take place again tomorrow so that I may once more feel myself to be a whole nation, which is much better than being just plain Mr. X. Since this is such an easy and convenient way of raising one's personality to a more exalted rank, mankind has always formed groups which made collective experiences of transformation—often of an ecstatic nature—possible. The regressive identification with lower and more primitive states of consciousness is invariably accompanied by a heightened sense of life; hence the quickening effect of regressive identifications with half-animal ancestors [21] in the Stone Age.

227 The inevitable psychological regression within the group is

21 The *alcheringamijina.* Cf. the rites of Australian tribes, in Spencer and Gillen, *The Northern Tribes of Central Australia;* also Lévy-Bruhl, *La Mythologie primitive.*

partially counteracted by ritual, that is to say through a cult ceremony which makes the solemn performance of sacred events the centre of group activity and prevents the crowd from relapsing into unconscious instinctuality. By engaging the individual's interest and attention, the ritual makes it possible for him to have a comparatively individual experience even within the group and so to remain more or less conscious. But if there is no relation to a centre which expresses the unconscious through its symbolism, the mass psyche inevitably becomes the hypnotic focus of fascination, drawing everyone under its spell. That is why masses are always breeding-grounds of psychic epidemics,[22] the events in Germany being a classic example of this.

228 It will be objected to this essentially negative evaluation of mass psychology that there are also positive experiences, for instance a positive enthusiasm which spurs the individual to noble deeds, or an equally positive feeling of human solidarity. Facts of this kind should not be denied. The group can give the individual a courage, a bearing, and a dignity which may easily get lost in isolation. It can awaken within him the memory of being a man among men. But that does not prevent something else from being added which he would not possess as an individual. Such unearned gifts may seem a special favour of the moment, but in the long run there is a danger of the gift becoming a loss, since human nature has a weak habit of taking gifts for granted; in times of necessity we demand them as a right instead of making the effort to obtain them ourselves. One sees this, unfortunately, only too plainly in the tendency to demand everything from the State, without reflecting that the State consists of those very individuals who make the demands. The logical development of this tendency leads to Communism, where each individual enslaves the community and the latter is represented by a dictator, the slave-owner. All primitive tribes characterized by a communistic order of society also have a chieftain over them with unlimited powers. The Communist State is nothing other than an absolute monarchy in which there are no subjects, but only serfs.

22 I would remind the reader of the catastrophic panic which broke out in New York on the occasion [1938] of a broadcast dramatization of H. G. Wells' *War of the Worlds* shortly before the second World War [see Cantril, *The Invasion from Mars* (1940)], and which was later [1949] repeated in Quito.

229 e. *Identification with a cult-hero.* Another important identification underlying the transformation experience is that with the god or hero who is transformed in the sacred ritual. Many cult ceremonies are expressly intended to bring this identity about, an obvious example being the *Metamorphosis* of Apuleius. The initiate, an ordinary human being, is elected to be Helios; he is crowned with a crown of palms and clad in the mystic mantle, whereupon the assembled crowd pays homage to him. The suggestion of the crowd brings about his identity with the god. The participation of the community can also take place in the following way: there is no apotheosis of the initiate, but the sacred action is recited, and then, in the course of long periods of time, psychic changes gradually occur in the individual participants. The Osiris cult offers an excellent example of this. At first only Pharaoh participated in the transformation of the god, since he alone "had an Osiris"; but later the nobles of the Empire acquired an Osiris too, and finally this development culminated in the Christian idea that everyone has an immortal soul and shares directly in the Godhead. In Christianity the development was carried still further when the outer God or Christ gradually became the inner Christ of the individual believer, remaining one and the same though dwelling in many. This truth had already been anticipated by the psychology of totemism: many exemplars of the totem animal are killed and consumed during the totem meals, and yet it is only the One who is being eaten, just as there is only one Christ-child and one Santa Claus.

230 In the mysteries, the individual undergoes an indirect transformation through his participation in the fate of the god. The transformation experience is also an indirect one in the Christian Church, inasmuch as it is brought about by participation in something acted or recited. Here the first form, the *dromenon*, is characteristic of the richly developed ritual of the Catholic Church; the second form, the recitation, the "Word" or "gospel," is practised in the "preaching of the Word" in Protestantism.

231 f. *Magical procedures.* A further form of transformation is achieved through a rite used directly for this purpose. Instead of the transformation experience coming to one through participation in the rite, the rite is used for the express purpose of

effecting the transformation. It thus becomes a sort of technique to which one submits oneself. For instance, a man is ill and consequently needs to be "renewed." The renewal must "happen" to him from outside, and to bring this about, he is pulled through a hole in the wall at the head of his sick-bed, and now he is reborn; or he is given another name and thereby another soul, and then the demons no longer recognize him; or he has to pass through a symbolical death; or, grotesquely enough, he is pulled through a leathern cow, which devours him, so to speak, in front and then expels him behind; or he undergoes an ablution or baptismal bath and miraculously changes into a semi-divine being with a new character and an altered metaphysical destiny.

232 g. *Technical transformation.* Besides the use of the rite in the magical sense, there are still other special techniques in which, in addition to the grace inherent in the rite, the personal endeavour of the initiate is needed in order to achieve the intended purpose. It is a transformation experience induced by technical means. The exercises known in the East as yoga and in the West as *exercitia spiritualia* come into this category. These exercises represent special techniques prescribed in advance and intended to achieve a definite psychic effect, or at least to promote it. This is true both of Eastern yoga and of the methods practised in the West.[23] They are, therefore, technical procedures in the fullest sense of the word; elaborations of the originally natural processes of transformation. The natural or spontaneous transformations that occurred earlier, before there were any historical examples to follow, were thus replaced by techniques designed to induce the transformation by imitating this same sequence of events. I will try to give an idea of the way such techniques may have originated by relating a fairy story:

233 There was once a queer old man who lived in a cave, where he had sought refuge from the noise of the villages. He was reputed to be a sorcerer, and therefore he had disciples who hoped to learn the art of sorcery from him. But he himself was not thinking of any such thing. He was only seeking to know what it was that he did not know, but which, he felt certain, was always happening. After meditating for a very long time on

[23] Cf. "The Psychology of Eastern Meditation."

that which is beyond meditation, he saw no other way of escape from his predicament than to take a piece of red chalk and draw all kinds of diagrams on the walls of his cave, in order to find out what that which he did not know might look like. After many attempts he hit on the circle. "That's right," he felt, "and now for a quadrangle inside it!"—which made it better still. His disciples were curious; but all they could make out was that the old man was up to something, and they would have given anything to know what he was doing. But when they asked him: "What are you doing there?" he made no reply. Then they discovered the diagrams on the wall and said: "That's it!"—and they all imitated the diagrams. But in so doing they turned the whole process upside down, without noticing it: they anticipated the result in the hope of making the process repeat itself which had led to that result. This is how it happened then and how it still happens today.

234 h. *Natural transformation (individuation).* As I have pointed out, in addition to the technical processes of transformation there are also natural transformations. All ideas of rebirth are founded on this fact. Nature herself demands a death and a rebirth. As the alchemist Democritus says: "Nature rejoices in nature, nature subdues nature, nature rules over nature." There are natural transformation processes which simply happen to us, whether we like it or not, and whether we know it or not. These processes develop considerable psychic effects, which would be sufficient in themselves to make any thoughtful person ask himself what really happened to him. Like the old man in our fairytale, he, too, will draw mandalas and seek shelter in their protective circle; in the perplexity and anguish of his self-chosen prison, which he had deemed a refuge, he is transformed into a being akin to the gods. Mandalas are birth-places, vessels of birth in the most literal sense, lotus-flowers in which a Buddha comes to life. Sitting in the lotus-seat, the yogi sees himself transfigured into an immortal.

235 Natural transformation processes announce themselves mainly in dreams. Elsewhere [24] I have presented a series of dream-symbols of the process of individuation. They were dreams which without exception exhibited rebirth symbolism. In this particular case there was a long-drawn-out process of

[24] Cf. *Psychology and Alchemy,* Part II.

inner transformation and rebirth into another being. This "other being" is the other person in ourselves—that larger and greater personality maturing within us, whom we have already met as the inner friend of the soul. That is why we take comfort whenever we find the friend and companion depicted in a ritual, an example being the friendship between Mithras and the sun-god. This relationship is a mystery to the scientific intellect, because the intellect is accustomed to regard these things unsympathetically. But if it made allowance for feeling, we would discover that it is the friend whom the sun-god takes with him on his chariot, as shown in the monuments. It is the representation of a friendship between two men which is simply the outer reflection of an inner fact: it reveals our relationship to that inner friend of the soul into whom Nature herself would like to change us—that other person who we also are and yet can never attain to completely. We are that pair of Dioscuri, one of whom is mortal and the other immortal, and who, though always together, can never be made completely one. The transformation processes strive to approximate them to one another, but our consciousness is aware of resistances, because the other person seems strange and uncanny, and because we cannot get accustomed to the idea that we are not absolute master in our own house. We should prefer to be always "I" and nothing else. But we are confronted with that inner friend or foe, and whether he is our friend or our foe depends on ourselves.

236 You need not be insane to hear his voice. On the contrary, it is the simplest and most natural thing imaginable. For instance, you can ask yourself a question to which "he" gives answer. The discussion is then carried on as in any other conversation. You can describe it as mere "associating" or "talking to oneself," or as a "meditation" in the sense used by the old alchemists, who referred to their interlocutor as *aliquem alium internum,* 'a certain other one, within.' [25] This form of colloquy with the friend of the soul was even admitted by Ignatius Loyola into the technique of his *Exercitia spiritualia,*[26] but with the limiting condition that only the person meditating is

[25] Cf. Ruland, *Lexicon* (1893 edn.), p. 226.

[26] Izquierdo, *Pratica di alcuni Esercitij spirituali di S. Ignatio* (Rome, 1686, p. 7): "A colloquy . . . is nothing else than to talk and communicate familiarly with Christ."

allowed to speak, whereas the inner responses are passed over as being merely human and therefore to be repudiated. This state of things has continued down to the present day. It is no longer a moral or metaphysical prejudice, but—what is much worse—an intellectual one. The "voice" is explained as nothing but "associating," pursued in a witless way and running on and on without sense or purpose, like the works of a clock that has no dial. Or we say "It is only my own thoughts!" even if, on closer inspection, it should turn out that they are thoughts which we either reject or had never consciously thought at all—as if everything psychic that is glimpsed by the ego had always formed part of it! Naturally this hybris serves the useful purpose of maintaining the supremacy of ego-consciousness, which must be safeguarded against dissolution into the unconscious. But it breaks down ignominiously if ever the unconscious should choose to let some nonsensical idea become an obsession or to produce other psychogenic symptoms, for which we would not like to accept responsibility on any account.

237 Our attitude towards this inner voice alternates between two extremes: it is regarded either as undiluted nonsense or as the voice of God. It does not seem to occur to any one that there might be something valuable in between. The "other" may be just as one-sided in one way as the ego is in another. And yet the conflict between them may give rise to truth and meaning—but only if the ego is willing to grant the other its rightful personality. It has, of course, a personality anyway, just as have the voices of insane people; but a real colloquy becomes possible only when the ego acknowledges the existence of a partner to the discussion. This cannot be expected of everyone, because, after all, not everyone is a fit subject for *exercitia spiritualia*. Nor can it be called a colloquy if one speaks only to oneself or only addresses the other, as is the case with George Sand in her conversations with a "spiritual friend": [26a] for thirty pages she talks exclusively to herself while one waits in vain for the other to reply. The colloquy of the *exercitia* may be followed by that silent grace in which the modern doubter no longer believes. But what if it were the supplicated Christ himself who gave immediate answer in the words of the sinful human heart? What fearful abysses of doubt would then be opened? What madness

[26a] ["Daily Conversations with Dr. Piffoel," in her *Intimate Journal*.—EDITORS.]

should we not then have to fear? From this one can understand that images of the gods are better mute, and that ego-consciousness had better believe in its own supremacy rather than go on "associating." One can also understand why that inner friend so often seems to be our enemy, and why he is so far off and his voice so low. For he who is near to him "is near to the fire."

238 Something of this sort may have been in the mind of the alchemist who wrote: "Choose for your Stone him through whom kings are honoured in their crowns, and through whom physicians heal their sick, for he is near to the fire." [27] The alchemists projected the inner event into an outer figure, so for them the inner friend appeared in the form of the "Stone," of which the *Tractatus aureus* says: "Understand, ye sons of the wise, what this exceeding precious Stone crieth out to you: Protect me and I will protect thee. Give me what is mine that I may help thee." [28] To this a scholiast adds: "The seeker after truth hears both the Stone and the Philosopher speaking as if out of one mouth." [29] The Philosopher is Hermes, and the Stone is identical with Mercurius, the Latin Hermes.[30] From the earliest times, Hermes was the mystagogue and psychopomp of the alchemists, their friend and counsellor, who leads them to the goal of their work. He is "like a teacher mediating between the stone and the disciple." [31] To others the friend appears in the shape of Christ or Khidr or a visible or invisible guru, or some other personal guide or leader figure. In this case the colloquy is distinctly one-sided: there is no inner dia-

27 A Pseudo-Aristotle quotation in *Rosarium philosophorum* (1550), fol. Q.

28 "Largiri vis mihi meum" is the usual reading, as in the first edition (1556) of *Ars chemica,* under the title "Septem tractatus seu capitula Hermetis Trismegisti aurei," and also in *Theatrum chemicum,* IV (1613), and Manget, *Bibliotheca chemica,* I (1702), pp. 400ff. In the *Rosarium philosophorum* (1550), fol. E^v, there is a different reading: "Largire mihi ius meum ut te adiuvem" (Give me my due that I may help thee). This is one of the interpretative readings for which the anonymous author of the *Rosarium* is responsible. Despite their arbitrariness they have an important bearing on the interpretation of alchemy. [Cf. *Psychology and Alchemy,* par. 139, n.17.]

29 *Biblio. chem.,* I, p. 430b.

30 Detailed documentation in *Psychology and Alchemy,* par. 84, and "The Spirit Mercurius," pars. 278ff., 287ff.

31 "Tanquam praeceptor intermedius inter lapidem et discipulum." (*Biblio. chem.,* I, p. 430b.) Cf. the beautiful prayer of Astrampsychos, beginning "Come to me, Lord Hermes," and ending "I am thou and thou art I." (Reitzenstein, *Poimandres,* p. 21.)

logue, but instead the response appears as the action of the other, i.e., as an outward event. The alchemists saw it in the transformation of the chemical substance. So if one of them sought transformation, he discovered it outside in matter, whose transformation cried out to him, as it were, "I am the transformation!" But some were clever enough to know, "It is my own transformation—not a personal transformation, but the transformation of what is mortal in me into what is immortal. It shakes off the mortal husk that I am and awakens to a life of its own; it mounts the sun-barge and may take me with it." [32]

239 This is a very ancient idea. In Upper Egypt, near Aswan, I once saw an ancient Egyptian tomb that had just been opened. Just behind the entrance-door was a little basket made of reeds, containing the withered body of a new-born infant, wrapped in rags. Evidently the wife of one of the workmen had hastily laid the body of her dead child in the nobleman's tomb at the last moment, hoping that, when he entered the sun-barge in order to rise anew, it might share in his salvation, because it had been buried in the holy precinct within reach of divine grace.

32 The stone and its transformation are represented:

(1) as the resurrection of the *homo philosophicus,* the Second Adam ("Aurea hora," *Artis auriferae,* 1593, I, p. 195);

(2) as the human soul ("Book of Krates," Berthelot, *La Chimie au moyen âge,* III, p. 50);

(3) as a being below and above man: "This stone is under thee, as to obedience; above thee, as to dominion; therefore from thee, as to knowledge; about thee, as to equals" ("Rosinus ad Sarratantam," *Art. aurif.,* I, p. 310);

(4) as life: "blood is soul and soul is life and life is our Stone" ("Tractatulus Aristotelis," ibid., p. 364),

(5) as the resurrection of the dead ("Calidis liber secretorum," ibid., p. 347; also "Rachaidibi fragmentum," ibid., p. 398);

(6) as the Virgin Mary ("De arte chymica," ibid., p. 582); and

(7) as man himself: "thou art its ore . . . and it is extracted from thee . . . and it remains inseparably with thee" ("Rosinus ad Sarratantam," ibid., p. 311).

3. A TYPICAL SET OF SYMBOLS ILLUSTRATING THE PROCESS OF TRANSFORMATION

240 I have chosen as an example a figure which plays a great role in Islamic mysticism, namely Khidr, "the Verdant One." He appears in the Eighteenth Sura of the Koran, entitled "The Cave."[1] This entire Sura is taken up with a rebirth mystery. The cave is the place of rebirth, that secret cavity in which one is shut up in order to be incubated and renewed. The Koran says of it: "You might have seen the rising sun decline to the right of their cavern, and as it set, go past them on the left, while they [the Seven Sleepers] stayed in the middle." The "middle" is the centre where the jewel reposes, where the incubation or the sacrificial rite or the transformation takes place. The most beautiful development of this symbolism is to be found on Mithraic altarpieces[2] and in alchemical pictures of the transformative substance,[3] which is always shown between sun and moon. Representations of the crucifixion frequently follow the same type, and a similar symbolical arrangement is also found in the transformation or healing ceremonies of the Navahos.[4] Just such a place of the centre or of transformation is the cave in which those seven had gone to sleep, little thinking that they would experience there a prolongation of life verging on immortality. When they awoke, they had slept 309 years.

241 The legend has the following meaning: Anyone who gets into that cave, that is to say into the cave which everyone has in himself, or into the darkness that lies behind consciousness, will find himself involved in an—at first—unconscious process of transformation. By penetrating into the unconscious he makes

1 [The Dawood trans. of the Koran is quoted, sometimes with modifications. The 18th Sura is at pp. 89–98.—EDITORS.]

2 Cumont, *Textes et monuments figurés relatifs aux mystères de Mithra*, II.

3 Cf. especially the crowning vision in the dream of Zosimos: "And another [came] behind him, bringing one adorned round with signs, clad in white and comely to see, who was named the Meridian of the Sun." Cf. "The Visions of Zosimos," par. 87 (III, v bis).

4 Matthews, *The Mountain Chant*, and Stevenson, *Ceremonial of Hasjelti Dailjis*.

a connection with his unconscious contents. This may result in a momentous change of personality in the positive or negative sense. The transformation is often interpreted as a prolongation of the natural span of life or as an earnest of immortality. The former is the case with many alchemists, notably Paracelsus (in his treatise *De vita longa* [5]), and the latter is exemplified in the Eleusinian mysteries.

242 Those seven sleepers indicate by their sacred number [6] that they are gods,[7] who are transformed during sleep and thereby enjoy eternal youth. This helps us to understand at the outset that we are dealing with a mystery legend. The fate of the numinous figures recorded in it grips the hearer, because the story gives expression to parallel processes in his own unconscious which in that way are integrated with consciousness again. The repristination of the original state is tantamount to attaining once more the freshness of youth.

243 The story of the sleepers is followed by some moral observations which appear to have no connection with it. But this apparent irrelevance is deceptive. In reality, these edifying comments are just what are needed by those who cannot be reborn themselves and have to be content with moral conduct, that is to

[5] An account of the secret doctrine hinted at in this treatise may be found in my "Paracelsus as a Spiritual Phenomenon," pars. 169ff.

[6] The different versions of the legend speak sometimes of seven and sometimes of eight disciples. According to the account given in the Koran, the eighth is a dog. The 18th Sura mentions still other versions: "Some will say: 'The sleepers were three: their dog was the fourth.' Others, guessing at the unknown, will say: 'They were five; their dog was the sixth.' And yet others: 'Seven; their dog was the eighth.' " It is evident, therefore, that the dog is to be taken into account. This would seem to be an instance of that characteristic wavering between seven and eight (or three and four, as the case may be), which I have pointed out in *Psychology and Alchemy*, pars. 200ff. There the wavering between seven and eight is connected with the appearance of Mephistopheles, who, as we know, materialized out of the black poodle. In the case of three and four, the fourth is the devil or the female principle, and on a higher level the Mater Dei. (Cf. "Psychology and Religion," pars. 124ff.) We may be dealing with the same kind of ambiguity as in the numbering of the Egyptian nonad (*paut* = 'company of gods'; cf. Budge, *The Gods of the Egyptians*, I, p. 88). The Khidr legend relates to the persecution of the Christians under Decius (*c.* A.D. 250). The scene is Ephesus, where St. John lay "sleeping," but not dead. The seven sleepers woke up again during the reign of Theodosius II (408–450); thus they had slept not quite 200 years.

[7] The seven are the planetary gods of the ancients. Cf. Bousset, *Hauptprobleme der Gnosis*, pp. 23ff.

say with adherence to the law. Very often behaviour prescribed by rule is a substitute for spiritual transformation.[8] These edifying observations are then followed by the story of Moses and his servant Joshua ben Nun:

And Moses said to his servant: "I will not cease from my wanderings until I have reached the place where the two seas meet, even though I journey for eighty years."

But when they had reached the place where the two seas meet, they forgot their fish, and it took its way through a stream to the sea.

And when they had journeyed past this place, Moses said to his servant: "Bring us our breakfast, for we are weary from this journey."

But the other replied: "See what has befallen me! When we were resting there by the rock, I forgot the fish. Only Satan can have put it out of my mind, and in wondrous fashion it took its way to the sea."

Then Moses said: "That is the place we seek." And they went back the way they had come. And they found one of Our servants, whom We had endowed with Our grace and Our wisdom. Moses said to him: "Shall I follow you, that you may teach me for my guidance some of the wisdom you have learnt?"

But he answered: "You will not bear with me, for how should you bear patiently with things you cannot comprehend?"

Moses said: "If Allah wills, you shall find me patient; I shall not in anything disobey you."

He said: "If you are bent on following me, you must ask no question about anything till I myself speak to you concerning it."

The two set forth, but as soon as they embarked, Moses' companion bored a hole in the bottom of the ship.

"A strange thing you have done!" exclaimed Moses. "Is it to drown her passengers that you have bored a hole in her?"

8 Obedience under the law on the one hand, and the freedom of the "children of God," the reborn, on the other, is discussed at length in the Epistles of St. Paul. He distinguishes not only between two different classes of men, who are separated by a greater or lesser development of consciousness, but also between the higher and lower man in one and the same individual. The *sarkikos* (carnal man) remains eternally under the law; the *pneumatikos* (spiritual man) alone is capable of being reborn into freedom. This is quite in keeping with what seems such an insoluble paradox: the Church demanding absolute obedience and at the same time proclaiming freedom from the law. So, too, in the Koran text, the legend appeals to the *pneumatikos* and promises rebirth to him that has ears to hear. But he who, like the *sarkikos*, has no inner ear will find satisfaction and safe guidance in blind submission to Allah's will.

"Did I not tell you," he replied, "that you would not bear with me?"

"Pardon my forgetfulness," said Moses. "Do not be angry with me on this account."

They journeyed on until they fell in with a certain youth. Moses' companion slew him, and Moses said: "You have killed an innocent man who has done no harm. Surely you have committed a wicked crime."

"Did I not tell you," he replied, "that you would not bear with me?"

Moses said: "If ever I question you again, abandon me; for then I should deserve it."

They travelled on until they came to a certain city. They asked the people for some food, but the people declined to receive them as their guests. There they found a wall on the point of falling down. The other raised it up, and Moses said: "Had you wished, you could have demanded payment for your labours."

"Now the time has arrived when we must part," said the other. "But first I will explain to you those acts of mine which you could not bear with in patience.

"Know that the ship belonged to some poor fishermen. I damaged it because in their rear was a king who was taking every ship by force.

"As for the youth, his parents both are true believers, and we feared lest he should plague them with his wickedness and unbelief. It was our wish that their Lord should grant them another in his place, a son more righteous and more filial.

"As for the wall, it belonged to two orphan boys in the city whose father was an honest man. Beneath it their treasure is buried. Your Lord decreed in His mercy that they should dig out their treasure when they grew to manhood. What I did was not done by caprice. That is the meaning of the things you could not bear with in patience."

244 This story is an amplification and elucidation of the legend of the seven sleepers and the problem of rebirth. Moses is the man who seeks, the man on the "quest." On this pilgrimage he is accompanied by his "shadow," the "servant" or "lower" man (*pneumatikos* and *sarkikos* in two individuals). Joshua is the son of Nun, which is a name for "fish," [9] suggesting that Joshua had his origin in the depths of the waters, in the darkness of the

[9] Vollers, "Chidher," *Archiv für Religionswissenschaft,* XII, p. 241. All quotations from the commentaries are extracted from this article.

shadow-world. The critical place is reached "where the two seas meet," which is interpreted as the isthmus of Suez, where the Western and the Eastern seas come close together. In other words, it is that "place of the middle" which we have already met in the symbolic preamble, but whose significance was not recognized at first by the man and his shadow. They had "forgotten their fish," the humble source of nourishment. The fish refers to Nun, the father of the shadow, of the carnal man, who comes from the dark world of the Creator. For the fish came alive again and leapt out of the basket in order to find its way back to its homeland, the sea. In other words, the animal ancestor and creator of life separates himself from the conscious man, an event which amounts to loss of the instinctive psyche. This process is a symptom of dissociation well known in the psychopathology of the neuroses; it is always connected with one-sidedness of the conscious attitude. In view of the fact, however, that neurotic phenomena are nothing but exaggerations of normal processes, it is not to be wondered at that very similar phenomena can also be found within the scope of the normal. It is a question of that well-known "loss of soul" among primitives, as described above in the section on diminution of the personality; in scientific language, an *abaissement du niveau mental.*

245 Moses and his servant soon notice what has happened. Moses had sat down, "worn out" and hungry. Evidently he had a feeling of insufficiency, for which a physiological explanation is given. Fatigue is one of the most regular symptoms of loss of energy or libido. The entire process represents something very typical, namely the *failure to recognize a moment of crucial importance,* a motif which we encounter in a great variety of mythical forms. Moses realizes that he has unconsciously found the source of life and then lost it again, which we might well regard as a remarkable intuition. The fish they had intended to eat is a content of the unconscious, by which the connection with the origin is re-established. He is the reborn one, who has awakened to new life. This came to pass, as the commentaries say, through the contact with the water of life: by slipping back into the sea, the fish once more becomes a content of the unconscious, and its offspring are distinguished by having only one eye and half a head.[10]

10 Ibid., p. 253.

246 The alchemists, too, speak of a strange fish in the sea, the "round fish lacking bones and skin," [11] which symbolizes the "round element," the germ of the "animate stone," of the *filius philosophorum*. The water of life has its parallel in the *aqua permanens* of alchemy. This water is extolled as "vivifying," besides which it has the property of dissolving all solids and coagulating all liquids. The Koran commentaries state that, on the spot where the fish disappeared, the sea was turned to solid ground, whereon the tracks of the fish could still be seen.[12] On the island thus formed Khidr was sitting, in the place of the middle. A mystical interpretation says that he was sitting "on a throne consisting of light, between the upper and the lower sea," [13] again in the middle position. The appearance of Khidr seems to be mysteriously connected with the disappearance of the fish. It looks almost as if he himself had been the fish. This conjecture is supported by the fact that the commentaries relegate the source of life to the "place of darkness." [14] The depths of the sea are dark (*mare tenebrositatis*). The darkness has its parallel in the alchemical *nigredo,* which occurs after the *coniunctio,* when the female takes the male into herself.[15] From the *nigredo* issues the Stone, the symbol of the immortal self; moreover, its first appearance is likened to "fish eyes." [16]

11 Cf. *Aion,* pars. 195ff. 12 Vollers, p. 244.

13 Ibid., p. 260. 14 Ibid., p. 258.

15 Cf. the myth in the "Visio Arislei," especially the version in the *Rosarium philosophorum (Art. aurif.,* II, p. 246), likewise the drowning of the sun in the Mercurial Fountain and the green lion who devours the sun (*Art. aurif.,* II, pp. 315, 366). Cf. "The Psychology of the Transference," pars. 467ff.

16 The white stone appears on the edge of the vessel, "like Oriental gems, like fish's eyes." Cf. Joannes Isaacus Hollandus, *Opera mineralia* (1600), p. 370. Also Lagneus, "Harmonica chemica." *Theatrum chemicum,* IV (1613), p. 870. The eyes appear at the end of the *nigredo* and with the beginning of the *albedo.* Another simile of the same sort is the *scintillae* that appear in the dark substance. This idea is traced back to Zacharias 4 : 10 (DV): "And they shall rejoice and see the tin plummet in the hand of Zorobabel. These are the seven eyes of the Lord that run to and fro through the whole earth." (Cf. Eirenaeus Orandus, in the introduction to Nicholas Flamel's *Exposition of the Hieroglyphicall Figures,* 1624, fol. A 5.) They are the seven eyes of God on the corner-stone of the new temple (Zach. 3 : 9). The number seven suggests the seven stars, the planetary gods, who were depicted by the alchemists in a cave under the earth (Mylius, *Philosophia reformata,* 1622, p. 167). They are the "sleepers enchained in Hades" (Berthelot, *Collection des anciens alchimistes grecs,* IV, xx, 8). This is an allusion to the legend of the seven sleepers.

247 Khidr may well be a symbol of the self. His qualities signalize him as such: he is said to have been born in a cave, i.e., in darkness. He is the "Long-lived One," who continually renews himself, like Elijah. Like Osiris, he is dismembered at the end of time, by Antichrist, but is able to restore himself to life. He is analogous to the Second Adam, with whom the reanimated fish is identified; [17] he is a counsellor, a Paraclete, "Brother Khidr." Anyway Moses accepts him as a higher consciousness and looks up to him for instruction. Then follow those incomprehensible deeds which show how ego-consciousness reacts to the superior guidance of the self through the twists and turns of fate. To the initiate who is capable of transformation it is a comforting tale; to the obedient believer, an exhortation not to murmur against Allah's incomprehensible omnipotence. Khidr symbolizes not only the higher wisdom but also a way of acting which is in accord with this wisdom and transcends reason.

248 Anyone hearing such a mystery tale will recognize himself in the questing Moses and the forgetful Joshua, and the tale shows him how the immortality-bringing rebirth comes about. Characteristically, it is neither Moses nor Joshua who is transformed, but the forgotten fish. Where the fish disappears, there is the birthplace of Khidr. The immortal being issues from something humble and forgotten, indeed, from a wholly improbable source. This is the familiar motif of the hero's birth and need not be documented here.[18] Anyone who knows the Bible will think of Isaiah 53:2ff., where the "servant of God" is described, and of the gospel stories of the Nativity. The nourishing character of the transformative substance or deity is borne out by numerous cult-legends: Christ is the bread, Osiris the wheat,

17 Vollers, p. 254. This may possibly be due to Christian influence: one thinks of the fish meals of the early Christians and of fish symbolism in general. Vollers himself stresses the analogy between Christ and Khidr. Concerning the fish symbolism, see *Aion*.

18 Further examples in *Symbols of Transformation*, Part II. I could give many more from alchemy, but shall content myself with the old verse:

"This is the stone, poor and of little price,
Spurned by the fool, but honoured by the wise."

(*Ros. phil.*, in *Art. aurif.*, II, p. 210.) The "lapis exilis" may be a connecting-link with the "lapsit exillis," the grail of Wolfram von Eschenbach.

Mondamin the maize,[19] etc. These symbols coincide with a psychic fact which obviously, from the point of view of consciousness, has the significance merely of something to be assimilated, but whose real nature is overlooked. The fish symbol shows immediately what this is: it is the "nourishing" influence of unconscious contents, which maintain the vitality of consciousness by a continual influx of energy; for consciousness does not produce its energy by itself. What is capable of transformation is just this root of consciousness, which—inconspicuous and almost invisible (i.e., unconscious) though it is—provides consciousness with all its energy. Since the unconscious gives us the feeling that it is something alien, a non-ego, it is quite natural that it should be symbolized by an alien figure. Thus, on the one hand, it is the most insignificant of things, while on the other, so far as it potentially contains that "round" wholeness which consciousness lacks, it is the most significant of all. This "round" thing is the great treasure that lies hidden in the cave of the unconscious, and its personification is this personal being who represents the higher unity of conscious and unconscious. It is a figure comparable to Hiranyagarbha, Purusha, Atman, and the mystic Buddha. For this reason I have elected to call it the "self," by which I understand a psychic totality and at the same time a centre, neither of which coincides with the ego but includes it, just as a larger circle encloses a smaller one.

249 The intuition of immortality which makes itself felt during the transformation is connected with the peculiar nature of the unconscious. It is, in a sense, non-spatial and non-temporal. The empirical proof of this is the occurrence of so-called telepathic phenomena, which are still denied by hypersceptical critics, although in reality they are much more common than is generally supposed.[20] The feeling of immortality, it seems to me, has its origin in a peculiar feeling of extension in space and time, and I am inclined to regard the deification rites in the mysteries as a projection of this same psychic phenomenon.

250 The character of the self as a personality comes out very

19 [The Ojibway legend of Mondamin was recorded by H. R. Schoolcraft and became a source for Longfellow's *Song of Hiawatha*. Cf. M. L. Williams, *Schoolcraft's Indian Legends*, pp. 58ff.—EDITORS.]

20 Rhine, *New Frontiers of the Mind*. [Cf. also "Synchronicity: An Acausal Connecting Principle."—EDITORS.]

plainly in the Khidr legend. This feature is most strikingly expressed in the non-Koranic stories about Khidr, of which Vollers gives some telling examples. During my trip through Kenya, the headman of our safari was a Somali who had been brought up in the Sufi faith. To him Khidr was in every way a living person, and he assured me that I might at any time meet Khidr, because I was, as he put it, a *M'tu-ya-kitabu,*[21] a 'man of the Book,' meaning the Koran. He had gathered from our talks that I knew the Koran better than he did himself (which was, by the way, not saying a great deal). For this reason he regarded me as "islamu." He told me I might meet Khidr in the street in the shape of a man, or he might appear to me during the night as a pure white light, or—he smilingly picked a blade of grass—the Verdant One might even look like that. He said he himself had once been comforted and helped by Khidr, when he could not find a job after the war and was suffering want. One night, while he slept, he dreamt he saw a bright white light near the door and he knew it was Khidr. Quickly leaping to his feet (in the dream), he reverentially saluted him with the words *salem aleikum,* 'peace be with you,' and then he knew that his wish would be fulfilled. He added that a few days later he was offered the post as headman of a safari by a firm of outfitters in Nairobi.

251 This shows that, even in our own day, Khidr still lives on in the religion of the people, as friend, adviser, comforter, and teacher of revealed wisdom. The position assigned to him by dogma was, according to my Somali, that of *maleika kwanza-ya-mungu,* 'First Angel of God'—a sort of "Angel of the Face," an *angelos* in the true sense of the word, a messenger.

252 Khidr's character as a friend explains the subsequent part of the Eighteenth Sura, which reads as follows:

> They will ask you about Dhulqarnein. Say: "I will give you an account of him.
>
> "We made him mighty in the land and gave him means to achieve all things. He journeyed on a certain road until he reached the West and saw the sun setting in a pool of black mud. Hard by he found a certain people.

21 He spoke in Kiswahili, the lingua franca of East Africa. It contains many words borrowed from Arabic, as shown by the above example: *kitab* = book.

" 'Dhulqarnein,' We said, 'you must either punish them or show them kindness.'

"He replied: 'The wicked We shall surely punish. Then they shall return to their Lord and be sternly punished by Him. As for those that have faith and do good works, we shall bestow on them a rich reward and deal indulgently with them.'

"He then journeyed along another road until he reached the East and saw the sun rising upon a people whom We had utterly exposed to its flaming rays. So he did; and We had full knowledge of all the forces at his command.

"Then he followed yet another route until he came between the Two Mountains and found a people who could barely understand a word. 'Dhulqarnein,' they said, 'Gog and Magog are ravaging this land. Build us a rampart against them and we will pay you tribute.'

"He replied: 'The power which my Lord has given me is better than any tribute. Lend me a force of labourers, and I will raise a rampart between you and them. Come, bring me blocks of iron.'

"He dammed up the valley between the Two Mountains, and said: 'Ply your bellows.' And when the iron blocks were red with heat, he said: 'Bring me molten brass to pour on them.'

"Gog and Magog could not scale it, nor could they dig their way through it. He said: 'This is a blessing from my Lord. But when my Lord's promise is fulfilled, He will level it to dust. The promise of my Lord is true.' "

On that day We will let them come in tumultuous throngs. The Trumpet shall be sounded and We will gather them all together.

On that day Hell shall be laid bare before the unbelievers, who have turned a blind eye to My admonition and a deaf ear to My warning.

253 We see here another instance of that lack of coherence which is not uncommon in the Koran. How are we to account for this apparently abrupt transition to Dhulqarnein, the Two-horned One, that is to say, Alexander the Great? Apart from the unheard-of anachronism (Mohammed's chronology in general leaves much to be desired), one does not quite understand why Alexander is brought in here at all. But it has to be borne in mind that Khidr and Dhulqarnein are *the* great pair of friends, altogether comparable to the Dioscuri, as Vollers rightly emphasizes. The psychological connection may therefore be presumed to be as follows: Moses has had a profoundly moving experience of the self, which brought unconscious processes before his eyes

with overwhelming clarity. Afterwards, when he comes to his people, the Jews, who are counted among the infidels, and wants to tell them about his experience, he prefers to use the form of a mystery legend. Instead of speaking about himself, he speaks about the Two-horned One. Since Moses himself is also "horned," the substitution of Dhulqarnein appears plausible. Then he has to relate the history of this friendship and describe how Khidr helped his friend. Dhulqarnein makes his way to the setting of the sun and then to its rising. That is, he describes the way of the renewal of the sun, through death and darkness to a new resurrection. All this again indicates that it is Khidr who not only stands by man in his bodily needs but also helps him to attain rebirth.[22] The Koran, it is true, makes no distinction in this narrative between Allah, who is speaking in the first person plural, and Khidr. But it is clear that this section is simply a continuation of the helpful actions described previously, from which it is evident that Khidr is a symbolization or "incarnation" of Allah. The friendship between Khidr and Alexander plays an especially prominent part in the commentaries, as does also the connection with the prophet Elijah. Vollers does not hesitate to extend the comparison to that other pair of friends, Gilgamesh and Enkidu.[23]

254 To sum up, then: Moses has to recount the deeds of the two friends to his people in the manner of an impersonal mystery legend. Psychologically this means that the transformation has to be described or felt as happening to the "other." Although it is Moses himself who, in his experience with Khidr, stands in Dhulqarnein's place, he has to name the latter instead of himself in telling the story. This can hardly be accidental, for the great psychic danger which is always connected with individuation, or the development of the self, lies in the identification of ego-consciousness with the self. This produces an inflation which threatens consciousness with dissolution. All the more primitive or older cultures show a fine sense for the "perils of the soul" and for the dangerousness and general

22 There are similar indications in the Jewish tales about Alexander. Cf. Bin Gorion, *Der Born Judas,* III, p. 133, for the legend of the "water of life," which is related to the 18th Sura.

23 [For a fuller discussion of these relationships, see *Symbols of Transformation,* pars. 282ff.—EDITORS.]

unreliability of the gods. That is, they have not yet lost their psychic instinct for the barely perceptible and yet vital processes going on in the background, which can hardly be said of our modern culture. To be sure, we have before our eyes as a warning just such a pair of friends distorted by inflation—Nietzsche and Zarathustra—but the warning has not been heeded. And what are we to make of Faust and Mephistopheles? The Faustian hybris is already the first step towards madness. The fact that the unimpressive beginning of the transformation in *Faust* is a dog and not an edible fish, and that the transformed figure is the devil and not a wise friend, "endowed with Our grace and Our wisdom," might, I am inclined to think, offer a key to our understanding of the highly enigmatic Germanic soul.

255 Without entering into other details of the text, I would like to draw attention to one more point: the building of the rampart against Gog and Magog (also known as Yajuj and Majuj). This motif is a repetition of Khidr's last deed in the previous episode, the rebuilding of the town wall. But this time the wall is to be a strong defence against Gog and Magog. The passage may possibly refer to Revelation 20:7f. (AV):

> And when the thousand years are expired, Satan shall be loosed out of his prison, and shall go out to deceive the nations which are in the four quarters of the earth, Gog and Magog, to gather them together for battle: the number of whom is as the sand of the sea. And they went up on the breadth of the earth, and compassed the camp of the saints about, and the beloved city.

256 Here Dhulqarnein takes over the role of Khidr and builds an unscalable rampart for the people living "between Two Mountains." This is obviously the same place in the middle which is to be protected against Gog and Magog, the featureless, hostile masses. Psychologically, it is again a question of the self, enthroned in the place of the middle, and referred to in Revelation as the beloved city (Jerusalem, the centre of the earth). The self is the hero, threatened already at birth by envious collective forces; the jewel that is coveted by all and arouses jealous strife; and finally the god who is dismembered by the old, evil power of darkness. In its psychological meaning, individuation is an *opus contra naturam,* which creates a *horror vacui* in the collective layer and is only too likely to collapse under the impact of

the collective forces of the psyche. The mystery legend of the two helpful friends promises protection[24] to him who has found the jewel on his quest. But there will come a time when, in accordance with Allah's providence, even the iron rampart will fall to pieces, namely, on the day when the world comes to an end, or psychologically speaking, when individual consciousness is extinguished in the waters of darkness, that is to say when a *subjective* end of the world is experienced. By this is meant the moment when consciousness sinks back into the darkness from which it originally emerged, like Khidr's island: the moment of death.

257 The legend then continues along eschatological lines: on that day (the day of the Last Judgment) the light returns to eternal light and the darkness to eternal darkness. The opposites are separated and a timeless state of permanence sets in, which, because of the absolute separation of opposites, is nevertheless one of supreme tension and therefore corresponds to the improbable initial state. This is in contrast to the view which sees the end as a *complexio oppositorum.*

258 With this prospect of eternity, Paradise, and Hell the Eighteenth Sura comes to an end. In spite of its apparently disconnected and allusive character, it gives an almost perfect picture of a psychic transformation or rebirth which today, with our greater psychological insight, we would recognize as an individuation process. Because of the great age of the legend and the Islamic prophet's primitive cast of mind, the process takes place entirely outside the sphere of consciousness and is projected in the form of a mystery legend of a friend or a pair of friends and the deeds they perform. That is why it is all so allusive and lacking in logical sequence. Nevertheless, the legend expresses the obscure archetype of transformation so admirably that the passionate religious *eros* of the Arab finds it completely satisfying. It is for this reason that the figure of Khidr plays such an important part in Islamic mysticism.

24 Just as the Dioscuri come to the aid of those who are in danger at sea.

IV

THE PSYCHOLOGY OF THE CHILD ARCHETYPE

THE PSYCHOLOGICAL ASPECTS OF THE KORE

[These two studies were first published, under the respective titles "Zur Psychologie des Kind-Archetypus" and "Zum psychologischen Aspekt der Kore-Figur," in two small volumes: *Das göttliche Kind* (Albae Vigiliae VI/VII, Amsterdam and Leipzig, 1940) and *Das göttliche Mädchen* (same series, VIII/IX, 1941). Each volume contained a companion essay by K. Kerényi. The two volumes were united, with additional material by Professor Kerényi, under the title *Einführung in das Wesen der Mythologie* (Amsterdam, Leipzig, and Zurich, 1941). This combined volume was translated by R. F. C. Hull as *Essays on a Science of Mythology* (Bollingen Series XXII; New York, 1949), of which the London (1950) edition was titled *Introduction to a Science of Mythology;* the text of the two studies here presented is a revision of that of 1949/50. The complete German volume was published in a new edition in 1951. In 1963, the English version appeared in Harper Torchbooks (New York; paperback), with the present Jung translation and a revised Kerényi translation—EDITORS.]

THE PSYCHOLOGY OF THE CHILD ARCHETYPE

I. INTRODUCTION

259 The author of the companion essay [1] on the mythology of the "child" or the child god has asked me for a psychological commentary on the subject of his investigations. I am glad to accede to his request, although the undertaking seems to me no small venture in view of the great significance of the child motif in mythology. Kerényi himself has enlarged upon the occurrence of this motif in Greece and Rome, with parallels drawn from Indian, Finnish, and other sources, thus indicating that the presentation of the theme would allow of yet further extensions. Though a comprehensive description would contribute nothing decisive in principle, it would nevertheless produce an overwhelming impression of the world-wide incidence and frequency of the motif. The customary treatment of mythological motifs so far in separate departments of science, such as philology, ethnology, the history of civilization, and comparative religion, was not exactly a help to us in recognizing their universality; and the psychological problems raised by this universality could easily be shelved by hypotheses of migration. Consequently Adolf Bastian's [2] ideas met with little success in their day. Even then there was sufficient empirical material available to permit far-reaching psychological conclusions, but the necessary premises were lacking. Although the psychological knowledge of that time included myth-formation in its province—witness Wundt's *Völkerpsychologie*—it was not in a position to demonstrate this same process as a living function actually present in the psyche of civilized man, any more than it could understand mythological motifs as structural elements of the psyche. True to its history, when psychology was metaphysics first of

1 Kerényi, "The Primordial Child in Primordial Times."
2 *Der Mensch in der Geschichte* (1860).

all, then the study of the senses and their functions, and then of the conscious mind and *its* functions, psychology identified its proper subject with the conscious psyche and its contents and thus completely overlooked the existence of a nonconscious psyche. Although various philosophers, among them Leibniz, Kant, and Schelling, had already pointed very clearly to the problem of the dark side of the psyche, it was a physician who felt impelled, from his scientific and medical experience, to point to the *unconscious* as the essential basis of the psyche. This was C. G. Carus,[3] the authority whom Eduard von Hartmann followed. In recent times it was, once again, medical psychology that approached the problem of the unconscious without philosophical preconceptions. It became clear from many separate investigations that the psychopathology of the neuroses and of many psychoses cannot dispense with the hypothesis of a dark side of the psyche, i.e., the unconscious. It is the same with the psychology of dreams, which is really the *terra intermedia* between normal and pathological psychology. In the dream, as in the products of psychoses, there are numberless interconnections to which one can find parallels only in mythological associations of ideas (or perhaps in certain poetic creations which are often characterized by a borrowing, not always conscious, from myths). Had thorough investigation shown that in the majority of such cases it was simply a matter of forgotten knowledge, the physician would not have gone to the trouble of making extensive researches into individual and collective parallels. But, in point of fact, typical mythologems were observed among individuals to whom all knowledge of this kind was absolutely out of the question, and where indirect derivation from religious ideas that might have been known to them, or from popular figures of speech, was impossible.[4] Such conclusions forced us to assume that we must be dealing with "autochthonous" revivals independent of all tradition, and, consequently, that "myth-forming" structural elements must be present in the unconscious psyche.[5]

3 *Psyche* (1846).

4 A working example in "The Concept of the Collective Unconscious," pars. 105ff., above.

5 Freud, in his *Interpretation of Dreams* (p. 261), paralleled certain aspects of infantile psychology with the Oedipus legend and observed that its "universal

260 These products are never (or at least very seldom) myths with a definite form, but rather mythological components which, because of their typical nature, we can call "motifs," "primordial images," types or—as I have named them—*archetypes*. The child archetype is an excellent example. Today we can hazard the formula that the archetypes appear in myths and fairytales just as they do in dreams and in the products of psychotic fantasy. The medium in which they are embedded is, in the former case, an ordered and for the most part immediately understandable context, but in the latter case a generally unintelligible, irrational, not to say delirious sequence of images which nonetheless does not lack a certain hidden coherence. In the individual, the archetypes appear as involuntary manifestations of unconscious processes whose existence and meaning can only be inferred, whereas the myth deals with traditional forms of incalculable age. They hark back to a prehistoric world whose spiritual preconceptions and general conditions we can still observe today among existing primitives. Myths on this level are as a rule tribal history handed down from generation to generation by word of mouth. Primitive mentality differs from the civilized chiefly in that the conscious mind is far less developed in scope and intensity. Functions such as thinking, willing, etc. are not yet differentiated; they are pre-conscious, and in the case of thinking, for instance, this shows itself in the circumstance that the primitive does not think *consciously*, but that thoughts *appear*. The primitive cannot assert that he thinks; it is rather that "something thinks in him." The spontaneity of the act of thinking does not lie, causally, in his conscious mind, but in his unconscious. Moreover, he is incapable of any conscious effort of will; he must put himself beforehand

validity" was to be explained in terms of the same infantile premise. The real working out of mythological material was then taken up by my pupils (A. Maeder, "Essai d'interprétation de quelques rêves," 1907, and "Die Symbolik in den Legenden, Märchen, Gebräuchen, und Träumen," 1908; F. Riklin, "Über Gefängnispsychosen," 1907, and *Wishfulfilment and Symbolism in Fairy Tales*, orig. 1908); and by K. Abraham, *Dreams and Myths*, orig. 1909. They were succeeded by Otto Rank of the Viennese school (*The Myth of the Birth of the Hero*, orig. 1922). In the *Psychology of the Unconscious* (orig. 1911; revised and expanded as *Symbols of Transformation*), I presented a somewhat more comprehensive examination of psychic and mythological parallels. Cf. also my essay in this volume, "Concerning the Archetypes, with Special Reference to the Anima Concept."

into the "mood of willing," or let himself be put—hence his *rites d'entrée et de sortie*. His consciousness is menaced by an almighty unconscious: hence his fear of magical influences which may cross his path at any moment; and for this reason, too, he is surrounded by unknown forces and must adjust himself to them as best he can. Owing to the chronic twilight state of his consciousness, it is often next to impossible to find out whether he merely dreamed something or whether he really experienced it. The spontaneous manifestation of the unconscious and its archetypes intrudes everywhere into his conscious mind, and the mythical world of his ancestors—for instance, the *alchera* or *bugari* of the Australian aborigines—is a reality equal if not superior to the material world.[6] It is not the world as we know it that speaks out of his unconscious, but the unknown world of the psyche, of which we know that it mirrors our empirical world only in part, and that, for the other part, it moulds this empirical world in accordance with its own psychic assumptions. The archetype does not proceed from physical facts, but describes how the psyche experiences the physical fact, and in so doing the psyche often behaves so autocratically that it denies tangible reality or makes statements that fly in the face of it.

261 The primitive mentality does not *invent* myths, it *experiences* them. Myths are original revelations of the preconscious psyche, involuntary statements about unconscious psychic happenings, and anything but allegories of physical processes.[7] Such allegories would be an idle amusement for an unscientific intellect. Myths, on the contrary, have a vital meaning. Not merely do they represent, they *are* the psychic life of the primitive tribe, which immediately falls to pieces and decays when it loses its mythological heritage, like a man who has lost his soul. A tribe's mythology is its living religion, whose loss is always and everywhere, even among the civilized, a moral catastrophe. But religion is a vital link with psychic processes independent of and beyond consciousness, in the dark hinterland of the psyche. Many of these unconscious processes may be indirectly occasioned by consciousness, but never by conscious choice. Others appear to arise spontaneously, that is to say, from no discernible or demonstrable conscious cause.

[6] This fact is well known, and the relevant ethnological literature is too extensive to be mentioned here.

[7] Cf. "The Structure of the Psyche," pars. 330ff.

262 Modern psychology treats the products of unconscious fantasy-activity as self-portraits of what is going on in the unconscious, or as statements of the unconscious psyche about itself. They fall into two categories. First, fantasies (including dreams) of a personal character, which go back unquestionably to personal experiences, things forgotten or repressed, and can thus be completely explained by individual anamnesis. Second, fantasies (including dreams) of an impersonal character, which cannot be reduced to experiences in the individual's past, and thus cannot be explained as something individually acquired. These fantasy-images undoubtedly have their closest analogues in mythological types. We must therefore assume that they correspond to certain *collective* (and not personal) structural elements of the human psyche in general, and, like the morphological elements of the human body, are *inherited.* Although tradition and transmission by migration certainly play a part, there are, as we have said, very many cases that cannot be accounted for in this way and drive us to the hypothesis of "autochthonous revival." These cases are so numerous that we are obliged to assume the existence of a collective psychic substratum. I have called this the *collective unconscious.*

263 The products of this second category resemble the types of structures to be met with in myth and fairytale so much that we must regard them as related. It is therefore wholly within the realm of possibility that both, the mythological types as well as the individual types, arise under quite similar conditions. As already mentioned, the fantasy-products of the second category (as also those of the first) arise in a state of reduced intensity of consciousness (in dreams, delirium, reveries, visions, etc.). In all these states the check put upon unconscious contents by the concentration of the conscious mind ceases, so that the hitherto unconscious material streams, as though from opened side-sluices, into the field of consciousness. This mode of origination is the general rule.[8]

264 Reduced intensity of consciousness and absence of concentration and attention, Janet's *abaissement du niveau mental,* correspond pretty exactly to the primitive state of consciousness

8 Except for certain cases of spontaneous vision, *automatismes téléologiques* (Flournoy), and the processes in the method of "active imagination" which I have described [e.g., in "The Transcendent Function" and *Mysterium Coniunctionis,* pars. 706, 753f.—EDITORS].

in which, we must suppose, myths were originally formed. It is therefore exceedingly probable that the mythological archetypes, too, made their appearance in much the same manner as the manifestations of archetypal structures among individuals today.

265 The methodological principle in accordance with which psychology treats the products of the unconscious is this: Contents of an archetypal character are manifestations of processes in the collective unconscious. Hence they do not refer to anything that is or has been conscious, but to something essentially unconscious. In the last analysis, therefore, it is impossible to say what they refer to. Every interpretation necessarily remains an "as-if." The ultimate core of meaning may be circumscribed, but not described. Even so, the bare circumscription denotes an essential step forward in our knowledge of the pre-conscious structure of the psyche, which was already in existence when there was as yet no unity of personality (even today the primitive is not securely possessed of it) and no consciousness at all. We can also observe this pre-conscious state in early childhood, and as a matter of fact it is the dreams of this early period that not infrequently bring extremely remarkable archetypal contents to light.[9]

266 If, then, we proceed in accordance with the above principle, there is no longer any question whether a myth refers to the sun or the moon, the father or the mother, sexuality or fire or water; all it does is to circumscribe and give an approximate description of an *unconscious core of meaning*. The ultimate meaning of this nucleus was never conscious and never will be. It was, and still is, only interpreted, and every interpretation that comes anywhere near the hidden sense (or, from the point of view of scientific intellect, nonsense, which comes to the same thing) has always, right from the beginning, laid claim not only to absolute truth and validity but to instant reverence and religious devotion. Archetypes were, and still are, living psychic forces that demand to be taken seriously, and they have a strange way of making sure of their effect. Always they were the bringers

[9] The relevant material can be found in the unpublished reports of the seminars I gave at the Federal Polytechnic Institute (ETH) in Zurich in 1936–39, and in Michael Fordham's book *The Life of Childhood.*

of protection and salvation, and their violation has as its consequence the "perils of the soul" known to us from the psychology of primitives. Moreover, they are the unfailing causes of neurotic and even psychotic disorders, behaving exactly like neglected or maltreated physical organs or organic functional systems.

267 An archetypal content expresses itself, first and foremost, in metaphors. If such a content should speak of the sun and identify with it the lion, the king, the hoard of gold guarded by the dragon, or the power that makes for the life and health of man, it is neither the one thing nor the other, but the unknown third thing that finds more or less adequate expression in all these similes, yet—to the perpetual vexation of the intellect—remains unknown and not to be fitted into a formula. For this reason the scientific intellect is always inclined to put on airs of enlightenment in the hope of banishing the spectre once and for all. Whether its endeavours were called euhemerism, or Christian apologetics, or Enlightenment in the narrow sense, or Positivism, there was always a myth hiding behind it, in new and disconcerting garb, which then, following the ancient and venerable pattern, gave itself out as ultimate truth. In reality we can never legitimately cut loose from our archetypal foundations unless we are prepared to pay the price of a neurosis, any more than we can rid ourselves of our body and its organs without committing suicide. If we cannot deny the archetypes or otherwise neutralize them, we are confronted, at every new stage in the differentiation of consciousness to which civilization attains, with the task of finding a new *interpretation* appropriate to this stage, in order to connect the life of the past that still exists in us with the life of the present, which threatens to slip away from it. If this link-up does not take place, a kind of rootless consciousness comes into being no longer oriented to the past, a consciousness which succumbs helplessly to all manner of suggestions and, in practice, is susceptible to psychic epidemics. With the loss of the past, now become "insignificant," devalued, and incapable of revaluation, the saviour is lost too, for the saviour is either the insignificant thing itself or else arises out of it. Over and over again in the "metamorphosis of the gods" he rises up as the prophet or first-born of a new

generation and appears unexpectedly in the unlikeliest places (sprung from a stone, tree, furrow, water, etc.) and in ambiguous form (Tom Thumb, dwarf, child, animal, and so on).

268 This archetype of the "child god" is extremely widespread and intimately bound up with all the other mythological aspects of the child motif. It is hardly necessary to allude to the still living "Christ-child," who, in the legend of Saint Christopher, also has the typical feature of being "smaller than small and bigger than big." In folklore the child motif appears in the guise of the *dwarf* or the *elf* as personifications of the hidden forces of nature. To this sphere also belongs the little metal man of late antiquity, the ἀνθρωπάριον,[10] who, till far into the Middle Ages, on the one hand inhabited the mine-shafts,[11] and on the other represented the alchemical metals,[12] above all Mercurius reborn in perfect form (as the hermaphrodite, *filius sapientiae,* or *infans noster*).[13] Thanks to the religious interpretation of the "child," a fair amount of evidence has come down to us from the Middle Ages showing that the "child" was not merely a traditional figure, but a vision spontaneously experienced (as a so-called "irruption of the unconscious"). I would mention Meister Eckhart's vision of the "naked boy" and the dream of Brother Eustachius.[14] Interesting accounts of these spontaneous experiences are also to be found in English ghost-stories, where we read of the vision of a "Radiant Boy" said to have been seen in a place where there are Roman remains.[15] This apparition was supposed to be of evil omen. It almost looks as though we were dealing with the figure of a *puer aeternus* who had become inauspicious through "metamorphosis," or in other words had shared the fate of the classical and the Germanic gods, who have all become bugbears. The mystical character of the experience is also confirmed in Part II of Goethe's *Faust,* where Faust him-

10 Berthelot, *Alchimistes grecs,* III, xxv.

11 Agricola, *De animantibus subterraneis* (1549); Kircher, *Mundus subterraneus* (1678), VIII, 4.

12 Mylius, *Philosophia reformata* (1622).

13 "Allegoria super librum Turbae" in *Artis auriferae,* I (1572), p. 161.

14 *Texte aus der deutschen Mystik des 14. und 15. Jahrhunderts,* ed. Spamer, pp. 143, 150.

15 Ingram, *The Haunted Homes and Family Traditions of Great Britain,* pp. 43ff.

self is transformed into a boy and admitted into the "choir of blessed youths," this being the "larval stage" of Doctor Marianus.[16]

269 In the strange tale called *Das Reich ohne Raum,* by Bruno Goetz, a *puer aeternus* named Fo (= Buddha) appears with whole troops of "unholy" boys of evil significance. (Contemporary parallels are better let alone.) I mention this instance only to demonstrate the enduring vitality of the child archetype.

270 The child motif not infrequently occurs in the field of psychopathology. The "imaginary" child is common among women with mental disorders and is usually interpreted in a Christian sense. Homunculi also appear, as in the famous Schreber case,[17] where they come in swarms and plague the sufferer. But the clearest and most significant manifestation of the child motif in the therapy of neuroses is in the maturation process of personality induced by the analysis of the unconscious, which I have termed the process of *individuation.*[18] Here we are confronted with preconscious processes which, in the form of more or less well-formed fantasies, gradually pass over into the conscious mind, or become conscious as dreams, or, lastly, are made conscious through the method of active imagination.[19] This material is rich in archetypal motifs, among them frequently that of the child. Often the child is formed after the Christian model; more often, though, it develops from earlier, altogether non-Christian levels—that is to say, out of chthonic animals such as crocodiles, dragons, serpents, or monkeys. Sometimes the child appears in the cup of a flower, or out of a golden egg, or as the centre of a mandala. In dreams it often appears as the dreamer's son or daughter or as a boy, youth, or young girl; occasionally it seems to be of exotic origin, Indian or Chinese, with a dusky skin, or, appearing more cosmically, surrounded by stars or with a starry

16 An old alchemical authority variously named Morienes, Morienus, Marianus ("De compositione alchemiae," Manget, *Bibliotheca chemica curiosa,* I, pp. 509ff.). In view of the explicitly alchemical character of *Faust,* Part II, such a connection would not be surprising.

17 Schreber, *Memoirs of My Nervous Illness.*

18 For a general presentation see infra, "Conscious, Unconscious, and Individuation." Special phenomena in the following text, also in *Psychology and Alchemy,* Part II.

19 "The Relations between the Ego and the Unconscious," Part II, ch. 3 [also "The Transcendent Function"—EDITORS].

coronet; or as the king's son or the witch's child with daemonic attributes. Seen as a special instance of "the treasure hard to attain" motif,[20] the child motif is extremely variable and assumes all manner of shapes, such as the jewel, the pearl, the flower, the chalice, the golden egg, the quaternity, the golden ball, and so on. It can be interchanged with these and similar images almost without limit.

II. THE PSYCHOLOGY OF THE CHILD ARCHETYPE

1. *The Archetype as a Link with the Past*

271 As to the *psychology* of our theme I must point out that every statement going beyond the purely phenomenal aspects of an archetype lays itself open to the criticism we have expressed above. Not for a moment dare we succumb to the illusion that an archetype can be finally explained and disposed of. Even the best attempts at explanation are only more or less successful translations into another metaphorical language. (Indeed, language itself is only an image.) The most we can do is to *dream the myth onwards* and give it a modern dress. And whatever explanation or interpretation does to it, we do to our own souls as well, with corresponding results for our own well-being. The archetype—let us never forget this—is a psychic organ present in all of us. A bad explanation means a correspondingly bad attitude to this organ, which may thus be injured. But the ultimate sufferer is the bad interpreter himself. Hence the "explanation" should always be such that the functional significance of the archetype remains unimpaired, so that an adequate and meaningful connection between the conscious mind and the archetypes is assured. For the archetype is an element of our psychic structure and thus a vital and necessary component in our psychic economy. It represents or personifies certain instinctive data of the dark, primitive psyche, the real but invisible roots of consciousness. Of what elementary importance the connection with these roots is, we see from the preoccupation of the primitive mentality with certain "magic" factors, which are nothing less than what we would call archetypes. This original form of

20 *Symbols of Transformation,* index, s.v.

religio ("linking back") is the essence, the working basis of all religious life even today, and always will be, whatever future form this life may take.

272 There is no "rational" substitute for the archetype any more than there is for the cerebellum or the kidneys. We can examine the physical organs anatomically, histologically, and embryologically. This would correspond to an outline of archetypal phenomenology and its presentation in terms of comparative history. But we only arrive at the *meaning* of a physical organ when we begin to ask teleological questions. Hence the query arises: What is the biological purpose of the archetype? Just as physiology answers such a question for the body, so it is the business of psychology to answer it for the archetype.

273 Statements like "The child motif is a vestigial memory of one's own childhood" and similar explanations merely beg the question. But if, giving this proposition a slight twist, we were to say, "The child motif is a picture of certain *forgotten* things in our childhood," we are getting closer to the truth. Since, however, the archetype is always an image belonging to the whole human race and not merely to the individual, we might put it better this way: "The child motif represents the preconscious, childhood aspect of the collective psyche." [21]

274 We shall not go wrong if we take this statement for the time being *historically,* on the analogy of certain psychological experiences which show that certain phases in an individual's life can become autonomous, can personify themselves to the extent

21 It may not be superfluous to point out that lay prejudice is always inclined to identify the child motif with the concrete experience "child," as though the real child were the cause and pre-condition of the existence of the child motif. In psychological reality, however, the empirical idea "child" is only the means (and not the only one) by which to express a psychic fact that cannot be formulated more exactly. Hence by the same token the mythological idea of the child is emphatically not a copy of the empirical child but a *symbol* clearly recognizable as such: it is a wonder-child, a divine child, begotten, born, and brought up in quite extraordinary circumstances, and not—this is the point—a human child. Its deeds are as miraculous or monstrous as its nature and physical constitution. Only on account of these highly unempirical properties is it necessary to speak of a "child motif" at all. Moreover, the mythological "child" has various forms: now a god, giant, Tom Thumb, animal, etc., and this points to a causality that is anything but rational or concretely human. The same is true of the "father" and "mother" archetypes which, mythologically speaking, are equally irrational symbols.

that they result in a *vision of oneself*—for instance, one sees oneself as a child. Visionary experiences of this kind, whether they occur in dreams or in the waking state, are, as we know, conditional on a dissociation having previously taken place between past and present. Such dissociations come about because of various incompatibilities; for instance, a man's present state may have come into conflict with his childhood state, or he may have violently sundered himself from his original character in the interests of some arbitrary persona[22] more in keeping with his ambitions. He has thus become unchildlike and artificial, and has lost his roots. All this presents a favourable opportunity for an equally vehement confrontation with the primary truth.

275 In view of the fact that men have not yet ceased to make statements about the child god, we may perhaps extend the individual analogy to the life of mankind and say in conclusion that humanity, too, probably always comes into conflict with its childhood conditions, that is, with its original, unconscious, and instinctive state, and that the danger of the kind of conflict which induces the vision of the "child" actually exists. Religious observances, i.e., the retelling and ritual repetition of the mythical event, consequently serve the purpose of bringing the image of childhood, and everything connected with it, again and again before the eyes of the conscious mind so that the link with the original condition may not be broken.

2. *The Function of the Archetype*

276 The child motif represents not only something that existed in the distant past but also something that exists *now;* that is to say, it is not just a vestige but a system functioning in the present whose purpose is to compensate or correct, in a meaningful manner, the inevitable one-sidednesses and extravagances of the conscious mind. It is in the nature of the conscious mind to concentrate on relatively few contents and to raise them to the highest pitch of clarity. A necessary result and precondition is the exclusion of other potential contents of consciousness. The exclusion is bound to bring about a certain one-sidedness of the conscious contents. Since the differentiated consciousness of

22 *Psychological Types,* Def. 48; and *Two Essays on Analytical Psychology,* index, s.v. "persona."

civilized man has been granted an effective instrument for the practical realization of its contents through the dynamics of his will, there is all the more danger, the more he trains his will, of his getting lost in one-sidedness and deviating further and further from the laws and roots of his being. This means, on the one hand, the possibility of human freedom, but on the other it is a source of endless transgressions against one's instincts. Accordingly, primitive man, being closer to his instincts, like the animal, is characterized by fear of novelty and adherence to tradition. To our way of thinking he is painfully backward, whereas we exalt progress. But our progressiveness, though it may result in a great many delightful wish-fulfilments, piles up an equally gigantic Promethean debt which has to be paid off from time to time in the form of hideous catastrophes. For ages man has dreamed of flying, and all we have got for it is saturation bombing! We smile today at the Christian hope of a life beyond the grave, and yet we often fall into chiliasms a hundred times more ridiculous than the notion of a happy Hereafter. Our differentiated consciousness is in continual danger of being uprooted; hence it needs compensation through the still existing state of childhood.

277 The symptoms of compensation are described, from the progressive point of view, in scarcely flattering terms. Since, to the superficial eye, it looks like a retarding operation, people speak of inertia, backwardness, scepticism, fault-finding, conservatism, timidity, pettiness, and so on. But inasmuch as man has, in high degree, the capacity for cutting himself off from his own roots, he may also be swept uncritically to catastrophe by his dangerous one-sidedness. The retarding ideal is always more primitive, more natural (in the good sense as in the bad), and more "moral" in that it keeps faith with law and tradition. The progressive ideal is always more abstract, more unnatural, and less "moral" in that it demands disloyalty to tradition. Progress enforced by will is always *convulsive.* Backwardness may be closer to naturalness, but in its turn it is always menaced by painful awakenings. The older view of things realized that progress is only possible *Deo concedente,* thus proving itself conscious of the opposites and repeating the age-old *rites d'entrée et de sortie* on a higher plane. The more differentiated consciousness becomes, the greater the danger of severance from the root-

condition. Complete severance comes when the *Deo concedente* is forgotten. Now it is an axiom of psychology that when a part of the psyche is split off from consciousness it is only *apparently* inactivated; in actual fact it brings about a possession of the personality, with the result that the individual's aims are falsified in the interests of the split-off part. If, then, the childhood state of the collective psyche is repressed to the point of total exclusion, the unconscious content overwhelms the conscious aim and inhibits, falsifies, even destroys its realization. Viable progress only comes from the co-operation of both.

3. *The Futurity of the Archetype*

278 One of the essential features of the child motif is its futurity. The child is potential future. Hence the occurrence of the child motif in the psychology of the individual signifies as a rule an anticipation of future developments, even though at first sight it may seem like a retrospective configuration. Life is a flux, a flowing into the future, and not a stoppage or a backwash. It is therefore not surprising that so many of the mythological saviours are child gods. This agrees exactly with our experience of the psychology of the individual, which shows that the "child" paves the way for a future change of personality. In the individuation process, it anticipates the figure that comes from the synthesis of conscious and unconscious elements in the personality. It is therefore a symbol which unites the opposites; [23] a mediator, bringer of healing, that is, one who makes whole. Because it has this meaning, the child motif is capable of the numerous transformations mentioned above: it can be expressed by roundness, the circle or sphere, or else by the quaternity as another form of wholeness.[24] I have called this wholeness that transcends consciousness the "self." [25] The goal of the individuation process is the synthesis of the self. From another point of view the term "entelechy" might be preferable to "synthesis." There is an empirical reason why "entelechy" is, in certain conditions, more fitting: the symbols

[23] *Psychological Types,* ch. V, 3: "The Significance of the Uniting Symbol."

[24] *Psychology and Alchemy,* pars. 327ff.; "Psychology and Religion," pars. 108ff.

[25] *Two Essays on Analytical Psychology,* pars. 399ff. [Cf. also *Aion* (Part II of this volume), ch. 4.—EDITORS.]

of wholeness frequently occur at the beginning of the individuation process, indeed they can often be observed in the first dreams of early infancy. This observation says much for the *a priori* existence of potential wholeness,[26] and on this account the idea of *entelechy* instantly recommends itself. But in so far as the individuation process occurs, empirically speaking, as a synthesis, it looks, paradoxically enough, as if something already existent were being put together. From this point of view, the term "synthesis" is also applicable.

4. *Unity and Plurality of the Child Motif*

279 In the manifold phenomenology of the "child" we have to distinguish between the *unity* and *plurality* of its respective manifestations. Where, for instance, numerous homunculi, dwarfs, boys, etc., appear, having no individual characteristics at all, there is the probability of a *dissociation.* Such forms are therefore found especially in schizophrenia, which is essentially a fragmentation of personality. The many children then represent the products of its dissolution. But if the plurality occurs in normal people, then it is the representation of an as yet incomplete synthesis of personality. The personality (viz., the "self") is still in the *plural stage,* i.e., an ego may be present, but it cannot experience its wholeness within the framework of its own personality, only within the community of the family, tribe, or nation; it is still in the stage of unconscious identification with the plurality of the group. The Church takes due account of this widespread condition in her doctrine of the *corpus mysticum,* of which the individual is by nature a member.

280 If, however, the child motif appears in the form of a unity, we are dealing with an unconscious and provisionally complete synthesis of the personality, which in practice, like everything unconscious, signifies no more than a possibility.

5. *Child God and Child Hero*

281 Sometimes the "child" looks more like a *child god,* sometimes more like a young *hero.* Common to both types is the

26 *Psychology and Alchemy,* pars. 328ff.

miraculous birth and the adversities of early childhood—abandonment and danger through persecution. The god is by nature wholly supernatural; the hero's nature is human but raised to the limit of the supernatural—he is "semi-divine." While the god, especially in his close affinity with the symbolic animal, personifies the collective unconscious which is not yet integrated into a human being, the hero's supernaturalness includes human nature and thus represents a synthesis of the ("divine," i.e., not yet humanized) unconscious and human consciousness. Consequently he signifies the potential anticipation of an individuation process which is approaching wholeness.

282 For this reason the various "child"-fates may be regarded as illustrating the kind of psychic events that occur in the entelechy or genesis of the "self." The "miraculous birth" tries to depict the way in which this genesis is experienced. Since it is a psychic genesis, everything must happen non-empirically, e.g., by means of a virgin birth, or by miraculous conception, or by birth from unnatural organs. The motifs of "insignificance," exposure, abandonment, danger, etc. try to show how precarious is the psychic possibility of wholeness, that is, the enormous difficulties to be met with in attaining this "highest good." They also signify the powerlessness and helplessness of the life-urge which subjects every growing thing to the law of maximum self-fulfilment, while at the same time the environmental influences place all sorts of insuperable obstacles in the way of individuation. More especially the threat to one's inmost self from dragons and serpents points to the danger of the newly acquired consciousness being swallowed up again by the instinctive psyche, the unconscious. The lower vertebrates have from earliest times been favourite symbols of the collective psychic substratum,[27] which is localized anatomically in the subcortical centres, the cerebellum and the spinal cord. These organs constitute the snake.[28] Snake-dreams usually occur, therefore, when the conscious mind is deviating from its instinctual basis.

283 The motif of "smaller than small yet bigger than big" complements the impotence of the child by means of its equally

27 Higher vertebrates symbolize mainly affects.

28 This interpretation of the snake is found as early as Hippolytus, *Elenchos,* IV, 49–51 (Legge trans., I, p. 117). Cf. also Leisegang, *Die Gnosis,* p. 146.

miraculous deeds. This paradox is the essence of the hero and runs through his whole destiny like a red thread. He can cope with the greatest perils, yet, in the end, something quite insignificant is his undoing: Baldur perishes because of the mistletoe, Maui because of the laughter of a little bird, Siegfried because of his one vulnerable spot, Heracles because of his wife's gift, others because of common treachery, and so on.

284 The hero's main feat is to overcome the monster of darkness: it is the long-hoped-for and expected triumph of consciousness over the unconscious. Day and light are synonyms for consciousness, night and dark for the unconscious. The coming of consciousness was probably the most tremendous experience of primeval times, for with it a world came into being whose existence no one had suspected before. "And God said: 'Let there be light!' " is the projection of that immemorial experience of the separation of the conscious from the unconscious. Even among primitives today the possession of a soul is a precarious thing, and the "loss of soul" a typical psychic malady which drives primitive medicine to all sorts of psychotherapeutic measures. Hence the "child" distinguishes itself by deeds which point to the conquest of the dark.

III. THE SPECIAL PHENOMENOLOGY OF THE CHILD ARCHETYPE

1. *The Abandonment of the Child*

285 Abandonment, exposure, danger, etc. are all elaborations of the "child's" insignificant beginnings and of its mysterious and miraculous birth. This statement describes a certain psychic experience of a creative nature, whose object is the emergence of a new and as yet unknown content. In the psychology of the individual there is always, at such moments, an agonizing situation of conflict from which there seems to be no way out—at least for the conscious mind, since as far as this is concerned, *tertium non datur*. But out of this collision of opposites the unconscious psyche always creates a third thing of an irrational nature,[29] which the conscious mind neither expects nor understands. It presents itself in a form that is neither a straight "yes"

[29] *Psychological Types*, Def. 51.

nor a straight "no," and is consequently rejected by both. For the conscious mind knows nothing beyond the opposites and, as a result, has no knowledge of the thing that unites them. Since, however, the solution of the conflict through the union of opposites is of vital importance, and is moreover the very thing that the conscious mind is longing for, some inkling of the creative act, and of the significance of it, nevertheless gets through. From this comes the numinous character of the "child." A meaningful but unknown content always has a secret fascination for the conscious mind. The new configuration is a nascent whole; it is on the way to wholeness, at least in so far as it excels in "wholeness" the conscious mind when torn by opposites and surpasses it in completeness. For this reason all uniting symbols have a redemptive significance.

286 Out of this situation the "child" emerges as a symbolic content, manifestly separated or even isolated from its background (the mother), but sometimes including the mother in its perilous situation, threatened on the one hand by the negative attitude of the conscious mind and on the other by the *horror vacui* of the unconscious, which is quite ready to swallow up all its progeny, since it produces them only in play, and destruction is an inescapable part of its play. Nothing in all the world welcomes this new birth, although it is the most precious fruit of Mother Nature herself, the most pregnant with the future, signifying a higher stage of self-realization. That is why Nature, the world of the instincts, takes the "child" under its wing: it is nourished or protected by animals.

287 "Child" means something evolving towards independence. This it cannot do without detaching itself from its origins: abandonment is therefore a necessary condition, not just a concomitant symptom. The conflict is not to be overcome by the conscious mind remaining caught between the opposites, and for this very reason it needs a symbol to point out the necessity of detaching itself from its origins. Because the symbol of the "child" fascinates and grips the conscious mind, its redemptive effect passes over into consciousness and brings about that separation from the conflict-situation which the conscious mind by itself was unable to achieve. The symbol anticipates a nascent state of consciousness. So long as this is not actually in being, the "child" remains a mythological projection which requires

religious repetition and renewal by ritual. The Christ Child, for instance, is a religious necessity only so long as the majority of men are incapable of giving psychological reality to the saying: "Except ye become as little children. . . ." Since all such developments and transitions are extraordinarily difficult and dangerous, it is no wonder that figures of this kind persist for hundreds or even thousands of years. Everything that man should, and yet cannot, be or do—be it in a positive or negative sense—lives on as a mythological figure and anticipation alongside his consciousness, either as a religious projection or—what is still more dangerous—as unconscious contents which then project themselves spontaneously into incongruous objects, e.g., hygienic and other "salvationist" doctrines or practices. All these are so many rationalized substitutes for mythology, and their unnaturalness does more harm than good.

288 The conflict-situation that offers no way out, the sort of situation that produces the "child" as the irrational third, is of course a formula appropriate only to a psychological, that is, modern stage of development. It is not strictly applicable to the psychic life of primitives, if only because primitive man's child-like range of consciousness still excludes a whole world of possible psychic experiences. Seen on the nature-level of the primitive, our modern *moral* conflict is still an *objective* calamity that threatens life itself. Hence not a few child-figures are culture-heroes and thus identified with things that promote culture, e.g., fire,[80] metal, corn, maize, etc. As bringers of light, that is, enlargers of consciousness, they overcome darkness, which is to say that they overcome the earlier unconscious state. Higher consciousness, or knowledge going beyond our present-day consciousness, is equivalent to being *all alone in the world.* This loneliness expresses the conflict between the bearer or symbol of higher consciousness and his surroundings. The conquerors of darkness go far back into primeval times, and, together with many other legends, prove that there once existed a state of *original psychic distress,* namely *unconsciousness.* Hence in all probability the "irrational" fear which primitive man has of the dark even today. I found a form of religion among a tribe living on Mount Elgon that corresponded to

80 Even Christ is of a fiery nature ("he that is near to me is near to the fire"—Origen, *In Jeremiam Homiliae,* XX, 3); likewise the Holy Ghost.

pantheistic optimism. Their optimistic mood was, however, always in abeyance between six o'clock in the evening and six o'clock in the morning, during which time it was replaced by fear, for in the night the dark being Ayik has his dominion—the "Maker of Fear." During the daytime there were no monster snakes anywhere in the vicinity, but at night they were lurking on every path. At night the whole of mythology was let loose.

2. *The Invincibility of the Child*

289 It is a striking paradox in all child myths that the "child" is on the one hand delivered helpless into the power of terrible enemies and in continual danger of extinction, while on the other he possesses powers far exceeding those of ordinary humanity. This is closely related to the psychological fact that though the child may be "insignificant," unknown, "a mere child," he is also divine. From the conscious standpoint we seem to be dealing with an insignificant content that has no releasing, let alone redeeming, character. The conscious mind is caught in its conflict-situation, and the combatant forces seem so overwhelming that the "child" as an isolated content bears no relation to the conscious factors. It is therefore easily overlooked and falls back into the unconscious. At least, this is what we should have to fear if things turned out according to our conscious expectations. Myth, however, emphasizes that it is not so, but that the "child" is endowed with superior powers and, despite all dangers, will unexpectedly pull through. The "child" is born out of the womb of the unconscious, begotten out of the depths of human nature, or rather out of living Nature herself. It is a personification of vital forces quite outside the limited range of our conscious mind; of ways and possibilities of which our one-sided conscious mind knows nothing; a wholeness which embraces the very depths of Nature. It represents the strongest, the most ineluctable urge in every being, namely the urge to realize itself. It is, as it were, an incarnation of *the inability to do otherwise,* equipped with all the powers of nature and instinct, whereas the conscious mind is always getting caught up in its supposed ability to do otherwise. The urge and compulsion to self-realization is a law of nature and thus of invincible power, even though its effect, at the start, is insignifi-

cant and improbable. Its power is revealed in the miraculous deeds of the child hero, and later in the *athla* ('works') of the bondsman or thrall (of the Heracles type), where, although the hero has outgrown the impotence of the "child," he is still in a menial position. The figure of the thrall generally leads up to the real epiphany of the semi-divine hero. Oddly enough, we have a similar modulation of themes in alchemy—in the synonyms for the *lapis*. As the *materia prima,* it is the *lapis exilis et vilis*. As a substance in process of transmutation, it is *servus rubeus* or *fugitivus;* and finally, in its true apotheosis, it attains the dignity of a *filius sapientiae* or *deus terrenus,* a "light above all lights," a power that contains in itself all the powers of the upper and nether regions. It becomes a *corpus glorificatum* which enjoys everlasting incorruptibility and is therefore a panacea ("bringer of healing").[31] The size and invincibility of the "child" are bound up in Hindu speculation with the nature of the atman, which corresponds to the "smaller than small yet bigger than big" motif. As an individual phenomenon, the self is "smaller than small"; as the equivalent of the cosmos, it is "bigger than big." The self, regarded as the counter-pole of the world, its "absolutely other," is the *sine qua non* of all empirical knowledge and consciousness of subject and object. Only because of this psychic "otherness" is consciousness possible at all. Identity does not make consciousness possible; it is only separation, detachment, and agonizing confrontation through opposition that produce consciousness and insight. Hindu introspection recognized this psychological fact very early and consequently equated the subject of cognition with the subject of ontology in general. In accordance with the predominantly introverted attitude of Indian thinking, the object lost the attribute of absolute reality and, in some systems, became a mere illusion. The Greek-Occidental type of mind could not free itself from the conviction of the world's absolute existence—at the cost, however, of the cosmic significance of the self. Even today Western man finds it hard to see the psychological necessity for a transcendental subject of cognition as the counter-pole of the empirical universe, although the postulate of a world-

31 The material is collected in *Psychology and Alchemy,* Parts II and III. For Mercurius as a servant, see the parable of Eirenaeus Philalethes, *Ripley Reviv'd: or, An Exposition upon Sir George Ripley's Hermetico-Poetical Works* (1678).

confronting self, at least as a *point of reflection,* is a logical necessity. Regardless of philosophy's perpetual attitude of dissent or only half-hearted assent, there is always a compensating tendency in our unconscious psyche to produce a symbol of the self in its cosmic significance. These efforts take on the archetypal forms of the hero myth such as can be observed in almost any individuation process.

290 The phenomenology of the "child's" birth always points back to an original psychological state of non-recognition, i.e., of darkness or twilight, of non-differentiation between subject and object, of unconscious identity of man and the universe. This phase of non-differentiation produces the *golden egg,* which is both man and universe and yet neither, but an irrational third. To the twilight consciousness of primitive man it seems as if the egg came out of the womb of the wide world and were, accordingly, a cosmic, objective, external occurrence. To a differentiated consciousness, on the other hand, it seems evident that this egg is nothing but a symbol thrown up by the psyche or—what is even worse—a fanciful speculation and therefore "nothing but" a primitive phantasm to which no "reality" of any kind attaches. Present-day medical psychology, however, thinks somewhat differently about these "phantasms." It knows only too well what dire disturbances of the bodily functions and what devastating psychic consequences can flow from "mere" fantasies. "Fantasies" are the natural expressions of the life of the unconscious. But since the unconscious is the psyche of all the body's autonomous functional complexes, its "fantasies" have an aetiological significance that is not to be despised. From the psychopathology of the individuation process we know that the formation of symbols is frequently associated with physical disorders of a psychic origin, which in some cases are felt as decidedly "real." In medicine, fantasies are *real things* with which the psychotherapist has to reckon very seriously indeed. He cannot therefore deprive of all justification those primitive phantasms whose content is so real that it is projected upon the external world. In the last analysis the human body, too, is built of the stuff of the world, the very stuff wherein fantasies become visible; indeed, without it they could not be experienced at all. Without this stuff they would be like a sort of abstract

crystalline lattice in a solution where the crystallization process had not yet started.

291 The symbols of the self arise in the depths of the body and they express its materiality every bit as much as the structure of the perceiving consciousness. The symbol is thus a living body, *corpus et anima;* hence the "child" is such an apt formula for the symbol. The uniqueness of the psyche can never enter wholly into reality, it can only be realized approximately, though it still remains the absolute basis of all consciousness. The deeper "layers" of the psyche lose their individual uniqueness as they retreat farther and farther into darkness. "Lower down," that is to say as they approach the autonomous functional systems, they become increasingly collective until they are universalized and extinguished in the body's materiality, i.e., in chemical substances. The body's carbon is simply carbon. Hence "at bottom" the psyche is simply "world." In this sense I hold Kerényi to be absolutely right when he says that in the symbol the *world itself* is speaking. The more archaic and "deeper," that is the more *physiological,* the symbol is, the more collective and universal, the more "material" it is. The more abstract, differentiated, and specific it is, and the more its nature approximates to conscious uniqueness and individuality, the more it sloughs off its universal character. Having finally attained full consciousness, it runs the risk of becoming a mere allegory which nowhere oversteps the bounds of conscious comprehension, and is then exposed to all sorts of attempts at rationalistic and therefore inadequate explanation.

3. *The Hermaphroditism of the Child*

292 It is a remarkable fact that perhaps the majority of cosmogonic gods are of a bisexual nature. The hermaphrodite means nothing less than a union of the strongest and most striking opposites. In the first place this union refers back to a primitive state of mind, a twilight where differences and contrasts were either barely separated or completely merged. With increasing clarity of consciousness, however, the opposites draw more and more distinctly and irreconcilably apart. If, therefore, the hermaphrodite were only a product of primitive non-differentiation, we would have to expect that it would soon be eliminated

with increasing civilization. This is by no means the case; on the contrary, man's imagination has been preoccupied with this idea over and over again on the high and even the highest levels of culture, as we can see from the late Greek and syncretic philosophy of Gnosticism. The hermaphroditic *rebis* has an important part to play in the natural philosophy of the Middle Ages. And in our own day we hear of Christ's androgyny in Catholic mysticism.[32]

293 We can no longer be dealing, then, with the continued existence of a primitive phantasm, or with an original contamination of opposites. Rather, as we can see from medieval writings,[33] the primordial idea has become a *symbol of the creative union of opposites,* a "uniting symbol" in the literal sense. In its functional significance the symbol no longer points back, but forward to a goal not yet reached. Notwithstanding its monstrosity, the hermaphrodite has gradually turned into a subduer of conflicts and a bringer of healing, and it acquired this meaning in relatively early phases of civilization. This vital meaning explains why the image of the hermaphrodite did not fade out in primeval times but, on the contrary, was able to assert itself with increasing profundity of symbolic content for thousands of years. The fact that an idea so utterly archaic could rise to such exalted heights of meaning not only points to the vitality of archetypal ideas, it also demonstrates the rightness of the principle that the archetype, because of its power to unite opposites, mediates between the unconscious substratum and the conscious mind. It throws a bridge between present-day consciousness, always in danger of losing its roots, and the natural, unconscious, instinctive wholeness of primeval times. Through this mediation the uniqueness, peculiarity, and one-sidedness of our present individual consciousness are linked up again with its natural, racial roots. Progress and development are ideals not lightly to be rejected, but they lose all meaning if man only arrives at his new state as a fragment of himself, having left his essential hinterland behind him in the shadow of the unconscious, in a state of primitivity or, indeed, barbarism. The conscious mind, split off from its origins, incapable of

32 Koepgen, *Die Gnosis des Christentums,* pp. 315ff.

33 For the *lapis* as mediator and medium, cf. *Tractatus aureus,* in Manget, *Bibliotheca chemica curiosa,* I, p. 408b, and *Artis auriferae* (1572), p. 641.

realizing the meaning of the new state, then relapses all too easily into a situation far worse than the one from which the innovation was intended to free it—*exempla sunt odiosa!* It was Friedrich Schiller who first had an inkling of this problem; but neither his contemporaries nor his successors were capable of drawing any conclusions. Instead, people incline more than ever to educate *children* and nothing more. I therefore suspect that the *furor paedogogicus* is a god-sent method of by-passing the central problem touched on by Schiller, namely the *education of the educator.* Children are educated by what the grown-up *is* and not by what he *says.* The popular faith in words is a veritable disease of the mind, for a superstition of this sort always leads farther and farther away from man's foundations and seduces people into a disastrous identification of the personality with whatever slogan may be in vogue. Meanwhile everything that has been overcome and left behind by so-called "progress" sinks deeper and deeper into the unconscious, from which there re-emerges in the end the primitive condition of *identity with the mass.* Instead of the expected progress, this condition now becomes reality.

294 As civilization develops, the bisexual primordial being turns into a symbol of the unity of personality, a symbol of the self, where the war of opposites finds peace. In this way the primordial being becomes the distant goal of man's self-development, having been from the very beginning a projection of his unconscious wholeness. Wholeness consists in the union of the conscious and the unconscious personality. Just as every individual derives from masculine and feminine genes, and the sex is determined by the predominance of the corresponding genes, so in the psyche it is only the conscious mind, in a man, that has the masculine sign, while the unconscious is by nature feminine. The reverse is true in the case of a woman. All I have done in my anima theory is to rediscover and reformulate this fact.[34] It had long been known.

295 The idea of the *coniunctio* of male and female, which became almost a technical term in Hermetic philosophy, appears in Gnosticism as the *mysterium iniquitatis,* probably not uninfluenced by the Old Testament "divine marriage" as

34 *Psychological Types,* Def. 48; and "Relations between the Ego and the Unconscious," pars. 296ff.

performed, for instance, by Hosea.[35] Such things are hinted at not only by certain traditional customs,[36] but by the quotation from the Gospel according to the Egyptians in the second epistle of Clement: "When the two shall be one, the outside as the inside, and the male with the female neither male nor female." [37] Clement of Alexandria introduces this logion with the words: "When ye have trampled on the garment of shame (with thy feet) . . . ," [38] which probably refers to the body; for Clement as well as Cassian (from whom the quotation was taken over), and the pseudo-Clement, too, interpreted the words in a spiritual sense, in contrast to the Gnostics, who would seem to have taken the *coniunctio* all too literally. They took care, however, through the practice of abortion and other restrictions, that the biological meaning of their acts did not swamp the religious significance of the rite. While, in Church mysticism, the primordial image of the *hieros gamos* was sublimated on a lofty plane and only occasionally—as for instance with Mechthild of Magdeburg [39]—approached the physical sphere in emotional intensity, for the rest of the world it remained very much alive and continued to be the object of especial psychic preoccupation. In this respect the symbolical drawings of Opicinus de Canistris [40] afford us an interesting glimpse of the way in which this primordial image was instrumental in uniting opposites, even in a pathological state. On the other hand, in the Hermetic philosophy that throve in the Middle Ages the *coniunctio* was performed wholly in the physical realm in the admittedly abstract theory of the *coniugium solis et lunae,* which despite this drawback gave the creative imagination much occasion for anthropomorphic flights.

296 Such being the state of affairs, it is readily understandable that the primordial image of the hermaphrodite should reappear in modern psychology in the guise of the male-female antithesis, in other words as *male* consciousness and personified *female* unconscious. But the psychological process of bringing things to consciousness has complicated the picture considerably. Whereas the old science was almost exclusively a field in

35 Hosea 1 : 2ff.

36 Cf. Fendt, *Gnostische Mysterien.*

37 James, *The Apocryphal New Testament,* p. 11.

38 Clement, *Stromata,* III, 13, 92, 2.

39 *The Flowing Light of the Godhead.*

40 Salomon, *Opicinus de Canistris.*

which only the man's unconscious could project itself, the new psychology had to acknowledge the existence of an autonomous female psyche as well. Here the case is reversed, and a feminine consciousness confronts a masculine personification of the unconscious, which can no longer be called *anima* but *animus*. This discovery also complicates the problem of the *coniunctio*.

297 Originally this archetype played its part entirely in the field of fertility magic and thus remained for a very long time a purely biological phenomenon with no other purpose than that of fecundation. But even in early antiquity the symbolical meaning of the act seems to have increased. Thus, for example, the physical performance of the *hieros gamos* as a sacred rite not only became a mystery—it faded to a mere conjecture.[41] As we have seen, Gnosticism, too, endeavoured in all seriousness to subordinate the physiological to the metaphysical. Finally, the Church severed the *coniunctio* from the physical realm altogether, and natural philosophy turned it into an abstract *theoria*. These developments meant the gradual transformation of the archetype into a psychological process which, in theory, we can call a combination of conscious and unconscious processes. In practice, however, it is not so simple, because as a rule the feminine unconscious of a man is projected upon a feminine partner, and the masculine unconscious of a woman is projected upon a man. The elucidation of these problems is a special branch of psychology and has no part in a discussion of the mythological hermaphrodite.

4. *The Child as Beginning and End*

298 Faust, after his death, is received as a boy into the "choir of blessed youths." I do not know whether Goethe was referring, with this peculiar idea, to the *cupids* on antique grave-stones. It is not unthinkable. The figure of the *cucullatus* points to the hooded, that is, the *invisible* one, the genius of the departed, who reappears in the child-like frolics of a new life, surrounded by the sea-forms of dolphins and tritons. The sea is the favourite

41 Cf. the diatribe by Bishop Asterius (Foucart, *Mystères of d'Eleusis*, pp. 477ff.). According to Hippolytus' account the hierophant actually made himself impotent by a draught of hemlock. The self-castration of priests in the worship of the Mother Goddess is of similar import.

symbol for the unconscious, the mother of all that lives. Just as the "child" is, in certain circumstances (e.g., in the case of Hermes and the Dactyls), closely related to the phallus, symbol of the begetter, so it comes up again in the sepulchral phallus, symbol of a renewed begetting.

299 The "child" is therefore *renatus in novam infantiam.* It is thus both beginning and end, an initial and a terminal creature. The initial creature existed before man was, and the terminal creature will be when man is not. Psychologically speaking, this means that the "child" symbolizes the pre-conscious and the post-conscious essence of man. His pre-conscious essence is the unconscious state of earliest childhood; his post-conscious essence is an anticipation by analogy of life after death. In this idea the all-embracing nature of psychic wholeness is expressed. Wholeness is never comprised within the compass of the conscious mind—it includes the indefinite and indefinable extent of the unconscious as well. Wholeness, empirically speaking, is therefore of immeasurable extent, older and younger than consciousness and enfolding it in time and space. This is no speculation, but an immediate psychic experience. Not only is the conscious process continually accompanied, it is often guided, helped, or interrupted, by unconscious happenings. The child had a psychic life before it had consciousness. Even the adult still says and does things whose significance he realizes only later, if ever. And yet he said them and did them as if he knew what they meant. Our dreams are continually saying things beyond our conscious comprehension (which is why they are so useful in the therapy of neuroses). We have intimations and intuitions from unknown sources. Fears, moods, plans, and hopes come to us with no visible causation. These concrete experiences are at the bottom of our feeling that we know ourselves very little; at the bottom, too, of the painful conjecture that we might have surprises in store for ourselves.

300 Primitive man is no puzzle to himself. The question "What is man?" is the question that man has always kept until last. Primitive man has so much psyche outside his conscious mind that the experience of something psychic outside him is far more familiar to him than to us. Consciousness hedged about by psychic powers, sustained or threatened or deluded by them, is the age-old experience of mankind. This experience has pro-

jected itself into the archetype of the child, which expresses man's wholeness. The "child" is all that is abandoned and exposed and at the same time divinely powerful; the insignificant, dubious beginning, and the triumphal end. The "eternal child" in man is an indescribable experience, an incongruity, a handicap, and a divine prerogative; an imponderable that determines the ultimate worth or worthlessness of a personality.

IV. CONCLUSION

301 I am aware that a psychological commentary on the child archetype without detailed documentation must remain a mere sketch. But since this is virgin territory for the psychologist, my main endeavour has been to stake out the possible extent of the problems raised by our archetype and to describe, at least cursorily, its different aspects. Clear-cut distinctions and strict formulations are quite impossible in this field, seeing that a kind of fluid interpenetration belongs to the very nature of all archetypes. They can only be roughly circumscribed at best. Their living meaning comes out more from their presentation as a whole than from a single formulation. Every attempt to focus them more sharply is immediately punished by the intangible core of meaning losing its luminosity. No archetype can be reduced to a simple formula. It is a vessel which we can never empty, and never fill. It has a potential existence only, and when it takes shape in matter it is no longer what it was. It persists throughout the ages and requires interpreting ever anew. The archetypes are the imperishable elements of the unconscious, but they change their shape continually.

302 It is a well-nigh hopeless undertaking to tear a single archetype out of the living tissue of the psyche; but despite their interwovenness they do form units of meaning that can be apprehended intuitively. Psychology, as one of the many expressions of psychic life, operates with ideas which in their turn are derived from archetypal structures and thus generate a somewhat more abstract kind of myth. Psychology therefore translates the archaic speech of myth into a modern mythologem—not yet, of course, recognized as such—which constitutes one element of the myth "science." This seemingly hopeless undertaking

is a *living and lived myth,* satisfying to persons of a corresponding temperament, indeed beneficial in so far as they have been cut off from their psychic origins by neurotic dissociation.

303 As a matter of experience, we meet the child archetype in spontaneous and in therapeutically induced individuation processes. The first manifestation of the "child" is as a rule a totally unconscious phenomenon. Here the patient identifies himself with his personal infantilism. Then, under the influence of therapy, we get a more or less gradual separation from and objectification of the "child," that is, the identity breaks down and is accompanied by an intensification (sometimes technically induced) of fantasy, with the result that archaic or mythological features become increasingly apparent. Further transformations run true to the hero myth. The theme of "mighty feats" is generally absent, but on the other hand the mythical dangers play all the greater part. At this stage there is usually another identification, this time with the hero, whose role is attractive for a variety of reasons. The identification is often extremely stubborn and dangerous to the psychic equilibrium. If it can be broken down and if consciousness can be reduced to human proportions, the figure of the hero can gradually be differentiated into a symbol of the self.

304 In practical reality, however, it is of course not enough for the patient merely to *know about* such developments; what counts is his experience of the various transformations. The initial stage of personal infantilism presents the picture of an "abandoned" or "misunderstood" and unjustly treated child with overweening pretensions. The epiphany of the hero (the second identification) shows itself in a corresponding inflation: the colossal pretension grows into a conviction that one is something extraordinary, or else the impossibility of the pretension ever being fulfilled only proves one's own inferiority, which is favourable to the role of the heroic sufferer (a negative inflation). In spite of their contradictoriness, both forms are identical, because conscious megalomania is balanced by unconscious compensatory inferiority and conscious inferiority by unconscious megalomania (you never get one without the other). Once the reef of the second identification has been successfully circumnavigated, conscious processes can be cleanly separated from the unconscious, and the latter observed objectively. This

leads to the possibility of an accommodation with the unconscious, and thus to a possible synthesis of the conscious and unconscious elements of knowledge and action. This in turn leads to a shifting of the centre of personality from the ego to the self.[42]

305 In this psychological framework the motifs of abandonment, invincibility, hermaphroditism, and beginning and end take their place as distinct categories of experience and understanding.

[42] A more detailed account of these developments is to be found in "The Relations between the Ego and the Unconscious."

THE PSYCHOLOGICAL ASPECTS OF THE KORE

306 Not only is the figure of Demeter and the Kore in its threefold aspect as maiden, mother, and Hecate not unknown to the psychology of the unconscious, it is even something of a practical problem. The "Kore" has her psychological counterpart in those archetypes which I have called the *self* or *supraordinate personality* on the one hand, and the *anima* on the other. In order to explain these figures, with which I cannot assume all readers to be familiar, I must begin with some remarks of a general nature.

307 The psychologist has to contend with the same difficulties as the mythologist when an exact definition or clear and concise information is demanded of him. The picture is concrete, clear, and subject to no misunderstandings only when it is seen in its habitual context. In this form it tells us everything it contains. But as soon as one tries to abstract the "real essence" of the picture, the whole thing becomes cloudy and indistinct. In order to understand its living function, we must let it remain an organic thing in all its complexity and not try to examine the anatomy of its corpse in the manner of the scientist, or the archaeology of its ruins in the manner of the historian. Naturally this is not to deny the justification of such methods when applied in their proper place.

308 In view of the enormous complexity of psychic phenomena, a purely phenomenological point of view is, and will be for a long time, the only possible one and the only one with any prospect of success. "Whence" things come and "what" they are, these, particularly in the field of psychology, are questions which are apt to call forth untimely attempts at explanation. Such speculations are moreover based far more on unconscious philosophical premises than on the nature of the phenomena themselves. Psychic phenomena occasioned by unconscious processes are so rich and so multifarious that I prefer to *describe* my findings and observations and, where possible, to classify them—

that is, to arrange them under certain definite types. That is the method of natural science, and it is applied wherever we have to do with multifarious and still unorganized material. One may question the utility or the appropriateness of the categories or types used in the arrangement, but not the correctness of the method itself.

309 Since for years I have been observing and investigating the products of the unconscious in the widest sense of the word, namely dreams, fantasies, visions, and delusions of the insane, I have not been able to avoid recognizing certain regularities, that is, *types*. There are types of *situations* and types of *figures* that repeat themselves frequently and have a corresponding meaning. I therefore employ the term "motif" to designate these repetitions. Thus there are not only typical dreams but typical motifs in the dreams. These may, as we have said, be situations or figures. Among the latter there are human figures that can be arranged under a series of archetypes, the chief of them being, according to my suggestion,[1] the *shadow,* the *wise old man,* the *child* (including the child hero), the *mother* ("Primordial Mother" and "Earth Mother") as a supraordinate personality ("daemonic" because supraordinate), and her counterpart the *maiden,* and lastly the *anima* in man and the *animus* in woman.

310 The above types are far from exhausting all the statistical regularities in this respect. The figure of the Kore that interests us here belongs, when observed in a man, to the *anima* type; and when observed in a woman to the type of *supraordinate personality*. It is an essential characteristic of psychic figures that they are duplex or at least capable of duplication; at all events they are bipolar and oscillate between their positive and negative meanings. Thus the "supraordinate" personality can appear in a despicable and distorted form, like for instance Mephistopheles, who is really more positive as a personality than the vapid and unthinking careerist Faust. Another negative figure

1 To the best of my knowledge, no other suggestions have been made so far. Critics have contented themselves with asserting that no such archetypes exist. Certainly they do not exist, any more than a botanical system exists in nature! But will anyone deny the existence of natural plant-families on that account? Or will anyone deny the occurrence and continual repetition of certain morphological and functional similarities? It is much the same thing in principle with the typical figures of the unconscious. They are forms existing *a priori,* or biological norms of psychic activity.

is the Tom Thumb or Tom Dumb of the folktales. The figure corresponding to the Kore in a woman is generally a double one, i.e., a mother and a maiden, which is to say that she appears now as the one, now as the other. From this I would conclude, for a start, that in the formation of the Demeter-Kore myth the feminine influence so far outweighed the masculine that the latter had practically no significance. The man's role in the Demeter myth is really only that of seducer or conqueror.

311 As a matter of practical observation, the Kore often appears in woman as an *unknown young girl,* not infrequently as Gretchen or the unmarried mother.[2] Another frequent modulation is the *dancer,* who is often formed by borrowings from classical knowledge, in which case the "maiden" appears as the *corybant, maenad,* or *nymph.* An occasional variant is the nixie or water-sprite, who betrays her superhuman nature by her fish-tail. Sometimes the Kore- and mother-figures slither down altogether to the animal kingdom, the favourite representatives then being the *cat* or the *snake* or the *bear,* or else some black monster of the underworld like the crocodile, or other salamander-like, saurian creatures.[3] The maiden's helplessness exposes her to all sorts of *dangers,* for instance of being devoured by reptiles or ritually slaughtered like a beast of sacrifice. Often there are bloody, cruel, and even obscene *orgies* to which the innocent child falls victim. Sometimes it is a true *nekyia,* a descent into Hades and a quest for the "treasure hard to attain," occasionally connected with orgiastic sexual rites or offerings of menstrual blood to the moon. Oddly enough, the various tortures and obscenities are carried out by an "Earth Mother." There are *drinkings of blood* and *bathings in blood,*[4] also cruci-

[2] The "personalistic" approach interprets such dreams as "wish-fulfilments." To many, this kind of interpretation seems the only possible one. These dreams, however, occur in the most varied circumstances, even in circumstances when the wish-fulfilment theory becomes entirely forced or arbitrary. The investigation of motifs in the field of dreams therefore seems to me the more cautious and the more appropriate procedure.

[3] The double vision of a salamander, of which Benvenuto Cellini tells in his autobiography, would be an anima-projection caused by the music his father was playing.

[4] One of my patients, whose principal difficulty was a negative mother-complex, developed a series of fantasies on a primitive mother-figure, an Indian woman,

fixions. The maiden who crops up in case histories differs not inconsiderably from the vaguely flower-like Kore in that the modern figure is more sharply delineated and not nearly so "unconscious," as the following examples will show.

312 The figures corresponding to Demeter and Hecate are supraordinate, not to say over-life-size "Mothers" ranging from the Pietà type to the Baubo type. The unconscious, which acts as a counterbalance to woman's conventional innocuousness, proves to be highly inventive in this latter respect. I can recall only very few cases where Demeter's own noble figure in its pure form breaks through as an image rising spontaneously from the unconscious. I remember a case, in fact, where a maiden-goddess appears clad all in purest white, but carrying a black monkey in her arms. The Earth Mother is always chthonic and is occasionally related to the moon, either through the blood-sacrifice already mentioned, or through a child-sacrifice, or else because she is adorned with a sickle moon.[5] In pictorial or plastic representations the Mother is dark deepening to *black,* or *red* (these being her principal colours), and with a primitive or animal expression of face; in form she not infrequently resembles the

who instructed her on the nature of woman in general. In these pronouncements a special paragraph is devoted to blood, running as follows: "A woman's life is close to the *blood.* Every month she is reminded of this, and birth is indeed a bloody business, destructive and creative. A woman is only *permitted* to give birth, but the new life is not *her* creation. In her heart of hearts she knows this and rejoices in the grace that has fallen to her. She is a little mother, not the *Great Mother.* But her little pattern is like the great pattern. If she understands this she is blessed by nature, because she has submitted in the right way and can thus partake of the nourishment of the Great Mother. . . ."

5 Often the moon is simply "there," as for instance in a fantasy of the chthonic mother in the shape of the "Woman of the Bees" (Josephine D. Bacon, *In the Border Country,* pp. 14ff.): "The path led to a tiny hut of the same colour as the *four great trees* that stood about it. Its door hung wide open, and in the middle of it, on a low stool, there sat an old woman wrapped in a long cloak, looking kindly at her. . . ." The hut was filled with the steady *humming of bees.* In the corner of the hut there was a deep cold *spring,* in which "a white moon and little stars" were reflected. The old woman exhorted the heroine to remember the duties of a woman's life. In Tantric yoga an "indistinct hum of swarms of love-mad bees" proceeds from the slumbering Shakti (*Shat-Chakra Nirupana,* in Avalon, *The Serpent Power,* p. 29). Cf. infra, the dancer who dissolves into a *swarm of bees.* Bees are also, as an allegory, connected with Mary, as the text for the consecration of the Easter candle shows. See Duchesne, *Christian Worship: Its Origin and Evolution,* p. 253.

neolithic ideal of the "Venus" of Brassempouy or that of Willendorf, or again the sleeper of Hal Saflieni.[6] Now and then I have come across *multiple breasts,* arranged like those of a sow. The Earth Mother plays an important part in the woman's unconscious, for all her manifestations are described as "powerful." This shows that in such cases the Earth Mother element in the conscious mind is abnormally weak and requires strengthening.

313 In view of all this it is, I admit, hardly understandable why such figures should be reckoned as belonging to the type of "supraordinate personality." In a scientific investigation, however, one has to disregard moral or aesthetic prejudices and let the facts speak for themselves. The *maiden* is often described as not altogether human in the usual sense; she is either of unknown or peculiar origin, or she looks strange or undergoes strange experiences, from which one is forced to infer the maiden's extraordinary, myth-like nature. Equally and still more strikingly, the Earth Mother is a divine being—in the classical sense. Moreover, she does not by any means always appear in the guise of Baubo, but, for instance, more like Queen Venus in the *Hypnerotomachia Poliphili,* though she is invariably heavy with destiny. The often unaesthetic forms of the Earth Mother are in keeping with a prejudice of the modern feminine unconscious; this prejudice was lacking in antiquity. The underworld nature of Hecate, who is closely connected with Demeter, and Persephone's fate both point nevertheless to the dark side of the human psyche, though not to the same extent as the modern material.

314 The "supraordinate personality" is the total man, i.e., man as he really is, not as he appears to himself. To this wholeness the unconscious psyche also belongs, which has its requirements and needs just as consciousness has. I do not want to interpret the unconscious personalistically and assert, for instance, that fantasy-images like those described above are the "wish-fulfilments" due to repression. These images were as such never conscious and consequently could never have been repressed. I understand the unconscious rather as an *impersonal* psyche common to all men, even though it expresses itself through a

6 [See Neumann, *The Great Mother,* Pls. 1a, 3. This entire work elucidates the present study.—EDITORS.]

personal consciousness. When anyone breathes, his breathing is not a phenomenon to be interpreted personally. The mythological images belong to the structure of the unconscious and are an impersonal possession; in fact, the great majority of men are far more *possessed by* them than possessing them. Images like those described above give rise under certain conditions to corresponding disturbances and symptoms, and it is then the task of medical therapy to find out whether and how and to what extent these impulses can be integrated with the conscious personality, or whether they are a secondary phenomenon which some defective orientation of consciousness has brought out of its normal potential state into actuality. Both possibilities exist in practice.

315 I usually describe the supraordinate personality as the "self," thus making a sharp distinction between the ego, which, as is well known, extends only as far as the conscious mind, and the *whole* of the personality, which includes the unconscious as well as the conscious component. The ego is thus related to the self as part to whole. To that extent the self is supraordinate. Moreover, the self is felt empirically not as subject but as object, and this by reason of its unconscious component, which can only come to consciousness indirectly, by way of projection. Because of its unconscious component the self is so far removed from the conscious mind that it can only be partially expressed by human figures; the other part of it has to be expressed by objective, abstract symbols. The human figures are father and son, mother and daughter, king and queen, god and goddess. Theriomorphic symbols are the dragon, snake, elephant, lion, bear, and other powerful animals, or again the spider, crab, butterfly, beetle, worm, etc. Plant symbols are generally flowers (lotus and rose). These lead on to geometrical figures like the circle, the sphere, the square, the quaternity, the clock, the firmament, and so on.[7] The indefinite extent of the unconscious component makes a comprehensive description of the human personality impossible. Accordingly, the unconscious supplements the picture with living figures ranging from the animal to the divine, as the two extremes outside man, and rounds out the animal extreme, through the addition of

[7] *Psychology and Alchemy*, Part II.

vegetable and inorganic abstractions, into a microcosm. These addenda have a high frequency in anthropomorphic divinities, where they appear as "attributes."

316 Demeter and Kore, mother and daughter, extend the feminine consciousness both upwards and downwards. They add an "older and younger," "stronger and weaker" dimension to it and widen out the narrowly limited conscious mind bound in space and time, giving it intimations of a greater and more comprehensive personality which has a share in the eternal course of things. We can hardly suppose that myth and mystery were invented for any conscious purpose; it seems much more likely that they were the involuntary revelation of a psychic, but unconscious, pre-condition. The psyche pre-existent to consciousness (e.g., in the child) participates in the maternal psyche on the one hand, while on the other it reaches across to the daughter psyche. We could therefore say that every mother contains her daughter in herself and every daughter her mother, and that every woman extends backwards into her mother and forwards into her daughter. This participation and intermingling give rise to that peculiar uncertainty as regards *time:* a woman lives earlier as a mother, later as a daughter. The conscious experience of these ties produces the feeling that her life is spread out over generations—the first step towards the immediate experience and conviction of being outside time, which brings with it a feeling of *immortality*. The individual's life is elevated into a type, indeed it becomes the archetype of woman's fate in general. This leads to a restoration or *apocatastasis* of the lives of her ancestors, who now, through the bridge of the momentary individual, pass down into the generations of the future. An experience of this kind gives the individual a place and a meaning in the life of the generations, so that all unnecessary obstacles are cleared out of the way of the life-stream that is to flow through her. At the same time the individual is rescued from her isolation and restored to wholeness. All ritual preoccupation with archetypes ultimately has this aim and this result.

317 It is immediately clear to the psychologist what cathartic and at the same rejuvenating effects must flow from the Demeter cult into the feminine psyche, and what a lack of psychic hygiene

characterizes our culture, which no longer knows the kind of wholesome experience afforded by Eleusinian emotions.

318 I take full account of the fact that not only the psychologically minded layman but the professional psychologist and psychiatrist as well, and even the psychotherapist, do not possess an adequate knowledge of their patients' archetypal material, in so far as they have not specially investigated this aspect of the phenomenology of the unconscious. For it is precisely in the field of psychiatric and psychotherapeutic observation that we frequently meet with cases characterized by a rich crop of archetypal symbols.[8] Since the necessary historical knowledge is lacking to the physician observing them, he is not in a position to perceive the parallelism between his observations and the findings of anthropology and the humane sciences in general. Conversely, an expert in mythology and comparative religion is as a rule no psychiatrist and consequently does not know that his mythologems are still fresh and living—for instance, in dreams and visions—in the hidden recesses of our most personal life, which we would on no account deliver up to scientific dissection. The archetypal material is therefore the great unknown, and it requires special study and preparation even to collect such material.

319 It does not seem to me superfluous to give a number of examples from my case histories which bring out the occurrence of archetypal images in dreams or fantasies. Time and again with my public I come across the difficulty that they imagine illustration by "a few examples" to be the simplest thing in the world. In actual fact it is almost impossible, with a few words and one or two images torn out of their context, to demonstrate anything. This only works when dealing with an expert. What Perseus has to do with the Gorgon's head would never occur to anyone who did not know the myth. So it is with the individual images: they need a context, and the context is not only a myth but an individual anamnesis. Such contexts, however, are of enormous extent. Anything like a complete series of images would require for its proper presentation a book of about two hundred pages. My own investigation of the Miller fantasies

8 I would refer to the thesis of my pupil Jan Nelken, "Analytische Beobachtungen über Phantasien eines Schizophrenen," as also to my own analysis of a series of fantasies in *Symbols of Transformation.*

gives some idea of this.[9] It is therefore with the greatest hesitation that I make the attempt to illustrate from case-histories. The material I shall use comes partly from normal, partly from slightly neurotic, persons. It is part dream, part vision, or dream mixed with vision. These "visions" are far from being hallucinations or ecstatic states; they are spontaneous, visual images of fantasy or so-called *active imagination.* The latter is a method (devised by myself) of introspection for observing the stream of interior images. One concentrates one's attention on some impressive but unintelligible dream-image, or on a spontaneous visual impression, and observes the changes taking place in it. Meanwhile, of course, all criticism must be suspended and the happenings observed and noted with absolute objectivity. Obviously, too, the objection that the whole thing is "arbitrary" or "thought up" must be set aside, since it springs from the anxiety of an ego-consciousness which brooks no master besides itself in its own house. In other words, it is the inhibition exerted by the conscious mind on the unconscious.

320 Under these conditions, long and often very dramatic series of fantasies ensue. The advantage of this method is that it brings a mass of unconscious material to light. Drawing, painting, and modelling can be used to the same end. Once a visual series has become dramatic, it can easily pass over into the auditive or linguistic sphere and give rise to dialogues and the like. With slightly pathological individuals, and particularly in the not infrequent cases of latent schizophrenia, the method may, in certain circumstances, prove to be rather dangerous and therefore requires medical control. It is based on a deliberate weakening of the conscious mind and its inhibiting effect, which either limits or suppresses the unconscious. The aim of the method is naturally therapeutic in the first place, while in the second it also furnishes rich empirical material. Some of our examples are taken from this. They differ from dreams only by reason of their better form, which comes from the fact that the contents were perceived not by a dreaming but by a waking consciousness. The examples are from women in middle life.

[9] Cf. *Symbols of Transformation.* H. G. Baynes' book, *The Mythology of the Soul,* runs to 939 pages and endeavours to do justice to the material provided by only two cases.

1. *Case X (spontaneous visual impressions, in chronological order)*

321 i. *"I saw a white bird with outstretched wings. It alighted on the figure of a woman, clad in blue, who sat there like an* antique statue. *The bird perched on her hand, and in it she held a* grain of wheat. *The bird took it in its beak and flew into the sky again."*

322 For this X painted a picture: a blue-clad, archaically simple "Mother"-figure on a white marble base. Her maternity is emphasized by the large breasts.

323 ii. *A bull lifts a child up from the ground and carries it to the antique statue of a woman. A naked young girl with a wreath of flowers in her hair appears, riding on a white bull. She takes the child and throws it into the air like a ball and catches it again. The white bull carries them both to a temple. The girl lays the child on the ground, and so on (initiation follows).*

324 In this picture the *maiden* appears, rather in the form of Europa. (Here a certain school knowledge is being made use of.) Her nakedness and the wreath of flowers point to Dionysian abandonment. The game of ball with the child is the motif of some secret rite which always has to do with "child-sacrifice." (Cf. the accusations of ritual murder levelled by the pagans against the Christians and by the Christians against the Jews and Gnostics; also the Phoenician child-sacrifices, rumours about the Black Mass, etc., and "the ball-game in church.")[10]

325 iii. *"I saw a golden* pig *on a pedestal. Beast-like beings* danced *round it in a circle. We made haste to dig* a hole in the ground. *I reached in and found* water. *Then a man appeared* in a golden carriage. *He jumped into the hole and began swaying back and forth, as if dancing. . . . I swayed in rhythm with him. Then he suddenly leaped out of the hole, raped me, and got me with child."*

326 X is identical with the young girl, who often appears as a *youth,* too. This youth is an animus-figure, the embodiment of the masculine element in a woman. Youth and young girl together form a syzygy or *coniunctio* which symbolizes the essence

10 [Cf. infra, "On the Psychology of the Trickster-Figure."—EDITORS.]

of wholeness (as also does the Platonic hermaphrodite, who later became the symbol of perfected wholeness in alchemical philosophy). X evidently dances with the rest, hence "*we* made haste." The parallel with the motifs stressed by Kerényi seems to me remarkable.

327 iv. *"I saw a beautiful youth with golden cymbals, dancing and leaping in joy and abandonment. . . . Finally he fell to the ground and buried his face in the flowers. Then he sank into the lap of a* very old mother. *After a time he got up and jumped into the water, where he sported like a* dolphin. . . . *I saw that his hair was golden. Now we were leaping together, hand in hand. So we came to a* gorge. . . ." *In leaping the gorge the youth falls into the chasm. X is left alone and comes to a river where a white* sea-horse *is waiting for her with a golden boat.*

328 In this scene X is the youth; therefore he disappears later, leaving her the sole heroine of the story. She is the child of the "very old mother," and is also the dolphin, the youth lost in the gorge, and the bride evidently expected by Poseidon. The peculiar overlapping and displacement of motifs in all this individual material is about the same as in the mythological variants. X found the youth in the lap of the mother so impressive that she painted a picture of it. The figure is the same as in item i; only, instead of the grain of wheat in her hand, there is the body of the youth lying completely exhausted in the lap of the gigantic mother.

329 v. *There now follows a sacrifice of sheep, during which a game of ball is likewise played with the sacrificial animal. The participants* smear themselves with the sacrificial blood, *and afterwards bathe in the pulsing gore. X is thereupon transformed into a* plant.

330 vi. *After that X comes to a* den of snakes, *and the snakes wind all round her.*

331 vii. *In a den of snakes beneath the sea there is a* divine woman, *asleep.* (She is shown in the picture as much larger than the others.) *She is wearing a blood-red garment that covers only the lower half of her body. She has a dark skin, full red lips, and seems to be of great physical strength. She kisses X, who is obviously in the role of the young girl, and hands her as a present to the many men who are standing by, etc.*

332 This chthonic goddess is the typical Earth Mother as she appears in so many modern fantasies.

333 viii. *As X emerged from the depths and saw the light again, she experienced a kind of illumination: white flames played about her head as she walked through waving* fields of grain.

334 With this picture the Mother-episode ended. Although there is not the slightest trace of any known myth being repeated, the motifs and the connections between them are all familiar to us from mythology. These images present themselves spontaneously and are based on no conscious knowledge whatever. I have applied the method of active imagination to myself over a long time and have observed numerous symbols and symbolic associations which in many cases I was only able to verify years afterwards in texts of whose existence I was totally ignorant. It is the same with dreams. Some years ago I dreamed for example that: *I was climbing slowly and toilsomely up a mountain. When I had reached, as I imagined, the top, I found that I was standing on the edge of a plateau. The crest that represented the real top of the mountain only rose far off in the distance. Night was coming on, and I saw, on the dark slope opposite, a brook flowing down with a metallic shimmer, and two paths leading upwards, one to the left, the other to the right, winding like serpents. On the crest, to the right, there was a hotel. Down below, the brook ran to the left with a bridge leading across.*

335 Not long afterwards I discovered the following "allegory" in an obscure alchemical treatise. In his *Speculativae philosophiae* [11] the Frankfurt physician Gerard Dorn, who lived in the second half of the sixteenth century, describes the "Mundi peregrinatio, quam erroris viam appellamus" (Tour of the world, which we call the way of error) on the one hand and the "Via veritatis" on the other. Of the first way the author says:

> The human race, whose nature it is to resist God, does not cease to ask how it may, by its own efforts, escape the pitfalls which it has laid for itself. But it does not ask help from Him on whom alone depends every gift of mercy. Hence it has come about that men have built for themselves a great Workshop on the left-hand side of the road . . . presided over by Industry. After this has been attained, they turn aside from Industry and bend their steps towards the

[11] *Theatrum chemicum,* I (1602), pp. 286ff.

second region of the world, making their crossing *on the bridge of infirmity.* . . . But because the good God desires to draw them back, He allows their infirmities to rule over them; then, seeking as before a remedy in themselves [industry!], they flock *to the great Hospital likewise built on the left,* presided over by Medicine. Here there is a great multitude of apothecaries, surgeons, and physicians, [etc.].[12]

336 Of the "way of truth," which is the "right" way, our author says: ". . . you will come to the camp of Wisdom and on being received there, you will be refreshed with food far more powerful than before." Even the brook is there: ". . . a stream of living water flowing with such wonderful artifice from the mountain peak. (From the Fountain of Wisdom the waters gush forth.)" [13]

337 An important difference, compared with my dream, is that here, apart from the situation of the hotel being reversed, the river of Wisdom is on the right and not, as in my dream, in the middle of the picture.

338 It is evident that in my dream we are not dealing with any known "myth" but with a group of ideas which might easily have been regarded as "individual," i.e., unique. A thorough analysis, however, could show without difficulty that it is an archetypal image such as can be reproduced over and over again in any age and any place. But I must admit that the archetypal nature of the dream-image only became clear to me when I read Dorn. These and similar incidents I have observed repeatedly not only in myself but in my patients. But, as this

12 "Humanum genus, cui Deo resistere iam innatum est, non desistit media quaerere, quibus proprio conatu laqueos evadat, quos sibimet posuit, ab eo non petens auxilium, a quo solo dependet omnis misericordiae munus. Hinc factum est, ut in sinistram viae partem officinam sibi maximam exstruxerint . . . huic domui praeest industria, etc. Quod postquam adepti fuerint, ab industria recedentes *in secundam mundi regionem* tendunt: *per infirmitatis pontem* facientes transitum. . . . At quia bonus Deus retrahere vellet, infirmitates in ipsis dominari permittit, tum rursus ut prius remedium [industria!] a se quaerentes, *ad xenodochium etiam a sinistris constructum* et permaximum confluunt, cui medicina praeest. Ibi pharmacopolarum, chirurgorum et physicorum ingens est copia." (p. 288.)

13 ". . . pervenietis ad Sophiae castra, quibus excepti, longe vehementiori quam antea cibo reficiemini. . . . viventis aquae fluvius tam admirando fluens artificio de montis apice. (De Sophiae fonte scaturiunt aquae!)" [Slightly modified by Professor Jung. Cf. Dorn, pp. 279–80.—EDITORS.]

example shows, it needs special attention if such parallels are not to be missed.

339 The antique Mother-image is not exhausted with the figure of Demeter. It also expresses itself in Cybele-Artemis. The next case points in this direction.

2. *Case Y (dreams)*

340 i. *"I am wandering over a great mountain; the way is lonely, wild, and difficult. A woman comes down from the sky to accompany and help me. She is all bright with light hair and shining eyes. Now and then she vanishes. After going on for some time alone I notice that I have left my stick somewhere, and must turn back to fetch it. To do this I have to pass a terrible monster, an enormous bear. When I came this way the first time I had to pass it, but then the sky-woman protected me. Just as I am passing the beast and he is about to come at me, she stands beside me again, and at her look the bear lies down quietly and lets us pass. Then the sky-woman vanishes."*

341 Here we have a maternally protective goddess related to bears, a kind of Diana or the Gallo-Roman Dea Artio. The sky-woman is the positive, the bear the negative aspect of the "supraordinate personality," which extends the conscious human being upwards into the celestial and downwards into the animal regions.

342 ii. *"We go through a door into a tower-like room, where we climb a long flight of steps. On one of the topmost steps I read an inscription:* 'Vis ut sis.' *The steps end in a temple situated on the crest of a wooded mountain, and there is no other approach. It is the shrine of* Ursanna, *the bear-goddess and Mother of God in one. The temple is of red stone. Bloody sacrifices are offered there. Animals are standing about the altar. In order to enter the temple precincts one has to be transformed into an animal—a beast of the forest. The temple has the form of a cross with equal arms and a circular space in the middle, which is not roofed, so that one can look straight up at the sky and the constellation of the Bear. On the altar in the middle of the open space there stands the moon-bowl, from which smoke or vapour continually rises. There is also a huge image of the goddess, but it cannot be seen clearly. The worshippers, who*

have been changed into animals and to whom I also belong, have to touch the goddess's foot with their own foot, whereupon the image gives them a sign or an oracular utterance like 'Vis ut sis.' "

343 In this dream the bear-goddess emerges plainly, although her statue "cannot be seen clearly." The relationship to the self, the supraordinate personality, is indicated not only by the oracle "Vis ut sis" but by the quaternity and the circular central precinct of the temple. From ancient times any relationship to the stars has always symbolized eternity. The soul comes "from the stars" and returns to the stellar regions. "Ursanna's" relation to the moon is indicated by the "moon-bowl."

344 The moon-goddess also appears in children's dreams. A girl who grew up in peculiarly difficult psychic circumstances had a recurrent dream between her seventh and tenth years: *"The moon-lady was always waiting for me down by the water at the landing-stage, to take me to her island."* Unfortunately she could never remember what happened there, but it was so beautiful that she often prayed she might have this dream again. Although, as is evident, the two dreamers are not identical, the *island motif* also occurred in the previous dream as the inaccessible mountain crest.

345 Thirty years later, the dreamer of the moon-lady had a dramatic fantasy:

346 *"I am climbing a steep dark mountain, on top of which stands a domed castle. I enter and go up a winding stairway to the left. Arriving inside the dome, I find myself in the presence of a woman wearing a head-dress of cow's horns. I recognize her immediately as the* moon-lady *of my childhood dreams. At her behest I look to the* right *and see a dazzlingly bright sun shining on the other side of a deep chasm. Over the chasm stretches a narrow, transparent bridge, upon which I step, conscious of the fact that in no circumstances must I look down. An uncanny fear seizes me, and I hesitate. Treachery seems to be in the air, but at last I go across and stand before the sun. The sun speaks: 'If you can approach me nine times without being burned, all will be well.' But I grow more and more afraid, finally I do look down, and I see a black tentacle like that of an octopus groping towards me from underneath the sun. I step back in fright and plunge into the abyss. But instead of being dashed*

to pieces I lie in the arms of the Earth Mother. When I try to look into her face, she turns to clay, and I find myself lying on the earth."

347 It is remarkable how the beginning of this fantasy agrees with the dream. The moon-lady above is clearly distinguished from the Earth Mother below. The former urges the dreamer to her somewhat perilous adventure with the sun; the latter catches her protectively in her maternal arms. The dreamer, as the one in danger, would therefore seem to be in the role of the Kore.

348 Let us now turn back to our dream-series:

349 iii. *Y sees two pictures in a dream, painted by the Scandinavian painter Hermann Christian Lund.*

I. *"The first picture is of a Scandinavian peasant room. Peasant girls in gay costumes are walking about arm in arm (that is, in a row). The middle one is smaller than the rest and, besides this, has a hump and keeps turning her head back. This, together with her peculiar glance, gives her a witchlike look."*

II. *"The second picture shows a dragon with its neck stretched out over the whole picture and especially over a girl, who is in the dragon's power and cannot move, for as soon as she moves, the dragon, which can make its body big or little at will, moves too; and when the girl wants to get away it simply stretches out its neck over her, and so catches her again. Strangely enough, the girl has no face, at least I couldn't see it."*

350 The painter is an invention of the dream. The animus often appears as a painter or has some kind of projection apparatus, or is a cinema-operator or owner of a picture-gallery. All this refers to the animus as the function mediating between conscious and unconscious: the unconscious contains pictures which are transmitted, that is, made manifest, by the animus, either as fantasies or, unconsciously, in the patient's own life and actions. The animus-projection gives rise to fantasied relations of love and hatred for "heroes" or "demons." The favourite victims are tenors, artists, movie-stars, athletic champions, etc. In the first picture the maiden is characterized as demonic, with a hump and an evil look "over her shoulder." (Hence amulets against the evil eye are often worn by primitives on the nape of the neck, for the vulnerable spot is at the back, where you can't see.)

351 In the second picture the "maiden" is portrayed as the innocent victim of the monster. Just as before there was a relationship of identity between the sky-woman and the bear, so here between the young girl and the dragon—which in practical life is often rather more than just a bad joke. Here it signifies a widening of the conscious personality, i.e., through the helplessness of the victim on the one hand and the dangers of the humpback's evil eye and the dragon's might on the other.

352 iv (part dream, part visual imagination). *"A magician is demonstrating his tricks to an Indian prince. He produces a beautiful young girl from under a cloth. She is a dancer, who has the power to change her shape or at least hold her audience spell-bound by faultless illusion. During the dance she dissolves with the music into a swarm of bees. Then she changes into a leopard, then into a jet of water, then into an octopus that has twined itself about a young pearl-fisher. Between times, she takes human form again at the dramatic moment. She appears as a she-ass bearing two baskets of wonderful fruits. Then she becomes a many-coloured peacock. The prince is beside himself with delight and calls her to him. But she dances on, now naked, and even tears the skin from her body, and finally falls down—a naked skeleton. This is buried, but at night a lily grows out of the grave, and from its cup there rises a* white lady, *who floats slowly up to the sky."*

353 This piece describes the successive transformations of the illusionist (artistry in illusion being a specifically feminine talent) until she becomes a transfigured personality. The fantasy was not invented as a sort of allegory; it was part dream, part spontaneous imagery.

354 v. *"I am in a church made of grey sandstone. The apse is built rather high. Near the tabernacle a girl in a red dress is hanging on the stone cross of the window. (Suicide?)"*

355 Just as in the preceding cases the sacrifice of a child or a sheep played a part, so here the sacrifice of the maiden hanging on the "cross." The death of the dancer is also to be understood in this sense, for these maidens are always doomed to die, because their exclusive domination of the feminine psyche hinders the individuation process, that is, the maturation of personality. The "maiden" corresponds to the anima of the man and makes use of it to gain her natural ends, in which illusion plays the

greatest role imaginable. But as long as a woman is content to be a *femme à homme,* she has no feminine individuality. She is empty and merely glitters—a welcome vessel for masculine projections. Woman as a personality, however, is a very different thing: here illusion no longer works. So that when the question of personality arises, which is as a rule the painful fact of the second half of life, the childish form of the self disappears too.

356 All that remains for me now is to describe the Kore as observable in man, the *anima.* Since a man's wholeness, in so far as he is not constitutionally homosexual, can only be a masculine personality, the feminine figure of the anima cannot be catalogued as a type of supraordinate personality but requires a different evaluation and position. In the products of unconscious activity, the anima appears equally as maiden and mother, which is why a personalistic interpretation always reduces her to the personal mother or some other female person. The real meaning of the figure naturally gets lost in the process, as is inevitably the case with all these reductive interpretations whether in the sphere of the psychology of the unconscious or of mythology. The innumerable attempts that have been made in the sphere of mythology to interpret gods and heroes in a solar, lunar, astral, or meteorological sense contribute nothing of importance to the understanding of them; on the contrary, they all put us on a false track. When, therefore, in dreams and other spontaneous products, we meet with an unknown female figure whose significance oscillates between the extremes of goddess and whore, it is advisable to let her keep her independence and not reduce her arbitrarily to something known. If the unconscious shows her as an "unknown," this attribute should not be got rid of by main force with a view to arriving at a "rational" interpretation. Like the "supraordinate personality," the anima is bipolar and can therefore appear positive one moment and negative the next; now young, now old; now mother, now maiden; now a good fairy, now a witch; now a saint, now a whore. Besides this ambivalence, the anima also has "occult" connections with "mysteries," with the world of darkness in general, and for that reason she often has a religious tinge. Whenever she emerges with some degree of clarity, she always has a peculiar relationship to *time:* as a rule she is more or less immortal, because outside time. Writers who have tried

their hand at this figure have never failed to stress the anima's peculiarity in this respect. I would refer to the classic descriptions in Rider Haggard's *She* and *The Return of She,* in Pierre Benoît's *L'Atlantide,* and above all in the novel of the young American author, William M. Sloane, *To Walk the Night.* In all these accounts, the anima is outside time as we know it and consequently immensely old or a being who belongs to a different order of things.

357 Since we can no longer or only partially express the archetypes of the unconscious by means of figures in which we religiously believe, they lapse into unconsciousness again and hence are unconsciously projected upon more or less suitable human personalities. To the young boy a clearly discernible anima-form appears in his mother, and this lends her the radiance of power and superiority or else a daemonic aura of even greater fascination. But because of the anima's ambivalence, the projection can be entirely negative. Much of the fear which the female sex arouses in men is due to the projection of the anima-image. An infantile man generally has a maternal anima; an adult man, the figure of a younger woman. The senile man finds compensation in a very young girl, or even a child.

[3. *Case Z*]

358 The anima also has affinities with animals, which symbolize her characteristics. Thus she can appear as a snake or a tiger or a bird. I quote by way of example a dream-series that contains transformations of this kind: [14]

359 i. *A white bird perches on a table. Suddenly it changes into a fair-haired seven-year-old girl and just as suddenly back into a bird, which now speaks with a human voice.*

360 ii. *In an underground house, which is really the underworld, there lives an old magician and prophet with his "daughter." She is, however, not really his daughter; she is a dancer, a very loose person, but is blind and seeks healing.*

361 iii. *A lonely house in a wood, where an old scholar is living. Suddenly his daughter appears, a kind of ghost, complaining that people only look upon her as a figment of fancy.*

[14] Only extracts from the dreams are given, so far as they bear on the anima.

362 iv. *On the façade of a church there is a Gothic Madonna, who is alive and is the "unknown and yet known woman." Instead of a child, she holds in her arms a sort of flame or a snake or a dragon.*

363 v. *A black-clad "countess" kneels in a dark chapel. Her dress is hung with costly pearls. She has red hair, and there is something uncanny about her. Moreover, she is surrounded by the spirits of the dead.*

364 vi. *A female snake comports herself tenderly and insinuatingly, speaking with a human voice. She is only "accidentally" shaped like a snake.*

365 vii. *A bird speaks with the same voice, but shows herself helpful by trying to rescue the dreamer from a dangerous situation.*

366 viii. *The unknown woman sits, like the dreamer, on the tip of a church-spire and stares at him uncannily across the abyss.*

367 ix. *The unknown woman suddenly appears as an old female attendant in an underground public lavatory with a temperature of 40° below zero.*

368 x. *The unknown woman leaves the house as a* petite bourgeoise *with a female relation, and in her place there is suddenly an over-life-size goddess clad in blue, looking like Athene.*

369 xi. *Then she appears in a church, taking the place of the altar, still over-life-size but with veiled face.*

370 In all these dreams [15] the central figure is a mysterious feminine being with qualities like those of no woman known to the dreamer. The unknown is described as such in the dreams themselves, and reveals her extraordinary nature firstly by her power to change shape and secondly by her paradoxical ambivalence. Every conceivable shade of meaning glitters in her, from the highest to the lowest.

371 *Dream i* shows the anima as elflike, i.e., only partially human. She can just as well be a bird, which means that she may belong wholly to nature and can vanish (i.e., become unconscious) from the human sphere (i.e., consciousness).

372 *Dream ii* shows the unknown woman as a mythological figure from the beyond (the unconscious). She is the *soror* or *filia mystica* of a hierophant or "philosopher," evidently a parallel to

[15] The following statements are not meant as "interpretations" of the dreams. They are intended only to sum up the various forms in which the anima appears.

those mystic syzygies which are to be met with in the figures of Simon Magus and Helen, Zosimus and Theosebeia, Comarius and Cleopatra, etc. Our dream-figure fits in best with Helen. A really admirable description of anima-psychology in a woman is to be found in Erskine's *Helen of Troy*.

373 *Dream iii* presents the same theme, but on a more "fairytale-like" plane. Here the anima is shown as rather spookish.

374 *Dream iv* brings the anima nearer to the Mother of God. The "child" refers to the mystic speculations on the subject of the redemptive serpent and the "fiery" nature of the redeemer.

375 In *dream v,* the anima is visualized somewhat romantically as the "distinguished" fascinating woman, who nevertheless has dealings with spirits.

376 *Dreams vi and vii* bring theriomorphic variations. The anima's identity is at once apparent to the dreamer because of the voice and what it says. The anima has "accidentally" taken the form of a snake, just as in *dream i* she changed with the greatest ease into a bird and back again. As a snake, she is playing the negative role, as a bird the positive.

377 *Dream viii* shows the dreamer confronted with his anima. This takes place high above the ground (i.e., above human reality). Obviously it is a case of dangerous fascination by the anima.

378 *Dream ix* signifies the anima's deep plunge into an extremely "subordinate" position, where the last trace of fascination has gone and only human sympathy is left.

379 *Dream x* shows the paradoxical double nature of the anima: banal mediocrity and Olympian divinity.

380 *Dream xi* restores the anima to the Christian church, not as an icon but as the altar itself. The altar is the place of sacrifice and also the receptacle for consecrated relics.

381 To throw even a moderate light on all these anima associations would require special and very extensive investigation, which would be out of place here because, as we have already said, the anima has only an indirect bearing on the interpretation of the Kore figure. I have presented this dream-series simply for the purpose of giving the reader some idea of the empirical material on which the idea of the anima is based.[16] From this series and others like it we get an average picture of that strange factor which has such an important part to play in the

16 Cf. the third paper in this volume.

masculine psyche, and which naïve presumption invariably identifies with certain women, imputing to them all the illusions that swarm in the male Eros.

382 It seems clear enough that the man's anima found occasion for projection in the Demeter cult. The Kore doomed to her subterranean fate, the two-faced mother, and the theriomorphic aspects of both afforded the anima ample opportunity to reflect herself, shimmering and equivocal, in the Eleusinian cult, or rather to experience herself there and fill the celebrants with her unearthly essence, to their lasting gain. For a man, anima experiences are always of immense and abiding significance.

383 But the Demeter-Kore myth is far too feminine to have been merely the result of an anima-projection. Although the anima can, as we have said, experience herself in Demeter-Kore, she is yet of a wholly different nature. She is in the highest degree *femme à homme,* whereas Demeter-Kore exists on the plane of mother-daughter experience, which is alien to man and shuts him out. In fact, the psychology of the Demeter cult bears all the features of a matriarchal order of society, where the man is an indispensable but on the whole disturbing factor.

V

THE PHENOMENOLOGY OF THE SPIRIT IN FAIRYTALES

ON THE PSYCHOLOGY OF THE TRICKSTER-FIGURE

THE PHENOMENOLOGY OF THE SPIRIT IN FAIRYTALES [1]

384 One of the unbreakable rules in scientific research is to take an object as known only so far as the inquirer is in a position to make scientifically valid statements about it. "Valid" in this sense simply means what can be verified by facts. The object of inquiry is the natural phenomenon. Now in psychology, one of the most important phenomena is the *statement,* and in particular its form and content, the latter aspect being perhaps the more significant with regard to the nature of the psyche. The first task that ordinarily presents itself is the description and arrangement of events, then comes the closer examination into the laws of their living behaviour. To inquire into the *substance* of what has been observed is possible in natural science only where there is an Archimedean point outside. For the psyche, no such outside standpoint exists—only the psyche can observe the psyche. Consequently, knowledge of the psychic substance is impossible for us, at least with the means at present available. This does not rule out the possibility that the atomic physics of the future may supply us with the said Archimedean point. For the time being, however, our subtlest lucubrations can establish no more than is expressed in the statement: this is how the psyche behaves. The honest investigator will piously refrain from meddling with questions of substance. I do not think it superfluous to acquaint my reader with the necessary limitations that psychology voluntarily imposes on itself, for he will then be in a position to appreciate the phenomenological standpoint of modern psychology, which is not always understood. This

1 [First published as a lecture, "Zur Psychologie des Geistes," in the *Eranos-Jahrbuch 1945*. Revised and published as "Zur Phänomenologie des Geistes im Märchen," in *Symbolik des Geistes* (Zurich, 1948), from which the present translation was made. This translation was published in a slightly different form in *Spirit and Nature* (Papers from the Eranos Yearbooks, 1; New York, 1953; London, 1954).—EDITORS.]

standpoint does not exclude the existence of faith, conviction, and experienced certainties of whatever description, nor does it contest their possible validity. Great as is their importance for the individual and for collective life, psychology completely lacks the means to prove their validity in the scientific sense. One may lament this incapacity on the part of science, but that does not enable it to jump over its own shadow.

I. CONCERNING THE WORD 'SPIRIT'

385 The word "spirit" possesses such a wide range of application that it requires considerable effort to make clear to oneself all the things it can mean. Spirit, we say, is the principle that stands in opposition to matter. By this we understand an immaterial substance or form of existence which on the highest and most universal level is called "God." We imagine this immaterial substance also as the vehicle of psychic phenomena or even of life itself. In contradiction to this view there stands the antithesis: spirit and nature. Here the concept of spirit is restricted to the supernatural or anti-natural, and has lost its substantial connection with psyche and life. A similar restriction is implied in Spinoza's view that spirit is an attribute of the One Substance. Hylozoism goes even further, taking spirit to be a quality of matter.

386 A very widespread view conceives spirit as a higher and psyche as a lower principle of activity, and conversely the alchemists thought of spirit as the *ligamentum animae et corporis,* obviously regarding it as a *spiritus vegetativus* (the later life-spirit or nerve-spirit). Equally common is the view that spirit and psyche are essentially the same and can be separated only arbitrarily. Wundt takes spirit as "the inner being, regardless of any connection with an outer being." Others restrict spirit to certain psychic capacities or functions or qualities, such as the capacity to think and reason in contradistinction to the more "soulful" sentiments. Here spirit means the sum-total of all the phenomena of rational thought, or of the intellect, including the will, memory, imagination, creative power, and aspirations motivated by ideals. Spirit has the further connotation of *sprightliness,* as when we say that a person is "spirited," mean-

ing that he is versatile and full of ideas, with a brilliant, witty, and surprising turn of mind. Again, spirit denotes a certain attitude or the principle underlying it, for instance, one is "educated in the spirit of Pestalozzi," or one says that the "spirit of Weimar is the immortal German heritage." A special instance is the time-spirit, or spirit of the age, which stands for the principle and motive force behind certain views, judgments, and actions of a collective nature. Then there is the "objective spirit," [2] by which is meant the whole stock of man's cultural possessions with particular regard to his intellectual and religious achievements.

387 As linguistic usage shows, spirit in the sense of an attitude has unmistakable leanings towards personification: the spirit of Pestalozzi can also be taken concretistically as his ghost or imago, just as the spirits of Weimar are the personal spectres of Goethe and Schiller; for spirit still has the spookish meaning of the soul of one departed. The "cold breath of the spirits" points on the one hand to the ancient affinity of ψυχή with ψυχρός and ψῦχος, which both mean 'cold,' and on the other hand to the original meaning of πνεῦμα, which simply denoted 'air in motion'; and in the same way animus and anima were connected with ἄνεμος, 'wind.' The German word *Geist* probably has more to do with something frothing, effervescing, or fermenting; hence affinities with *Gischt* (foam), *Gäscht* (yeast), *ghost,* and also with the emotional *ghastly* and *aghast,* are not to be rejected. From time immemorial emotion has been regarded as possession, which is why we still say today, of a hot-tempered person, that he is possessed of a devil or that an evil spirit has entered into him.[3] Just as, according to the old view, the spirits or souls of the dead are of a subtle disposition like a vapour or a smoke, so to the alchemist *spiritus* was a subtle, volatile, active, and vivifying essence, such as alcohol was understood to be, and all the arcane substances. On this level, spirit includes spirits of salts, spirits of ammonia, formic spirit, etc.

388 This score or so of meanings and shades of meaning attributable to the word "spirit" make it difficult for the psychologist to delimit his subject conceptually, but on the other hand they lighten the task of describing it, since the many different aspects

2 [An Hegelian term, roughly equivalent to our "spirit of man."—TRANS.]

3 See my "Spirit and Life."

go to form a vivid and concrete picture of the phenomenon in question. We are concerned with a functional complex which originally, on the primitive level, was felt as an invisible, breath-like "presence." William James has given us a lively account of this primordial phenomenon in his *Varieties of Religious Experience*. Another well-known example is the wind of the Pentecostal miracle. The primitive mentality finds it quite natural to personify the invisible presence as a ghost or demon. The souls or spirits of the dead are identical with the psychic activity of the living; they merely continue it. The view that the psyche is a spirit is implicit in this. When therefore something psychic happens in the individual which he feels as belonging to himself, that something is his own spirit. But if anything psychic happens which seems to him strange, then it is somebody else's spirit, and it may be causing a possession. The spirit in the first case corresponds to the subjective attitude, in the latter case to public opinion, to the time-spirit, or to the original, not yet human, anthropoid disposition which we also call the *unconscious*.

389 In keeping with its original wind-nature, spirit is always an active, winged, swift-moving being as well as that which vivifies, stimulates, incites, fires, and inspires. To put it in modern language, spirit is the dynamic principle, forming for that very reason the classical antithesis of matter—the antithesis, that is, of its stasis and inertia. Basically it is the contrast between life and death The subsequent differentiation of this contrast leads to the actually very remarkable opposition of spirit and nature. Even though spirit is regarded as essentially alive and enlivening, one cannot really feel nature as unspiritual and dead. We must therefore be dealing here with the (Christian) postulate of a spirit whose life is so vastly superior to the life of nature that in comparison with it the latter is no better than death.

390 This special development in man's idea of spirit rests on the recognition that its invisible presence is a psychic phenomenon, i.e., one's own spirit, and that this consists not only of uprushes of life but of formal products too. Among the first, the most prominent are the images and shadowy presentations that occupy our inner field of vision; among the second, thinking and reason, which organize the world of images. In this way a tran-

scendent spirit superimposed itself upon the original, natural life-spirit and even swung over to the opposite position, as though the latter were merely naturalistic. The transcendent spirit became the supranatural and transmundane cosmic principle of order and as such was given the name of "God," or at least it became an attribute of the One Substance (as in Spinoza) or one Person of the Godhead (as in Christianity).

391 The corresponding development of spirit in the reverse, hylozoistic direction—*a maiori ad minus*—took place under anti-Christian auspices in materialism. The premise underlying this reaction is the exclusive certainty of the spirit's identity with psychic functions, whose dependence upon brain and metabolism became increasingly clear. One had only to give the One Substance another name and call it "matter" to produce the idea of a spirit which was entirely dependent on nutrition and environment, and whose highest form was the intellect or reason. This meant that the original pneumatic presence had taken up its abode in man's physiology, and a writer like Klages could arraign the spirit as the "adversary of the soul." [4] For it was into this latter concept that the original spontaneity of the spirit withdrew after it had been degraded to a servile attribute of matter. Somewhere or other the *deus ex machina* quality of spirit had to be preserved—if not in the spirit itself, then in its synonym the soul, that glancing, Aeolian [5] thing, elusive as a butterfly (anima, ψυχή).

392 Even though the materialistic conception of the spirit did not prevail everywhere, it still persisted, outside the sphere of religion, in the realm of conscious phenomena. Spirit as "subjective spirit" came to mean a purely endopsychic phenomenon, while "objective spirit" did not mean the universal spirit, or God, but merely the sum total of intellectual and cultural possessions which make up our human institutions and the content of our libraries. Spirit had forfeited its original nature, its autonomy and spontaneity over a very wide area, with the solitary exception of the religious field, where, at least in principle, its pristine character remained unimpaired.

4 Ludwig Klages, *Der Geist als Widersacher der Seele.*

5 *Soul,* from Old German *saiwalô,* may be cognate with αἰόλος, 'quick-moving, changeful of hue, shifting.' It also has the meaning of 'wily' or 'shifty'; hence an air of probability attaches to the alchemical definition of *anima* as Mercurius.

In this résumé we have described an entity which presents itself to us as an immediate psychic phenomenon distinguished from other psychisms whose existence is naïvely believed to be causally dependent upon physical influences. A connection between spirit and physical conditions is not immediately apparent, and for this reason it was credited with immateriality to a much higher degree than was the case with psychic phenomena in the narrower sense. Not only is a certain physical dependence attributed to the latter, but they are themselves thought of as possessing a kind of materiality, as the idea of the subtle body and the Chinese *kuei*-soul clearly show. In view of the intimate connection that exists between certain psychic processes and their physical parallels we cannot very well accept the total immateriality of the psyche. As against this, the *consensus omnium* insists on the immateriality of spirit, though not everyone would agree that it also has a reality of its own. It is, however, not easy to see why our hypothetical "matter," which looks quite different from what it did even thirty years ago, alone should be real, and spirit not. Although the idea of immateriality does not in itself exclude that of reality, popular opinion invariably associates reality with materiality. Spirit and matter may well be forms of one and the same transcendental being. For instance the Tantrists, with as much right, say that matter is nothing other than the concreteness of God's thoughts. The sole immediate reality is the psychic reality of conscious contents, which are as it were labelled with a spiritual or material origin as the case may be.

393 The hallmarks of spirit are, firstly, the principle of spontaneous movement and activity; secondly, the spontaneous capacity to produce images independently of sense perception; and thirdly, the autonomous and sovereign manipulation of these images. This spiritual entity approaches primitive man from outside; but with increasing development it gets lodged in man's consciousness and becomes a subordinate function, thus apparently forfeiting its original character of autonomy. That character is now retained only in the most conservative views, namely in the religions. The descent of spirit into the sphere of human consciousness is expressed in the myth of the divine νοῦς caught in the embrace of φύσις. This process, con-

tinuing over the ages, is probably an unavoidable necessity, and the religions would find themselves in a very forlorn situation if they believed in the attempt to hold up evolution. Their task, if they are well advised, is not to impede the ineluctable march of events, but to guide it in such a way that it can proceed without fatal injury to the soul. The religions should therefore constantly recall to us the origin and original character of the spirit, lest man should forget what he is drawing into himself and with what he is filling his consciousness. He himself did not create the spirit, rather the spirit makes *him* creative, always spurring him on, giving him lucky ideas, staying power, "enthusiasm" and "inspiration." So much, indeed, does it permeate his whole being that he is in gravest danger of thinking that he actually created the spirit and that he "has" it. In reality, however, the primordial phenomenon of the spirit takes possession of *him,* and, while appearing to be the willing object of human intentions, it binds his freedom, just as the physical world does, with a thousand chains and becomes an obsessive *idée-force.* Spirit threatens the naïve-minded man with inflation, of which our own times have given us the most horribly instructive examples. The danger becomes all the greater the more our interest fastens upon external objects and the more we forget that the differentiation of our relation to nature should go hand in hand with a correspondingly differentiated relation to the spirit, so as to establish the necessary balance. If the outer object is not offset by an inner, unbridled materialism results, coupled with maniacal arrogance or else the extinction of the autonomous personality, which is in any case the ideal of the totalitarian mass state.

394 As can readily be seen, the common modern idea of spirit ill accords with the Christian view, which regards it as the *summum bonum,* as God himself. To be sure, there is also the idea of an evil spirit. But the modern idea cannot be equated with that either, since for us spirit is not necessarily evil; we would have to call it morally indifferent or neutral. When the Bible says "God is spirit," it sounds more like the definition of a substance, or like a qualification. But the devil too, it seems, is endowed with the same peculiar spiritual substance, albeit an evil and corrupt one. The original identity of substance is

still expressed in the idea of the fallen angel, as well as in the close connection between Jehovah and Satan in the Old Testament. There may be an echo of this primitive connection in the Lord's Prayer, where we say "Lead us not into temptation"—for is not this really the business of the *tempter,* the devil himself?

395 This brings us to a point we have not considered at all in the course of our observations so far. We have availed ourselves of cultural and everyday conceptions which are the product of human consciousness and its reflections, in order to form a picture of the psychic modes of manifestation of the factor "spirit." But we have yet to consider that because of its original autonomy,[6] about which there can be no doubt in the psychological sense, the spirit is quite capable of staging its own manifestations spontaneously.

II. SELF-REPRESENTATION OF THE SPIRIT IN DREAMS

396 The psychic manifestations of the spirit indicate at once that they are of an archetypal nature—in other words, the phenomenon we call spirit depends on the existence of an autonomous primordial image which is universally present in the preconscious makeup of the human psyche. As usual, I first came up against this problem when investigating the dreams of my patients. It struck me that a certain kind of father-complex has a "spiritual" character, so to speak, in the sense that the father-image gives rise to statements, actions, tendencies, impulses, opinions, etc., to which one could hardly deny the attribute "spiritual." In men, a positive father-complex very often produces a certain credulity with regard to authority and a distinct willingness to bow down before all spiritual dogmas and values; while in women, it induces the liveliest spiritual aspirations and interests. In dreams, it is always the father-figure from whom the decisive convictions, prohibitions, and wise counsels ema-

6 Even if one accepts the view that a self-revelation of spirit—an apparition for instance—is nothing but an hallucination, the fact remains that this is a spontaneous psychic event not subject to our control. At any rate it is an autonomous complex, and that is quite sufficient for our purpose.

nate. The invisibility of this source is frequently emphasized by the fact that it consists simply of an authoritative voice which passes final judgments.[7] Mostly, therefore, it is the figure of a "wise old man" who symbolizes the spiritual factor. Sometimes the part is played by a "real" spirit, namely the ghost of one dead, or, more rarely, by grotesque gnomelike figures or talking animals. The dwarf forms are found, at least in my experience, mainly in women; hence it seems to me logical that in Ernst Barlach's play *Der tote Tag* (1912), the gnomelike figure of Steissbart ("Rumpbeard") is associated with the mother, just as Bes is associated with the mother-goddess at Karnak. In both sexes the spirit can also take the form of a boy or a youth. In women he corresponds to the so-called "positive" animus who indicates the possibility of conscious spiritual effort. In men his meaning is not so simple. He can be positive, in which case he signifies the "higher" personality, the self or *filius regius* as conceived by the alchemists.[8] But he can also be negative, and then he signifies the infantile shadow.[9] In both cases the boy means some form of spirit.[10] Graybeard and boy belong together. The pair of them play a considerable role in alchemy as symbols of Mercurius.

397 It can never be established with one-hundred-per-cent certainty whether the spirit-figures in dreams are morally good. Very often they show all the signs of duplicity, if not of outright malice. I must emphasize, however, that the grand plan on which the unconscious life of the psyche is constructed is so inaccessible to our understanding that we can never know what evil may not be necessary in order to produce good by enantiodromia, and what good may very possibly lead to evil. Sometimes the *probate spiritus* recommended by John cannot, with the best will in the world, be anything other than a cautious and patient waiting to see how things will finally turn out.

398 The figure of the wise old man can appear so plastically, not only in dreams but also in visionary meditation (or what we call

7 Cf. *Psychology and Alchemy*, par. 115.

8 Cf. the vision of the "naked boy" in Meister Eckhart (trans. by Evans, I, p. 438).

9 I would remind the reader of the "boys" in Bruno Goetz's novel *Das Reich ohne Raum*.

10 Cf. the paper on the "Child Archetype" in this volume, pars. 268f.

"active imagination"), that, as is sometimes apparently the case in India, it takes over the role of a guru.[11] The wise old man appears in dreams in the guise of a magician, doctor, priest, teacher, professor, grandfather, or any other person possessing authority. The archetype of spirit in the shape of a man, hobgoblin, or animal always appears in a situation where insight, understanding, good advice, determination, planning, etc., are needed but cannot be mustered on one's own resources. The archetype compensates this state of spiritual deficiency by contents designed to fill the gap. An excellent example of this is the dream about the white and black magicians, which tried to compensate the spiritual difficulties of a young theological student. I did not know the dreamer myself, so the question of my personal influence is ruled out. He dreamed *he was standing in the presence of a sublime hieratic figure called the "white magician," who was nevertheless clothed in a long black robe. This magician had just ended a lengthy discourse with the words "And for that we require the help of the black magician." Then the door suddenly opened and another old man came in, the "black magician," who however was dressed in a white robe. He too looked noble and sublime. The black magician evidently wanted to speak with the white, but hesitated to do so in the presence of the dreamer. At that the white magician, pointing to the dreamer, said, "Speak, he is an innocent." So the black magician began to relate a strange story of how he had found the lost keys of Paradise and did not know how to use them. He had, he said, come to the white magician for an explanation of the secret of the keys. He told him that the king of the country in which he lived was seeking a suitable tomb for himself. His subjects had chanced to dig up an old sarcophagus containing the mortal remains of a virgin. The king opened the sarcophagus, threw away the bones, and had the empty sarcophagus buried again for later use. But no sooner had the bones seen the light of day than the being to whom they once had belonged*

11 Hence the many miraculous stories about rishis and mahatmas. A cultured Indian with whom I once conversed on the subject of gurus told me, when I asked him who his guru had been, that it was Shankaracharya (who lived in the 8th and 9th cents.) "But that's the celebrated commentator," I remarked in amazement. Whereupon he replied, "Yes, so he was; but naturally it was his spirit," not in the least perturbed by my Western bewilderment.

—the virgin—changed into a black horse that galloped off into the desert. The black magician pursued it across the sandy wastes and beyond, and there after many vicissitudes and difficulties he found the lost keys of Paradise. That was the end of his story, and also, unfortunately, of the dream.

399 Here the compensation certainly did not fall out as the dreamer would wish, by handing him a solution on a plate; rather it confronted him with a problem to which I have already alluded, and one which life is always bringing us up against: namely, the uncertainty of all moral valuation, the bewildering interplay of good and evil, and the remorseless concatenation of guilt, suffering, and redemption. This path to the primordial religious experience is the right one, but how many can recognize it? It is like a still small voice, and it sounds from afar. It is ambiguous, questionable, dark, presaging danger and hazardous adventure; a razor-edged path, to be trodden for God's sake only, without assurance and without sanction.

III. THE SPIRIT IN FAIRYTALES

400 I would gladly present the reader with some more modern dream-material, but I fear that the individualism of dreams would make too high a demand upon our exposition and would claim more space than is here at our disposal. We shall therefore turn to folklore, where we need not get involved in the grim confrontations and entanglements of individual case histories and can observe the variations of the spirit motif without having to consider conditions that are more or less unique. In myths and fairytales, as in dreams, the psyche tells its own story, and the interplay of the archetypes is revealed in its natural setting as "formation, transformation / the eternal Mind's eternal recreation."

401 The frequency with which the spirit-type appears as an old man is about the same in fairytales as in dreams.[12] The old man always appears when the hero is in a hopeless and desperate situation from which only profound reflection or a lucky idea —in other words, a spiritual function or an endopsychic autom-

12 I am indebted to Mrs. H. von Roques and Dr. Marie-Louise von Franz for the fairytale material used here.

atism of some kind—can extricate him. But since, for internal and external reasons, the hero cannot accomplish this himself, the knowledge needed to compensate the deficiency comes in the form of a personified thought, i.e., in the shape of this sagacious and helpful old man. An Estonian fairytale,[13] for instance, tells how an ill-treated little orphan boy who had let a cow escape was afraid to return home again for fear of more punishment. So he ran away, chancing to luck. He naturally got himself into a hopeless situation, with no visible way out. Exhausted, he fell into a deep sleep. When he awoke, "it seemed to him that he had something liquid in his mouth, and he saw a little old man with a long grey beard standing before him, who was in the act of replacing the stopper in his little milk-flask. 'Give me some more to drink,' begged the boy. 'You have had enough for today,' replied the old man. 'If my path had not chanced to lead me to you, that would assuredly have been your last sleep, for when I found you, you were half dead.' Then the old man asked the boy who he was and where he wanted to go. The boy recounted everything he could remember happening to him up to the beating he had received the previous evening. 'My dear child,' said the old man, 'you are no better and no worse off than many others whose dear protectors and comforters rest in their coffins under the earth. You can no longer turn back. Now that you have run away, you must seek a new fortune in the world. As I have neither house nor home, nor wife nor child, I cannot take further care of you, but I will give you some good advice for nothing.' "

402 So far the old man has been expressing no more than what the boy, the hero of the tale, could have thought out for himself. Having given way to the stress of emotion and simply run off like that into the blue, he would at least have had to reflect that he needed food. It would also have been necessary, at such a moment, to consider his position. The whole story of his life up to the recent past would then have passed before his mind, as is usual in such cases. An anamnesis of this kind is a purpose-

13 *Finnische und estnische Volksmärchen,* No. 68, p. 208 ["How an Orphan Boy Unexpectedly Found His Luck"]. [All German collections of tales here cited are listed under "Folktales" in the bibliography, q.v. English titles of tales are given in brackets, though no attempt has been made to locate published translations. —EDITORS.]

ful process whose aim is to gather the assets of the whole personality together at the critical moment, when all one's spiritual and physical forces are challenged, and with this united strength to fling open the door of the future. No one can help the boy to do this; he has to rely entirely on himself. There is no going back. This realization will give the necessary resolution to his actions. By forcing him to face the issue, the old man saves him the trouble of making up his mind. Indeed the old man is himself this purposeful reflection and concentration of moral and physical forces that comes about spontaneously in the psychic space outside consciousness when conscious thought is not yet—or is no longer—possible. The concentration and tension of psychic forces have something about them that always looks like magic: they develop an unexpected power of endurance which is often superior to the conscious effort of will. One can observe this experimentally in the artificial concentration induced by hypnosis: in my demonstrations I used regularly to put an hysteric, of weak bodily build, into a deep hypnotic sleep and then get her to lie with the back of her head on one chair and her heels resting on another, stiff as a board, and leave her there for about a minute. Her pulse would gradually go up to 90. A husky young athlete among the students tried in vain to imitate this feat with a conscious effort of will. He collapsed in the middle with his pulse racing at 120.

403 When the clever old man had brought the boy to this point he could begin his good advice, i.e., the situation no longer looked hopeless. He advised him to continue his wanderings, always to the eastward, where after seven years he would reach the great mountain that betokened his good fortune. The bigness and tallness of the mountain are allusions to his adult personality.[14] Concentration of his powers brings assurance and is therefore the best guarantee of success.[15] From now on he will

14 The mountain stands for the goal of the pilgrimage and ascent, hence it often has the psychological meaning of the self. The *I Ching* describes the goal thus: "The king introduces him / To the Western Mountain" (Wilhelm/Baynes trans., 1967, p. 74—Hexagram 17, *Sui,* "Following"). Cf. Honorius of Autun (*Expositio in Cantica canticorum,* col. 389): "The mountains are prophets." Richard of St. Victor says: "Vis videre Christum transfiguratum? Ascende in montem istum, disce cognoscere te ipsum" (Do you wish to see the transfigured Christ? Ascend that mountain and learn to know yourself). (*Benjamin minor,* cols. 53–56.)

15 In this respect we would call attention to the phenomenology of yoga.

lack for nothing. "Take my scrip and my flask," says the old man, "and each day you will find in them all the food and drink you need." At the same time he gave him a burdock leaf that could change into a boat whenever the boy had to cross water.

404 Often the old man in fairytales asks questions like who? why? whence? and whither?[16] for the purpose of inducing self-reflection and mobilizing the moral forces, and more often still he gives the necessary magical talisman,[17] the unexpected and improbable power to succeed, which is one of the peculiarities of the unified personality in good or bad alike. But the intervention of the old man—the spontaneous objectivation of the archetype—would seem to be equally indispensable, since the conscious will by itself is hardly ever capable of uniting the personality to the point where it acquires this extraordinary power to succeed. For that, not only in fairytales but in life generally, the objective intervention of the archetype is needed, which checks the purely affective reactions with a chain of inner confrontations and realizations. These cause the who? where? how? why? to emerge clearly and in this wise bring knowledge of the immediate situation as well as of the goal. The resultant enlightenment and untying of the fatal tangle often has something positively magical about it—an experience not unknown to the psychotherapist.

405 The tendency of the old man to set one thinking also takes the form of urging people to "sleep on it." Thus he says to the girl who is searching for her lost brothers: "Lie down:

16 There are numerous examples of this: *Spanische und Portugiesische Volksmärchen*, pp. 158, 199 ["The White Parrot" and "Queen Rose, or Little Tom"]; *Russische Volksmärchen*, p. 149 ["The Girl with No Hands"]; *Balkanmärchen*, p. 64 ["The Shepherd and the Three Samovilas (Nymphs)"]; *Märchen aus Iran*, pp. 150ff. ["The Secret of the Bath of Windburg"]; *Nordische Volksmärchen*, I, p. 231 ["The Werewolf"].

17 To the girl looking for her brothers he gives a ball of thread that rolls towards them (*Finnische und Estnische Volksmärchen*, p. 260 ["The Contending Brothers"]). The prince who is searching for the kingdom of heaven is given a boat that goes by itself (*Deutsche Märchen seit Grimm*, pp. 381f. ["The Iron Boots"]). Other gifts are a flute that sets everybody dancing (*Balkanmärchen*, p. 173 ["The Twelve Crumbs"]), or the path-finding ball, the staff of invisibility (*Nordische Volksmärchen*, I, p. 97 ["The Princess with Twelve Pairs of Golden Shoes"]), miraculous dogs (ibid., p. 287 ["The Three Dogs"]), or a book of secret wisdom (*Chinesische Volksmärchen*, p. 258 ["Jang Liang"]).

morning is cleverer than evening." [18] He also sees through the gloomy situation of the hero who has got himself into trouble, or at least can give him such information as will help him on his journey. To this end he makes ready use of animals, particularly birds. To the prince who has gone in search of the kingdom of heaven the old hermit says: "I have lived here for three hundred years, but never yet has anybody asked me about the kingdom of heaven. I cannot tell you myself; but up there, on another floor of the house, live all kinds of birds, and they can surely tell you." [19] The old man knows what roads lead to the goal and points them out to the hero.[20] He warns of dangers to come and supplies the means of meeting them effectively. For instance, he tells the boy who has gone to fetch the silver water that the well is guarded by a lion who has the deceptive trick of sleeping with his eyes open and watching with his eyes shut;[21] or he counsels the youth who is riding to a magic fountain in order to fetch the healing draught for the king, only to draw the water at a trot because of the lurking witches who lasso everybody that comes to the fountain.[22] He charges the princess whose lover has been changed into a werewolf to make a fire and put a cauldron of tar over it. Then she must plunge her beloved white lily into the boiling tar, and when the werewolf comes, she must empty the cauldron over its head, which will release her lover from the spell.[23] Occasionally the old man is a very critical old man, as in the Caucasian tale of the youngest prince who wanted to build a flawless church for his father, so as to inherit the kingdom. This he does, and nobody can discover a single flaw, but then an old man comes along and says, "That's a fine church you've built, to be sure! What a pity the main wall is a bit crooked!" The prince has the church pulled down again

18 *Finnische und estnische Volksmärchen,* loc. cit.

19 *Deutsche Märchen seit Grimm,* p. 382 [op. cit.]. In one Balkan tale (*Balkanmärchen,* p. 65 ["The Shepherd and the Three Samovilas"]) the old man is called the "Czar of all the birds." Here the magpie knows all the answers. Cf. the mysterious "master of the dovecot" in Gustav Meyrink's novel *Der weisse Dominikaner.*

20 *Märchen aus Iran,* p. 152 [op. cit.].

21 *Spanische und Portugiesische Märchen,* p. 158 ["The White Parrot"].

22 Ibid., p. 199 ["Queen Rose, or Little Tom"].

23 *Nordische Volksmärchen,* Vol. I, p. 231f. ["The Werewolf"].

and builds a new one, but here too the old man discovers a flaw, and so on for the third time.[24]

406 The old man thus represents knowledge, reflection, insight, wisdom, cleverness, and intuition on the one hand, and on the other, moral qualities such as goodwill and readiness to help, which make his "spiritual" character sufficiently plain. Since the archetype is an autonomous content of the unconscious, the fairytale, which usually concretizes the archetypes, can cause the old man to appear in a dream in much the same way as happens in modern dreams. In a Balkan tale the old man appears to the hard-pressed hero in a dream and gives him good advice about accomplishing the impossible tasks that have been imposed upon him.[25] His relation to the unconscious is clearly expressed in one Russian fairytale, where he is called the "King of the Forest." As the peasant sat down wearily on a tree stump, a little old man crept out: "all wrinkled he was and a green beard hung down to his knees." "Who are you?" asked the peasant. "I am Och, King of the Forest," said the manikin. The peasant hired out his profligate son to him, "and the King of the Forest departed with the young man, and conducted him to that other world under the earth and brought him to a green hut. . . . In the hut everything was green: the walls were green and the benches, Och's wife was green and the children were green . . . and the little water-women who waited on him were as green as rue." Even the food was green. The King of the Forest is here a vegetation or tree numen who reigns in the woods and, through the nixies, also has connections with water, which clearly shows his relation to the unconscious since the latter is frequently expressed through wood and water symbols.

407 There is equally a connection with the unconscious when the old man appears as a dwarf. The fairytale about the princess who was searching for her lover says: "Night came and the darkness, and still the princess sat in the same place and wept. As she sat there lost in thought, she heard a voice greeting her: 'Good evening, pretty maid! Why are you sitting here so lonely and sad?' She sprang up hastily and felt very confused, and that was no wonder. But when she looked round there was only a tiny little old man standing before her, who nodded his head at her

24 *Kaukasische Märchen,* pp. 35f. ["The False and the True Nightingale"].

25 *Balkanmärchen,* p. 217 ["The Lubi (She-Devil) and the Fair of the Earth"].

and looked so kind and simple." In a Swiss fairytale, the peasant's son who wants to bring the king's daughter a basket of apples encounters "es chlis isigs Männdli, das frogt-ne, was er do i dem Chratte häig?" (a little iron man who asked what he had there in the basket). In another passage the "Männdli" has "es isigs Chlaidli a" (iron clothes on). By "isig" presumably "eisern" (iron) is meant, which is more probable than "eisig" (icy). In the latter case it would have to be "es Chlaidli vo Is" (clothes of ice).[26] There are indeed little ice men, and little metal men too; in fact, in a modern dream I have even come across a little black iron man who appeared at a critical juncture, like the one in this fairytale of the country bumpkin who wanted to marry the princess.

408 In a modern series of visions in which the figure of the wise old man occurred several times, he was on one occasion of normal size and appeared at the very bottom of a crater surrounded by high rocky walls; on another occasion he was a tiny figure on the top of a mountain, inside a low, stony enclosure. We find the same motif in Goethe's tale of the dwarf princess who lived in a casket.[27] In this connection we might also mention the Anthroparion, the little leaden man of the Zosimos vision,[28] as well as the metallic men who dwell in the mines, the crafty dactyls of antiquity, the homunculi of the alchemists, and the gnomic throng of hobgoblins, brownies, gremlins, etc. How "real" such conceptions are became clear to me on the occasion of a serious mountaineering accident: after the catastrophe two of the climbers had the collective vision, in broad daylight, of a little hooded man who scrambled out of an inaccessible crevasse in the ice face and passed across the glacier, creating a regular panic in the two beholders. I have often encountered motifs which made me think that the unconscious must be the world of the infinitesimally small. Such an idea could be derived rationalistically from the obscure feeling that in all these visions we are dealing with something endopsychic, the inference being that a thing must be exceedingly small in order to fit

26 This occurs in the tale of the griffin, No. 84 in the volume of children's fairytales collected by the brothers Grimm (1912), II, pp. 84ff. The text swarms with phonetic mistakes. [The English text (trans. by Margaret Hunt, rev. by James Stern, no. 165) has "hoary."—TRANS.]

27 Goethe, "Die neue Melusine."

28 Cf. "The Visions of Zosimos," par. 87 (III, i, 2–3).

inside the head. I am no friend of any such "rational" conjectures, though I would not say that they are all beside the mark. It seems to me more probable that this liking for diminutives on the one hand and for superlatives—giants, etc.—on the other is connected with the queer uncertainty of spatial and temporal relations in the unconscious.[29] Man's sense of proportion, his rational conception of big and small, is distinctly anthropomorphic, and it loses its validity not only in the realm of physical phenomena but also in those parts of the collective unconscious beyond the range of the specifically human. The atman is "smaller than small and bigger than big," he is "the size of a thumb" yet he "encompasses the earth on every side and rules over the ten-finger space." And of the Cabiri Goethe says: "little in length / mighty in strength." In the same way, the archetype of the wise old man is quite tiny, almost imperceptible, and yet it possesses a fateful potency, as anyone can see when he gets down to fundamentals. The archetypes have this peculiarity in common with the atomic world, which is demonstrating before our eyes that the more deeply the investigator penetrates into the universe of microphysics the more devastating are the explosive forces he finds enchained there. That the greatest effects come from the smallest causes has become patently clear not only in physics but in the field of psychological research as well. How often in the critical moments of life everything hangs on what appears to be a mere nothing!

409 In certain primitive fairytales, the illuminating quality of our archetype is expressed by the fact that the old man is identified with the sun. He brings a firebrand with him which he uses for roasting a pumpkin. After he has eaten, he takes the fire away again, which causes mankind to steal it from him.[30] In a North American Indian tale, the old man is a witch-doctor who owns the fire.[31] Spirit too has a fiery aspect, as we know from the language of the Old Testament and from the story of the Pentecostal miracle.

29 In one Siberian fairytale (*Märchen aus Sibirien,* no. 13 ["The Man Turned to Stone"]) the old man is a white shape towering up to heaven.

30 *Indianermärchen aus Südamerika,* p. 285 ["The End of the World and the Theft of Fire"—Bolivian].

31 *Indianermärchen aus Nordamerika,* p. 74 [Tales of Manabos: "The Theft of Fire"].

410 Apart from his cleverness, wisdom, and insight, the old man, as we have already mentioned, is also notable for his moral qualities; what is more, he even tests the moral qualities of others and makes his gifts dependent on this test. There is a particularly instructive example of this in the Estonian fairytale of the stepdaughter and the real daughter. The former is an orphan distinguished for her obedience and good behaviour. The story begins with her distaff falling into a well. She jumps in after it, but does not drown, and comes to a magic country where, continuing her quest, she meets a cow, a ram, and an appletree whose wishes she fulfils. She now comes to a washhouse where a dirty old man is sitting who wants her to wash him. The following dialogue develops: "Pretty maid, pretty maid, wash me, do, it is hard for me to be so dirty!" "What shall I heat the stove with?" "Collect wooden pegs and crows' dung and make a fire with that." But she fetches sticks, and asks, "Where shall I get the bath-water?" "Under the barn there stands a white mare. Get her to piss into the tub!" But she takes clean water, and asks, "Where shall I get a bath-switch?" "Cut off the white mare's tail and make a bath-switch of that!" But she makes one out of birch-twigs, and asks, "Where shall I get soap?" "Take a pumice-stone and scrub me with that!" But she fetches soap from the village and with that she washes the old man.

411 As a reward he gives her a bag full of gold and precious stones. The daughter of the house naturally becomes jealous, throws her distaff into the well, where she finds it again instantly. Nevertheless she goes on and does everything wrong that the stepdaughter had done right, and is rewarded accordingly. The frequency of this motif makes further examples superfluous.

412 The figure of the superior and helpful old man tempts one to connect him somehow or other with God. In the German tale of the soldier and the black princess [32] it is related how the princess, on whom a curse has been laid, creeps out of her iron coffin every night and devours the soldier standing guard over the tomb. One soldier, when his turn came, tried to escape. "That evening he stole away, fled over the fields and mountains,

32 *Deutsche Märchen seit Grimm,* pp. 189ff.

and came to a beautiful meadow. Suddenly a little man stood before him with a long grey beard, but it was none other than the Lord God himself, who could no longer go on looking at all the mischief the devil wrought every night. 'Whither away?' said the little grey man, 'may I come with you?' And because the little old man looked so friendly the soldier told him that he had run away and why he had done so." Good advice follows, as always. In this story the old man is taken for God in the same naïve way that the English alchemist, Sir George Ripley,[33] describes the "old king" as "antiquus dierum"—"the Ancient of Days."

413 Just as all archetypes have a positive, favourable, bright side that points upwards, so also they have one that points downwards, partly negative and unfavourable, partly chthonic, but for the rest merely neutral. To this the spirit archetype is no exception. Even his dwarf form implies a kind of limitation and suggests a naturalistic vegetation-numen sprung from the underworld. In one Balkan tale, the old man is handicapped by the loss of an eye. It has been gouged out by the Vili, a species of winged demon, and the hero is charged with the task of getting them to restore it to him. The old man has therefore lost part of his eyesight—that is, his insight and enlightenment—to the daemonic world of darkness; this handicap is reminiscent of the fate of Osiris, who lost an eye at the sight of a black pig (his wicked brother Set), or again of Wotan, who sacrificed his eye at the spring of Mimir. Characteristically enough, the animal ridden by the old man in our fairytale is a goat, a sign that he himself has a dark side. In a Siberian tale, he appears as a one-legged, one-handed, and one-eyed greybeard who wakens a dead man with an iron staff. In the course of the story the latter, after being brought back to life several times, kills the old man by a mistake, and thus throws away his good fortune. The story is entitled "The One-sided Old Man," and in truth his handicap shows that he consists of one half only. The other half is invisible, but appears in the shape of a murderer who seeks the hero's life. Eventually the hero succeeds in killing his persistent murderer, but in the struggle he also kills the one-sided old man, so that the identity of the two victims is clearly revealed. It is thus possible that the old man is his own opposite, a life-

33 In his "Cantilena" (15 cent.). [Cf. *Mysterium Coniunctionis*, par. 374.].

bringer as well as a death-dealer—"ad utrumque peritus" (skilled in both), as is said of Hermes.[34]

414 In these circumstances, whenever the "simple" and "kindly" old man appears, it is advisable for heuristic and other reasons to scrutinize the context with some care. For instance, in the Estonian tale we first mentioned, about the hired boy who lost the cow, there is a suspicion that the helpful old man who happened to be on the spot so opportunely had surreptitiously made away with the cow beforehand in order to give his protégé an excellent reason for taking to flight. This may very well be, for everyday experience shows that it is quite possible for a superior, though subliminal, foreknowledge of fate to contrive some annoying incident for the sole purpose of bullying our Simple Simon of an ego-consciousness into the way he should go, which for sheer stupidity he would never have found by himself. Had our orphan guessed that it was the old man who had whisked off his cow as if by magic, he would have seemed like a spiteful troll or a devil. And indeed the old man has a wicked aspect too, just as the primitive medicine-man is a healer and helper and also the dreaded concocter of poisons. The very word φάρμακον means 'poison' as well as 'antidote,' and poison can in fact be both.

415 The old man, then, has an ambiguous elfin character—witness the extremely instructive figure of Merlin—seeming, in certain of his forms, to be good incarnate and in others an aspect of evil. Then again, he is the wicked magician who, from sheer egoism, does evil for evil's sake. In a Siberian fairytale, he is an evil spirit "on whose head were two lakes with two ducks swimming in them." He feeds on human flesh. The story relates how the hero and his companions go to a feast in the next village, leaving their dogs at home. These, acting on the principle "when the cat's away the mice do play," also arrange a feast, at the climax of which they all hurl themselves on the stores of meat. The men return home and chase out the dogs, who dash off into the wilderness. "Then the Creator spoke to Ememqut [the hero of the tale]: 'Go and look for the dogs with your wife.' " But he gets caught in a terrible snow-storm and has to seek shelter in the hut of the evil spirit. There now follows the

34 Prudentius, *Contra Symmachum*, I, 94 (trans. by Thomson, I, p. 356). See Hugo Rahner, "Die seelenheilende Blume."

well-known motif of the biter bit. The "Creator" is Ememqut's father, but the father of the Creator is called the "Self-created" because he created himself. Although we are nowhere told that the old man with the two lakes on his head lured the hero and his wife into the hut in order to satisfy his hunger, it may be conjectured that a very peculiar spirit must have got into the dogs to cause them to celebrate a feast like the men and afterwards—contrary to their nature—to run away, so that Ememqut had to go out and look for them; and that the hero was then caught in a snow-storm in order to drive him into the arms of the wicked old man. The fact that the Creator, son of the Self-created, was a party to the advice raises a knotty problem whose solution we had best leave to the Siberian theologians.

416 In a Balkan fairytale the old man gives the childless Czarina a magic apple to eat, from which she becomes pregnant and bears a son, it being stipulated that the old man shall be his godfather. The boy, however, grows up into a horrid little tough who bullies all the children and slaughters the cattle. For ten years he is given no name. Then the old man appears, sticks a knife into his leg, and calls him the "Knife Prince." The boy now wants to set forth on his adventures, which his father, after long hesitation, finally allows him to do. The knife in his leg is of vital importance: if he draws it out himself, he will live; if anybody else does so, he will die. In the end the knife becomes his doom, for an old witch pulls it out when he is asleep. He dies, but is restored to life by the friends he has won.[35] Here the old man is a helper, but also the contriver of a dangerous fate which might just as easily have turned out for the bad. The evil showed itself early and plainly in the boy's villainous character.

417 In another Balkan tale, there is a variant of our motif that is worth mentioning: A king is looking for his sister who has been abducted by a stranger. His wanderings bring him to the hut of an old woman, who warns him against continuing the search. But a tree laden with fruit, ever receding before him, lures him away from the hut. When at last the tree comes to a halt, an old man climbs down from the branches. He regales the king and takes him to a castle, where the sister is living with the old man as his wife. She tells her brother that the old man is a wicked

35 *Balkanmärchen*, pp. 34ff. ["The Deeds of the Czar's Son and His Two Companions"].

spirit who will kill him. And sure enough, three days afterwards, the king vanishes without trace. His younger brother now takes up the search and kills the wicked spirit in the form of a dragon. A handsome young man is thereby released from the spell and forthwith marries the sister. The old man, appearing at first as a tree-numen, is obviously connected with the sister. He is a murderer. In an interpolated episode, he is accused of enchanting a whole city by turning it to iron, i.e., making it immovable, rigid, and locked up.[36] He also holds the king's sister a captive and will not let her return to her relatives. This amounts to saying that the sister is animus-possessed. The old man is therefore to be regarded as her animus. But the manner in which the king is drawn into this possession, and the way he seeks for his sister, make us think that she has an anima significance for her brother. The fateful archetype of the old man has accordingly first taken possession of the king's anima—in other words, robbed him of the archetype of life which the anima personifies—and forced him to go in search of the lost charm, the "treasure hard to attain," thus making him the mythical hero, the higher personality who is an expression of the self. Meanwhile, the old man acts the part of the villain and has to be forcibly removed, only to appear at the end as the husband of the sister-anima, or more properly as the bridegroom of the soul, who celebrates the sacred incest that symbolizes the union of opposites and equals. This bold enantiodromia, a very common occurrence, not only signifies the rejuvenation and transformation of the old man, but hints at a secret inner relation of evil to good and vice versa.

418 So in this story we see the archetype of the old man in the guise of an evil-doer, caught up in all the twists and turns of an individuation process that ends suggestively with the *hieros gamos*. Conversely, in the Russian tale of the Forest King, he starts by being helpful and benevolent, but then refuses to let his hired boy go, so that the main episodes in the story deal with the boy's repeated attempts to escape from the clutches of the magician. Instead of the quest we have flight, which nonetheless appears to win the same reward as adventures valiantly sought, for in the end the hero marries the king's daughter. The

36 Ibid., pp. 177ff. ["The Son-in-Law from Abroad"].

magician, however, must rest content with the role of the biter bit.

IV. THERIOMORPHIC SPIRIT SYMBOLISM IN FAIRYTALES

419 The description of our archetype would not be complete if we omitted to consider one special form of its manifestation, namely its animal form. This belongs essentially to the theriomorphism of gods and demons and has the same psychological significance. The animal form shows that the contents and functions in question are still in the extrahuman sphere, i.e., on a plane beyond human consciousness, and consequently have a share on the one hand in the daemonically superhuman and on the other in the bestially subhuman. It must be remembered, however, that this division is only true within the sphere of consciousness, where it is a necessary condition of thought. Logic says *tertium non datur,* meaning that we cannot envisage the opposites in their oneness. In other words, while the abolition of an obstinate antinomy can be no more than a postulate for us, this is by no means so for the unconscious, whose contents are without exception paradoxical or antinomial by nature, not excluding the category of being. If anyone unacquainted with the psychology of the unconscious wants to get a working knowledge of these matters, I would recommend a study of Christian mysticism and Indian philosophy, where he will find the clearest elaboration of the antinomies of the unconscious.

420 Although the old man has, up to now, looked and behaved more or less like a human being, his magical powers and his spiritual superiority suggest that, in good and bad alike, he is outside, or above, or below the human level. Neither for the primitive nor for the unconscious does his animal aspect imply any devaluation, for in certain respects the animal is superior to man. It has not yet blundered into consciousness nor pitted a self-willed ego against the power from which it lives; on the contrary, it fulfils the will that actuates it in a well-nigh perfect manner. Were it conscious, it would be morally better than man. There is deep doctrine in the legend of the fall: it is the expression of a dim presentiment that the emancipation of ego-consciousness was a Luciferian deed. Man's whole history con-

sists from the very beginning in a conflict between his feeling of inferiority and his arrogance. Wisdom seeks the middle path and pays for this audacity by a dubious affinity with daemon and beast, and so is open to moral misinterpretation.

421 Again and again in fairytales we encounter the motif of helpful animals. These act like humans, speak a human language, and display a sagacity and a knowledge superior to man's. In these circumstances we can say with some justification that the archetype of the spirit is being expressed through an animal form. A German fairytale [37] relates how a young man, while searching for his lost princess, meets a wolf, who says, "Do not be afraid! But tell me, where is your way leading you?" The young man recounts his story, whereupon the wolf gives him as a magic gift a few of his hairs, with which the young man can summon his help at any time. This intermezzo proceeds exactly like the meeting with the helpful old man. In the same story, the archetype also displays its other, wicked side. In order to make this clear I shall give a summary of the story:

422 While the young man is watching his pigs in the wood, he discovers a large tree, whose branches lose themselves in the clouds. "How would it be," says he to himself, "if you were to look at the world from the top of that great tree?" So he climbs up, all day long he climbs, without even reaching the branches. Evening comes, and he has to pass the night in a fork of the tree. Next day he goes on climbing and by noon has reached the foliage. Only towards evening does he come to a village nestling in the branches. The peasants who live there give him food and shelter for the night. In the morning he climbs still further. Towards noon, he reaches a castle in which a young girl lives. Here he finds that the tree goes no higher. She is a king's daughter, held prisoner by a wicked magician. So the young man stays with the princess, and she allows him to go into all the rooms of the castle: one room alone she forbids him to enter. But curiosity is too strong. He unlocks the door, and there in the room he finds a raven fixed to the wall with three nails. One nail goes through his throat, the two others through the wings. The raven complains of thirst and the young man, moved by pity, gives him water to drink. At each sip a nail falls out,

37 *Deutsche Märchen seit Grimm*, pp. 1ff. ["The Princess in the Tree"].

and at the third sip the raven is free and flies out at the window. When the princess hears of it she is very frightened and says, "That was the devil who enchanted me! It won't be long now before he fetches me again." And one fine morning she has indeed vanished.

423 The young man now sets out in search of her and, as we have described above, meets the wolf. In the same way he meets a bear and a lion, who also give him some hairs. In addition the lion informs him that the princess is imprisoned nearby in a hunting-lodge. The young man finds the house and the princess, but is told that flight is impossible, because the hunter possesses a three-legged white horse that knows everything and would infallibly warn its master. Despite that, the young man tries to flee away with her, but in vain. The hunter overtakes him but, because he had saved his life as a raven, lets him go and rides off again with the princess. When the hunter has disappeared into the wood, the young man creeps back to the house and persuades the princess to wheedle from the hunter the secret of how he obtained his clever white horse. This she successfully does in the night, and the young man, who has hidden himself under the bed, learns that about an hour's journey from the hunting-lodge there dwells a witch who breeds magic horses. Whoever was able to guard the foals for three days might choose a horse as a reward. In former times, said the hunter, she used to make a gift of twelve lambs into the bargain, in order to satisfy the hunger of the twelve wolves who lived in the woods near the farmstead, and prevent them from attacking; but to him she gave no lambs. So the wolves followed him as he rode away, and while crossing the borders of her domain they succeeded in tearing off one of his horse's hoofs. That was why it had only three legs.

424 Then the young man made haste to seek out the witch and agreed to serve her on condition that she gave him not only a horse of his own choosing but twelve lambs as well. To this she consented. Instantly she commanded the foals to run away, and, to make him sleepy, she gave him brandy. He drinks, falls asleep, and the foals escape. On the first day he catches them with the help of the wolf, on the second day the bear helps him, and on the third the lion. He can now go and choose his reward. The witch's little daughter tells him which horse her mother rides.

This is naturally the best horse, and it too is white. Hardly has he got it out of the stall when the witch pierces the four hoofs and sucks the marrow out of the bones. From this she bakes a cake and gives it to the young man for his journey. The horse grows deathly weak, but the young man feeds it on the cake, whereupon the horse recovers its former strength. He gets out of the woods unscathed after quieting the twelve wolves with the twelve lambs. He then fetches the princess and rides away with her. But the three-legged horse calls out to the hunter, who sets off in pursuit and quickly catches up with them, because the four-legged horse refuses to gallop. As the hunter approaches, the four-legged horse cries out to the three-legged, "Sister, throw him off!" The magician is thrown and trampled to pieces by the two horses. The young man sets the princess on the three-legged horse, and the pair of them ride away to her father's kingdom, where they get married. The four-legged horse begs him to cut off both their heads, for otherwise they would bring disaster upon him. This he does, and the horses are transformed into a handsome prince and a wonderfully beautiful princess, who after a while repair "to their own kingdom." They had been changed into horses by the hunter, long ago.

425 Apart from the theriomorphic spirit symbolism in this tale, it is especially interesting to note that the function of knowing and intuition is represented by a riding-animal. This is as much as to say that the spirit can be somebody's property. The three-legged white horse is thus the property of the demonic hunter, and the four-legged one the property of the witch. Spirit is here partly a function, which like any other object (horse) can change its owner, and partly an autonomous subject (magician as owner of the horse). By obtaining the four-legged horse from the witch, the young man frees a spirit or a thought of some special kind from the grip of the unconscious. Here as elsewhere, the witch stands for a *mater natura* or the original "matriarchal" state of the unconscious, indicating a psychic constitution in which the unconscious is opposed only by a feeble and still-dependent consciousness. The four-legged horse shows itself superior to the three-legged, since it can command the latter. And since the quaternity is a symbol of wholeness and wholeness plays a considerable role in the picture-world of the uncon-

scious,[38] the victory of four-leggedness over three-leggedness is not altogether unexpected. But what is the meaning of the opposition between threeness and fourness, or rather, what does threeness mean as compared with wholeness? In alchemy this problem is known as the axiom of Maria and runs all through alchemical philosophy for more than a thousand years, finally to be taken up again in the Cabiri scene in *Faust*. The earliest literary version of it is to be found in the opening words of Plato's *Timaeus,*[39] of which Goethe gives us a reminder. Among the alchemists we can see clearly how the divine Trinity has its counterpart in a lower, chthonic triad (similar to Dante's three-headed devil). This represents a principle which, by reason of its symbolism, betrays affinities with evil, though it is by no means certain that it expresses nothing but evil. Everything points rather to the fact that evil, or its familiar symbolism, belongs to the family of figures which describe the dark, nocturnal, lower, chthonic element. In this symbolism the lower stands to the higher as a correspondence [40] in reverse; that is to say it is conceived, like the upper, as a triad. Three, being a masculine number, is logically correlated with the wicked hunter, who can be thought of alchemically as the lower triad. Four, a feminine number, is assigned to the old woman. The two horses are miraculous animals that talk and know and thus represent the unconscious spirit, which in one case is subordinated to the wicked magician and in the other to the old witch.

426 Between the three and the four there exists the primary opposition of male and female, but whereas fourness is a symbol of wholeness, threeness is not. The latter, according to alchemy, denotes polarity, since one triad always presupposes another, just as high presupposes low, lightness darkness, good evil. In terms of energy, polarity means a potential, and wherever a

38 With reference to the quaternity I would call attention to my earlier writings, and in particular to *Psychology and Alchemy* and "Psychology and Religion."

39 The oldest representation I know of this problem is that of the four sons of Horus, three of whom are occasionally depicted with the heads of animals, and the other with the head of a man. Chronologically this links up with Ezekiel's vision of the four creatures, which then reappear in the attributes of the four evangelists. Three have animal heads and one a human head (the angel). [Cf. frontispiece to *Psychology and Religion: West and East*.—EDITORS.]

40 According to the dictum in the "Tabula smaragdina," "Quod est inferius, est sicut quod est superius" (That which is below is like that which is above).

potential exists there is the possibility of a current, a flow of events, for the tension of opposites strives for balance. If one imagines the quaternity as a square divided into two halves by a diagonal, one gets two triangles whose apices point in opposite directions. One could therefore say metaphorically that if the wholeness symbolized by the quaternity is divided into equal halves, it produces two opposing triads. This simple reflection shows how three can be derived from four, and in the same way the hunter of the captured princess explains how his horse, from being four-legged, became three-legged, through having one hoof torn off by the twelve wolves. The three-leggedness is due to an accident, therefore, which occurred at the very moment when the horse was leaving the territory of the dark mother. In psychological language we should say that when the unconscious wholeness becomes manifest, i.e., leaves the unconscious and crosses over into the sphere of consciousness, one of the four remains behind, held fast by the *horror vacui* of the unconscious. There thus arises a triad, which as we know—not from the fairytale but from the history of symbolism—constellates a corresponding triad in opposition to it [41]—in other words, a conflict ensues. Here too we could ask with Socrates, "One, two, three—but, my dear Timaeus, of those who yesterday were the banqueters and today are the banquet-givers, where is the fourth?" [42] He has remained in the realm of the dark mother, caught by the wolfish greed of the unconscious, which is unwilling to let anything escape from its magic circle save at the cost of a sacrifice.

427 The hunter or old magician and the witch correspond to the negative parental imagos in the magic world of the unconscious. The hunter first appears in the story as a black raven. He has stolen away the princess and holds her a prisoner. She describes him as "the devil." But it is exceedingly odd that he himself is locked up in the one forbidden room of the castle and fixed to the wall with three nails, as though *crucified.* He is imprisoned, like all jailers, in his own prison, and bound like all who curse. The prison of both is a magic castle at the top of a gigantic tree, presumably the world-tree. The princess belongs to the upper

41 Cf. *Psychology and Alchemy,* fig. 54 and par. 539; and, for a more detailed account, "The Spirit Mercurius," par. 271.

42 This unexplained passage has been put down to Plato's "drollery."

region of light near the sun. Sitting there in captivity on the world-tree, she is a kind of *anima mundi* who has got herself into the power of darkness. But this catch does not seem to have done the latter much good either, seeing that the captor is crucified and moreover with three nails. The crucifixion evidently betokens a state of agonizing bondage and suspension, fit punishment for one foolhardy enough to venture like a Prometheus into the orbit of the opposing principle. This was what the raven, who is identical with the hunter, did when he ravished a precious soul from the upper world of light; and so, as a punishment, he is nailed to the wall in that upper world. That this is an inverted reflection of the primordial Christian image should be obvious enough. The Saviour who freed the soul of humanity from the dominion of the prince of this world was nailed to a cross down below on earth, just as the thieving raven is nailed to the wall in the celestial branches of the world-tree for his presumptuous meddling. In our fairytale, the peculiar instrument of the magic spell is the triad of nails. Who it was that made the raven captive is not told in the tale, but it sounds as if a spell had been laid upon him in the triune name.[43]

428 Having climbed up the world-tree and penetrated into the magic castle where he is to rescue the princess, our young hero is permitted to enter all the rooms but one, the very room in which the raven is imprisoned. Just as in paradise there was one tree of which it was forbidden to eat, so here there is one room that is not to be opened, with the natural result that it is entered at once. Nothing excites our interest more than a prohibition. It is the surest way of provoking disobedience. Obviously there is some secret scheme afoot to free not so much the princess as the raven. As soon as the hero catches sight of him, the raven begins to cry piteously and to complain of thirst,[44] and the

43 In *Deutsche Märchen seit Grimm* (I, p. 256 ["The Mary-Child"]) it is said that the "Three-in-One" is in the forbidden room, which seems to me worth noting.

44 Aelian (*De natura animalium*, I, 47) relates that Apollo condemned the ravens to perpetual thirst because a raven sent to fetch water dallied too long. In German folklore it is said that the raven has to suffer from thirst in June or August, the reason given being that he alone did not mourn at the death of Christ, and that he failed to return when Noah sent him forth from the ark. (Köhler, *Kleinere Schriften zur Märchenforschung*, p. 3.) For the raven as an allegory of evil, see the exhaustive account by Hugo Rahner, "Earth Spirit and Divine Spirit in Patristic Theology." On the other hand the raven is closely connected with Apollo

young man, moved by the virtue of compassion, slakes it, not with hyssop and gall, but with quickening water, whereupon the three nails fall out and the raven escapes through the open window. Thus the evil spirit regains his freedom, changes into the hunter, steals the princess for the second time, but this time locks her up in his hunting-lodge on earth. The secret scheme is partially unveiled: the princess must be brought down from the upper world to the world of men, which was evidently not possible without the help of the evil spirit and man's disobedience.

429 But since in the human world, too, the hunter of souls is the princess's master, the hero has to intervene anew, to which end, as we have seen, he filches the four-legged horse from the witch and breaks the three-legged spell of the magician. It was the triad that first transfixed the raven, and the triad also represents the power of the evil spirit. These are the two triads that point in opposite directions.

430 Turning now to quite another field, the realm of psychological experience, we know that three of the four functions of consciousness can become differentiated, i.e., conscious, while the other remains connected with the matrix, the unconscious, and is known as the "inferior" function. It is the Achilles heel of even the most heroic consciousness: somewhere the strong man is weak, the clever man foolish, the good man bad, and the reverse is also true. In our fairytale the triad appears as a mutilated quaternity. If only one leg could be added to the other three, it would make a whole. The enigmatic axiom of Maria runs: ". . . from the third comes the one as the fourth" (ἐκ τοῦ τρίτου τὸ ἓν τέταρτον)—which presumably means, when the third produces the fourth it at once produces unity. The lost component which is in the possession of the wolves belonging to the Great Mother is indeed only a quarter, but, together with the three, it makes a whole which does away with division and conflict.

as his sacred animal, and in the Bible too he has a positive significance. See Psalm 147 : 9: "He giveth to the beast his food, and to the young ravens which cry"; Job 38 : 41: "Who provideth for the raven his food? when his young ones cry unto God, they wander for lack of meat." Cf. also Luke 12 : 24. Ravens appear as true "ministering spirits" in I Kings 17 : 6, where they bring Elijah the Tishbite his daily fare.

431 But how is it that a quarter, on the evidence of symbolism, is at the same time a triad? Here the symbolism of our fairytale leaves us in the lurch, and we are obliged to have recourse to the facts of psychology. I have said previously that three functions can become differentiated, and only one remains under the spell of the unconscious. This statement must be defined more closely. It is an empirical fact that only *one* function becomes more or less successfully differentiated, which on that account is known as the superior or main function, and together with extraversion or introversion constitutes the type of conscious attitude. This function has associated with it one or two partially differentiated auxiliary functions which hardly ever attain the same degree of differentiation as the main function, that is, the same degree of applicability by the will. Accordingly they possess a higher degree of spontaneity than the main function, which displays a large measure of reliability and is amenable to our intentions. The fourth, inferior function proves on the other hand to be inaccessible to our will. It appears now as a teasing and distracting imp, now as a *deus ex machina.* But always it comes and goes of its own volition. From this it is clear that even the differentiated functions have only partially freed themselves from the unconscious; for the rest they are still rooted in it and to that extent they operate under its rule. Hence the three "differentiated" functions at the disposal of the ego have three corresponding unconscious components that have not yet broken loose from the unconscious.[45] And just as the three conscious and differentiated parts of these functions are confronted by a fourth, undifferentiated function which acts as a painfully disturbing factor, so also the superior function seems to have its worst enemy in the unconscious. Nor should we omit to mention one final turn of the screw: like the devil who delights in disguising himself as an angel of light, the inferior function secretly and mischievously influences the superior function most of all, just as the latter represses the former most strongly.[46]

432 These unfortunately somewhat abstract formulations are necessary in order to throw some light on the tricky and allusive

[45] Pictured as three princesses, buried neck deep, in *Nordische Volksmärchen,* II, pp. 126ff. ["The Three Princesses in the White Land"].

[46] For the function theory, see *Psychological Types.*

associations in our—save the mark!—"childishly simple" fairytale. The two antithetical triads, the one banning and the other representing the power of evil, tally to a hair's breadth with the functional structure of the conscious and unconscious psyche. Being a spontaneous, naïve, and uncontrived product of the psyche, the fairytale cannot very well express anything except what the psyche actually is. It is not only *our* fairytale that depicts these structural psychic relations, but countless other fairytales do the same.[47]

433 Our fairytale reveals with unusual clarity the essentially antithetical nature of the spirit archetype, while on the other hand it shows the bewildering play of antinomies all aiming at the great goal of higher consciousness. The young swineherd who climbs from the animal level up to the top of the giant world-tree and there, in the upper world of light, discovers his captive anima, the high-born princess, symbolizes the ascent of consciousness, rising from almost bestial regions to a lofty perch with a broad outlook, which is a singularly appropriate image for the enlargement of the conscious horizon.[48] Once the masculine consciousness has attained this height, it comes face to face with its feminine counterpart, the anima.[49] She is a personification of the unconscious. The meeting shows how inept it is to designate the latter as the "subconscious": it is not merely "below" consciousness but also above it, so far above it indeed that the hero has to climb up to it with considerable effort. This "upper" unconscious, however, is far from being a "superconscious" in the sense that anyone who reaches it, like our hero, would stand as high above the "subconscious" as above the earth's surface. On the contrary, he makes the disagreeable discovery that his high and mighty anima, the Princess Soul, is bewitched up there and no freer than a bird in a golden cage.

47 I would like to add, for the layman's benefit, that the theory of the psyche's structure was not derived from fairytales and myths, but is grounded on empirical observations made in the field of medico-psychological research and was corroborated only secondarily through the study of comparative symbology, in spheres very far removed from ordinary medical practice.

48 A typical enantiodromia is played out here: as one cannot go any higher along this road, one must now realize the other side of one's being, and climb down again.

49 The young man asks himself, on catching sight of the tree, "How would it be if you were to look at the world from the top of that great tree?"

He may pat himself on the back for having soared up from the flatlands and from almost bestial stupidity, but his soul is in the power of an evil spirit, a sinister father-imago of subterrene nature in the guise of a raven, the celebrated theriomorphic figure of the devil. What use now is his lofty perch and his wide horizon, when his own dear soul is languishing in prison? Worse, she plays the game of the underworld and ostensibly tries to stop the young man from discovering the secret of her imprisonment, by forbidding him to enter that one room. But secretly she leads him to it by the very fact of her veto. It is as though the unconscious had two hands of which one always does the opposite of the other. The princess wants and does not want to be rescued. But the evil spirit too has got himself into a fix, by all accounts: he wanted to filch a fine soul from the shining upper world—which he could easily do as a winged being—but had not bargained on being shut up there himself. Black spirit though he is, he longs for the light. That is his secret justification, just as his being spellbound is a punishment for his transgression. But so long as the evil spirit is caught in the upper world, the princess cannot get down to earth either, and the hero remains lost in paradise. So now he commits the sin of disobedience and thereby enables the robber to escape, thus causing the abduction of the princess for the second time—a whole chain of calamities. In the result, however, the princess comes down to earth and the devilish raven assumes the human shape of the hunter. The other-worldly anima and the evil principle both descend to the human sphere, that is, they dwindle to human proportions and thus become approachable. The three-legged, all-knowing horse represents the hunter's own power: it corresponds to the unconscious components of the differentiated functions.[50] The hunter himself personifies the inferior function, which also manifests itself in the hero as his inquisitiveness and love of adventure. As the story unfolds, he becomes more and more like the hunter: he too obtains his horse from the witch. But, unlike him, the hunter omitted to

50 The "omniscience" of the unconscious components is naturally an exaggeration. Nevertheless they do have at their disposal—or are influenced by—subliminal perceptions and memories of the unconscious, as well as by its instinctive archetypal contents. It is these that give unconscious activities their unexpectedly accurate information.

obtain the twelve lambs in order to feed the wolves, who then injured his horse. He forgot to pay tribute to the chthonic powers because he was nothing but a robber. Through this omission the hero learns that the unconscious lets its creatures go only at the cost of sacrifice.[51] The number 12 is presumably a time symbol, with the subsidiary meaning of the twelve labours (ἆθλα) [52] that have to be performed for the unconscious before one can get free.[53] The hunter looks like a previous unsuccessful attempt of the hero to gain possession of his soul through robbery and violence. But the conquest of the soul is in reality a work of patience, self-sacrifice, and devotion. By gaining possession of the four-legged horse the hero steps right into the shoes of the hunter and carries off the princess as well. The quaternity in our tale proves to be the greater power, for it integrates into its totality that which it still needed in order to become whole.

434 The archetype of the spirit in this, be it said, by no means primitive fairytale is expressed theriomorphically as a system of three functions which is subordinated to a unity, the evil spirit, in the same way that some unnamed authority has crucified the raven with a triad of three nails. The two supraordinate unities correspond in the first case to the inferior function which is the arch-enemy of the main function, namely to the hunter; and in the second case to the main function, namely to the hero. Hunter and hero are ultimately equated with one another, so that the hunter's function is resolved in the hero. As a matter of fact, the hero lies dormant in the hunter from the very beginning, egging him on, with all the unmoral means at his disposal, to carry out the rape of the soul, and then causing him to play her into the hero's hands against the hunter's will. On the surface a furious conflict rages between them, but down below the one goes about the other's business. The knot is unravelled directly the hero succeeds in capturing the quaternity—or in psychological language, when he assimilates the inferior function

51 The hunter has reckoned without his host, as generally happens. Seldom or never do we think of the price exacted by the spirit's activity.

52 Cf. the Heracles cycle.

53 The alchemists stress the long duration of the work and speak of the "longissima via," "diuturnitas immensae meditationis," etc. The number 12 may be connected with the ecclesiastical year, in which the redemptive work of Christ is fulfilled. The lamb-sacrifice probably comes from this source too.

into the ternary system. That puts an end to the conflict at one blow, and the figure of the hunter melts into thin air. After this victory, the hero sets his princess upon the three-legged steed and together they ride away to her father's kingdom. From now on she rules and personifies the realm of spirit that formerly served the wicked hunter. Thus the anima is and remains the representative of that part of the unconscious which can never be assimilated into a humanly attainable whole.

435 *Postscript.* Only after the completion of my manuscript was my attention drawn by a friend to a Russian variant of our story. It bears the title "Maria Morevna." [54] The hero of the story is no swineherd, but Czarevitch Ivan. There is an interesting explanation of the three helpful animals: they correspond to Ivan's three sisters and their husbands, who are really birds. The three sisters represent an unconscious triad of functions related to both the animal and spiritual realms. The bird-men are a species of angel and emphasize the auxiliary nature of the unconscious functions. In the story they intervene at the critical moment when the hero—unlike his German counterpart—gets into the power of the evil spirit and is killed and dismembered (the typical fate of the God-man!).[55] The evil spirit is an old man who is often shown naked and is called Koschei [56] the Deathless. The corresponding witch is the well-known Baba Yaga. The three helpful animals of the German variant are doubled here, appearing first as the bird-men and then as the lion, the strange bird, and the bees. The princess is Queen Maria Morevna, a redoubtable martial leader—Mary the queen of heaven is lauded in the Russian Orthodox hymnal as "leader of hosts"!—who has chained up the evil spirit with twelve chains in the forbidden room in her castle. When Ivan slakes the old devil's thirst he makes off with the queen. The magic riding animals do not in the end turn into human beings. This Russian story has a distinctly more primitive character.

[54] "Daughter of the sea."—Afanas'ev, *Russian Fairy Tales*, pp. 553ff.

[55] The old man puts the dismembered body into a barrel which he throws into the sea. This is reminiscent of the fate of Osiris (head and phallus).

[56] From *kost*, 'bone,' and *pakost, kapost*, 'disgusting, dirty.'

V. SUPPLEMENT

436 The following remarks lay no claim to general interest, being in the main technical. I wanted at first to delete them from this revised version of my essay, but then I changed my mind and appended them in a supplement. The reader who is not specifically interested in psychology can safely skip this section. For, in what follows, I have dealt with the abstruse-looking problem of the three- and four-leggedness of the magic horses, and presented my reflections in such a way as to demonstrate the method I have employed. This piece of psychological reasoning rests firstly on the irrational data of the material, that is, of the fairytale, myth, or dream, and secondly on the conscious realization of the "latent" rational connections which these data have with one another. That such connections exist at all is something of a hypothesis, like that which asserts that dreams have a meaning. The truth of this assumption is not established *a priori:* its usefulness can only be proved by application. It therefore remains to be seen whether its methodical application to irrational material enables one to interpret the latter in a meaningful way. Its application consists in approaching the material as if it had a coherent inner meaning. For this purpose most of the data require a certain amplification, that is, they need to be clarified, generalized, and approximated to a more or less general concept in accordance with Cardan's rule of interpretation. For instance, the three-leggedness, in order to be recognized for what it is, has first to be separated from the horse and then approximated to its specific principle—the principle of threeness. Likewise, the four-leggedness in the fairytale, when raised to the level of a general concept, enters into relationship with the threeness, and as a result we have the enigma mentioned in the *Timaeus,* the problem of three and four. Triads and tetrads represent archetypal structures that play a significant part in all symbolism and are equally important for the investigation of myths and dreams. By raising the irrational datum (three-leggedness and four-leggedness) to the level of a general concept we elicit the universal meaning of this motif and encourage the inquiring mind to tackle the problem seriously. This task involves a series of reflections and deductions of a

technical nature which I would not wish to withhold from the psychologically interested reader and especially from the professional, the less so as this labour of the intellect represents a typical unravelling of symbols and is indispensable for an adequate understanding of the products of the unconscious. Only in this way can the nexus of unconscious relationships be made to yield their own meaning, in contrast to those deductive interpretations derived from a preconceived theory, e.g., interpretations based on astronomy, meteorology, mythology, and—last but not least—the sexual theory.

437 The three-legged and four-legged horses are in truth a recondite matter worthy of closer examination. The three and the four remind us not only of the dilemma we have already met in the theory of psychological functions, but also of the axiom of Maria Prophetissa, which plays a considerable role in alchemy. It may therefore be rewarding to examine more closely the meaning of the miraculous horses.

438 The first thing that seems to me worthy of note is that the three-legged horse which is assigned to the princess as her mount is a mare, and is moreover herself a bewitched princess. Threeness is unmistakably connected here with femininity, whereas from the dominating religious standpoint of consciousness it is an exclusively masculine affair, quite apart from the fact that 3, as an uneven number, is masculine in the first place. One could therefore translate threeness as "masculinity" outright, this being all the more significant when one remembers the ancient Egyptian triunity of God, Ka-mutef,[57] and Pharaoh.

439 Three-leggedness, as the attribute of some animal, denotes the unconscious masculinity immanent in a female creature. In a real woman it would correspond to the animus who, like the magic horse, represents "spirit." In the case of the anima, however, threeness does not coincide with any Christian idea of the Trinity but with the "lower triangle," the inferior function triad that constitutes the "shadow." The inferior half of the personality is for the greater part unconscious. It does not denote the whole of the unconscious, but only the personal segment of it. The anima, on the other hand, so far as she is distinguished from the shadow, personifies the collective un-

[57] Ka-mutef means "bull of his mother." See Jacobsohn, "Die dogmatische Stellung des Königs in der Theologie der alten Aegypter," pp. 17, 35, 41ff.

conscious. If threeness is assigned to her as a riding-animal, it means that she "rides" the shadow, is related to it as the *mar*.[58] In that case she possesses the shadow. But if she herself is the horse, then she has lost her dominating position as a personification of the collective unconscious and is "ridden"—possessed—by Princess A, spouse of the hero. As the fairytale rightly says, she has been changed by witchcraft into the three-legged horse (Princess B).

We can sort out this imbroglio more or less as follows:

440 1. Princess A is the anima[59] of the hero. She rides—that is, possesses—the three-legged horse, who is the shadow, the inferior function-triad of her later spouse. To put it more simply: she has taken possession of the inferior half of the hero's personality. She has caught him on his weak side, as so often happens in ordinary life, for where one is weak one needs support and completion. In fact, a woman's place is on the weak side of a man. This is how we would have to formulate the situation if we regarded the hero and Princess A as two ordinary people. But since it is a fairy-story played out mainly in the world of magic, we are probably more correct in interpreting Princess A as the hero's anima. In that case the hero has been wafted out of the profane world through his encounter with the anima, like Merlin by his fairy: as an ordinary man he is like one caught in a marvellous dream, viewing the world through a veil of mist.

441 2. The matter is now considerably complicated by the unexpected fact that the three-legged horse is a mare, an equivalent of Princess A. She (the mare) is Princess B, who in the shape of a horse corresponds to Princess A's shadow (i.e., her inferior function-triad). Princess B, however, differs from Princess A in that, unlike her, she does not ride the horse but is contained in it: she is bewitched and has thus come under the spell of a masculine triad. Therefore, she is possessed by a shadow.

442 3. The question now is, *whose* shadow? It cannot be the shadow of the hero, for this is already taken up by the latter's

[58] Cf. *Symbols of Transformation*, pars. 370ff., 421.

[59] The fact that she is no ordinary girl, but is of royal descent and moreover the *electa* of the evil spirit, proves her nonhuman, mythological nature. I must assume that the reader is acquainted with the idea of the anima.

anima. The fairytale gives us the answer: it is the hunter or magician who has bewitched her. As we have seen, the hunter is somehow connected with the hero, since the latter gradually puts himself in his shoes. Hence one could easily arrive at the conjecture that the hunter is at bottom none other than the shadow of the hero. But this supposition is contradicted by the fact that the hunter stands for a formidable power which extends not only to the hero's anima but much further, namely to the royal brother-sister pair of whose existence the hero and his anima have no notion, and who appear very much out of the blue in the story itself. The power that extends beyond the orbit of the individual has a more than individual character and cannot therefore be identified with the shadow, if we conceive and define this as the dark half of the personality. As a supra-individual factor the numen of the hunter is a dominant of the collective unconscious, and its characteristic features—hunter, magician, raven, miraculous horse, crucifixion or suspension high up in the boughs of the world-tree [60]—touch the Germanic psyche very closely. Hence the Christian *Weltanschauung,* when reflected in the ocean of the (Germanic) unconscious, logically takes on the features of Wotan.[61] In the figure of the hunter we meet an *imago dei,* a God-image, for Wotan is also a god of winds and spirits, on which account the Romans fittingly interpreted him as Mercury.

443 4. The Prince and his sister, Princess B, have therefore been seized by a pagan god and changed into horses, i.e., thrust down to the animal level, into the realm of the unconscious. The inference is that in their proper human shape the pair of them

60 "I ween that I hung / on the windy tree,
Hung there for nights full nine;
With the spear I was wounded, / and offered I was
To Othin, myself to myself,
On the tree that none / may ever know
What root beneath it runs."
—*Hovamol,* 139 (trans. by H. A. Bellows, p. 60).

61 Cf. the experience of God as described by Nietzsche in "Ariadne's Lament":
"I am but thy quarry,
Cruellest of hunters!
Thy proudest captive,
Thou brigand back of the clouds!"
—*Gedichte und Sprüche,* pp. 155ff.

once belonged to the sphere of collective consciousness. But who are they?

444 In order to answer this question we must proceed from the fact that these two are an undoubted counterpart of the hero and Princess A. They are connected with the latter also because they serve as their mounts, and in consequence they appear as their lower, animal halves. Because of its almost total unconsciousness, the animal has always symbolized the psychic sphere in man which lies hidden in the darkness of the body's instinctual life. The hero rides the stallion, characterized by the even (feminine) number 4; Princess A rides the mare who has only three legs (3 = a masculine number). These numbers make it clear that the transformation into animals has brought with it a modification of sex character: the stallion has a feminine attribute, the mare a masculine one. Psychology can confirm this development as follows: to the degree that a man is overpowered by the (collective) unconscious there is not only a more unbridled intrusion of the instinctual sphere, but a certain feminine character also makes its appearance, which I have suggested should be called "anima." If, on the other hand, a woman comes under the domination of the unconscious, the darker side of her feminine nature emerges all the more strongly, coupled with markedly masculine traits. These latter are comprised under the term "animus." [62]

445 5. According to the fairytale, however, the animal form of the brother-sister pair is "unreal" and due simply to the magic influence of the pagan hunter-god. If they were nothing but animals, we could rest content with this interpretation. But that would be to pass over in unmerited silence the singular allusion to a modification of sex character. The white horses are no ordinary horses: they are miraculous beasts with supernatural powers. Therefore the human figures out of which the horses were magically conjured must likewise have had something supernatural about them. The fairytale makes no comment here, but if our assumption is correct that the two animal forms correspond to the subhuman components of hero and princess, then it follows that the human forms—Prince and Princess B—must correspond to their superhuman components. The

62 Cf. Emma Jung, "On the Nature of the Animus."

superhuman quality of the original swineherd is shown by the fact that he becomes a hero, practically a half-god, since he does not stay with his swine but climbs the world-tree, where he is very nearly made its prisoner, like Wotan. Similarly, he could not have become like the hunter if he did not have a certain resemblance to him in the first place. In the same way the imprisonment of Princess A on the top of the world-tree proves her electness, and in so far as she shares the hunter's bed, as stated by the tale, she is actually the bride of God.

446 It is these extraordinary forces of heroism and election, bordering on the superhuman, which involve two quite ordinary humans in a superhuman fate. Accordingly, in the profane world a swineherd becomes a king, and a princess gets an agreeable husband. But since, for fairytales, there is not only a profane but also a magical world, human fate does not have the final word. The fairytale therefore does not omit to point out what happens in the world of magic. There too a prince and princess have got into the power of the evil spirit, who is himself in a tight corner from which he cannot extricate himself without extraneous help. So the human fate that befalls the swineherd and Princess A is paralleled in the world of magic. But in so far as the hunter is a pagan God-image and thus exalted above the world of heroes and paramours of the gods, the parallelism goes beyond the merely magical into a divine and spiritual sphere, where the evil spirit, the Devil himself—or at least *a* devil—is bound by the spell of an equally mighty or even mightier counter-principle indicated by the three nails. This supreme tension of opposites, the mainspring of the whole drama, is obviously the conflict between the upper and lower triads, or, to put it in theological terms, between the Christian God and the devil who has assumed the features of Wotan.[63]

447 6. We must, it seems, start from this highest level if we want to understand the story correctly, for the drama takes its rise from the initial transgression of the evil spirit. The immediate consequence of this is his crucifixion. In that distressing situation he needs outside help, and as it is not forthcoming from above, it can only be summoned from below. A young swine-

[63] As regards the triadic nature of Wotan cf. Ninck, *Wodan und germanischer Schicksalsglaube,* p. 142. His horse is also described as, among other things, three-legged.

herd, possessed with the boyish spirit of adventure, is reckless and inquisitive enough to climb the world-tree. Had he fallen and broken his neck, no doubt everybody would have said, "What evil spirit could have given him the crazy idea of climbing up an enormous tree like that!" Nor would they have been altogether wrong, for that is precisely what the evil spirit was after. The capture of Princess A was a transgression in the profane world, and the bewitching of the—as we may suppose—semidivine brother-sister pair was just such an enormity in the magical world. We do not know, but it is possible, that this heinous crime was committed before the bewitching of Princess A. At any rate, both episodes point to a transgression of the evil spirit in the magical world as well as in the profane.

448 It is assuredly not without a deeper meaning that the rescuer or redeemer should be a swineherd, like the Prodigal Son. He is of lowly origin and has this much in common with the curious conception of the redeemer in alchemy. His first liberating act is to deliver the evil spirit from the divine punishment meted out to him. It is from this act, representing the first stage of the lysis, that the whole dramatic tangle develops.

449 7. The moral of this story is in truth exceedingly odd. The finale satisfies in so far as the swineherd and Princess A are married and become the royal pair. Prince and Princess B likewise celebrate their wedding, but this—in accordance with the archaic prerogative of kings—takes the form of incest, which, though somewhat repellent, must be regarded as more or less habitual in semidivine circles.[64] But what, we may ask, happens to the evil spirit, whose rescue from condign punishment sets the whole thing in motion? The wicked hunter is trampled to pieces by the horses, which presumably does no lasting damage to a spirit. Apparently he vanishes without trace, but only apparently, for he does after all leave a trace behind him, namely a hard-won happiness in both the profane and the magical world. Two halves of the quaternity, represented on one side by the swineherd and Princess A and on the other by

64 The assumption that they are a brother-sister pair is supported by the fact that the stallion addresses the mare as "sister." This may be just a figure of speech; on the other hand sister means sister, whether we take it figuratively or non-figuratively. Moreover, incest plays a significant part in mythology as well as in alchemy.

Prince and Princess B, have each come together and united: two marriage-pairs now confront one another, parallel but otherwise divided, inasmuch as the one pair belongs to the profane and the other to the magical world. But in spite of this indubitable division, secret psychological connections, as we have seen, exist between them which allow us to derive the one pair from the other.

450 Speaking in the spirit of the fairytale, which unfolds its drama from the highest point, one would have to say that the world of half-gods is anterior to the profane world and produces it out of itself, just as the world of half-gods must be thought of as proceeding from the world of gods. Conceived in this way, the swineherd and Princess A are nothing less than earthly simulacra of Prince and Princess B, who in their turn would be the descendants of divine prototypes. Nor should we forget that the horse-breeding witch belongs to the hunter as his female counterpart, rather like an ancient Epona (the Celtic goddess of horses). Unfortunately we are not told how the magical conjuration into horses happened. But it is evident that the witch had a hand in the game because both the horses were raised from her stock and are thus, in a sense, her productions. Hunter and witch form a pair—the reflection, in the nocturnal-chthonic part of the magical world, of a divine parental pair. The latter is easily recognized in the central Christian idea of *sponsus et sponsa,* Christ and his bride, the Church.

451 If we wanted to explain the fairytale personalistically, the attempt would founder on the fact that archetypes are not whimsical inventions but autonomous elements of the unconscious psyche which were there before any invention was thought of. They represent the unalterable structure of a psychic world whose "reality" is attested by the determining effects it has upon the conscious mind. Thus, it is a significant psychic reality that the human pair [65] is matched by another pair in the unconscious, the latter pair being only in appearance a reflection of the first. In reality the royal pair invariably comes first, as an *a priori,* so that the human pair has far more the significance of an individual concretization, in space and time, of

65 Human in so far as the anima is replaced by a human person.

an eternal and primordial image—at least in its mental structure, which is imprinted upon the biological continuum.

452 We could say, then, that the swineherd stands for the "animal" man who has a soul-mate somewhere in the upper world. By her royal birth she betrays her connection with the pre-existent, semidivine pair. Looked at from this angle, the latter stands for everything a man can become if only he climbs high enough up the world-tree.[66] For to the degree that the young swineherd gains possession of the patrician, feminine half of himself, he approximates to the pair of half-gods and lifts himself into the sphere of royalty, which means universal validity. We come across the same theme in Christian Rosencreutz's *Chymical Wedding,* where the king's son must first free his bride from the power of a Moor, to whom she has voluntarily given herself as a concubine. The Moor represents the alchemical *nigredo* in which the arcane substance lies hidden, an idea that forms yet another parallel to our mythologem, or, as we would say in psychological language, another variant of this archetype.

453 As in alchemy, our fairytale describes the unconscious processes that compensate the conscious, Christian situation. It depicts the workings of a spirit who carries our Christian thinking beyond the boundaries set by ecclesiastical concepts, seeking an answer to questions which neither the Middle Ages nor the present day have been able to solve. It is not difficult to see in the image of the second royal pair a correspondence to the ecclesiastical conception of bridegroom and bride, and in that of the hunter and witch a distortion of it, veering towards an atavistic, unconscious Wotanism. The fact that it is a *German* fairytale makes the position particularly interesting, since this same Wotanism was the psychological godfather of National Socialism, a phenomenon which carried the distortion to the lowest pitch before the eyes of the world.[67] On the other hand, the fairytale makes it clear that it is possible for a man to attain totality, to become whole, only with the co-operation of the spirit of darkness, indeed that the latter is actually a *causa*

66 The great tree corresponds to the *arbor philosophica* of the alchemists. The meeting between an earthly human being and the anima, swimming down in the shape of a mermaid, is to be found in the so-called "Ripley Scrowle." Cf. *Psychology and Alchemy,* fig. 257.

67 Cf. my "Wotan."

instrumentalis of redemption and individuation. In utter perversion of this goal of spiritual development, to which all nature aspires and which is also prefigured in Christian doctrine, National Socialism destroyed man's moral autonomy and set up the nonsensical totalitarianism of the State. The fairytale tells us how to proceed if we want to overcome the power of darkness: we must turn his own weapons against him, which naturally cannot be done if the magical underworld of the hunter remains unconscious, and if the best men in the nation would rather preach dogmatisms and platitudes than take the human psyche seriously.

VI. CONCLUSION

454 When we consider the spirit in its archetypal form as it appears to us in fairytales and dreams, it presents a picture that differs strangely from the conscious idea of spirit, which is split up into so many meanings. Spirit was originally a spirit in human or animal form, a *daimonion* that came upon man from without. But our material already shows traces of an expansion of consciousness which has gradually begun to occupy that originally unconscious territory and to transform those *daimonia,* at least partially, into voluntary acts. Man conquers not only nature, but spirit also, without realizing what he is doing. To the man of enlightened intellect it seems like the correction of a fallacy when he recognizes that what he took to be spirits is simply the human spirit and ultimately his own spirit. All the superhuman things, whether good or bad, that former ages predicated of the *daimonia,* are reduced to "reasonable" proportions as though they were pure exaggeration, and everything seems to be in the best possible order. But were the unanimous convictions of the past really and truly only exaggerations? If they were not, then the integration of the spirit means nothing less than its demonization, since the superhuman spiritual agencies that were formerly tied up in nature are introjected into human nature, thus endowing it with a power which extends the bounds of the personality *ad infinitum,* in the most perilous way. I put it to the enlightened rationalist: has his rational

reduction led to the beneficial control of matter and spirit? He will point proudly to the advances in physics and medicine, to the freeing of the mind from medieval stupidity and—as a well-meaning Christian—to our deliverance from the fear of demons. But we continue to ask: what have all our other cultural achievements led to? The fearful answer is there before our eyes: man has been delivered from no fear, a hideous nightmare lies upon the world. So far reason has failed lamentably, and the very thing that everybody wanted to avoid rolls on in ghastly progression. Man has achieved a wealth of useful gadgets, but, to offset that, he has torn open the abyss, and what will become of him now—where can he make a halt? After the last World War we hoped for reason: we go on hoping. But already we are fascinated by the possibilities of atomic fission and promise ourselves a Golden Age—the surest guarantee that the abomination of desolation will grow to limitless dimensions. And who or what is it that causes all this? It is none other than that harmless (!), ingenious, inventive, and sweetly reasonable human spirit who unfortunately is abysmally unconscious of the demonism that still clings to him. Worse, this spirit does everything to avoid looking himself in the face, and we all help him like mad. Only, heaven preserve us from psychology—*that* depravity might lead to self-knowledge! Rather let us have wars, for which somebody else is always to blame, nobody seeing that all the world is driven to do just what all the world flees from in terror.

455 It seems to me, frankly, that former ages did not exaggerate, that the spirit has not sloughed off its demonisms, and that mankind, because of its scientific and technological development, has in increasing measure delivered itself over to the danger of possession. True, the archetype of the spirit is capable of working for good as well as for evil, but it depends upon man's free—i.e., conscious—decision whether the good also will be perverted into something satanic. Man's worst sin is unconsciousness, but it is indulged in with the greatest piety even by those who should serve mankind as teachers and examples. When shall we stop taking man for granted in this barbarous manner and in all seriousness seek ways and means to exorcize him, to rescue him from possession and unconsciousness, and

make this the most vital task of civilization? Can we not understand that all the outward tinkerings and improvements do not touch man's inner nature, and that everything ultimately depends upon whether the man who wields the science and the technics is capable of responsibility or not? Christianity has shown us the way, but, as the facts bear witness, it has not penetrated deeply enough below the surface. What depths of despair are still needed to open the eyes of the world's responsible leaders, so that at least they can refrain from leading themselves into temptation?

ON THE PSYCHOLOGY OF THE TRICKSTER-FIGURE [1]

456 It is no light task for me to write about the figure of the trickster in American Indian mythology within the confined space of a commentary. When I first came across Adolf Bandelier's classic on this subject, *The Delight Makers,* many years ago, I was struck by the European analogy of the carnival in the medieval Church, with its reversal of the hierarchic order, which is still continued in the carnivals held by student societies today. Something of this contradictoriness also inheres in the medieval description of the devil as *simia dei* (the ape of God), and in his characterization in folklore as the "simpleton" who is "fooled" or "cheated." A curious combination of typical trickster motifs can be found in the alchemical figure of Mercurius; for instance, his fondness for sly jokes and malicious pranks, his powers as a shape-shifter, his dual nature, half animal, half divine, his exposure to all kinds of tortures, and—last but not least—his approximation to the figure of a saviour. These qualities make Mercurius seem like a daemonic being resurrected from primitive times, older even than the Greek Hermes. His rogueries relate him in some measure to various figures met with in folklore and universally known in fairytales: Tom Thumb, Stupid Hans, or the buffoon-like Hanswurst, who is an altogether negative hero and yet manages to achieve through his stupidity what others fail to accomplish with their best efforts. In Grimm's fairytale, the "Spirit Mercurius" lets himself be outwitted by a peasant lad, and then has to buy his freedom with the precious gift of healing.

1 [Originally published as part 5 of *Der göttliche Schelm,* by Paul Radin, with commentaries by C. G. Jung and Karl Kerényi (Zurich, 1954). The present translation then appeared in the English version of the volume: *The Trickster: A Study in American Indian Mythology* (London and New York, 1956); it is republished here with only minor revisions.—EDITORS.]

457 Since all mythical figures correspond to inner psychic experiences and originally sprang from them, it is not surprising to find certain phenomena in the field of parapsychology which remind us of the trickster. These are the phenomena connected with poltergeists, and they occur at all times and places in the ambience of pre-adolescent children. The malicious tricks played by the poltergeist are as well known as the low level of his intelligence and the fatuity of his "communications." Ability to change his shape seems also to be one of his characteristics, as there are not a few reports of his appearance in animal form. Since he has on occasion described himself as a soul in hell, the motif of subjective suffering would seem not to be lacking either. His universality is co-extensive, so to speak, with that of shamanism, to which, as we know, the whole phenomenology of spiritualism belongs. There is something of the trickster in the character of the shaman and medicine-man, for he, too, often plays malicious jokes on people, only to fall victim in his turn to the vengeance of those whom he has injured. For this reason, his profession sometimes puts him in peril of his life. Besides that, the shamanistic techniques in themselves often cause the medicine-man a good deal of discomfort, if not actual pain. At all events the "making of a medicine-man" involves, in many parts of the world, so much agony of body and soul that permanent psychic injuries may result. His "approximation to the saviour" is an obvious consequence of this, in confirmation of the mythological truth that the wounded wounder is the agent of healing, and that the sufferer takes away suffering.

458 These mythological features extend even to the highest regions of man's spiritual development. If we consider, for example, the daemonic features exhibited by Yahweh in the Old Testament, we shall find in them not a few reminders of the unpredictable behaviour of the trickster, of his senseless orgies of destruction and his self-imposed sufferings, together with the same gradual development into a saviour and his simultaneous humanization. It is just this transformation of the meaningless into the meaningful that reveals the trickster's compensatory relation to the "saint." In the early Middle Ages, this led to some strange ecclesiastical customs based on memories of the ancient saturnalia. Mostly they were celebrated on the days immediately following the birth of Christ—that is, in

the New Year—with singing and dancing. The dances were the originally harmless *tripudia* of the priests, lower clergy, children, and subdeacons and took place in church. An *episcopus puerorum* (children's bishop) was elected on Innocents' Day and dressed in pontifical robes. Amid uproarious rejoicings he paid an official visit to the palace of the archbishop and bestowed the episcopal blessing from one of the windows. The same thing happened at the *tripudium hypodiaconorum,* and at the dances for other priestly grades. By the end of the twelfth century, the subdeacons' dance had degenerated into a real *festum stultorum* (fools' feast). A report from the year 1198 says that at the Feast of the Circumcision in Notre Dame, Paris, "so many abominations and shameful deeds" were committed that the holy place was desecrated "not only by smutty jokes, but even by the shedding of blood." In vain did Pope Innocent III inveigh against the "jests and madness that make the clergy a mockery," and the "shameless frenzy of their play-acting." Two hundred and fifty years later (March 12, 1444), a letter from the Theological Faculty of Paris to all the French bishops was still fulminating against these festivals, at which "even the priests and clerics elected an archbishop or a bishop or pope, and named him the Fools' Pope" (*fatuorum papam*). "In the very midst of divine service masqueraders with grotesque faces, disguised as women, lions, and mummers, performed their dances, sang indecent songs in the choir, ate their greasy food from a corner of the altar near the priest celebrating mass, got out their games of dice, burned a stinking incense made of old shoe leather, and ran and hopped about all over the church." [2]

459 It is not surprising that this veritable witches' sabbath was uncommonly popular, and that it required considerable time and effort to free the Church from this pagan heritage.[3]

2 Du Cange, *Glossarium,* s.v. Kalendae, p. 1666. Here there is a note to the effect that the French title "sou-diacres" means literally 'saturi diaconi' or 'diacres saouls' (drunken deacons).

3 These customs seem to be directly modelled on the pagan feast known as "Cervula" or "Cervulus." It took place on the kalends of January and was a kind of New Year's festival, at which people exchanged *strenae* (étrennes, 'gifts'), dressed up as animals or old women, and danced through the streets singing, to the applause of the populace. According to Du Cange (s.v. cervulus), sacrilegious songs were sung. This happened even in the immediate vicinity of St. Peter's in Rome.

460 In certain localities even the priests seem to have adhered to the "libertas decembrica," as the Fools' Holiday was called, in spite (or perhaps because?) of the fact that the older level of consciousness could let itself rip on this happy occasion with all the wildness, wantonness, and irresponsibility of paganism.[4] These ceremonies, which still reveal the spirit of the trickster in his original form, seem to have died out by the beginning of the sixteenth century. At any rate, the various conciliar decrees issued from 1581 to 1585 forbade only the *festum puerorum* and the election of an *episcopus puerorum.*

461 Finally, we must also mention in this connection the *festum asinorum,* which, so far as I know, was celebrated mainly in France. Although considered a harmless festival in memory of Mary's flight into Egypt, it was celebrated in a somewhat curious manner which might easily have given rise to misunderstandings. In Beauvais, the ass procession went right into the church.[5] At the conclusion of each part (Introit, Kyrie, Gloria, etc.) of the high mass that followed, the whole congregation *brayed,* that is, they all went "Y-a" like a donkey ("hac modulatione hinham concludebantur"). A codex dating apparently from the eleventh century says: "At the end of the mass, instead of the words 'Ite missa est,' the priest shall bray three times (*ter hinhamabit*), and instead of the words 'Deo gratias,' the congregation shall answer 'Y-a' (*hinham*) three times."

462 Du Cange cites a hymn from this festival:

Orientis partibus
Adventavit Asinus
Pulcher et fortissimus
Sarcinis aptissimus.

Each verse was followed by the French refrain:

4 Part of the *festum fatuorum* in many places was the still unexplained ballgame played by the priests and captained by the bishop or archbishop, "ut etiam sese ad lusum pilae demittent" (that they also may indulge in the game of pelota). *Pila* or *pelota* is the ball which the players throw to one another. See Du Cange, s.v. Kalendae and pelota.

5 "Puella, quae cum asino a parte Evangelii prope altare collocabatur" (the girl who stationed herself with the ass at the side of the altar where the gospel is read). Du Cange, s.v. festum asinorum.

Hez, Sire Asnes, car chantez
Belle bouche rechignez
Vous aurez du foin assez
Et de l'avoine à plantez.

The hymn had nine verses, the last of which was:

Amen, dicas, Asine (*hic genuflectebatur*)
Jam satur de gramine.
Amen, amen, itera
Aspernare vetera.[6]

463 Du Cange says that the more ridiculous this rite seemed, the greater the enthusiasm with which it was celebrated. In other places the ass was decked with a golden canopy whose corners were held "by distinguished canons"; the others present had to "don suitably festive garments, as at Christmas." Since there were certain tendencies to bring the ass into symbolic relationship with Christ, and since, from ancient times, the god of the Jews was vulgarly conceived to be an ass—a prejudice which extended to Christ himself,[7] as is shown by the mock crucifixion scratched on the wall of the Imperial Cadet School on the Palatine [8]—the danger of theriomorphism lay uncomfortably close. Even the bishops could do nothing to stamp out this custom, until finally it had to be suppressed by the "auctoritas supremi Senatus." The suspicion of blasphemy becomes quite

[6] *Caetera* instead of *vetera*? [Trans. by A. S. B. Glover:

From the furthest Eastern clime
Came the Ass in olden time,
Comely, sturdy for the road,
Fit to bear a heavy load.

Sing then loudly, master Ass,
Let the tempting titbit pass:
You shall have no lack of hay
And of oats find good supply.

Say Amen, Amen, good ass, (*here a genuflection is made*)
Now you've had your fill of grass;
Ancient paths are left behind:
Sing Amen with gladsome mind.]

[7] Cf. also Tertullian, *Apologeticus adversus gentes*, XVI.

[8] [Reproduced in *Symbols of Transformation*, pl. XLIII.—EDITORS.]

open in Nietzsche's "Ass Festival," which is a deliberately blasphemous parody of the mass.[9]

464 These medieval customs demonstrate the role of the trickster to perfection, and, when they vanished from the precincts of the Church, they appeared again on the profane level of Italian theatricals, as those comic types who, often adorned with enormous ithyphallic emblems, entertained the far from prudish public with ribaldries in true Rabelaisian style. Callot's engravings have preserved these classical figures for posterity—the Pulcinellas, Cucorognas, Chico Sgarras, and the like.[10]

465 In picaresque tales, in carnivals and revels, in magic rites of healing, in man's religious fears and exaltations, this phantom of the trickster haunts the mythology of all ages, sometimes in quite unmistakable form, sometimes in strangely modulated guise.[11] He is obviously a "psychologem," an archetypal psychic structure of extreme antiquity. In his clearest manifestations he is a faithful reflection of an absolutely undifferentiated human consciousness, corresponding to a psyche that has hardly left the animal level. That this is how the trickster figure originated can hardly be contested if we look at it from the causal and historical angle. In psychology as in biology we cannot afford to overlook or underestimate this question of origins, although the answer usually tells us nothing about the functional meaning. For this reason biology should never forget the question of purpose, for only by answering that can we get at the meaning of a phenomenon. Even in pathology, where we are concerned with lesions which have no meaning in themselves, the exclusively causal approach proves to be inadequate, since there are a number of pathological phenomena which only give up their meaning when we inquire into their purpose. And where we are concerned with the normal phenomena of life, this question of purpose takes undisputed precedence.

9 *Thus Spake Zarathustra*, Part. IV, ch. LXXVIII.

10 I am thinking here of the series called "Balli di Sfessania." The name is probably a reference to the Etrurian town of Fescennia, which was famous for its lewd songs. Hence "Fescennina licentia" in Horace, Fescenninus being the equivalent of φαλλικός.

11 Cf. the article "Daily Paper Pantheon," by A. McGlashan, in *The Lancet* (1953), p. 238, pointing out that the figures in comic-strips have remarkable archetypal analogies.

466 When, therefore, a primitive or barbarous consciousness forms a picture of itself on a much earlier level of development and continues to do so for hundreds or even thousands of years, undeterred by the contamination of its archaic qualities with differentiated, highly developed mental products, then the causal explanation is that the older the archaic qualities are, the more conservative and pertinacious is their behaviour. One simply cannot shake off the memory-image of things as they were, and drags it along like a senseless appendage.

467 This explanation, which is facile enough to satisfy the rationalistic requirements of our age, would certainly not meet with the approval of the Winnebagos, the nearest possessors of the trickster cycle. For them the myth is not in any sense a remnant—it is far too amusing for that, and an object of undivided enjoyment. For them it still "functions," provided that they have not been spoiled by civilization. For them there is no earthly reason to theorize about the meaning and purpose of myths, just as the Christmas-tree seems no problem at all to the naïve European. For the thoughtful observer, however, both trickster and Christmas-tree afford reason enough for reflection. Naturally it depends very much on the mentality of the observer what he thinks about these things. Considering the crude primitivity of the trickster cycle, it would not be surprising if one saw in this myth simply the reflection of an earlier, rudimentary stage of consciousness, which is what the trickster obviously seems to be.[12]

468 The only question that would need answering is whether such personified reflections exist at all in empirical psychology. As a matter of fact they do, and these experiences of split or double personality actually form the core of the earliest psychopathological investigations. The peculiar thing about these dissociations is that the split-off personality is not just a random one, but stands in a complementary or compensatory relationship to the ego-personality. It is a personification of traits of

12 Earlier stages of consciousness seem to leave perceptible traces behind them. For instance, the chakras of the Tantric system correspond by and large to the regions where consciousness was earlier localized, *anahata* corresponding to the breast region, *manipura* to the abdominal region, *svadhistana* to the bladder region, and *visuddha* to the larynx and the speech-consciousness of modern man. Cf. Avalon, *The Serpent Power.*

character which are sometimes worse and sometimes better than those the ego-personality possesses. A collective personification like the trickster is the product of an aggregate of individuals and is welcomed by each individual as something known to him, which would not be the case if it were just an individual outgrowth.

469 Now if the myth were nothing but an historical remnant, one would have to ask why it has not long since vanished into the great rubbish-heap of the past, and why it continues to make its influence felt on the highest levels of civilization, even where, on account of his stupidity and grotesque scurrility, the trickster no longer plays the role of a "delight-maker." In many cultures his figure seems like an old river-bed in which the water still flows. One can see this best of all from the fact that the trickster motif does not crop up only in its mythical form but appears just as naïvely and authentically in the unsuspecting modern man—whenever, in fact, he feels himself at the mercy of annoying "accidents" which thwart his will and his actions with apparently malicious intent. He then speaks of "hoodoos" and "jinxes" or of the "mischievousness of the object." Here the trickster is represented by counter-tendencies in the unconscious, and in certain cases by a sort of second personality, of a puerile and inferior character, not unlike the personalities who announce themselves at spiritualistic séances and cause all those ineffably childish phenomena so typical of poltergeists. I have, I think, found a suitable designation for this character-component when I called it the *shadow*.[13] On the civilized level, it is regarded as a personal "gaffe," "slip," "faux pas," etc., which are then chalked up as defects of the conscious personality. We are no longer aware that in carnival customs and the like there are remnants of a collective shadow figure which prove that the personal shadow is in part descended from a numinous collective figure. This collective figure gradually breaks up under the impact of civilization, leaving traces in folklore which are difficult to recognize. But the main part of him gets personalized and is made an object of personal responsibility.

470 Radin's trickster cycle preserves the shadow in its pristine mythological form, and thus points back to a very much earlier

[13] The same idea can be found in the Church Father Irenaeus, who calls it the "umbra." *Adversus haereses,* I, ii, 1.

stage of consciousness which existed before the birth of the myth, when the Indian was still groping about in a similar mental darkness. Only when his consciousness reached a higher level could he detach the earlier state from himself and objectify it, that is, say anything about it. So long as his consciousness was itself trickster-like, such a confrontation could obviously not take place. It was possible only when the attainment of a newer and higher level of consciousness enabled him to look back on a lower and inferior state. It was only to be expected that a good deal of mockery and contempt should mingle with this retrospect, thus casting an even thicker pall over man's memories of the past, which were pretty unedifying anyway. This phenomenon must have repeated itself innumerable times in the history of his mental development. The sovereign contempt with which our modern age looks back on the taste and intelligence of earlier centuries is a classic example of this, and there is an unmistakable allusion to the same phenomenon in the New Testament, where we are told in Acts 17:30 that God looked down from above (ὑπεριδών, *despiciens*) on the χρόνοι τῆς ἀγνοίας, the times of ignorance (or unconsciousness).

471 This attitude contrasts strangely with the still commoner and more striking idealization of the past, which is praised not merely as the "good old days" but as the Golden Age—and not just by uneducated and superstitious people, but by all those legions of theosophical enthusiasts who resolutely believe in the former existence and lofty civilization of Atlantis.

472 Anyone who belongs to a sphere of culture that seeks the perfect state somewhere in the past must feel very queerly indeed when confronted by the figure of the trickster. He is a forerunner of the saviour, and, like him, God, man, and animal at once. He is both subhuman and superhuman, a bestial and divine being, whose chief and most alarming characteristic is his unconsciousness. Because of it he is deserted by his (evidently human) companions, which seems to indicate that he has fallen below their level of consciousness. He is so unconscious of himself that his body is not a unity, and his two hands fight each other. He takes his anus off and entrusts it with a special task. Even his sex is optional despite its phallic qualities: he can turn himself into a woman and bear children. From his penis he makes all kinds of useful plants. This is a reference to

his original nature as a Creator, for the world is made from the body of a god.

473 On the other hand he is in many respects stupider than the animals, and gets into one ridiculous scrape after another. Although he is not really evil, he does the most atrocious things from sheer unconsciousness and unrelatedness. His imprisonment in animal unconsciousness is suggested by the episode where he gets his head caught inside the skull of an elk, and the next episode shows how he overcomes this condition by imprisoning the head of a hawk inside his own rectum. True, he sinks back into the former condition immediately afterwards, by falling under the ice, and is outwitted time after time by the animals, but in the end he succeeds in tricking the cunning coyote, and this brings back to him his saviour nature. The trickster is a primitive "cosmic" being of *divine-animal* nature, on the one hand superior to man because of his superhuman qualities, and on the other hand inferior to him because of his unreason and unconsciousness. He is no match for the animals either, because of his extraordinary clumsiness and lack of instinct. These defects are the marks of his *human* nature, which is not so well adapted to the environment as the animal's but, instead, has prospects of a much higher development of consciousness based on a considerable eagerness to learn, as is duly emphasized in the myth.

474 What the repeated telling of the myth signifies is the therapeutic anamnesis of contents which, for reasons still to be discussed, should never be forgotten for long. If they were nothing but the remnants of an inferior state it would be understandable if man turned his attention away from them, feeling that their reappearance was a nuisance. This is evidently by no means the case, since the trickster has been a source of amusement right down to civilized times, where he can still be recognized in the carnival figures of Pulcinella and the clown. That is one important reason for his still continuing to function. But it is not the only one, and certainly not the reason why this reflection of an extremely primitive state of consciousness solidified into a mythological personage. Mere vestiges of an early state that is dying out usually lose their energy at an increasing rate, otherwise they would never disappear. The last thing we would expect is that they would have the strength to solidify into a

mythological figure with its own cycle of legends—unless, of course, they received energy from outside, in this case from a higher level of consciousness or from sources in the unconscious which are not yet exhausted. To take a legitimate parallel from the psychology of the individual, namely the appearance of an impressive shadow figure antagonistically confronting a personal consciousness: this figure does not appear merely because it *still* exists in the individual, but because it rests on a dynamism whose existence can only be explained in terms of his actual situation, for instance because the shadow is so disagreeable to his ego-consciousness that it has to be repressed into the unconscious. This explanation does not quite meet the case here, because the trickster obviously represents a vanishing level of consciousness which increasingly lacks the power to take express and assert itself. Furthermore, repression would prevent it from vanishing, because repressed contents are the very ones that have the best chance of survival, as we know from experience that nothing is corrected in the unconscious. Lastly, the story of the trickster is not in the least disagreeable to the Winnebago consciousness or incompatible with it but, on the contrary, pleasurable and therefore not conducive to repression. It looks, therefore, as if the myth were actively sustained and fostered by consciousness. This may well be so, since that is the best and most successful method of keeping the shadow figure conscious and subjecting it to conscious criticism. Although, to begin with, this criticism has more the character of a positive evaluation, we may expect that with the progressive development of consciousness the cruder aspects of the myth will gradually fall away, even if the danger of its rapid disappearance under the stress of white civilization did not exist. We have often seen how certain customs, originally cruel or obscene, became mere vestiges in the course of time.[14]

475 The process of rendering this motif harmless takes an extremely long time, as its history shows; one can still detect traces of it even at a high level of civilization. Its longevity could also be explained by the strength and vitality of the state of consciousness described in the myth, and by the secret attrac-

14 For instance, the ducking of the "Ueli" (from Udalricus = Ulrich, yokel, oaf, fool) in Basel during the second half of January was, if I remember correctly, forbidden by the police in the 1860's, after one of the victims died of pneumonia.

tion and fascination this has for the conscious mind. Although purely causal hypotheses in the biological sphere are not as a rule very satisfactory, due weight must nevertheless be given to the fact that in the case of the trickster a higher level of consciousness has covered up a lower one, and that the latter was already in retreat. His recollection, however, is mainly due to the interest which the conscious mind brings to bear on him, the inevitable concomitant being, as we have seen, the gradual civilizing, i.e., assimilation, of a primitive daemonic figure who was originally autonomous and even capable of causing possession.

476 To supplement the causal approach by a final one therefore enables us to arrive at more meaningful interpretations not only in medical psychology, where we are concerned with individual fantasies originating in the unconscious, but also in the case of collective fantasies, that is myths and fairytales.

477 As Radin points out, the civilizing process begins within the framework of the trickster cycle itself, and this is a clear indication that the original state has been overcome. At any rate the marks of deepest unconsciousness fall away from him; instead of acting in a brutal, savage, stupid, and senseless fashion, the trickster's behaviour towards the end of the cycle becomes quite useful and sensible. The devaluation of his earlier unconsciousness is apparent even in the myth, and one wonders what has happened to his evil qualities. The naïve reader may imagine that when the dark aspects disappear they are no longer there in reality. But that is not the case at all, as experience shows. What actually happens is that the conscious mind is then able to free itself from the fascination of evil and is no longer obliged to live it compulsively. The darkness and the evil have not gone up in smoke, they have merely withdrawn into the unconscious owing to loss of energy, where they remain unconscious so long as all is well with the conscious. But if the conscious should find itself in a critical or doubtful situation, then it soon becomes apparent that the shadow has not dissolved into nothing but is only waiting for a favourable opportunity to reappear as a projection upon one's neighbour. If this trick is successful, there is immediately created between them that world of primordial darkness where everything that is characteristic of the trickster can happen—even on the highest plane of

civilization. The best examples of these "monkey tricks," as popular speech aptly and truthfully sums up this state of affairs in which everything goes wrong and nothing intelligent happens except by mistake at the last moment, are naturally to be found in politics.

478 The so-called civilized man has forgotten the trickster. He remembers him only figuratively and metaphorically, when, irritated by his own ineptitude, he speaks of fate playing tricks on him or of things being bewitched. He never suspects that his own hidden and apparently harmless shadow has qualities whose dangerousness exceeds his wildest dreams. As soon as people get together in masses and submerge the individual, the shadow is mobilized, and, as history shows, may even be personified and incarnated.

479 The disastrous idea that everything comes to the human psyche from outside and that it is born a *tabula rasa* is responsible for the erroneous belief that under normal circumstances the individual is in perfect order. He then looks to the State for salvation, and makes society pay for his inefficiency. He thinks the meaning of existence would be discovered if food and clothing were delivered to him gratis on his own doorstep, or if everybody possessed an automobile. Such are the puerilities that rise up in place of an unconscious shadow and keep it unconscious. As a result of these prejudices, the individual feels totally dependent on his environment and loses all capacity for introspection. In this way his code of ethics is replaced by a knowledge of what is permitted or forbidden or ordered. How, under these circumstances, can one expect a soldier to subject an order received from a superior to ethical scrutiny? He has not yet made the discovery that he might be capable of spontaneous ethical impulses, and of performing them—even when no one is looking.

480 From this point of view we can see why the myth of the trickster was preserved and developed: like many other myths, it was supposed to have a therapeutic effect. It holds the earlier low intellectual and moral level before the eyes of the more highly developed individual, so that he shall not forget how things looked yesterday. We like to imagine that something which we do not understand does not help us in any way. But that is not always so. Seldom does a man understand with his

head alone, least of all when he is a primitive. Because of its numinosity the myth has a direct effect on the unconscious, no matter whether it is understood or not. The fact that its repeated telling has not long since become obsolete can, I believe, be explained by its usefulness. The explanation is rather difficult because two contrary tendencies are at work: the desire on the one hand to get out of the earlier condition and on the other hand not to forget it.[15] Apparently Radin has also felt this difficulty, for he says: "Viewed psychologically, it might be contended that the history of civilization is largely the account of the attempts of man to forget his transformation from an animal into a human being." [16] A few pages further on he says (with reference to the Golden Age): "So stubborn a refusal to forget is not an accident." [17] And it is also no accident that we are forced to contradict ourselves as soon as we try to formulate man's paradoxical attitude to myth. Even the most enlightened of us will set up a Christmas-tree for his children without having the least idea what this custom means, and is invariably disposed to nip any attempt at interpretation in the bud. It is really astonishing to see how many so-called superstitions are rampant nowadays in town and country alike, but if one took hold of the individual and asked him, loudly and clearly, "Do you believe in ghosts? in witches? in spells and magic?" he would deny it indignantly. It is a hundred to one he has never heard of such things and thinks it all rubbish. But in secret he is all for it, just like a jungle-dweller. The public knows very little of these things anyway, for everyone is convinced that in our enlightened society that kind of superstition has long since been eradicated, and it is part of the general convention to act as though one had never heard of such things, not to mention believing in them.

481 But nothing is ever lost, not even the blood pact with the devil. Outwardly it is forgotten, but inwardly not at all. We act like the natives on the southern slopes of Mount Elgon, in East Africa, one of whom accompanied me part of the way into the bush. At a fork in the path we came upon a brand new "ghost trap," beautifully got up like a little hut, near the cave where

15 Not to forget something means keeping it in consciousness. If the enemy disappears from my field of vision, then he may possibly be behind me—and even more dangerous.

16 Radin, *The World of Primitive Man*, p. 3.

17 Ibid., p. 5.

he lived with his family. I asked him if he had made it. He denied it with all the signs of extreme agitation, asserting that only children would make such a "ju-ju." Whereupon he gave the hut a kick, and the whole thing fell to pieces.

482 This is exactly the reaction we can observe in Europe today. Outwardly people are more or less civilized, but inwardly they are still primitives. Something in man is profoundly disinclined to give up his beginnings, and something else believes it has long since got beyond all that. This contradiction was once brought home to me in the most drastic manner when I was watching a "Strudel" (a sort of local witch-doctor) taking the spell off a stable. The stable was situated immediately beside the Gotthard railway line, and several international expresses sped past during the ceremony. Their occupants would hardly have suspected that a primitive ritual was being performed a few yards away.

483 The conflict between the two dimensions of consciousness is simply an expression of the polaristic structure of the psyche, which like any other energic system is dependent on the tension of opposites. That is also why there are no general psychological propositions which could not just as well be reversed; indeed, their reversibility proves their validity. We should never forget that in any psychological discussion we are not saying anything *about* the psyche, but that the psyche is always speaking about *itself*. It is no use thinking we can ever get beyond the psyche by means of the "mind," even though the mind asserts that it is not dependent on the psyche. How could it prove that? We can say, if we like, that one statement comes from the psyche, is psychic and nothing but psychic, and that another comes from the mind, is "spiritual" and therefore superior to the psychic one. Both are mere assertions based on the postulates of belief.

484 The fact is, that this old trichotomous hierarchy of psychic contents (hylic, psychic, and pneumatic) represents the polaristic structure of the psyche, which is the only immediate object of experience. The unity of our psychic nature lies in the middle, just as the living unity of the waterfall appears in the dynamic connection between above and below. Thus, the living effect of the myth is experienced when a higher consciousness, rejoicing in its freedom and independence, is confronted by the autonomy of a mythological figure and yet cannot flee from its

fascination, but must pay tribute to the overwhelming impression. The figure works, because secretly it participates in the observer's psyche and appears as its reflection, though it is not recognized as such. It is split off from his consciousness and consequently behaves like an autonomous personality. The trickster is a collective shadow figure, a summation of all the inferior traits of character in individuals. And since the individual shadow is never absent as a component of personality, the collective figure can construct itself out of it continually. Not always, of course, as a mythological figure, but, in consequence of the increasing repression and neglect of the original mythologems, as a corresponding projection on other social groups and nations.

485 If we take the trickster as a parallel of the individual shadow, then the question arises whether that trend towards meaning, which we saw in the trickster myth, can also be observed in the subjective and personal shadow. Since this shadow frequently appears in the phenomenology of dreams as a well-defined figure, we can answer this question positively: the shadow, although by definition a negative figure, sometimes has certain clearly discernible traits and associations which point to a quite different background. It is as though he were hiding meaningful contents under an unprepossessing exterior. Experience confirms this; and what is more important, the things that are hidden usually consist of increasingly numinous figures. The one standing closest behind the shadow is the anima,[18] who is endowed with considerable powers of fascination and possession. She often appears in rather too youthful form, and hides in her turn the powerful archetype of the wise old man (sage, magician, king, etc.). The series could be extended, but it would be pointless to do so, as psychologically one only understands what one has experienced oneself. The concepts of complex psychology are, in essence, not intellectual formula-

18 By the metaphor "standing behind the shadow" I am attempting to illustrate the fact that, to the degree in which the shadow is recognized and integrated, the problem of the anima, i.e., of relationship, is constellated. It is understandable that the encounter with the shadow should have an enduring effect on the relations of the ego to the inside and outside world, since the integration of the shadow brings about an alteration of personality. Cf. *Aion,* Part II of this vol., pars. 13ff.

tions but names for certain areas of experience, and though they can be described they remain dead and irrepresentable to anyone who has not experienced them. Thus, I have noticed that people usually have not much difficulty in picturing to themselves what is meant by the shadow, even if they would have preferred instead a bit of Latin or Greek jargon that sounds more "scientific." But it costs them enormous difficulties to understand what the anima is. They accept her easily enough when she appears in novels or as a film star, but she is not understood at all when it comes to seeing the role she plays in their own lives, because she sums up everything that a man can never get the better of and never finishes coping with. Therefore it remains in a perpetual state of emotionality which must not be touched. The degree of unconsciousness one meets with in this connection is, to put it mildly, astounding. Hence it is practically impossible to get a man who is afraid of his own femininity to understand what is meant by the anima.

486 Actually, it is not surprising that this should be so, since even the most rudimentary insight into the shadow sometimes causes the greatest difficulties for the modern European. But since the shadow is the figure nearest his consciousness and the least explosive one, it is also the first component of personality to come up in an analysis of the unconscious. A minatory and ridiculous figure, he stands at the very beginning of the way of individuation, posing the deceptively easy riddle of the Sphinx, or grimly demanding answer to a "quaestio crocodilina." [19]

487 If, at the end of the trickster myth, the saviour is hinted at, this comforting premonition or hope means that some calamity or other has happened and been consciously understood. Only out of disaster can the longing for the saviour arise—in other words, the recognition and unavoidable integration of the shadow create such a harrowing situation that nobody but a saviour can undo the tangled web of fate. In the case of the individual, the problem constellated by the shadow is answered on the plane of the anima, that is, through relatedness. In the

[19] A crocodile stole a child from its mother. On being asked to give it back to her, the crocodile replied that he would grant her wish if she could give a true answer to his question: "Shall I give the child back?" If she answers "Yes," it is not true, and she won't get the child back. If she answers "No," it is again not true, so in either case the mother loses the child.

history of the collective as in the history of the individual, everything depends on the development of consciousness. This gradually brings liberation from imprisonment in ἀγνοία, 'unconsciousness,' [20] and is therefore a bringer of light as well as of healing.

488 As in its collective, mythological form, so also the individual shadow contains within it the seed of an enantiodromia, of a conversion into its opposite.

20 Neumann, *The Origins and History of Consciousness*, passim.

VI

CONSCIOUS, UNCONSCIOUS, AND INDIVIDUATION

A STUDY IN THE PROCESS OF INDIVIDUATION

CONCERNING MANDALA SYMBOLISM

CONSCIOUS, UNCONSCIOUS, AND INDIVIDUATION[1]

489 The relation between the conscious and the unconscious on the one hand, and the individuation process on the other, are problems that arise almost regularly during the later stages of analytical treatment. By "analytical" I mean a procedure that takes account of the existence of the unconscious. These problems do not arise in a procedure based on suggestion. A few preliminary words may not be out of place in order to explain what is meant by "individuation."

490 I use the term "individuation" to denote the process by which a person becomes a psychological "in-dividual," that is, a separate, indivisible unity or "whole."[2] It is generally assumed that consciousness is the whole of the psychological individual. But knowledge of the phenomena that can only be explained on the hypothesis of unconscious psychic processes makes it doubtful whether the ego and its contents are in fact identical with the "whole." If unconscious processes exist at all, they must surely belong to the totality of the individual, even though they are not components of the conscious ego. If they were part of the ego they would necessarily be conscious, because everything that is directly related to the ego is conscious. Consciousness can even be equated with the relation between the ego and the psychic contents. But unconscious phenomena

1 [Originally written in English as "The Meaning of Individuation," the introductory chapter of *The Integration of the Personality* (New York, 1939; London, 1940), a collection of papers otherwise translated by Stanley Dell. Professor Jung afterward rewrote the paper, with considerable revision, in German and published it as "Bewusstsein, Unbewusstes und Individuation," *Zentralblatt für Psychotherapie und ihre Grenzgebiete* (Leipzig), XI (1939) : 5, 257–70. The original English version was slightly longer, owing to material which Mr. Dell edited into it from other writings of Jung's, for the special requirements of the *Integration* volume. It is the basis of the present version, together with the 1939 German version.—EDITORS.]

2 Modern physicists (Louis de Broglie, for instance) use instead of this the concept of something "discontinuous."

are so little related to the ego that most people do not hesitate to deny their existence outright. Nevertheless, they manifest themselves in an individual's behaviour. An attentive observer can detect them without difficulty, while the observed person remains quite unaware of the fact that he is betraying his most secret thoughts or even things he has never thought consciously. It is, however, a great prejudice to suppose that something we have never thought consciously does not exist in the psyche. There is plenty of evidence to show that consciousness is very far from covering the psyche in its totality. Many things occur semiconsciously, and a great many more remain entirely unconscious. Thorough investigation of the phenomena of dual and multiple personalities, for instance, has brought to light a mass of material with observations to prove this point. (I would refer the reader to the writings of Pierre Janet, Théodore Flournoy, Morton Prince, and others.[3])

491 The importance of such phenomena has made a deep impression on medical psychology, because they give rise to all sorts of psychic and physiological symptoms. In these circumstances, the assumption that the ego expresses the totality of the psyche has become untenable. It is, on the contrary, evident that the whole must necessarily include not only consciousness but the illimitable field of unconscious occurrences as well, and that the ego can be no more than the centre of the field of consciousness.

492 You will naturally ask whether the unconscious possesses a centre too. I would hardly venture to assume that there is in the unconscious a ruling principle analogous to the ego. As a matter of fact, everything points to the contrary. If there were such a centre, we could expect almost regular signs of its existence. Cases of dual personality would then be frequent occurrences instead of rare curiosities. As a rule, unconscious phenomena manifest themselves in fairly chaotic and unsystematic form. Dreams, for instance, show no apparent order and no tendency to systematization, as they would have to do if there were a personal consciousness at the back of them. The philosophers Carus and von Hartmann treat the unconscious as a metaphysical principle, a sort of universal mind, without any trace of personality or ego-consciousness, and similarly

3 [See also Jung's *Psychiatric Studies,* index, s. vv.—EDITORS.]

Schopenhauer's "Will" is without an ego. Modern psychologists, too, regard the unconscious as an egoless function below the threshold of consciousness. Unlike the philosophers, they tend to derive its subliminal functions from the conscious mind. Janet thinks that there is a certain weakness of consciousness which is unable to hold all the psychic processes together. Freud, on the other hand, favours the idea of conscious factors that suppress certain incompatible tendencies. Much can be said for both theories, since there are numerous cases where a weakness of consciousness actually causes certain contents to fall below the threshold, or where disagreeable contents are repressed. It is obvious that such careful observers as Janet and Freud would not have constructed theories deriving the unconscious mainly from conscious sources had they been able to discover traces of an independent personality or of an autonomous will in the manifestations of the unconscious.

493 If it were true that the unconscious consists of nothing but contents accidentally deprived of consciousness but otherwise indistinguishable from the conscious material, then one could identify the ego more or less with the totality of the psyche. But actually the situation is not quite so simple. Both theories are based mainly on observations in the field of neurosis. Neither Janet nor Freud had any specifically psychiatric experience. If they had, they would surely have been struck by the fact that the unconscious displays contents that are utterly different from conscious ones, so strange, indeed, that nobody can understand them, neither the patient himself nor his doctors. The patient is inundated by a flood of thoughts that are as strange to him as they are to a normal person. That is why we call him "crazy": we cannot understand his ideas. We understand something only if we have the necessary premises for doing so. But here the premises are just as remote from our consciousness as they were from the mind of the patient before he went mad. Otherwise he would never have become insane.

494 There is, in fact, no field directly known to us from which we could derive certain pathological ideas. It is not a question of more or less normal contents that became unconscious just by accident. They are, on the contrary, products whose nature is at first completely baffling. They differ in every respect from neurotic material, which cannot be said to be at all bizarre. The

material of a neurosis is understandable in human terms, but that of a psychosis is not.[4]

495 This peculiar psychotic material cannot be derived from the conscious mind, because the latter lacks the premises which would help to explain the strangeness of the ideas. Neurotic contents can be integrated without appreciable injury to the ego, but psychotic ideas cannot. They remain inaccessible, and ego-consciousness is more or less swamped by them. They even show a distinct tendency to draw the ego into their "system."

496 Such cases indicate that under certain conditions the unconscious is capable of taking over the role of the ego. The consequence of this exchange is insanity and confusion, because the unconscious is not a second personality with organized and centralized functions but in all probability a decentralized congeries of psychic processes. However, nothing produced by the human mind lies absolutely outside the psychic realm. Even the craziest idea must correspond to something in the psyche. We cannot suppose that certain minds contain elements that do not exist at all in other minds. Nor can we assume that the unconscious is capable of becoming autonomous only in certain people, namely in those predisposed to insanity. It is very much more likely that the tendency to autonomy is a more or less general peculiarity of the unconscious. Mental disorder is, in a sense, only one outstanding example of a hidden but none the less general condition. This tendency to autonomy shows itself above all in affective states, including those of normal people. When in a state of violent affect one says or does things which exceed the ordinary. Not much is needed: love and hate, joy and grief, are often enough to make the ego and the unconscious change places. Very strange ideas indeed can take possession of otherwise healthy people on such occasions. Groups, communities, and even whole nations can be seized in this way by psychic epidemics.

497 The autonomy of the unconscious therefore begins where emotions are generated. Emotions are instinctive, involuntary reactions which upset the rational order of consciousness by their elemental outbursts. Affects are not "made" or wilfully

4 By this I mean only certain cases of schizophrenia, such as the famous Schreber case (*Memoirs of My Nervous Illness*) or the case published by Nelken ("Analytische Beobachtungen über Phantasien eines Schizophrenen," 1912).

produced; they simply happen. In a state of affect a trait of character sometimes appears which is strange even to the person concerned, or hidden contents may irrupt involuntarily. The more violent an affect the closer it comes to the pathological, to a condition in which the ego-consciousness is thrust aside by autonomous contents that were unconscious before. So long as the unconscious is in a dormant condition, it seems as if there were absolutely nothing in this hidden region. Hence we are continually surprised when something unknown suddenly appears "from nowhere." Afterwards, of course, the psychologist comes along and shows that things had to happen as they did for this or that reason. But who could have said so beforehand?

498 We call the unconscious "nothing," and yet it is a reality *in potentia*. The thought we shall think, the deed we shall do, even the fate we shall lament tomorrow, all lie unconscious in our today. The unknown in us which the affect uncovers was always there and sooner or later would have presented itself to consciousness. Hence we must always reckon with the presence of things not yet discovered. These, as I have said, may be unknown quirks of character. But possibilities of future development may also come to light in this way, perhaps in just such an outburst of affect which sometimes radically alters the whole situation. The unconscious has a Janus-face: on one side its contents point back to a preconscious, prehistoric world of instinct, while on the other side it potentially anticipates the future—precisely because of the instinctive readiness for action of the factors that determine man's fate. If we had complete knowledge of the ground plan lying dormant in an individual from the beginning, his fate would be in large measure predictable.

499 Now, to the extent that unconscious tendencies—be they backward-looking images or forward-looking anticipations—appear in dreams, dreams have been regarded, in all previous ages, less as historical regressions than as anticipations of the future, and rightly so. For everything that will be happens on the basis of what has been, and of what—consciously or unconsciously—still exists as a memory-trace. In so far as no man is born totally new, but continually repeats the stage of development last reached by the species, he contains unconsciously, as an *a priori* datum, the entire psychic structure developed both

upwards and downwards by his ancestors in the course of the ages. That is what gives the unconscious its characteristic "historical" aspect, but it is at the same time the *sine qua non* for shaping the future. For this reason it is often very difficult to decide whether an autonomous manifestation of the unconscious should be interpreted as an *effect* (and therefore historical) or as an *aim* (and therefore teleological and anticipatory). The conscious mind thinks as a rule without regard to ancestral preconditions and without taking into account the influence this *a priori* factor has on the shaping of the individual's fate. Whereas we think in periods of years, the unconscious thinks and lives in terms of millennia. So when something happens that seems to us an unexampled novelty, it is generally a very old story indeed. We still forget, like children, what happened yesterday. We are still living in a wonderful new world where man thinks himself astonishingly new and "modern." This is unmistakable proof of the youthfulness of human consciousness, which has not yet grown aware of its historical antecedents.

500 As a matter of fact, the "normal" person convinces me far more of the autonomy of the unconscious than does the insane person. Psychiatric theory can always take refuge behind real or alleged organic disorders of the brain and thus detract from the importance of the unconscious. But such a view is no longer applicable when it comes to normal humanity. What one sees happening in the world is not just a "shadowy vestige of activities that were once conscious," but the expression of a living psychic condition that still exists and always will exist. Were that not so, one might well be astonished. But it is precisely those who give least credence to the autonomy of the unconscious who are the most surprised by it. Because of its youthfulness and vulnerability, our consciousness tends to make light of the unconscious. This is understandable enough, for a young man should not let himself be overawed by the authority of his parents if he wants to start something on his own account. Historically as well as individually, our consciousness has developed out of the darkness and somnolence of primordial unconsciousness. There were psychic processes and functions long before any ego-consciousness existed. "Thinking" existed long before man was able to say: "I am conscious of thinking."

501 The primitive "perils of the soul" consist mainly of dangers to consciousness. Fascination, bewitchment, "loss of soul," possession, etc. are obviously phenomena of the dissociation and suppression of consciousness caused by unconscious contents. Even civilized man is not yet entirely free of the darkness of primeval times. The unconscious is the mother of consciousness. Where there is a mother there is also a father, yet he seems to be unknown. Consciousness, in the pride of its youth, may deny its father, but it cannot deny its mother. That would be too unnatural, for one can see in every child how hesitantly and slowly its ego-consciousness evolves out of a fragmentary consciousness lasting for single moments only, and how these islands gradually emerge from the total darkness of mere instinctuality.

502 Consciousness grows out of an unconscious psyche which is older than it, and which goes on functioning together with it or even in spite of it. Although there are numerous cases of conscious contents becoming unconscious again (through being repressed, for instance), the unconscious as a whole is far from being a mere remnant of consciousness. Or are the psychic functions of animals remnants of consciousness?

503 As I have said, there is little hope of our finding in the unconscious an order equivalent to that of the ego. It certainly does not look as if we were likely to discover an unconscious ego-personality, something in the nature of a Pythagorean "counter-earth." Nevertheless, we cannot overlook the fact that, just as consciousness arises from the unconscious, the ego-centre, too, crystallizes out of a dark depth in which it was somehow contained *in potentia.* Just as a human mother can only produce a human child, whose deepest nature lay hidden during its potential existence within her, so we are practically compelled to believe that the unconscious cannot be an entirely chaotic accumulation of instincts and images. There must be something to hold it together and give expression to the whole. Its centre cannot possibly be the ego, since the ego was born out of it into consciousness and turns its back on the unconscious, seeking to shut it out as much as possible. Or can it be that the unconscious loses its centre with the birth of the ego? In that case we would expect the ego to be far superior to the unconscious in influence and importance. The unconscious would

then follow meekly in the footsteps of the conscious, and that would be just what we wish.

504 Unfortunately, the facts show the exact opposite: consciousness succumbs all too easily to unconscious influences, and these are often truer and wiser than our conscious thinking. Also, it frequently happens that unconscious motives overrule our conscious decisions, especially in matters of vital importance. Indeed, the fate of the individual is largely dependent on unconscious factors. Careful investigation shows how very much our conscious decisions depend on the undisturbed functioning of memory. But memory often suffers from the disturbing interference of unconscious contents. Moreover, it functions as a rule automatically. Ordinarily it uses the bridges of association, but often in such an extraordinary way that another thorough investigation of the whole process of memory-reproduction is needed in order to find out how certain memories managed to reach consciousness at all. And sometimes these bridges cannot be found. In such cases it is impossible to dismiss the hypothesis of the spontaneous activity of the unconscious. Another example is intuition, which is chiefly dependent on unconscious processes of a very complex nature. Because of this peculiarity, I have defined intuition as "perception via the unconscious."

505 Normally the unconscious collaborates with the conscious without friction or disturbance, so that one is not even aware of its existence. But when an individual or a social group deviates too far from their instinctual foundations, they then experience the full impact of unconscious forces. The collaboration of the unconscious is intelligent and purposive, and even when it acts in opposition to consciousness its expression is still compensatory in an intelligent way, as if it were trying to restore the lost balance.

506 There are dreams and visions of such an impressive character that some people refuse to admit that they could have originated in an unconscious psyche. They prefer to assume that such phenomena derive from a sort of "superconsciousness." Such people make a distinction between a quasi-physiological or instinctive unconscious and a psychic sphere or layer "above" consciousness, which they style the "superconscious." As a matter of fact, this psyche, which in Indian philosophy is

called the "higher" consciousness, corresponds to what we in the West call the "unconscious." Certain dreams, visions, and mystical experiences do, however, suggest the existence of a consciousness in the unconscious. But, if we assume a consciousness in the unconscious, we are at once faced with the difficulty that no consciousness can exist without a subject, that is, an ego to which the contents are related. Consciousness needs a centre, an ego to which something is conscious. We know of no other kind of consciousness, nor can we imagine a consciousness without an ego. There can be no consciousness when there is no one to say: "*I* am conscious."

507 It is unprofitable to speculate about things we cannot know. I therefore refrain from making assertions that go beyond the bounds of science. It was never possible for me to discover in the unconscious anything like a personality comparable with the ego. But although a "second ego" cannot be discovered (except in the rare cases of dual personality), the manifestations of the unconscious do at least show *traces of personalities.* A simple example is the dream, where a number of real or imaginary people represent the dream-thoughts. In nearly all the important types of dissociation, the manifestations of the unconscious assume a strikingly personal form. Careful examination of the behaviour and mental content of these personifications, however, reveals their fragmentary character. They seem to represent complexes that have split off from a greater whole, and are the very reverse of a personal centre of the unconscious.

508 I have always been greatly impressed by the character of dissociated fragments as personalities. Hence I have often asked myself whether we are not justified in assuming that, if such fragments have personality, the whole from which they were broken off must have personality to an even higher degree. The inference seemed logical, since it does not depend on whether the fragments are large or small. Why, then, should not the whole have personality too? *Personality need not imply consciousness. It can just as easily be dormant or dreaming.*

509 The general aspect of unconscious manifestations is in the main chaotic and irrational, despite certain symptoms of intelligence and purposiveness. The unconscious produces dreams, visions, fantasies, emotions, grotesque ideas, and so forth. This

is exactly what we would expect a dreaming personality to do. It seems to be a personality that was never awake and was never conscious of the life it had lived and of its own continuity. The only question is whether the hypothesis of a dormant and hidden personality is possible or not. It may be that all of the personality to be found in the unconscious is contained in the fragmentary personifications mentioned before. Since this is very possible, all my conjectures would be in vain—unless there were evidence of much less fragmentary and more complete personalities, even though they are hidden.

510 I am convinced that such evidence exists. Unfortunately, the material to prove this belongs to the subtleties of psychological analysis. It is therefore not exactly easy to give the reader a simple and convincing idea of it.

511 I shall begin with a brief statement: in the unconscious of every man there is hidden a feminine personality, and in that of every woman a masculine personality.

512 It is a well-known fact that sex is determined by a majority of male or female genes, as the case may be. But the minority of genes belonging to the other sex does not simply disappear. A man therefore has in him a feminine side, an unconscious feminine figure—a fact of which he is generally quite unaware. I may take it as known that I have called this figure the "anima," and its counterpart in a woman the "animus." In order not to repeat myself, I must refer the reader to the literature.[5] This figure frequently appears in dreams, where one can observe all the attributes I have mentioned in earlier publications.

513 Another, no less important and clearly defined figure is the "shadow." Like the anima, it appears either in projection on suitable persons, or personified as such in dreams. The shadow coincides with the "personal" unconscious (which corresponds to Freud's conception of the unconscious). Again like the anima, this figure has often been portrayed by poets and writers. I would mention the Faust-Mephistopheles relationship and E. T. A. Hoffmann's tale *The Devil's Elixir* as two especially typical descriptions. The shadow personifies everything that the subject refuses to acknowledge about himself and yet is always

[5] *Psychological Types,* Def. 48; "The Relations between the Ego and the Unconscious," pars. 296ff.; *Psychology and Alchemy,* Part II. Cf. also the third paper in this volume.

thrusting itself upon him directly or indirectly—for instance, inferior traits of character and other incompatible tendencies.[6]

514 The fact that the unconscious spontaneously personifies certain affectively toned contents in dreams is the reason why I have taken over these personifications in my terminology and formulated them as names.

515 Besides these figures there are still a few others, less frequent and less striking, which have likewise undergone poetic as well as mythological formulation. I would mention, for instance, the figure of the hero [7] and of the wise old man,[8] to name only two of the best known.

516 All these figures irrupt autonomously into consciousness as soon as it gets into a pathological state. With regard to the anima, I would particularly like to draw attention to the case described by Nelken.[9] Now the remarkable thing is that these figures show the most striking connections with the poetic, religious, or mythological formulations, though these connections are in no way factual. That is to say, they are spontaneous products of analogy. One such case even led to the charge of plagiarism: the French writer Benoît gave a description of the anima and her classic myth in his book *L'Atlantide,* which is an exact parallel of Rider Haggard's *She.* The lawsuit proved unsuccessful; Benoît had never heard of *She.* (It might, in the last analysis, have been an instance of cryptomnesic deception, which is often extremely difficult to rule out.) The distinctly "historical" aspect of the anima and her condensation with the figures of the sister, wife, mother, and daughter, plus the associated incest motif, can be found in Goethe ("You were in times gone by my wife or sister"),[10] as well as in the anima figure of the *regina* or *femina alba* in alchemy. The English alchemist Eirenaeus Philalethes ("lover of truth"), writing about 1645, remarks that the "Queen" was the King's "sister, mother, or wife." [11] The same idea can be found, ornately elaborated, in

6 Toni Wolff, "Einführung in die Grundlagen der Komplexen Psychologie," p. 107. [Also *Aion,* ch. 2.—EDITORS.]

7 *Symbols of Transformation,* Part II.

8 Cf. supra, "The Phenomenology of the Spirit in Fairytales."

9 See n. 4, above.

10 [Untitled poem ("Warum gabst du uns die tiefen Blicke") in *Werke,* II, p. 43. —EDITORS.]

11 *Ripley Reviv'd; or, An Exposition upon Sir George Ripley's Hermetico-Poetical Works* (1678), trans. into German in 1741 and possibly known to Goethe.

Nelken's patient and in a whole series of cases observed by me, where I was able to rule out with certainty any possibility of literary influence. For the rest, the anima complex is one of the oldest features of Latin alchemy.[12]

517 When one studies the archetypal personalities and their behaviour with the help of the dreams, fantasies, and delusions of patients,[13] one is profoundly impressed by their manifold and unmistakable connections with mythological ideas completely unknown to the layman. They form a species of singular beings whom one would like to endow with ego-consciousness; indeed, they almost seem capable of it. And yet this idea is not borne out by the facts. There is nothing in their behaviour to suggest that they have an ego-consciousness as we know it. They show, on the contrary, all the marks of fragmentary personalities. They are masklike, wraithlike, without problems, lacking self-reflection, with no conflicts, no doubts, no sufferings; like gods, perhaps, who have no philosophy, such as the Brahma-gods of the *Samyutta-nikāya,* whose erroneous views needed correction by the Buddha. Unlike other contents, they always remain strangers in the world of consciousness, unwelcome intruders saturating the atmosphere with uncanny forebodings or even with the fear of madness.

518 If we examine their content, i.e., the fantasy material constituting their phenomenology, we find countless archaic and "historical" associations and images of an archetypal nature.[14] This peculiar fact permits us to draw conclusions about the "localization" of anima and animus in the psychic structure. They evidently live and function in the deeper layers of the unconscious, especially in that phylogenetic substratum which I have called the collective unconscious. This localization explains a good deal of their strangeness: they bring into our ephemeral consciousness an unknown psychic life belonging to a remote past. It is the mind of our unknown ancestors, their way of thinking and feeling, their way of experiencing life and

12 Cf. the celebrated "Visio Arislei" (*Artis auriferae,* 1593, II, pp. 246ff.), also available in German: Ruska, *Die Vision des Arisleus,* p. 22.

13 For an example of the method, see *Psychology and Alchemy,* Part II.

14 In my *Symbols of Transformation,* I have described the case of a young woman with a "hero-story," i.e., an animus fantasy that yielded a rich harvest of mythological material. Rider Haggard, Benoît, and Goethe (in *Faust*) have all stressed the historical character of the anima.

the world, gods and men. The existence of these archaic strata is presumably the source of man's belief in reincarnations and in memories of "previous existences." Just as the human body is a museum, so to speak, of its phylogenetic history, so too is the psyche. We have no reason to suppose that the specific structure of the psyche is the only thing in the world that has no history outside its individual manifestations. Even the conscious mind cannot be denied a history reaching back at least five thousand years. It is only our ego-consciousness that has forever a new beginning and an early end. The unconscious psyche is not only immensely old, it is also capable of growing into an equally remote future. It moulds the human species and is just as much a part of it as the human body, which, though ephemeral in the individual, is collectively of immense age.

519 The anima and animus live in a world quite different from the world outside—in a world where the pulse of time beats infinitely slowly, where the birth and death of individuals count for little. No wonder their nature is strange, so strange that their irruption into consciousness often amounts to a psychosis. They undoubtedly belong to the material that comes to light in schizophrenia.

520 What I have said about the collective unconscious may give you a more or less adequate idea of what I mean by this term. If we now turn back to the problem of individuation, we shall see ourselves faced with a rather extraordinary task: the psyche consists of two incongruous halves which together should form a whole. One is inclined to think that ego-consciousness is capable of assimilating the unconscious, at least one hopes that such a solution is possible. But unfortunately the unconscious really is unconscious; in other words, it is unknown. And how can you assimilate something unknown? Even if you can form a fairly complete picture of the anima and animus, this does not mean that you have plumbed the depths of the unconscious. One hopes to control the unconscious, but the past masters in the art of self-control, the yogis, attain perfection in *samādhi,* a state of ecstasy, which so far as we know is equivalent to a state of unconsciousness. It makes no difference whether they call our unconscious a "universal consciousness"; the fact remains that in their case the unconscious has swallowed up ego-consciousness. They do not realize that a "universal consciousness" is a

contradiction in terms, since exclusion, selection, and discrimination are the root and essence of everything that lays claim to the name "consciousness." "Universal consciousness" is logically identical with unconsciousness. It is nevertheless true that a correct application of the methods described in the Pāli Canon or in the *Yoga-sūtra* induces a remarkable extension of consciousness. But, with increasing extension, the contents of consciousness lose in clarity of detail. In the end, consciousness becomes all-embracing, but nebulous; an infinite number of things merge into an indefinite whole, a state in which subject and object are almost completely identical. This is all very beautiful, but scarcely to be recommended anywhere north of the Tropic of Cancer.

521 For this reason we must look for a different solution. We believe in ego-consciousness and in what we call reality. The realities of a northern climate are somehow so convincing that we feel very much better off when we do not forget them. For us it makes sense to concern ourselves with reality. Our European ego-consciousness is therefore inclined to swallow up the unconscious, and if this should not prove feasible we try to suppress it. But if we understand anything of the unconscious, we know that it cannot be swallowed. We also know that it is dangerous to suppress it, because the unconscious is life and this life turns against us if suppressed, as happens in neurosis.

522 Conscious and unconscious do not make a whole when one of them is suppressed and injured by the other. If they must contend, let it at least be a fair fight with equal rights on both sides. Both are aspects of life. Consciousness should defend its reason and protect itself, and the chaotic life of the unconscious should be given the chance of having its way too—as much of it as we can stand. This means open conflict and open collaboration at once. That, evidently, is the way human life should be. It is the old game of hammer and anvil: between them the patient iron is forged into an indestructible whole, an "individual."

523 This, roughly, is what I mean by the individuation process. As the name shows, it is a process or course of development arising out of the conflict between the two fundamental psychic facts. I have described the problems of this conflict, at least in their essentials, in my essay "The Relations between the Ego

and the Unconscious." A special chapter, however, is the *symbolism* of the process, which is of the utmost importance for understanding the final stages of the encounter between conscious and unconscious, in practice as well as in theory. My investigations during these last years have been devoted mainly to this theme. It turned out, to my own great astonishment, that the symbol formation has the closest affinities with alchemical ideas, and especially with the conceptions of the "uniting symbol," [15] which yield highly significant parallels. Naturally these are processes which have no meaning in the initial stages of psychological treatment. On the other hand, more difficult cases, such as cases of unresolved transference, develop these symbols. Knowledge of them is of inestimable importance in treating cases of this kind, especially when dealing with cultured patients.

524 How the harmonizing of conscious and unconscious data is to be undertaken cannot be indicated in the form of a recipe. It is an irrational life-process which expresses itself in definite symbols. It may be the task of the analyst to stand by this process with all the help he can give. In this case, knowledge of the symbols is indispensable, for it is in them that the union of conscious and unconscious contents is consummated. Out of this union emerge new situations and new conscious attitudes. I have therefore called the union of opposites the "transcendent function." [16] This rounding out of the personality into a whole may well be the goal of any psychotherapy that claims to be more than a mere cure of symptoms.

15 [*Psychological Types*, Def. 51 and ch. V, 3c. In the *Collected Works*, the term "uniting symbol" supersedes the earlier translation "reconciling symbol." —EDITORS]

16 [Cf. "The Transcendent Function."—EDITORS.]

A STUDY IN THE PROCESS OF INDIVIDUATION [1]

Tao's working of things is vague and obscure.
Obscure! Oh vague!
In it are images.
Vague! Oh obscure!
In it are things.
Profound! Oh dark indeed!
In it is seed.
Its seed is very truth.
In it is trustworthiness.
From the earliest Beginning until today
Its name is not lacking
By which to fathom the Beginning of all things.
How do I know it is the Beginning of all things?
Through *it!*

LAO-TZU, *Tao Teh Ching,* ch. 21.

Introductory

525 During the 1920's, I made the acquaintance in America of a lady with an academic education—we will call her Miss X—who had studied psychology for nine years. She had read all the more recent literature in this field. In 1928, at the age of fifty-five, she came to Europe in order to continue her studies under my guidance. As the daughter of an exceptional father she had varied interests, was extremely cultured, and possessed a lively turn of mind. She was unmarried, but lived with the unconscious equivalent of a human partner, namely the animus (the personification of everything masculine in a woman), in that

1 [Translated from "Zur Empirie des Individuationsprozesses," *Gestaltungen des Unbewussten* (Zurich, 1950), where it carries the author's note that it is a "thoroughly revised and enlarged version of the lecture of the same title first published in the *Eranos-Jahrbuch 1933,*" i.e., in 1934. The original version was translated by Stanley Dell and published in *The Integration of the Personality* (New York, 1939; London, 1940). The motto by Lao-tzu is from a translation by Carol Baumann in her article "Time and Tao," *Spring,* 1951, p. 30.—EDITORS.]

characteristic liaison so often met with in women with an academic education. As frequently happens, this development of hers was based on a positive father complex: she was "fille à papa" and consequently did not have a good relation to her mother. Her animus was not of the kind to give her cranky ideas. She was protected from this by her natural intelligence and by a remarkable readiness to tolerate the opinions of other people. This good quality, by no means to be expected in the presence of an animus, had, in conjunction with some difficult experiences that could not be avoided, enabled her to realize that she had reached a limit and "got stuck," and this made it urgently necessary for her to look round for ways that might lead her out of the impasse. That was one of the reasons for her trip to Europe. Associated with this there was another—not accidental—motive. On her mother's side she was of Scandinavian descent. Since her relation to her mother left very much to be desired, as she herself clearly realized, the feeling had gradually grown up in her that this side of her nature might have developed differently if only the relation to her mother had given it a chance. In deciding to go to Europe she was conscious that she was turning back to her own origins and was setting out to reactivate a portion of her childhood that was bound up with the mother. Before coming to Zurich she had gone back to Denmark, her mother's country. There the thing that affected her most was the landscape, and unexpectedly there came over her the desire to paint—above all, landscape motifs. Till then she had noticed no such aesthetic inclinations in herself, also she lacked the ability to paint or draw. She tried her hand at watercolours, and her modest landscapes filled her with a strange feeling of contentment. Painting them, she told me, seemed to fill her with new life. Arriving in Zurich, she continued her painting efforts, and on the day before she came to me for the first time she began another landscape—this time from memory. While she was working on it, a fantasy-image suddenly thrust itself between her and the picture: she saw herself with the lower half of her body in the earth, stuck fast in a block of rock. The region round about was a beach strewn with boulders. In the background was the sea. She felt caught and helpless. Then she suddenly saw me in the guise of a medieval sorcerer. She shouted for help, I came along and touched the rock with a magic wand. The stone instantly burst open, and she stepped out uninjured. She then painted this fantasy-image instead of the landscape and brought it to me on the following day.

Picture 1

526 As usually happens with beginners and people with no skill of hand, the drawing of the picture cost her considerable difficulties. In such cases it is very easy for the unconscious to slip its subliminal images into the painting. Thus it came about that the big boulders would not appear on the paper in their real form but took on unexpected shapes. They looked, some of them, like hardboiled eggs cut in two, with the yolk in the middle. Others were like pointed pyramids. It was in one of these that Miss X was stuck. Her hair, blown out behind her, and the movement of the sea suggested a strong wind.

527 The picture shows first of all her imprisoned state, but not yet the act of liberation. So it was there that she was attached to the earth, in the land of her mother. Psychologically this state means being caught in the unconscious. Her inadequate relation to her mother had left behind something dark and in need of development. Since she succumbed to the magic of her motherland and tried to express this by painting, it is obvious that she is still stuck with half her body in Mother Earth: that is, she is still partly identical with the mother and, what is more, through that part of the body which contains just that secret of the mother which she had never inquired into.

528 Since Miss X had discovered all by herself the method of active imagination I have long been accustomed to use, I was able to approach the problem at just the point indicated by the picture: she is caught in the unconscious and expects magical help from me, as from a sorcerer. And since her psychological knowledge had made her completely *au fait* with certain possible interpretations, there was no need of even an understanding wink to bring to light the apparent *sous-entendu* of the liberating magician's wand. The sexual symbolism, which for many naïve minds is of such capital importance, was no discovery for her. She was far enough advanced to know that explanations of this kind, however true they might be in other respects, had no significance in her case. She did not want to know how liberation might be possible in a *general* way, but

how and in what way it could come about for *her*. And about this I knew as little as she. I know that such solutions can only come about in an individual way that cannot be foreseen. One cannot think up ways and means artificially, let alone know them in advance, for such knowledge is merely collective, based on average experience, and can therefore be completely inadequate, indeed absolutely wrong, in individual cases. And when, on top of that, we consider the patient's age, we would do well to abandon from the start any attempt to apply ready-made solutions and warmed-up generalities of which the patient knows just as much as the doctor. Long experience has taught me not to know anything in advance and not to know better, but to let the unconscious take precedence. Our instincts have ridden so infinitely many times, unharmed, over the problems that arise at this stage of life that we may be sure the transformation processes which make the transition possible have long been prepared in the unconscious and are only waiting to be released.

529 I had already seen from her previous history how the unconscious made use of the patient's inability to draw in order to insinuate its own suggestions. I had not overlooked the fact that the boulders had surreptitiously transformed themselves into *eggs*. The egg is a germ of life with a lofty symbolical significance. It is not just a cosmogonic symbol—it is also a "philosophical" one. As the former it is the Orphic egg, the world's beginning; as the latter, the philosophical egg of the medieval natural philosophers, the vessel from which, at the end of the *opus alchymicum,* the homunculus emerges, that is, the Anthropos, the spiritual, inner and complete man, who in Chinese alchemy is called the *chen-yen* (literally, "perfect man").[2]

530 From this hint, therefore, I could already see what solution the unconscious had in mind, namely individuation, for this is the transformation process that loosens the attachment to the unconscious. It is a definitive solution, for which all other ways serve as auxiliaries and temporary makeshifts. This knowledge, which for the time being I kept to myself, bade me act with caution. I therefore advised Miss X not to let it go at a mere fantasy-image of the act of liberation, but to try to make a

2 Cf. *Psychology and Alchemy,* pars. 138f., 306, and Wei Po-yang, "An Ancient Chinese Treatise on Alchemy."

picture of it. How this would turn out I could not guess, and that was a good thing, because otherwise I might have put Miss X on the wrong track from sheer helpfulness. She found this task terribly difficult owing to her artistic inhibitions. So I counselled her to content herself with what was possible and to use her fantasy for the purpose of circumventing technical difficulties. The object of this advice was to introduce as much fantasy as possible into the picture, for in that way the unconscious has the best chance of revealing its contents. I also advised her not to be afraid of bright colours, for I knew from experience that vivid colours seem to attract the unconscious. Thereupon, a new picture arose.

Picture 2

531 Again there are boulders, the round and pointed forms; but the round ones are no longer eggs, they are complete circles, and the pointed ones are tipped with golden light. One of the round forms has been blasted out of its place by a golden flash of lightning. The magician and magic wand are no longer there. The personal relationship to me seems to have ceased: the picture shows an impersonal natural process.

532 While Miss X was painting this picture she made all sorts of discoveries. Above all, she had no notion of what picture she was going to paint. She tried to reimagine the initial situation; the rocky shore and the sea are proof of this. But the eggs turned into abstract spheres or circles, and the magician's touch became a flash of lightning cutting through her unconscious state. With this transformation she had rediscovered the historical synonym of the philosophical egg, namely the *rotundum,* the round, original form of the Anthropos (or στοιχεῖον στρογγύλον, 'round element,' as Zosimos calls it). This is an idea that has been associated with the Anthropos since ancient times.[3] The soul, too, according to tradition, has a round form. As the Monk of Heisterbach says, it is not only "like to the sphere of the moon, but is furnished on all sides with eyes" (*ex omni parte oculata*). We shall come back to this motif of polyophthalmia later on. His remark refers in all probability to certain parapsychological phenomena, the "globes of light" or globular

3 *Psychology and Alchemy,* par. 109, n. 38.

luminosities which, with remarkable consistency, are regarded as "souls" in the remotest parts of the world.[4]

533 The liberating flash of lightning is a symbol also used by Paracelsus [5] and the alchemists for the same thing. Moses' rock-splitting staff, which struck forth the living water and afterwards changed into a serpent, may have been an unconscious echo in the background.[6] Lightning signifies a sudden, unexpected, and overpowering change of psychic condition.[7]

534 "In this Spirit of the Fire-flash consists the Great Almighty Life," says Jakob Böhme.[8] "For when you strike upon the *sharp* part of the stone, the bitter sting of Nature sharpens itself, and is stirred in the highest degree. For Nature is dissipated or *broken asunder* in the sharpness, so that the *Liberty shines forth as a Flash.*" [9] The flash is the *"Birth of the light."* [10] It has transformative power: "For if I could in my Flesh comprehend the Flash, which I very well see and know how it is, I could clarify or transfigure my Body therewith, so that it would shine with a bright light and glory. And then it would no more resemble and be conformed to the bestial Body, but to the angels of God." [11] Elsewhere Böhme says: "As when the Flash of Life

4 Caesarius of Heisterbach, *The Dialogue on Miracles,* trans. by Scott and Bland, Dist. IV, c. xxxiv (p. 231) and Dist. I, c. xxxii (p. 42): "His soul was like a glassy spherical vessel, that had eyes before and behind." A collection of similar reports in Bozzano, *Popoli primitivi e Manifestazioni supernormali.*

5 Cf. my "Paracelsus as a Spiritual Phenomenon," par. 190. It is Hermes Kyllenios, who calls up the souls. The caduceus corresponds to the phallus. Cf. Hippolytus, *Elenchos,* V, 7, 30.

6 The same association in *Elenchos,* V, 16, 8: serpent = δύναμις of Moses.

7 Ruland (*Lexicon,* 1612) speaks of "the gliding of the mind or spirit into another world." In the *Chymical Wedding* of Rosencreutz the lightning causes the royal pair to come alive. The Messiah appears as lightning in the Syrian Apocalypse of Baruch (Charles, *Apocrypha,* II, p. 510). Hippolytus (*Elenchos,* VIII, 10, 3) says that, in the view of the Docetists, the Monogenes drew together "like the greatest lightning-flash into the smallest body" (because the Aeons could not stand the effulgence of the Pleroma), or like "light under the eyelids." In this form he came into the world through Mary (VIII, 10, 5). Lactantius (*Works,* trans. by Fletcher, I, p. 470) says: ". . . the light of the descending God may be manifest in all the world as lightning." This refers to Luke 17 : 24: ". . . as the lightning that lighteneth . . so shall the Son of man be in his day." Similarly Zach. 9 : 14: "And the Lord God . . . his dart shall go forth as lightning" (DV).

8 *Forty Questions concerning the Soul* (*Works,* ed. Ward and Langcake, II, p. 17).

9 *The High and Deep Searching of the Threefold Life of Man* (*Works,* II), p. 11.

10 *Aurora* (*Works,* I), X. 17, p. 84.

11 Ibid., X. 38, p. 86.

rises up in the centre of the Divine Power, wherein all the spirits of God attain their life, and highly rejoice." [12] Of the "Source-spirit" *Mercurius*, he says that it "arises in the Fire-flash." Mercurius is the "animal spirit" which, from *Lucifer's* body, "struck into the Salniter [13] of God like a *fiery serpent* from its hole, as if there went a fiery Thunder-bolt into God's Nature, or a fierce Serpent, which tyrannizes, raves, and rages, as if it would tear and rend Nature all to pieces." [14] Of the "innermost *birth of the soul*" the bestial body "attains only a glimpse, just as if it lightened." [15] "The triumphing *divine Birth* lasteth in us men only so long as the flash lasteth; therefore our knowledge is but in part, whereas in God the flash stands unchangeably, always eternally thus." [16] (Cf. Fig. 1.)

535 In this connection I would like to mention that Böhme associates lightning with something else too. That is the *quaternity*, which plays a great role in the following pictures. When caught and assuaged in the four "Qualities" or four "Spirits," [17] "the Flash, or the Light, subsists in the *Midst or Centre as a Heart.*[18] Now when that Light, which stands in the Midst or Centre, shines into the four Spirits, then the Power of the four Spirits rises up in the Light, and they become Living, and love the Light; that is, they take it into them, and are *impregnated* with it." [19] "The Flash, or *Stock,* [20] or Pith, or the Heart, which is generated in the Powers, remains standing in the Midst or Centre, and that is the *Son*. . . . And this is the true *Holy Ghost,* whom we Christians honour and adore for the third

12 Ibid., X. 53, p. 87.

13 Salniter = *sal nitri* = Saltpetre; like salt, *the prima materia. Three Principles of the Divine Essence* (*Works,* I), I. 9, p. 10.

14 *Aurora,* XV. 84, p. 154. Here the lightning is not a revelation of God's will but a Satanic change of state. Lightning is also a manifestation of the devil (Luke 10 : 18).

15 Ibid., XIX. 19, p. 185.

16 Ibid., XI. 10, p. 93.

17 For Böhme the four "qualities" coincide partly with the four elements but also with dry, wet, warm, cold, the four qualities of taste (e.g., sharp, bitter, sweet, sour), and the four colours.

18 A heart forms the centre of the mandala in the *Forty Questions*. See Fig. 1.

19 *Aurora,* XI. 27–28, p. 94.

20 "Stock" in this context can mean tree or cross (*σταυρός*, 'stake, pole, post'), but it could also refer to a staff or stick. It would then be the magical wand that, in the subsequent development of these pictures, begins to sprout like a tree. Cf. infra, par. 570.

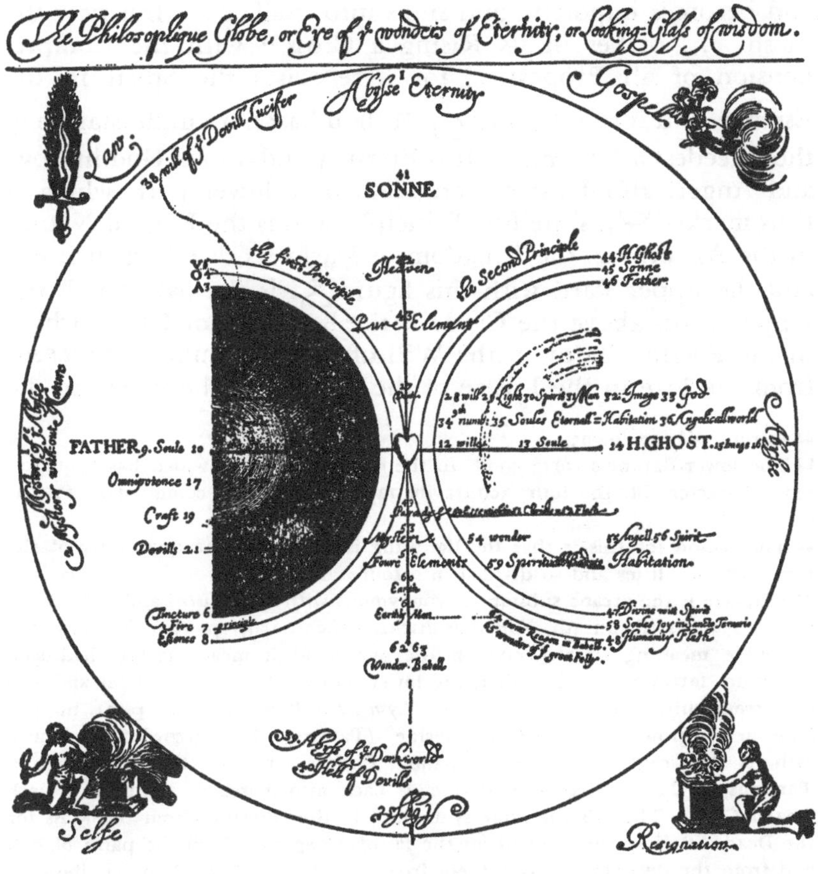

Fig. 1. Mandala from Jakob Böhme's *XL Questions concerning the Soule* (1620)

The picture is taken from the English edition of 1647. The quaternity consists of *Father, H. Ghost, Sonne,* and *Earth* or *Earthly Man.* It is characteristic that the two semicircles are turned back to back instead of closing.

Person in the Deity."[21] Elsewhere Böhme says: "When the Fire-flash reaches the dark substance,[22] it is a great terror, from which the Cold Fire draws back in affright as if it would perish, and becomes impotent, and sinks into itself. . . . But now the Flash . . . makes in its Rising a Cross[23] with the Comprehension of all Properties; for here arises the Spirit in the Essence, and it stands thus: . If thou hast here understanding, thou needest ask no more; it is Eternity and Time, God in Love and Anger, also Heaven and Hell. The lower part, which is thus marked , is the first Principle, and is the Eternal Nature in the Anger, viz. the Kingdom of Darkness dwelling in itself; and the upper Part, with this figure , is the Salniter;[24] the Upper Cross above the Circle is the Kingdom of Glory, which in the Flagrat of Joy in the Will of the free Lubet[25] proceeds from the Fire in the Lustre of the Light into the power of the

21 *Aurora,* XI. 37, p. 95.

22 The lower darkness corresponds to the elemental world, which has a quaternary character. Cf. the four Achurayim mentioned in the commentary to Picture 7.

23 The reason for this is that the lightning is caught by the quaternity of elements and qualities and so divided into four.

24 Saltpetre is the arcane substance, synonymous with *Sal Saturni* and *Sal Tartari mundi maioris* (Khunrath, *Von hylealischen Chaos,* 1597, p. 263). Tartarus has a double meaning in alchemy: on the one hand it means tartar (hydrogen potassium tartrate); on the other, the lower half of the cooking vessel and also the arcane substance (Eleazar, *Uraltes Chymisches Werk,* 1760, II, p. 91, no. 32). The metals grow in the "cavitates terrae" (Tartarus). Salt, according to Khunrath, is the "centrum terrae physicum." Eleazar says that the "Heaven and Tartarus of the wise" change all metals back into mercury. Saturn is a dark "malefic" star. There is the same symbolism in the Offertory from the Mass for the Dead: "Deliver the souls of all the faithful departed from the pains of hell and from the deep pit; deliver them from the mouth of the lion [attribute of Ialdabaoth, Saturn], lest Tartarus lay hold on them, and they fall into darkness." Saturn "maketh darkness" (Böhme, *Threefold Life,* IX. 85, p. 96) and is one aspect of the Salniter (*Signatura rerum,* XIV. 46–48, p. 118). Salniter is the "dried" or "fixed" form and embodiment of the seven "Source Spirits" of God, who are all contained in the seventh, Mercury, the "Word of God" (*Aurora,* XI. 86f., p. 99 and XV. 49, p. 151; *Sig. rer.,* IV. 35, p. 28). Salniter, like mercury, is the mother and cause of all metals and salts (*Sig. rer.,* XIV. 46 and III. 16, pp. 118 and 19). It is a subtle body, the paradisal earth and the spotless state of the body before the Fall, and hence the epitome of the *prima materia.*

25 ["Flagrat" and "lubet" are used by Böhme to signify respectively "flash, flame, burning" and "desire, affect."—EDITORS.]

Liberty; and this spiritual Water[26] . . . is the Corporality of the free Lubet . . . wherein the Lustre from the Fire and Light makes a Tincture, viz. a budding and growing and a Manifestation of Colours from the Fire and Light." [27]

536 I have purposely dwelt at some length on Böhme's disquisition on the lightning, because it throws a good deal of light on the psychology of our pictures. However, it anticipates some things that will only become clear when we examine the pictures themselves. I must therefore ask the reader to bear Böhme's views in mind in the following commentary. I have put the most important points in italics. It is clear from the quotations what the lightning meant to Böhme and what sort of a role it plays in the present case. The last quotation in particular deserves special attention, as it anticipates various key motifs in the subsequent pictures done by my patient, namely the cross, the quaternity, the divided mandala, the lower half of which is virtually equivalent to hell and the upper half to the lighter realm of the "Salniter." For Böhme the lower half signifies the "everlasting darkness" that "extends into the fire," [28] while the upper, "salnitrous" half corresponds to the third Principle, the "visible, elemental world, which is an emanation of the first and other Principle." [29] The cross, in turn, corresponds to the second Principle, the "Kingdom of Glory," which is revealed through "magic fire," the lightning, which he calls a "Revelation of Divine Motion." [30] The "lustre of the fire" comes from the "unity of God" and reveals his will. The mandala therefore represents the "Kingdom of Nature," which "in itself is the great everlasting Darkness." The "Kingdom of God," on the other hand, or the "Glory" (i.e., the Cross), is the Light of which John 1 : 5 speaks: "And the light shineth in the darkness, and the darkness comprehendeth it not." The Life that "breaks itself off from the eternal Light and enters into the Object, as into the selfhood of Properties," is "only fantastic and foolish, even such as the Devils were, and the souls of the damned are; as can be seen . . . from the fourth number." [31]

26 Reference to the "waters which were above the firmament" (Gen. 1 : 7).

27 *Sig. rer.*, XIV. 32–33, p. 116.

28 *Tabula principiorum*, 3 (Amsterdam edn., 1682, p. 271).

29 Ibid., 5, p. 271. 30 Ibid., 42, p. 279.

31 *Four Tables of Divine Revelation*, p. 14.

For the "fire of Nature" is called by Böhme the *fourth form,* and he understands it as a "spiritual Life-Fire, that exists from a continual conjunction . . . of Hardness [i.e., the solidified, dry Salniter] and Motion [the Divine Will]." [32] Quite in keeping with John 1 : 5 the quaternity of the lightning, the Cross, pertains to the Kingdom of Glory, whereas Nature, the visible world and the dark abyss remain untouched by the fourfold light and abide in darkness.

537 For the sake of completeness I should mention that  is the sign for *cinnabar,* the most important quicksilver ore (HgS).[33] The coincidence of the two symbols can hardly be accidental in view of the significance which Böhme attributes to Mercurius. Ruland finds it rather hard to define exactly what was meant by cinnabar.[34] The only certain thing is that there was a κιννάβαρις τῶν φιλοσόφων (cinnabar of the philosophers) in Greek alchemy, and that it stood for the *rubedo* stage of the transforming substance. Thus Zosimos says: "(After the preceding process) you will find the gold coloured fiery red like blood. That is the cinnabar of the philosophers and the copper man (χαλκάνθρωπος), turned to gold." [35] Cinnabar was also supposed to be identical with the uroboros dragon.[36] Even in Pliny, cinnabar is called *sanguis draconis,* 'dragon's blood,' a term that lasted all through the Middle Ages.[37] On account of its redness it was often identified with the philosophical sulphur. A special difficulty is the fact that the wine-red cinnabar crystals were classed with the ἄνθρακες, *carbons,* to which belong all reddish and red-tinted stones like *rubies,* garnets, amethysts, etc. They all shine like glowing coals.[38] The λιθάνθρακες (anthracites), on the other hand, were

32 Ibid., p. 13.

33 Its official name is *hydrargyrum sulfuratum rubrum.* Another version of its sign is : cf. Lüdy, *Alchemistische und Chemische Zeichen,* and Gessmann, *Die Geheimsymbole der Alchymie, Arzneikunde und Astrologie des Mittelalters.*

34 "There is very great doubt among doctors as to what is actually signified by Cinnabar, for the term is applied by different authorities to very diverse substances." Ruland, *Lexicon,* p. 102.

35 Berthelot, *Alch. grecs,* III, xxix, 24.

36 Ibid., I, v, 1. It may be remarked that the dragon has three ears and four legs (The axiom of Maria! Cf. *Psychology and Alchemy,* pars. 209f.)

37 *Hist. nat.,* Lib. XXXIII, cap. vii.

38 The medical term *anthrax* means 'carbuncle, abscess.'

regarded as "quenched" coals. These associations explain the similarity of the alchemical signs for gold, antimony, and garnet. Gold ♁, after mercury the most important "philosophical" substance, shares its sign with what is known as "regulus" or "button" antimony,[39] and during the two decades prior to the writing of *Signatura rerum* (1622), from which our quotation comes, this had enjoyed particular fame as the new transformative substance[40] and panacea.[41] Basilius Valentinus' *Triumphal Car of Antimony* was published about the first decade of the seventeenth century (the first edition possibly in 1611) and soon found the widest acclaim.[42] The sign for garnet is ♁, and ⊖ means salt. A cross with a little circle in it ⌖ means copper (from the "Cyprian," Venus ♀). Medicinal tartaric acid is denoted by ♀, and hydrogen potassium tartrate (tartar) has the signs ⊖ ♀.[43] Tartar settles on the bottom of the vessel, which in the language of the alchemists means: in the underworld, Tartarus.[44]

538 I will not attempt here any interpretation of Böhme's symbols, but will only point out that in our picture the lightning, striking into the darkness and "hardness," has blasted a *rotundum* out of the dark *massa confusa* and kindled a light in it. There can be no doubt that the dark stone means the blackness, i.e., the unconscious, just as the sea and sky and the upper half of the woman's figure indicate the sphere of consciousness. We may safely assume that Böhme's symbol refers to a similar situation. The lightning has released the spherical form from the rock and so caused a kind of liberation. But, just as the magician has been replaced by the lightning, so the patient has been replaced by the sphere. The unconscious has thus presented her

39 Antimony is also denoted by ♁. Regulus = "The impure mass of metal formed beneath the slag in melting and reducing ores" (Merriam-Webster).

40 Michael Maier (*Symbola aureae mensae*, 1617, p. 380) says: "The true antimony of the Philosophers lies hidden in the deep sea, like the son of the King."

41 Praised as Hercules Morbicida, "slayer of diseases" (ibid., p. 378).

42 The book was (first?) mentioned by Maier, ibid., pp. 379ff.

43 Also ⊡, a pure quaternity.

44 Τάρταρος, like βόρβορος, βάρβαρος, etc. is probably onomatopoeic, expressing terror. Τόργανον means 'vinegar, spoilt wine.' Derived from ταράσσω, 'to stir up, disturb, frighten' (τάραγμα, 'trouble, confusion') and τάρβος, 'terror, awe.'

with ideas which show that she had gone on thinking without the aid of consciousness and that this radically altered the initial situation. It was again her inability to draw that led to this result. Before finding this solution, she had made two attempts to portray the act of liberation with human figures, but with no success. She had overlooked the fact that the initial situation, her imprisonment in the rock, was already irrational and symbolic and therefore could not be solved in a rational way. It had to be done by an equally irrational process. That was why I advised her, should she fail in her attempt to draw human figures, to use some kind of hieroglyph. It then suddenly struck her that the sphere was a suitable symbol for the individual human being. That it was a chance idea (*Einfall*) is proved by the fact that it was not her conscious mind that thought up this typification, but the unconscious, for an *Einfall* "falls in" quite of its own accord. It should be noted that she represents only herself as a sphere, not me. I am represented only by the lightning, purely functionally, so that for her I am simply the "precipitating" cause. As a magician I appeared to her in the apt role of Hermes Kyllenios, of whom the Odyssey says: "Meanwhile Cyllenian Hermes was gathering in the souls of the suitors, armed with the splendid golden wand that he can use at will to cast a spell on our eyes or wake us from the soundest sleep." [45] Hermes is the ψυχῶν αἴτιος, 'originator of souls.' He is also the ἡγήτωρ ὀνείρων, 'guide of dreams.' [46] For the following pictures it is of special importance that Hermes has the number 4 attributed to him. Martianus Capella says: "The number four is assigned to the Cyllenian, for he alone is held to be a fourfold god." [47]

539 The form the picture had taken was not unreservedly welcome to the patient's conscious mind. Luckily, however, while painting it Miss X had discovered that two factors were involved. These, in her own words, were *reason* and the *eyes*. Reason always wanted to make the picture as *it* thought it ought to be; but the eyes held fast to their vision and finally forced the picture to come out as it actually did and not in accordance with rationalistic expectations. Her reason, she said, had really intended a daylight scene, with the sunshine melting the sphere

45 Rieu trans., p. 351.
46 Hippolytus, *Elenchos*, V, 7, 30; Kerényi, "Hermes der Seelenführer," p. 29.
47 Ibid., p. 30.

free, but the eyes favoured a nocturne with "shattering, dangerous lightning." This realization helped her to acknowledge the actual result of her artistic efforts and to admit that it was in fact an objective and impersonal process and not a personal relationship.

540 For anyone with a personalistic view of psychic events, such as a Freudian, it will not be easy to see in this anything more than an elaborate repression. But if there was any repression here we certainly cannot make the conscious mind responsible for it, because the conscious mind would undoubtedly have preferred a personal imbroglio as being far more interesting. The repression must have been manoeuvred by the unconscious from the start. One should consider what this means: instinct, the most original force of the unconscious, is suppressed or turned back on itself by an arrangement stemming from this same unconscious! It would be idle indeed to talk of "repression" here, since we know that the unconscious goes straight for its goal and that this does not consist solely in pairing two animals but in allowing an individual to become whole. For this purpose wholeness—represented by the sphere—is emphasized as the essence of personality, while I am reduced to the fraction of a second, the duration of a lightning flash.

541 The patient's association to lightning was that it might stand for *intuition,* a conjecture that is not far off the mark, since intuitions often come "like a flash." Moreover, there are good grounds for thinking that Miss X was a *sensation* type. She herself thought she was one. The "inferior" function would then be intuition. As such, it would have the significance of a releasing or "redeeming" function. We know from experience that the inferior function always compensates, complements, and balances the "superior" function.[48] My psychic peculiarity would make me a suitable projection carrier in this respect. The inferior function is the one of which least conscious use is made. This is the reason for its undifferentiated quality, but also for its freshness and vitality. It is not at the disposal of the conscious mind, and even after long use it never loses its autonomy and spontaneity, or only to a very limited degree. Its role is therefore mostly that of a *deus ex machina.* It depends not on the

[48] The pairs of functions are thinking/feeling, sensation/intuition. See *Psychological Types,* definitions.

ego but on the *self*. Hence it hits consciousness unexpectedly, like lightning, and occasionally with devastating consequences. It thrusts the ego aside and makes room for a supraordinate factor, the totality of a person, which consists of conscious and unconscious and consequently extends far beyond the ego. This self was always present,[49] but sleeping, like Nietzsche's "image in the stone." [50] It is, in fact, the secret of the stone, of the *lapis philosophorum*, in so far as this is the *prima materia*. In the stone sleeps the spirit *Mercurius*, the "circle of the moon," the "round and square," [51] the homunculus, Tom Thumb and Anthropos at once,[52] whom the alchemists also symbolized as their famed *lapis philosophorum*.[53]

542 All these ideas and inferences were naturally unknown to my patient, and they were known to me at the time only in so far as I was able to recognize the circle as a *mandala*,[54] the psychological expression of the totality of the self. Under these circumstances there could be no question of my having unintentionally infected her with alchemical ideas. The pictures are, in all essentials, genuine creations of the unconscious; their inessential aspects (landscape motifs) are derived from conscious contents.

543 Although the sphere with its glowing red centre and the golden flash of lightning play the chief part, it should not be overlooked that there are several other eggs or spheres as well. If the sphere signifies the self of the patient, we must apply this interpretation to the other spheres, too. They must therefore represent other people who, in all probability, were her intimates. In both the pictures two other spheres are clearly indicated. So I must mention that Miss X had two women friends who shared her intellectual interests and were joined to her in a lifelong friendship. All three of them, as if bound together by fate, are rooted in the same "earth," i.e., in the collective unconscious, which is one and the same for all. It is probably for this reason that the second picture has the decidedly *nocturnal*

[49] Cf. *Psychology and Alchemy*, par. 329, for the *a priori* presence of the mandala symbol. [50] Details in ibid., par. 406.

[51] Preisendanz, *Papyri Graecae Magicae*, II, p. 139.

[52] "The Spirit Mercurius," pars. 267ff.

[53] *Psychology and Alchemy*, Part III, ch. 5.

[54] Cf. Wilhelm and Jung, *The Secret of the Golden Flower*.

character intended by the unconscious and asserted against the wishes of the conscious mind. It should also be mentioned that the pointed pyramids of the first picture reappear in the second, where their points are actually gilded by the lightning and strongly emphasized. I would interpret them as unconscious contents "pushing up" into the light of consciousness, as seems to be the case with many contents of the collective unconscious.[55] In contrast to the first picture, the second is painted in more vivid colours, red and gold. Gold expresses sunlight, value, divinity even. It is therefore a favourite synonym for the *lapis,* being the *aurum philosophicum* or *aurum potabile* or *aurum vitreum.*[56]

544 As already pointed out, I was not at that time in a position to reveal anything of these ideas to Miss X, for the simple reason that I myself knew nothing of them. I feel compelled to mention this circumstance yet again, because the third picture, which now follows, brings a motif that points unmistakably to alchemy and actually gave me the definitive incentive to make a thorough study of the works of the old adepts.

Picture 3

545 The third picture, done as spontaneously as the first two, is distinguished most of all by its light colours. Free-floating in space, among clouds, is a dark blue sphere with a wine-red border. Round the middle runs a wavy silver band, which keeps the sphere balanced by "equal and opposite forces," as the patient explained. To the right, above the sphere, floats a snake with golden rings, its head pointing at the sphere—an obvious development of the golden lightning in Picture 2. But she drew the snake in afterwards, on account of certain "reflections." The whole is "a planet in the making." In the middle of the silver band is the number 12. The band was thought of as being in rapid vibratory motion; hence the wave motif. It is like a vibrating belt that keeps the sphere afloat. Miss X compared it to the ring of Saturn. But unlike this, which is composed of

55 Though we talk a great deal and with some justice about the resistance which the unconscious puts up against becoming conscious, it must also be emphasized that it has a kind of gradient towards consciousness, and this acts as an urge to become conscious.

56 The last-named refers to Rev. 21 : 21.

disintegrated satellites, her ring was the origin of future moons such as Jupiter possesses. The black lines in the silver band she called "lines of force"; they were meant to indicate that it was in motion. As if asking a question, I made the remark: "Then it is the vibrations of the band that keep the sphere floating?" "Naturally," she said, "they are the wings of Mercury, the messenger of the gods. The silver is *quicksilver!*" She went on at once: "Mercury, that is Hermes, is the Nous, the mind or reason, and that is the animus, who is here outside instead of inside. He is like a veil that hides the true personality." [57] We shall leave this latter remark alone for the moment and turn first to the wider context, which, unlike that of the two previous pictures, is especially rich.

546 While Miss X was painting this picture, she felt that two earlier dreams were mingling with her vision. They were the two "big" dreams of her life. She knew of the attribute "big" from my stories of the dream life of African primitives I had visited. It has become a kind of "colloquial term" for characterizing archetypal dreams, which as we know have a peculiar numinosity. It was used in this sense by the dreamer. Several years previously, she had undergone a major operation. Under narcosis she had the following dream-vision: *She saw a grey globe of the world. A silver band rotated about the equator and, according to the frequency of its vibrations, formed alternate zones of condensation and evaporation. In the zones of condensation appeared the numbers 1 to 3, but they had the tendency to increase up to 12.* These numbers signified "nodal points" or "great personalities" who played a part in man's historical development. "The number 12 meant the most important nodal point or great man (still to come), because it denotes the climax or turning point of the process of development." (These are her own words.)

547 The other dream that intervened had occurred a year before the first one: *She saw a golden snake in the sky. It demanded the sacrifice, from among a great crowd of people, of a young man, who obeyed this demand with an expression of sorrow.* The dream was repeated a little later, but this time *the snake*

[57] Miss X was referring to my remarks in "The Relations between the Ego and the Unconscious," which she knew in its earlier version in *Collected Papers on Analytical Psychology* (2nd. edn., 1920).

picked on the dreamer herself. The assembled people regarded her compassionately, but she took her fate "proudly" on herself.

548 She was, as she told me, born immediately after midnight, so soon afterwards, indeed, that there was some doubt as to whether she came into the world on the 28th or on the 29th. Her father used to tease her by saying that she was obviously born before her time, since she came into the world just at the beginning of a new day, but "only just," so that one could almost believe she was born "at the twelfth hour." The number 12, as she said, meant for her the culminating point of her life, which she had only now reached. That is, she felt the "liberation" as the climax of her life. It is indeed an hour of birth—not of the dreamer but of the self. This distinction must be borne in mind.

549 The context to Picture 3 here established needs a little commentary. First, it must be emphasized that the patient felt the moment of painting this picture as the "climax" of her life and also described it as such. Second, two "big" dreams have amalgamated in the picture, which heightens its significance still more. The sphere blasted from the rock in Picture 2 has now, in the brighter atmosphere, floated up to heaven. The nocturnal darkness of the earth has vanished. The increase of light indicates conscious realization: the liberation has become a fact that is integrated into consciousness. The patient has understood that the floating sphere symbolizes the "true personality." At present, however, it is not quite clear how she understands the relation of the ego to the "true personality." The term chosen by her coincides in a remarkable way with the Chinese *chen-yen,* the "true" or "complete" man, who has the closest affinity with the *homo quadratus* [58] of alchemy.[59] As we pointed out in the analysis of Picture 2, the *rotundum* of alchemy is identical with Mercurius, the "round and square." [60] In Picture 3 the connection is shown concretely through the

58 The expressions "square," "four-square," are used in English in this sense.

59 The "squared figure" in the centre of the alchemical mandala, symbolizing the *lapis,* and whose midpoint is Mercurius, is called the "mediator making peace between the enemies or elements." [Cf. *Aion* (Part II of this vol.), pars. 377f.—EDITORS.]

60 So called in an invocation to Hermes. Cf. Preisendanz, II, p. 139. Further particulars in *Psychology and Alchemy,* par. 172; fig. 214 is a repetition of the *quadrangulum secretum sapientum* from the *Tractatus aureus* (1610), p. 43. Cf. also my "The Spirit Mercurius," par. 272.

mediating idea of the wings of Mercury, who, it is evident, has entered the picture in his own right and not because of any non-existent knowledge of Böhme's writings.[61]

550 For the alchemists the process of individuation represented by the *opus* was an analogy of the creation of the world, and the *opus* itself an analogy of God's work of creation. Man was seen as a microcosm, a complete equivalent of the world in miniature. In our picture, we see what it is in man that corresponds to the cosmos, and what kind of evolutionary process is compared with the creation of the world and the heavenly bodies: it is the *birth of the self,* the latter appearing as a microcosm.[62] It is not the empirical man that forms the "correspondentia" to the world, as the medievalists thought, but rather the indescribable totality of the psychic or spiritual man, who cannot be described because he is compounded of consciousness as well as of the indeterminable extent of the unconscious.[63] The term microcosm proves the existence of a common intuition (also present in my patient) that the "total" man is as big as the world, like an Anthropos. The cosmic analogy had already appeared in the much earlier dream under narcosis, which likewise contained the problem of personality: the nodes of the vibrations were great personalities of historical importance. As early as 1916, I had observed a similar individuation process, illustrated by pictures, in another woman patient. In her case too there was a world creation, depicted as follows (see Fig. 2):

551 To the left, from an unknown source, three drops fall, dissolving into four lines,[64] or two pairs of lines. These lines move and form four separate paths, which then unite periodically in a nodal point and thus build a system of vibrations. The nodes are "great personalities and founders of religions," as my erstwhile patient told me. It is obviously the same conception as in our case, and we can call it archetypal in so far as there exist

61 Despite my efforts I could find no other source for the "mercury." Naturally cryptomnesia cannot be ruled out. Considering the definiteness of the idea and the astonishing coincidence of its appearance (as in Böhme), I incline to the hypothesis of spontaneous emergence, which does not eliminate the archetype but, on the contrary, presupposes it.

62 Cf. the "innermost Birth of the Soul" in Böhme.

63 This *homo interior* or *altus* was Mercurius, or was at least derived from him. Cf. "The Spirit Mercurius," pars. 284ff.

64 The lines are painted in the classical four colours.

Picture 1

Picture 2

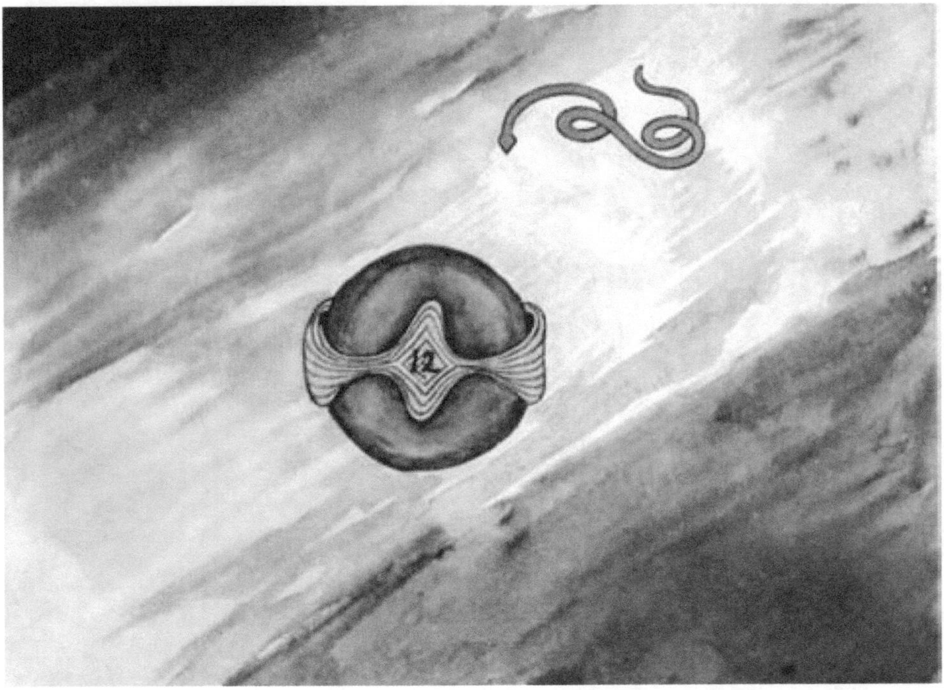

Picture 3

Picture 4

Picture 5

Picture 6

Picture 7

Picture 8

Picture 9

Picture 10

Picture 11

Picture 12

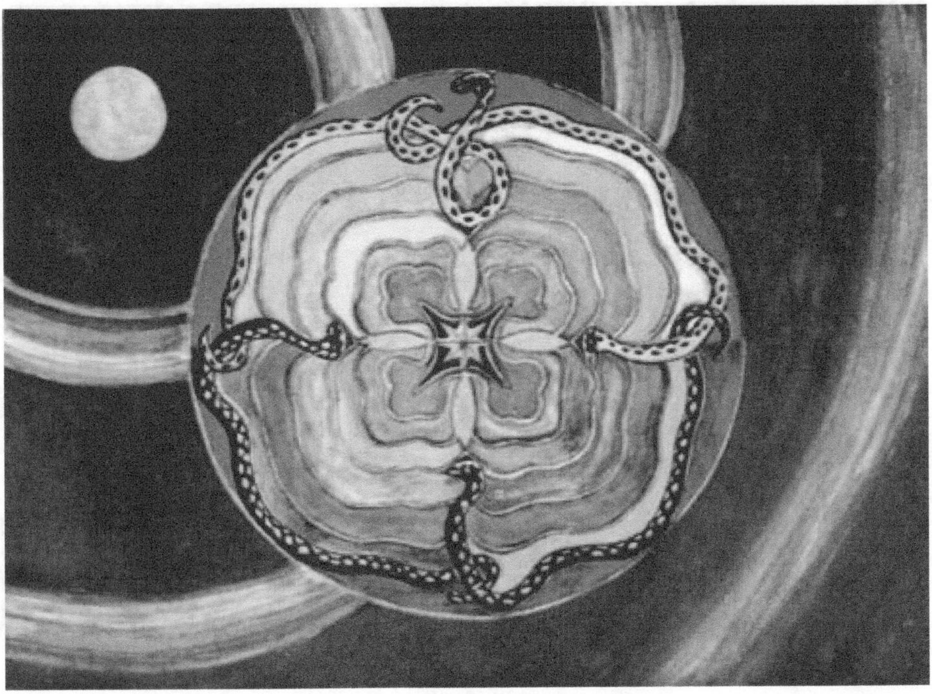

Picture 13

Picture 14

Picture 15

Picture 16

Picture 17

Picture 18

Picture 19

Picture 20

Picture 21

Picture 22

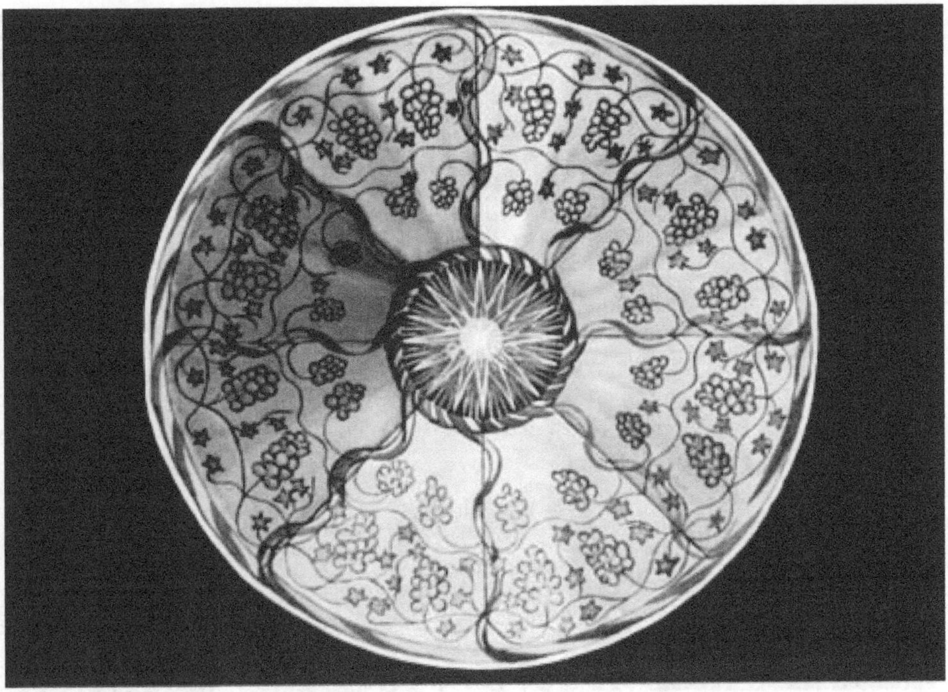

Picture 23

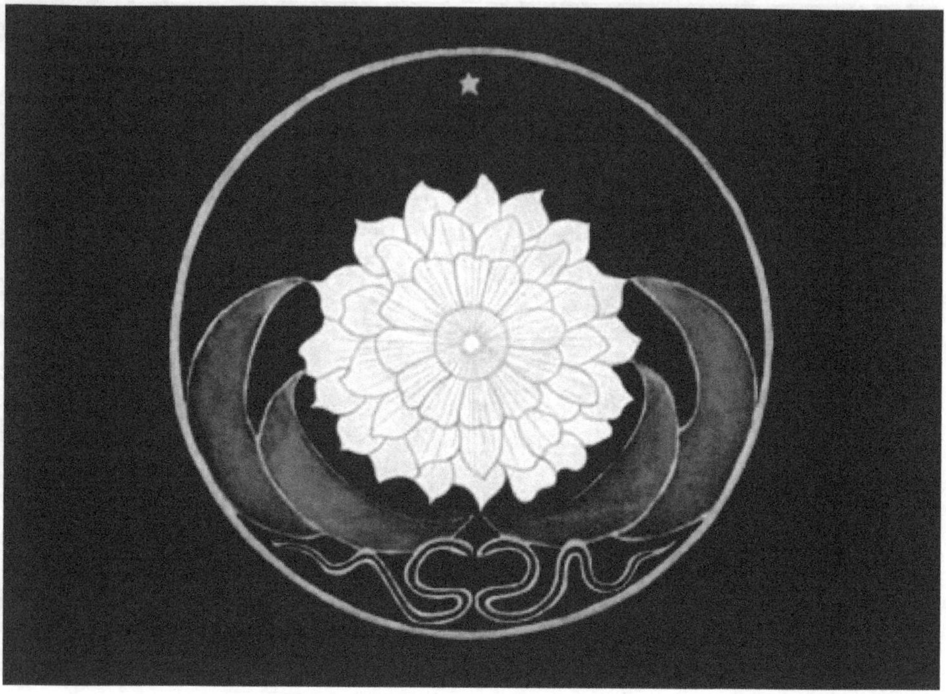

Picture 24

Fig. 2. Sketch of a picture from the year 1916

At the top, the sun, surrounded by a rainbow-coloured halo divided into twelve parts, like the zodiac. To the left, the descending, to the right, the ascending, transformation process.

universal ideas of world periods, critical transitions, gods and half gods who personify the aeons. The unconscious naturally does not produce its images from conscious reflections, but from the worldwide propensity of the human system to form such conceptions as the world periods of the Parsees, the yugas and avatars of Hinduism, and the Platonic months of astrology with their bull and ram deities and the "great" Fish of the Christian aeon.[65]

552 That the nodes in our patient's picture signify or contain numbers is a bit of unconscious number mysticism that is not always easy to unravel. So far as I can see, there are two stages in this arithmetical phenomenology: the first, earlier stage goes up to 3, the second, later stage up to 12. Two numbers, 3 and 12, are expressly mentioned. Twelve is four times three. I think we have here stumbled again on the axiom of Maria, that peculiar dilemma of three and four,[66] which I have discussed many times before because it plays such a great role in alchemy.[67] I would hazard that we have to do here with a *tetrameria* (as in Greek alchemy), a transformation process divided into four stages[68] of three parts each, analogous to the twelve transformations of the zodiac and its division into four. As not infrequently happens, the number 12 would then have a not merely individual significance (as the patient's birth number, for instance), but a time-conditioned one too, since the present aeon of the Fishes is drawing to its end and is at the same time the twelfth house of the zodiac. One is reminded of similar Gnostic ideas, such as those in the gnosis of Justin: The "Father" (Elohim) begets with Edem, who was half woman and half snake, twelve "fatherly" angels, and Edem gives birth besides these to twelve "motherly" angels, who—in psychological parlance—represent the shadows of the twelve "fatherly" ones. The "motherly" angels divide themselves into four categories (μέρη) of three each, corresponding to the four rivers of

65 The "giant" fish of the Abercius inscription (*c.* A.D. 200). [Cf. *Aion,* par. 127, n. 4.—EDITORS.]

66 Cf. Frobenius, *Schicksalskunde,* pp. 119f. The author's interpretations seem to me questionable in some respects.

67 *Psychology and Alchemy,* par. 204; "The Phenomenology of the Spirit in Fairytales," pars. 425 and 430; and *Psychology and Religion,* par. 184.

68 *Psychology and Alchemy,* index, s.v. "quartering."

Paradise. These angels dance round in a circle (ἐν χόρῳ κυκλικῷ).[69] It is legitimate to bring these seemingly remote associations into hypothetical relationship, because they all spring from a common root, i.e., the collective unconscious.

553 In our picture Mercurius forms a world-encircling band, usually represented by a snake.[70] Mercurius is a serpent or dragon in alchemy ("serpens mercurialis"). Oddly enough, this serpent is some distance away from the sphere and is aiming down at it, as if to strike. The sphere, we are told, is kept afloat by equal and opposite forces, represented by the quicksilver or somehow connected with it. According to the old view, Mercurius is duplex, i.e., he is himself an antithesis.[71] Mercurius or Hermes is a magician and god of magicians. As Hermes Trismegistus he is the patriarch of alchemy. His magician's wand, the caduceus, is entwined by two snakes. The same attribute distinguishes Asklepios, the god of physicians.[72] The archetype of these ideas was projected on to me by the patient before ever the analysis had begun.

554 The primordial image underlying the sphere girdled with quicksilver is probably that of the world egg encoiled by a snake.[73] But in our case the snake symbol of Mercurius is replaced by a sort of pseudo-physicistic notion of a field of vibrating molecules of quicksilver. This looks like an intellectual disguising of the true situation, that the self, or its symbol, is

69 Hippolytus, *Elenchos,* V, 26, 1ff.

70 Cf. the "account . . . of a many-coloured and many-shaped sphere" from the Cod. Vat. 190 (cited by Cumont in *Textes et monuments figurés relatifs aux mystères de Mithra*), which says: "The all-wise God fashioned an immensely great dragon of gigantic length, breadth and thickness, having its dark-coloured head . . . towards sunrise, and its tail . . . towards sunset." Of the dragon the text says: "Then the all-wise Demiurge, by his highest command, set in motion the great dragon with the spangled crown, I mean the twelve signs of the zodiac which it carried on its back." Eisler (*Weltenmantel und Himmelszelt,* p. 389) connects this zodiacal serpent with Leviathan. For the dragon as symbol of the year, see the Mythographus Vaticanus III, in *Classicorum Auctorum e Vaticanis Codicibus Editorum,* VI (1831), p. 162. There is a similar association in Horapollo, *Hieroglyphica,* trans. by Boas, p. 57.

71 "The Spirit Mercurius," ch. 6.

72 Meier, *Antike Inkubation und moderne Psychotherapie.*

73 Vishnu is described as *dāmodara,* 'bound about the body with a rope.' I am not sure whether this symbol should be considered here; I mention it only for the sake of completeness.

entwined by the mercurial serpent. As the patient remarked more or less correctly, the "true personality" is veiled by it. This, presumably, would then be something like an Eve in the coils of the paradisal serpent. In order to avoid giving this appearance, Mercurius has obligingly split into his two forms, according to the old-established pattern: the *mercurius crudus* or *vulgi* (crude or ordinary quicksilver), and the *Mercurius Philosophorum* (the *spiritus mercurialis* or the spirit Mercurius, Hermes-Nous), who hovers in the sky as the golden lightning-snake or Nous Serpent, at present inactive. In the vibrations of the quicksilver band we may discern a certain tremulous excitement, just as the suspension expresses tense expectation: "Hover and haver suspended in pain!" For the alchemists quicksilver meant the concrete, material manifestation of the spirit Mercurius, as the above-mentioned mandala in the scholia to the *Tractatus aureus* shows: the central point is Mercurius, and the square is Mercurius divided into the four elements. He is the *anima mundi,* the innermost point and at the same time the encompasser of the world, like the atman in the Upanishads. And just as quicksilver is a materialization of Mercurius, so the gold is a materialization of the sun in the earth.[74]

555 A circumstance that never ceases to astonish one is this: that at all times and in all places alchemy brought its conception of the *lapis* or its *minera* (raw material) together with the idea of the *homo altus* or *maximus,* that is, with the Anthropos.[75] Equally, one must stand amazed at the fact that here too the conception of the dark round stone blasted out of the rock should represent such an abstract idea as the psychic totality of man. The earth and in particular the heavy cold stone is the epitome of materiality, and so is the metallic quicksilver which, the patient thought, meant the animus (mind, *nous*). We would expect pneumatic symbols for the idea of the self and the animus, images of air, breath, wind. The ancient formula λίθος οὐ λίθος (the stone that is no stone) expresses this dilemma: we are dealing with a *complexio oppositorum,* with something like the nature of light, which under some conditions behaves like particles and under others like waves, and is obviously in

74 Michael Maier, *De circulo physico quadrato* (1616), ch. I.

75 Christ in medieval alchemy. Cf. *Psychology and Alchemy,* Part III, ch. 5.

its essence both at once. Something of this kind must be conjectured with regard to these paradoxical and hardly explicable statements of the unconscious. They are not inventions of any conscious mind, but are spontaneous manifestations of a psyche not controlled by consciousness and obviously possessing all the freedom it wants to express views that take no account of our conscious intentions. The duplicity of Mercurius, his simultaneously metallic and pneumatic nature, is a parallel to the symbolization of an extremely spiritual idea like the Anthropos by a corporeal, indeed metallic, substance (gold). One can only conclude that the unconscious tends to regard spirit and matter not merely as equivalent but as actually identical, and this in flagrant contrast to the intellectual one-sidedness of consciousness, which would sometimes like to spiritualize matter and at other times to materialize spirit. That the *lapis,* or in our case the floating sphere, has a double meaning is clear from the circumstance that it is characterized by two symbolical colours: red means blood and affectivity, the physiological reaction that joins spirit to body, and blue means the spiritual process (mind or *nous*). This duality reminds one of the alchemical duality *corpus* and *spiritus,* joined together by a third, the *anima* as the *ligamentum corporis et spiritus.* For Böhme a "high deep blue" mixed with green signifies "Liberty," that is, the inner "Kingdom of Glory" of the reborn soul. Red leads to the region of fire and the "abyss of darkness," which forms the periphery of Böhme's mandala (see Fig. 1).

Picture 4

556 Picture 4, which now follows, shows a significant change: the sphere has divided into an outer membrane and an inner nucleus. The outer membrane is flesh coloured, and the originally rather nebulous red nucleus in Picture 2 now has a differentiated internal structure of a decidedly ternary character. The "lines of force" that originally belonged to the band of quicksilver now run through the whole nuclear body, indicating that the excitation is no longer external only but has seized the innermost core. "An enormous inner activity now began," the patient told me. The nucleus with its ternary structure is presumably the female organ, stylized to look like a plant, in the act of fecundation: the spermatozoon is penetrating the

nuclear membrane. Its role is played by the mercurial serpent: the snake is black, dark, chthonic, a subterranean and ithyphallic Hermes; but it has the golden wings of Mercury and consequently possesses his pneumatic nature. The alchemists accordingly represented their *Mercurius duplex* as the winged and wingless dragon, calling the former feminine and the latter masculine.

557 The serpent in our picture represents not so much the spermatozoon but, more accurately, the phallus. Leone Ebreo,[76] in his *Dialoghi d'amore,* calls the planet Mercury the *membrum virile* of heaven, that is, of the macrocosm conceived as the *homo maximus.*[77] The spermatozoon seems, rather, to correspond to the golden substance which the snake is injecting into the invaginated ectoderm of the nucleus.[78] The two silver petals (?) probably represent the receptive vessel, the moon-bowl in which the sun's seed (gold) is destined to rest.[79] Underneath the flower is a small violet circle inside the ovary, indicating by its colour that it is a "united double nature," spirit and body (blue and red).[80] The snake has a pale yellow halo, which is meant to express its numinosity.

558 Since the snake evolved out of the flash of lightning or is a modulated form of it, I would like to instance a parallel where the lightning has the same illuminating, vivifying, fertilizing, transforming and healing function that in our case falls to the snake (cf. Fig. 3). Two phases are represented: first, a black sphere, signifying a state of profound depression; and second, the lightning that strikes into this sphere. Ordinary speech

76 The writings of the physician and philosopher Leone Ebreo (*c.* 1460–1520) enjoyed widespread popularity in the sixteenth century and exercised a far-reaching influence on his contemporaries and their successors. His work is a continuation of the Neoplatonist thought developed by the physician and alchemist Marsilio Ficino (1433–99) in his commentary on Plato's *Symposium.* Ebreo's real name was Don Judah Abrabanel, of Lisbon. (Sometimes the texts have Abrabanel, sometimes Abarbanel.)

77 Cf. the English version, *The Philosophy of Love,* trans. by Friedeberg-Seeley and Barnes, pp. 92 and 94. The source of this view can be found in the cabalistic interpretation of Yesod (Knorr von Rosenroth, *Kabbala Denudata,* 1677–84).

78 This pseudo-biological terminology fits in with the patient's scientific education.

79 Another alchemical idea: the *synodos Lunae cum Sole,* or hierogamy of sun and moon. Cf. "The Psychology of the Transference," par. 421, n. 17.

80 More on this in "On the Nature of the Psyche," par. 498.

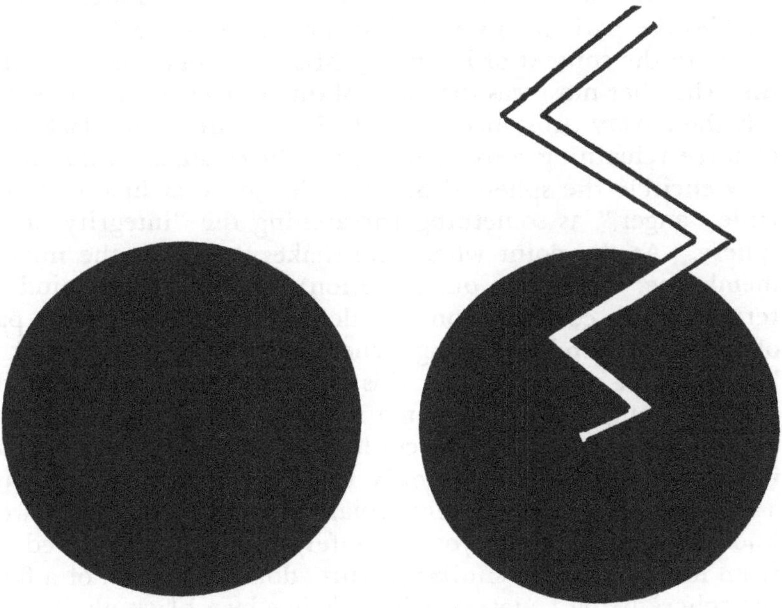

I II

Fig. 3. Sketch of a drawing by a young woman patient with psychogenic depression from the beginning of the treatment

I. State of black hopelessness / II. Beginning of the therapeutic effect

In an earlier picture the sphere lay on the bottom of the sea. As a series of pictures shows, it arose in the first place because a black snake had swallowed the sun. There then followed an eight-rayed, completely black mandala with a wreath of eight silver stars. In the centre was a black homunculus. Next the black sphere developed a red centre, from which red rays, or streams of blood, ran out into tentacle-like extremities. The whole thing looked rather like a crab or an octopus. As the later pictures showed, the patient herself was shut up in the sphere.

makes use of the same imagery: something "strikes home" in a "flash of revelation." The only difference is that generally the image comes first, and only afterwards the realization which enables the patient to say: "This has struck home."

559 As to the context of Picture 4, Miss X emphasized that what disturbed her most was the band of quicksilver in Picture 3. She felt the silvery substance ought to be "inside," the black lines of force remaining outside to form a black snake. This would now encircle the sphere.[81] She felt the snake at first as a "terrible danger," as something threatening the "integrity of the sphere." At the point where the snake penetrates the nuclear membrane, fire breaks out (emotion). Her conscious mind interpreted this conflagration as a defensive reaction on the part of the sphere, and accordingly she tried to depict the attack as having been repulsed. But this attempt failed to satisfy the "eyes," though she showed me a pencil sketch of it. She was obviously in a dilemma: she could not accept the snake, because its sexual significance was only too clear to her without any assistance from me. I merely remarked to her: "This is a well-known process [82] which you can safely accept," and showed her from my collection a similar picture, done by a man, of a floating sphere being penetrated *from below* by a black phallus-like object. Later she said: "I suddenly understood the whole process in a more impersonal way." It was the realization of a law of life to which sex is subordinated. "The ego was not the centre, but, following a universal law, I circled round a sun." Thereupon she was able to accept the snake "as a necessary part of the process of growth" and finish the picture quickly and satisfactorily. Only one thing continued to give difficulty: she had to put the snake, she said, "One hundred per cent at the top, in the middle, in order to satisfy the eyes." Evidently the unconscious would only be satisfied with the most important position at the top and in the middle—in direct contrast to the picture

81 Here one must think of the world-encircling Ocean and the world-snake hidden in it: Leviathan, the "dragon in the sea," which, in accordance with the Egyptian tradition of Typhon (Set) and the sea he rules over, is the devil. "The devil . . . surrounds the seas and the ocean on all sides" (St. Jerome, *Epistolae,* Part I, p. 12). Further particulars in Rahner, "Antenna Crucis II: Das Meer der Welt," pp. 89ff.

82 We find the same motif in the two mandalas published by Esther Harding in *Psychic Energy: Its Source and Its Transformation* [Pls. XVI, XVII].

I had previously shown her. This, as I said, was done by a man and showed the menacing black symbol entering the mandala from below. For a woman, the typical danger emanating from the unconscious comes *from above,* from the "spiritual" sphere personified by the animus, whereas for a man it comes from the chthonic realm of the "world and woman," i.e., the anima projected on to the world.

560 Once again we must recall similar ideas found in Justin's gnosis: the third of the fatherly angels is Baruch. He is also the tree of life in paradise. His counterpart on the motherly side is Naas, the serpent, who is the tree of knowledge of good and evil.[83] When Elohim left Edem, because, as the second member, he had retreated to the first member of the divine triad (which consisted of the "Good," the "Father," and Edem), Edem pursued the pneuma of the Father, which he had left behind in man, and caused it to be tormented by Naas (ἵνα πάσαις κολάσεσι κολάζῃ τὸ ὂν πνεῦμα τοῦ Ἐλωεὶμ τὸ ἐν τοῖς ἀνθρώποις). Naas defiled Eve and also used Adam as a catamite. Edem, however, is the soul; Elohim is spirit. "The soul is against the spirit, and the spirit against the soul" (κατὰ τῆς ψυχῆς τετάκται).[84] This idea sheds light on the polarity of red and blue in our mandala, and also on the attack by the snake, who represents knowledge. That is why we fear knowledge of the truth, in this case, of the shadow. Therefore Baruch sent to mankind Jesus, that they might be led back to the "Good." But the "Good One is Priapus."[85] Elohim is the swan, Edem is Leda; he the gold, she Danae. Nor should we forget that the god of revelation has from of old the form of a snake—e.g., the *agathodaimon.* Edem too, as a snake-maiden, has a dual nature, "two-minded, two-bodied" (δίγνωμος, δίσωμος), and in medieval alchemy her figure became the symbol of the androgynous Mercurius.[86]

561 Let us remember that in Picture 3 *Mercurius vulgi,* ordinary quicksilver, encircles the sphere. This means that the mysterious

[83] Naas is the same as the snakelike Nous and mercurial serpent of alchemy.

[84] Hippolytus, *Elenchos,* V, 26, 21ff. This tale of Adam and Eve and the serpent was preserved until well into the Middle Ages.

[85] Apparently a play on the words Πρίαπος and ἐπριοποίησε τὰ πάντα ('created all'). *Elenchos,* V, 26, 33.

[86] See the illustration from Reusner's *Pandora* (1588) in my "Paracelsus as a Spiritual Phenomenon," Fig. B4.

sphere is enveloped or veiled by a "vulgar" or crude understanding. The patient herself opined that "the animus veils the true personality." We shall hardly be wrong in assuming that a banal, everyday view of the world, allegedly biological, has here got hold of the sexual symbol and concretized it after the approved pattern. A pardonable error! Another, more correct view is so much more subtle that one naturally prefers to fall back on something well-known and ready to hand, thus gratifying one's own "rational" expectations and earning the applause of one's contemporaries—only to discover that one has got hopelessly stuck and has arrived back at the point from which one set forth on the great adventure. It is clear what is meant by the ithyphallic serpent: from above comes all that is aerial, intellectual, spiritual, and from below all that is passionate, corporeal, and dark. The snake, contrary to expectation, turns out to be a pneumatic symbol,[87] a *Mercurius spiritualis*—a realization which the patient herself formulated by saying that the ego, despite its capricious manipulation of sexuality, is subject to a universal law. Sex in this case is therefore no problem at all, as it has been subjected to a higher transformation process and is contained in it; not repressed, only without an object.

562 Miss X subsequently told me that she felt Picture 4 was the most difficult, as if it denoted the turning point of the whole process. In my view she may not have been wrong in this, because the clearly felt, ruthless setting aside of the so beloved and so important ego is no light matter. Not for nothing is this "letting go" the *sine qua non* of all forms of higher spiritual development, whether we call it meditation, contemplation, yoga, or spiritual exercises. But, as this case shows, relinquishing the ego is not an act of the will and not a result arbitrarily produced; it is an event, an occurrence, whose inner, compelling logic can be disguised only by wilful self-deception.

563 In this case and at this moment the ability to "let go" is of decisive importance. But since everything passes, the moment may come when the relinquished ego must be reinstated in its functions. Letting go gives the unconscious the opportunity it

87 In accordance with the classical view that the snake is πνευματικώτατον ζῶον, 'the most spiritual animal.' For this reason it was a symbol for the Nous and the Redeemer.

has been waiting for. But since it consists of opposites—day and night, bright and dark, positive and negative—and is good and evil and therefore ambivalent, the moment will infallibly come when the individual, like the exemplary Job, must hold fast so as not to be thrown catastrophically off balance—when the wave rebounds. The holding fast can be achieved only by a conscious will, i.e., by the ego. That is the great and irreplaceable significance of the ego, but one which, as we see here, is nonetheless relative. Relative, too, is the gain won by integrating the unconscious. We add to ourselves a bright and a dark, and more light means more night.[88] The urge of consciousness towards wider horizons, however, cannot be stopped; they must needs extend the scope of the personality, if they are not to shatter it.

Picture 5

564 Picture 5, Miss X said, followed naturally from Picture 4, with no difficulty. The sphere and the snake have drawn apart. The snake is sinking downwards and seems to have lost its threateningness. But the sphere has been fecundated with a vengeance: it has not only got bigger, but blossoms in the most vivid colours.[89] The nucleus has divided into four; something like a segmentation has occurred. This is not due to any conscious reflection, such as might come naturally to a biologically educated person; the division of the process or of the central symbol into four has always existed, beginning with the four sons of Horus, or the four seraphim of Ezekiel, or the birth of the four Aeons from the Metra (uterus) impregnated by the pneuma in Barbelo-Gnosis, or the cross formed by the lightning (snake) in Böhme's system,[90] and ending with the tetrameria of the *opus alchymicum* and its components (the four elements, qualities, stages, etc.).[91] In each case the quaternity forms a

88 Cf. what St. John of the Cross says about the "dark night of the soul." His interpretation is as helpful as it is psychological.

89 Hence the alchemical mandala was likened to a *rosarium* (rose-garden).

90 In Buddhism the "four great kings" (*lokapata*), the world-guardians, form the quaternity. Cf. the *Samyutta-Nikaya*, in *Dialogues of the Buddha*, Part II, p. 242.

91 "God separated and divided this primordial water by a kind of mystical distillation into four parts and regions" (Sendivogius, *Epist. XIII*, in Manget, *Bibliotheca chemica*, 1702, II, p. 496). In Christianos (Berthelot, *Alch. grecs*, VI, ix, 1 and x, 1) the egg, and matter itself, consist of four components. (Cited from Xenocrates, ibid., VI, xv, 8.)

unity; here it is the green circle at the centre of the four. The four are undifferentiated, and each of them forms a vortex, apparently turning to the left. I think I am not mistaken in regarding it as probable that, in general, a leftward movement indicates movement towards the unconscious, while a rightward (clockwise) movement goes towards consciousness.[92] The one is "sinister," the other "right," "rightful," "correct." In Tibet, the leftward-moving swastika is a sign of the Bön religion, of black magic. Stupas and chörtens must therefore be circumambulated clockwise. The leftward-spinning eddies spin into the unconscious; the rightward-spinning ones spin out of the unconscious chaos. The rightward-moving swastika in Tibet is therefore a Buddhist emblem.[93] (Cf. also Fig. 4.)

565 For our patient the process appeared to mean, first and foremost, a differentiation of consciousness. From the treasures of her psychological knowledge she interpreted the four as the four orienting functions of consciousness: thinking, feeling, sensation, intuition. She noticed, however, that the four were all alike, whereas the four functions are all unlike. This raised no question for her, but it did for me. What are these four if they are *not* the four functional aspects of consciousness? I doubted whether this could be a sufficient interpretation of them. They seemed to be much more than that, and that is probably the reason why they are not different but identical. They do not form four functions, different by definition, but they might well represent the *a priori* possibility for the formation of the four functions. In this picture we have the quaternity, the archetypal 4, which is capable of numerous interpretations, as history shows and as I have demonstrated elsewhere. It illustrates the coming to consciousness of an un-

92 In Taoist philosophy, movement to the right means a "falling" life-process, as the spirit is then under the influence of the feminine *p'o*-soul, which embodies the *yin* principle and is by nature passionate. Its designation as the anima (cf. my "Commentary on *The Secret of the Golden Flower,*" pars. 57ff.) is psychologically correct, although this touches only one aspect of it. The *p'o*-soul entangles *hun,* the spirit, in the world-process and in reproduction. A leftward or backward movement, on the other hand, means the "rising" movement of life. A "deliverance from outward things" occurs and the spirit obtains control over the anima. This idea agrees with my findings, but it does not take account of the fact that a person can easily have the spirit outside and the anima inside.

93 This was told to me by the Rimpoche of Bhutia Busty, Sikkim.

Fig. 4. Neolithic relief from Tarxien, Malta

The spirals represent vine tendrils.

conscious content; hence it frequently occurs in cosmogonic myths. What is the precise significance of the fact that the four eddies are apparently turning to the left, when the division of the mandala into four denotes a process of becoming conscious, is a point about which I would rather not speculate. I lack the necessary material. Blue means air or pneuma, and the leftward movement an intensification of the unconscious influence. Possibly this should be taken as a pneumatic compensation for the strongly emphasized red colour, which signifies affectivity.

566 The mandala itself is bright red, but the four eddies have in the main a cool, greenish-blue colour, which the patient associated with "water." This might hang together with the leftward movement, since water is a favourite symbol for the unconscious.[94] The green of the circle in the middle signifies life in the chthonic sense. It is the "benedicta viriditas" of the alchemists.

567 The problematical thing about this picture is the fact that the black snake is outside the totality of the symbolic circle. In order to make the totality actual, it ought really to be inside. But if we remember the unfavourable significance of the snake, we shall understand why its assimilation into the symbol of psychic wholeness presents certain difficulties. If our conjecture about the leftward movement of the four eddies is correct, this would denote a trend towards the deep and dark side of the spirit,[95] by means of which the black snake could be assimilated. The snake, like the devil in Christian theology, represents the shadow, and one which goes far beyond anything personal and could therefore best be compared with a principle, such as the principle of evil.[96] It is the colossal shadow thrown by man, of which our age had to have such a devastating experience. It is no easy matter to fit this shadow into our cosmos. The view that we can simply turn our back on evil and in this way eschew it belongs to the long list of antiquated naïveties. This is sheer ostrich policy and does not affect the reality of evil in the slight-

94 Water also symbolizes the "materiality" of the spirit when it has become a "fixed" doctrine. One is reminded, too, of the blue-green colour in Böhme, signifying "Liberty."

95 For the double nature of the spirit (*Mercurius duplex* of the alchemists) see "The Phenomenology of the Spirit in Fairytales," supra.

96 Cf. the fiery serpent of Lucifer in Böhme.

est. Evil is the necessary opposite of good, without which there would be no good either. It is impossible even to think evil out of existence. Hence the fact that the black snake remains outside expresses the critical position of evil in our traditional view of the world.[97]

568 The background of the picture is pale, the colour of parchment. I mention this fact in particular, as the pictures that follow show a characteristic change in this respect.

Picture 6

569 The background of Picture 6 is a cloudy grey. The mandala itself is done in the vividest colours, bright red, green, and blue. Only where the red outer membrane enters the blue-green nucleus does the red deepen to blood colour and the pale blue to a dark ultramarine. The wings of Mercury, missing in the previous picture, reappear here at the neck of the blood-red pistons (as previously on the neck of the black snake in Picture 4). But the most striking thing is the appearance of a swastika, undoubtedly wheeling to the right. (I should add that these pictures were painted in 1928 and had no direct connection with contemporary fantasies, which at that time were still unknown to the world at large.) Because of its green colour, the swastika suggests something plantlike, but at the same time it has the wavelike character of the four eddies in the previous picture.

570 In this mandala an attempt is made to unite the opposites red and blue, outside and inside. Simultaneously, the rightward movement aims at bringing about an ascent into the light of consciousness, presumably because the background has become noticeably darker. The black snake has disappeared, but has begun to impart its darkness to the entire background. To compensate this, there is in the mandala an upwards movement towards the light, apparently an attempt to rescue consciousness from the darkening of the environment. The picture was associated with a dream that occurred a few days before. Miss X dreamt that *she returned to the city after a holiday in the country. To her astonishment she found a tree growing in the middle of the room where she worked. She thought: "Well, with its thick bark this tree can withstand the heat of an apart-*

[97] Cf. "A Psychological Approach to the Dogma of the Trinity," pars. 243ff.

ment." Associations to the tree led to its maternal significance. The tree would explain the plant motif in the mandala, and its sudden growth represents the higher level or freeing of consciousness induced by the movement to the right. For the same reason the "philosophical" tree is a symbol of the alchemical *opus,* which as we know is an individuation process.

571 We find similar ideas in Justin's gnosis. The angel Baruch stands for the pneuma of Elohim, and the "motherly" angel Naas for the craftiness of Edem. But both angels, as I have said, were also trees: Baruch the tree of life, Naas the tree of knowledge. Their division and polarity are in keeping with the spirit of the times (second–third centuries A.D.). But in those days, too, they knew of an individuation process, as we can see from Hippolytus.[98] Elohim, we are told, set the "prophet" Heracles the task of delivering the "Father" (the pneuma) from the power of the twelve wicked angels. This resulted in his twelve labours. Now the Heracles myth has in fact all the characteristic features of an individuation process: the journeys to the four directions,[99] four sons, submission to the feminine principle (Omphale) that symbolizes the unconscious, and the self-sacrifice and rebirth caused by Deianeira's robe.

572 The "thick bark" of the tree suggests the motif of protection, which appears in the mandala as the "formation of skins" (see par. 576). This is expressed in the motif of the protective black bird's wings, which shield the contents of the mandala from outside influences. The piston-shaped prolongations of the peripheral red substance are phallic symbols, indicating the entry of affectivity into the pneumatic interior. They are obviously meant to activate and enrich the spirit dwelling within. This "spirit" has of course nothing to do with intellect, rather with something that we would have to call spiritual substance (pneuma) or—in modern terms—"spiritual life." The underlying symbolical thought is no doubt the same as the view developed in the Clementine Homilies, that πνεῦμα (spirit) and σῶμα (body) are one in God.[100] The mandala, though only a symbol of the self as the psychic totality, is at the same time a God-image, for the central point, circle, and quaternity are

98 *Elenchos,* V, 26, 27ff.

99 *Psychology and Alchemy,* par. 457.

100 Hauck, *Realencyclopädie für protestantische Theologie,* IV, p. 173, li. 59.

well-known symbols for the deity. The impossibility of distinguishing empirically between "self" and "God" leads, in Indian theosophy, to the identity of the personal and suprapersonal Purusha-Atman. In ecclesiastical as in alchemical literature the saying is often quoted: "God is an infinite circle (or sphere) whose centre is everywhere and the circumference nowhere." [101] This idea can be found in full development as early as Parmenides. I will cite the passage, because it alludes to the same motifs that underlie our mandala: "For the narrower rings [102] were filled with unmixed Fire, and those next to them with Night, but between these rushes the portion of Flame. And in the centre of these is the goddess [103] who guides everything; for throughout she rules over cruel Birth and Mating, sending the female to mate with the male, and conversely again the male with the female." [104]

573 The learned Jesuit, Nicholas Caussin, apropos the report in Clement of Alexandria that, on certain occasions, wheels were rolled round in the Egyptian temples,[105] comments that Democritus of Abdera called God νοῦν ἐν πυρὶ σφαιροειδεῖ [106] (*mentem in igne orbiculari,* 'mind in the spherical fire'). He goes on: "This was the view also of Parmenides, who defined God as στεφάνην,

101 Baumgartner (*Die Philosophie des Alanus de Insulis,* II, Part 4, p. 118) traces this saying to a *liber Hermetis* or *liber Trismegisti,* Cod. Par. 6319 and Cod. Vat. 3060.

102 Στεφάναι = *coronae.*

103 Δαίμων ἣ πάντα κυβέρναι, a feminine *daemonium.*

104 Freeman, *Ancilla to the Pre-Socratic Philosophers,* p. 45.

105 *Writings of Clement of Alexandria,* trans. by Wilson, II, p. 248: "Also Dionysius Thrax, the grammarian, in his book *Respecting the Exposition of the Symbolical Signification of Circles,* says expressly, 'Some signified actions not by words only, but also by symbols: . . . as the wheel that is turned in the temples of the gods [by] the Egyptians, and the branches that are given to the worshippers. For the Thracian Orpheus says:

> For the works of mortals on earth are like branches,
> Nothing has but one fate in the mind, but all things
> Revolve in a circle, nor is it lawful to abide in one place,
> But each keeps its own course wherewith it began.' "

[Verses translated from the Overbeck version in German quoted by the author.—TRANS.]

106 Diels, *Fragmente der Vorsokratiker,* II, p. 102. Aetius, *De plac. phil.,* I, 7, 16.

'crown,' a circle consisting of glowing light.[107] And it has been very clearly established by Iamblichus, in his book on the mysteries, that the Egyptians customarily represent God, the Lord of the world, as sitting in the lotus, a water-plant, the fruits as well as the leaves of which are round,[108] thereby indicating the circular motion of the mind, which everywhere returns into itself." This is also the origin, he says, of the ritual transformations or circuits ("circuitiones") that imitate the motion of the heavens. But the Stoics named the heavens a "round and revolving God" (*rotundum et volubilem Deum*). Caussin says it is to this that the "mystical" (*mystice* = symbolical) explanation of Psalm 12 : 8 refers: "In circuitu impii ambulant" (the ungodly wander in a circle); [109] they only walk round the periphery without ever reaching the centre, which is God. Here I would mention the wheel motif in mandala symbolism only in passing, as I have dealt with it in detail elsewhere.[110]

Picture 7

574 In Picture 7 it has indeed turned to night: the entire sheet which the mandala is painted on is black. All the light is concentrated in the sphere. The colours have lost their brightness but have gained in intensity. It is especially striking that the black has penetrated as far as the centre, so that something of what we feared has already occurred: the blackness of the snake and of the sombre surroundings has been assimilated by the nucleus and, at the same time, as the picture shows, is compensated by a golden light radiating out from the centre. The rays form an equal-armed cross, to replace the swastika of the previous picture, which is here represented only by four hooks

107 A reference to Cicero, *De natura deorum* (trans. by Rackham, p. 31): "Parmenides . . . invents a purely fanciful something resembling a crown—*stephane* is his name for it—an unbroken ring of glowing lights encircling the sky, which he entitles god; but no one can imagine this to possess divine form, or sensation." This ironic remark of Cicero's shows that he was the child of another age, already very far from the primordial images.

108 There are innumerable representations of the sun-child sitting in the lotus. Cf. Erman, *Die Religion der Aegypter*, p. 62 and *Handbook of Egyptian Religion*, p. 26. It is also found on Gnostic gems [*Psychology and Alchemy*, fig. 52]. The lotus is the customary seat of the gods in India.

109 [Or, as in the DV, "The wicked walk round about."—EDITORS.]

110 *Psychology and Alchemy*, pars. 214f.

suggesting a rightwards rotation. With the attainment of absolute blackness, and particularly its presence in the centre, the upward movement and rightward rotation seem to have come to an end. On the other hand, the wings of Mercury have undergone a noticeable differentiation, which presumably means that the sphere has sufficient power to keep itself afloat and not sink down into total darkness. The golden rays forming the cross bind the four together.[111] This produces an inner bond and consolidation as a defence against destructive influences [112] emanating from the black substance that has penetrated to the centre. For us the cross symbol always has the connotation of *suffering,* so we are probably not wrong in assuming that the mood of this picture is one of more or less painful *suspension*—remember the wings!—over the dark abyss of inner loneliness.

575 Earlier, I mentioned Böhme's lightning that "makes a cross," and I brought this cross into connection with the four elements. As a matter of fact, John Dee symbolizes the elements by an equal-armed cross.[113] As we said, the cross with a little circle in it is the alchemical sign for copper (*cuprum,* from Kypris, Aphrodite), and the sign for Venus is ♀. Remarkably enough, ⊕ is the old apothecary's sign for *spiritus Tartari* (tartaric acid), which, literally translated, means 'spirit of the underworld.' -⊕- is also the sign for red hematite (bloodstone). Hence there seems to be not only a cross that comes from above, as in Böhme's case and in our mandala, but also one that comes from below. In other words, the lightning—to keep to Böhme's image—can come from below out of the blood, from Venus or from Tartarus. Böhme's neutral "Salniter" is identical with salt in general, and one of the signs for this is +⊕+ (with crosses above and below). One can hardly imagine a better sign for the arcane substance, which salt was

111 This interpretation was confirmed for me by my Tibetan mentor, Lingdam Gomchen, abbot of Bhutia Busty: the swastika, he said, is that which "cannot be broken, divided, or spoilt." Accordingly, it would amount to an inner consolidation of the mandala.

112 Cf. the similar motif in the mandala of the *Amitāyur-dhyāna Sūtra,* in "The Psychology of Eastern Meditation," pars. 917, 930.

113 "Monas hieroglyphica," *Theatr. chem.* (1602), II, p. 220. Dee also associates the cross with fire.

considered to be by the sixteenth- and seventeenth-century alchemists. Salt, in ecclesiastical as well as alchemical usage, is the symbol for Sapientia and also for the distinguished or elect *personality,* as in Matthew 5 : 13: "Ye are the salt of the earth."

576 The numerous wavy lines or layers in the mandala could be interpreted as representing the formation of *layers of skin,* giving protection against outside influences. They serve the same purpose as the inner consolidation. These cortices probably have something to do with the dream of the tree in the workroom, which had a "thick bark." The formation of skins is also found in other mandalas, and it denotes a hardening or sealing off against the outside, the production of a regular rind or "hide." It is possible that this phenomenon would account for the cortices or *putamina* ('shards') mentioned in the cabala.[114] "For such is the name for that which abides outside holiness," such as the seven fallen kings and the four Achurayim.[115] From them come the "klippoth" or cortices. As in alchemy, these are the scoriae or slag, to which adheres the quality of plurality and of death. In our mandala the cortices are boundary lines marking off the inner unity and protecting it against the outer blackness with its disintegrating influences, personified by the snake.[116] The same motif is expressed by the petals of the lotus and by the skins of the onion: the outer layers are withered and desiccated, but they protect the softer, inner layers. The lotus seat of the Horus-child, of the Indian divinities, and of

114 [Cf. "Answer to Job," *Psychology and Religion,* par. 595, n. 8.—EDITORS.]

115 The seven kings refer to previous aeons, "perished" worlds, and the four Achurayim are the so-called "back of God": "All belong to Malkhuth; which is so called because it is last in the system of Aziluth . . . they exist in the depths of the Shekinah" (*Kabbala Denudata,* I, p. 72). They form a masculine-feminine quaternio "of the Father and Mother of the highest, and of the Senex Israel and Tebhunah" (I, p. 675). The Senex is Ain-Soph or Kether (I, p. 635), Tebhunah is Binah, intelligence (I, p. 726). The shards also mean unclean spirits.

116 *Kabbala Denudata,* I, pp. 675f. The shards also stand for evil. (*Zohar,* I, 137aff., II, 34b.). According to a Christian interpretation from the 17th century, Adam Belial is the body of the Messiah, the "entire body or the host of shards." (Cf. II Cor. 6 : 15.) In consequence of the Fall, the host of shards irrupted into Adam's body, its outer layers being more infected than the inner ones. The "Anima Christi" fought and finally destroyed the shards, which signify matter. In connection with Adam Belial the text refers to Proverbs 6 : 12: "A naughty person, a wicked man, walketh with a froward mouth" (AV). (*Kabbala Denudata,* II, Appendix, cap. IX, sec. 2, p. 56.)

the Buddha must be understood in this sense. Hölderlin makes use of the same image:

> Fateless, like the sleeping
> Infant, breathe the heavenly ones,
> Chastely guarded
> In modest bud; their spirits
> Blossom eternally . . .[117]

577 In Christian metaphor, Mary is the flower in which God lies hidden; or again, the rose window in which the *rex gloriae* and judge of the world is enthroned.

578 The idea of circular layers is to be found, by implication, in Böhme, for the outermost ring of his three-dimensional mandala [118] is labelled "will of ye Devill Lucifer," "Abysse (of) Eternity," "Abyss of ye Darkness," "Hell of Devills," etc. (See Fig. 1.) Böhme says of this in his *Aurora* (ch. XVII, sec. 6): "Behold, when Lucifer with his hosts aroused the Wrath-fire in God's nature, so that God waxed wroth in Nature in the place of Lucifer, the outermost Birth in Nature acquired another Quality, wholly wrathful, dry, cold, vehement, bitter, and sour. The raging Spirit, that before had a subtle, gentle Quality in Nature, became in his outermost Birth wholly presumptuous and terrible, and now in his outermost Birth is called the Wind, or the element Air." In this way the four elements arose—the earth, in particular, by a process of contraction and desiccation.

579 Cabalistic influences may be conjectured here, though Böhme knew not much more about the Cabala than did Paracelsus. He regarded it as a species of magic. The four elements correspond to the four Achurayim.[119] They constitute a sort of

117 "Hyperion's Song of Fate," in *Gedichte,* p. 315. (Trans. as in Jung, *Symbols of Transformation,* p. 399.)

118 Concerning the total vision of the "Life of Spirit and Nature," Böhme says: "We may then liken it to a round spherical Wheel, which goes on all sides, as the Wheel in Ezekiel shows" (*Mysterium pansophicum,* Sämmtliche Werke, ed. Schiebler, VI, p. 416).

119 *Quaestiones Theosophicae* (Amsterdam edn., 1682), p. 23. *Aurora,* XVII. 9, p. 168, mentions the "seven Spirits, which kindled themselves in their outermost Birth or Geniture." They are the Spirits of God, "Source-Spirits" of eternal and timeless Nature, corresponding to the seven planets and forming the "Wheel of the Centre" (*Sig. rer.,* IX, 8ff., p. 60). These seven Spirits are the seven above-mentioned "Qualities" which all come from one mother. She is the "twofold

second quaternity, proceeding from the inner, pneumatic quaternity but of a physical nature. The alchemists, too, allude to the Achurayim. Mennens,[120] for instance, says: "And although the holy name of God reveals the Tetragrammaton or the Four Letters, yet if you should look at it aright, only three Letters are found in it. The letter *he* [ה] is found twice, since they are the same, namely Air and Water, which signifies the Son; Earth the Father, and Fire the Holy Ghost. Thus the Four Letters of God's name manifestly signify the Most Holy Trinity and Matter, which likewise is threefold (*triplex*) [121] . . . and which is also called the shadow of the same [i.e., of God], and is named by Moyses [122] the back of God [*Dei posteriora*], which seems to be created out of it [matter]." [123] This statement bears out Böhme's view.

580 To return to our mandala. The original four eddies have coalesced into the wavy squares in the middle of the picture. Their place is taken by golden points at the outer rim (developed from the previous picture), emitting rainbow colours. These are the colours of the *peacock's eye*, which play a great role as the *cauda pavonis* in alchemy.[124] The appearance of these

Source, evil and good in all things" (*Aurora*, p. 27). Cf. the "goddess" in Parmenides and the two-bodied Edem in Justin's gnosis.

120 Gulielmus Mennens (1525–1608), a learned Flemish alchemist, wrote a book entitled *Aurei velleris, sive sacrae philosophiae, naturae et artis admirabilium libri tres* (Antwerp, 1604). Printed in *Theatr. chem.*, V (1622), pp. 267ff.

121 "As therefore God is three and one, so also the matter from which he created all things is triplex and one." This is the alchemical equivalent of the conscious and unconscious triads of functions in psychology. Cf. supra, "The Phenomenology of the Spirit in Fairytales," pars. 425 and 436ff.

122 Mennens seems to refer not to the Cabala direct, but to a text ascribed to Moses, which I have not been able to trace. It is certainly not a reference to the Greek text called by Berthelot "Chimie de Moise" (*Alch. grecs*, IV, xxii). Moses is mentioned now and then in the old literature, and Lenglet du Fresnoy (*Histoire de la philosophie hermétique*, 1742, III, p. 22) cites under No. 26 a MS from the Vienna Bibliothek entitled: "Moysis Prophetae et Legislatoris Hebraeorum secretum Chimicum" (Ouvrage supposé).

123 "Aurei velleris," I, cap. X, in *Theatr. chem.*, V, pp. 334f.

124 The *cauda pavonis* is identified by Khunrath with Iris, the "nuncia Dei." Dorn ("De transmutatione metallorum," *Theatr. chem.*, I, p. 599) explains it as follows: "This is the bird which flies by night without wings, which the early dew of heaven, continually acting by upward and downward ascent and descent, turns into the head of a crow (*caput corvi*), then into the tail of a peacock, and

colours in the *opus* represents an intermediate stage preceding the definitive end result. Böhme speaks of a "love-desire or a Beauty of Colours; and here all Colours arise." [125] In our mandala, too, the rainbow colours spring from the red layer that means affectivity. Of the "life of Nature and Spirit" that is united in the "spherical wheel" [126] Böhme says: "Thus is made known to us an eternal Essence of Nature, like to Water and Fire, which stand as it were mixed into one another. For there comes a *bright-blue* colour, like the *Lightning* of the Fire; and then it has a form like a *Ruby* [127] mingled with Crystals into one Essence, or like *yellow, white, red,* and *blue* mingled in *dark Water:* for it is like blue in green, since each still has its brightness and shines, and the Water only resists their Fire, so that there is no wasting anywhere, but one eternal Essence in two Mysteries mingled together, notwithstanding the difference of two Principles, viz. two kinds of life." The phenomenon of the colours owes its existence to the "Imagination of the great Mystery, where a wondrous essential Life is born." [128]

---

afterwards it acquires the bright wings of a swan, and lastly an extreme redness, an index of its fiery nature." In Basilides (Hippolytus, *Elenchos,* X, 14, 1) the peacock's egg is synonymous with the *sperma mundi,* the κόκκος σινάπεως. It contains the "fullness of colours," 365 of them. The golden colour should be produced from the peacock's eggs, we are told in the Cyranides (Delatte, *Textes latins et vieux français relatifs aux Cyranides,* p. 171). The light of Mohammed has the form of a peacock, and the angels were made out of the peacock's sweat (Aptowitzer, "Arabisch-Jüdische Schöpfungstheorien," pp. 209, 233).

125 *Sig. rer.,* XIV, 10ff., pp. 112f.

126 See n. 118.

127 The carbuncle is a synonym for the *lapis.* "The king bright as a carbuncle" (Lilius, an old source in the "Rosarium philosophorum," *Art. aurif.,* 1593, II, p. 329). "A ray . . . in the earth, shining in the darkness after the manner of a carbuncle gathered into itself" (from Michael Maier's exposition of the theory of Thomas Aquinas, in *Symbola aureae mensae,* p. 377). "I found a certain stone, red, shining, transparent, and brilliant, and in it I saw all the forms of the elements and also their contraries" (quotation from Thomas in Mylius, *Philosophia reformata,* p. 42). For heaven, gold, and carbuncle as synonyms for the *rubedo,* see ibid., p. 104. The *lapis* is "shimmering carbuncle light" (Khunrath, *Von hyleal. Chaos,* p. 237). Ruby or carbuncle is the name for the *corpus glorificatum* (Glauber, *Tractatus de natura salium,* Part I, p. 42). In Rosencreutz's *Chemical Wedding* (1616) the bed-chamber of Venus is lit by carbuncles (p. 97). Cf. what was said above about *anthrax* (ruby and cinnabar).

128 *Mysterium pansophicum,* pp. 416f.

581 It is abundantly clear from this that Böhme was preoccupied with the same psychic phenomenon that fascinated Miss X—and many other patients too. Although Böhme took the idea of the *cauda pavonis* and the tetrameria from alchemy,[129] he, like the alchemists, was working on an empirical basis which has since been rediscovered by modern psychology. There are products of active imagination, and also dreams, which reproduce the same patterns and arrangements with a spontaneity that cannot be influenced. A good example is the following dream: A patient dreamt that *she was in a drawing-room. There was a table with* three chairs *beside it. An unknown man standing beside her invited her to sit down. For this purpose she fetched a* fourth *chair that stood further off. She then sat at the table and began turning over the pages of a book, containing pictures of* blue *and* red *cubes, as for a building game. Suddenly it occurred to her that she had something else to attend to. She left the room and went to a* yellow *house. It was raining in torrents, and she sought shelter under a* green *laurel tree.*

582 The table, the three chairs, the invitation to sit down, the other chair that had to be fetched to make four chairs, the cubes, and the building game all suggest a process of *composition.* This takes place in stages: a combination first of blue and red, then of yellow and green. These four colours symbolize four qualities, as we have seen, which can be interpreted in various ways. Psychologically this quaternity points to the orienting functions of consciousness, of which at least one is unconscious and therefore not available for conscious use. Here it would be the green, the sensation function,[130] because the patient's relation to the real world was uncommonly complicated and clumsy. The "inferior" function, however, just because of its unconsciousness, has the great advantage of being contaminated with the collective unconscious and can be used as a bridge to span the gulf between conscious and unconscious and thus restore the vital connection with the latter. This is the deeper reason why the dream represents the inferior function as a laurel. The laurel in this dream has the same connection with

129 The chemical causes of the *cauda pavonis* are probably the iridiscent skin on molten metals and the vivid colours of certain compounds of mercury and lead. These two metals were often used as the primary material.

130 Statistically, at least, green is correlated with the sensation function.

the processes of inner growth as the tree that Miss X dreamt grew in her room. It is essentially the same tree as the *arbor philosophica* of the alchemists, about which I have written in *Psychology and Alchemy*.[131] We should also remember that, according to tradition, the laurel is not injured either by lightning or by cold—"intacta triumphat." Hence it symbolized the Virgin Mary,[132] the model for all women, just as Christ is the model for men. In view of its historical interpretation the laurel, like the alchemical tree, should be taken in this context as a symbol of the self.[133] The ingenuousness of patients who produce such dreams is always very impressive.

583 To turn back again to our mandala. The golden lines that end in pistons recapitulate the spermatozoon motif and therefore have a spermatic significance, suggesting that the quaternity will be reproduced in a new and more distinct form. In so far as the quaternity has to do with conscious realization, we can infer from these symptoms an intensification of the latter, as is also suggested by the golden light radiating from the centre. Probably a kind of inner illumination is meant.

584 Two days before painting this picture, Miss X dreamt that *she was in her father's room in their country house. "But my mother had moved my bed away from the wall into the middle of the room and had slept in it. I was furious, and moved the bed back to its former place. In the dream the bed-cover was red—exactly the red reproduced in the picture."*

585 The mother significance of the tree in her previous dream has here been taken up by the unconscious: this time the mother has slept in the middle of the room. This seems to be for Miss X an annoying intrusion into her sphere, symbolized by the room of her father, who has an animus significance for her. Her sphere is therefore a spiritual one, and she has usurped it just as she usurped her father's room. She has thus identified with the "spirit." Into this sphere her mother has intruded and installed herself in the centre, at first under the symbol of the

131 [See the index, s.v.; also Jung, "The Philosophical Tree."—EDITORS.]

132 "Lovely laurel, evergreen in all its parts, standing midmost among many trees smitten by lightning, bears the inscription: 'Untouched it triumphs.' This similitude refers to Mary the Virgin, alone among all creatures undefiled by any lightning-flash of sin." Picinelli, *Mondo simbolico* (1669), Lib. IX, cap. XVI.

133 Cf. "The Spirit Mercurius," par. 241.

tree. She therefore stands for physis opposed to spirit, i.e., for the natural feminine being which the dreamer also is, but which she would not accept because it appeared to her as a black snake. Although she remedied the intrusion at once, the dark chthonic principle, the black substance, has nevertheless penetrated to the centre of her mandala, as Picture 7 shows. But just because of this the golden light can appear: "e tenebris lux!" We have to relate the mother to Böhme's idea of the matrix. For him the matrix is the *sine qua non* of all differentiation or realization, without which the spirit remains suspended and never comes down to earth. The collision between the paternal and the maternal principle (spirit and nature) works like a shock.

586 After this picture, she felt the renewed penetration of the red colour, which she associated with feeling, as something disturbing, and she now discovered that her "rapport" with me, her analyst (= father), was unnatural and unsatisfactory. She was giving herself airs, she said, and was posing as an intelligent, understanding pupil (usurpation of spirituality!). But she had to admit that she felt very silly and was very silly, regardless of what I thought about it. This admission brought her a feeling of great relief and helped her to see at last that sex was "not, on the one hand, merely a mechanism for producing children and not, on the other, only an expression of supreme passion, but was also banally physiological and autoerotic." This belated realization led her straight into a fantasy state where she became conscious of a series of obscene images. At the end she saw the image of a large bird, which she called the "earth bird," and which alighted on the earth. Birds, as aerial beings, are well-known spirit symbols. It represented the transformation of the "spiritual" image of herself into a more earthy version that is more characteristic of women. This "tailpiece" confirms our suspicion that the intensive upward and rightward movement has come to a halt: the bird is coming down to earth. This symbolization denotes a further and necessary differentiation of what Böhme describes in general as "Love-desire." Through this differentiation consciousness is not only widened but also brought face to face with the reality of things, so that the inner experience is tied, so to speak, to a definite spot.

587 On the days following, the patient was overcome by feelings of self-pity. It became clear to her how much she regretted never having had any children. She felt like a neglected animal or a lost child. This mood grew into a regular *Weltschmerz,* and she felt like the "all-compassionate Tathagata" (Buddha). Only when she had completely given way to these feelings could she bring herself to paint another picture. Real liberation comes not from glossing over or repressing painful states of feeling, but only from experiencing them to the full.

Picture 8

588 The thing that strikes us at once in Picture 8 is that almost the whole interior is filled with the black substance. The blue-green of the water has condensed to a dark blue quaternity, and the golden light in the centre turns in the reverse direction, anti-clockwise: the bird is coming down to earth. That is, the mandala is moving towards the dark, chthonic depths. It is still floating—the wings of Mercury show this—but it has come much closer to the blackness. The inner, undifferentiated quaternity is balanced by an outer, differentiated one, which Miss X equated with the four functions of consciousness. To these she assigned the following colours: yellow = intuition, light blue = thinking, flesh pink = feeling, brown = sensation.[134] Each of these quarters is divided into three, thus producing the number 12 again. The separation and characterization of the two quaternities is worth noting. The outer quaternity of wings appears as a differentiated realization [135] of the undifferentiated inner one, which really represents the archetype. In the cabala this relationship corresponds to the quaternity of Merkabah [136] on the one hand and of the Achurayim on the other, and in Böhme they are the four Spirits of God [137] and the four elements.

134 The colour correlated with sensation in the mandalas of other persons is usually green.

135 Cf. the Achurayim quaternity.

136 Chochmah (= face of the man), Binah (= eagle), Gedulah (= lion), Gebhurah (= bull), the four symbolical angels in Ezekiel's vision.

137 He gives them the names of planets and describes them as the "four Bailiffs, who hold government in the Mother, the Birth-giver." They are Jupiter, Saturn, Mars, and Sun. "In these four Forms the Spirit's Birth consists, viz. the true Spirit both in the inward and outward Being" (*Sig. rer.,* IX, 9ff., p. 61).

589 The plantlike form of the cross in the middle of the mandala, also noted by the patient, refers back to the tree ("tree of the cross") and the mother.[138] She thus makes it clear that this previously taboo element has been accepted and now holds the central place. She was fully conscious of this—which of course was a great advance on her previous attitude.

590 In contrast to the previous picture there are no inner cortices. This is a logical development, because the thing they were meant to exclude is now in the centre, and defence has become superfluous. Instead, the cortices spread out into the darkness as golden rings, expanding concentrically like waves. This would mean a far-reaching influence on the environment emanating from the sealed-off self.

591 Four days before she painted this mandala she had the following dream: *"I drew a young man to the window and, with a brush dipped in white oil, removed a black fleck from the cornea of his eye. A little golden lamp then became visible in the centre of the pupil. The young man felt greatly relieved, and I told him he should come again for treatment. I woke up saying the words: 'If therefore thine eye be single, thy whole body shall be full of light.'"* (Matthew 6 : 22.)

592 This dream describes the change: the patient is no longer identical with her animus. The animus has, so to speak, become *her* patient, since he has eye trouble. As a matter of fact the animus usually sees things "cock-eyed" and often very unclearly. Here a black fleck on the cornea obscures the golden light shining from inside the eye. He has "seen things too blackly." The eye is the prototype of the mandala, as is evident from Böhme, who calls his mandala "The Philosophique Globe, or Eye of ye Wonders of Eternity, or Looking-Glass of Wisdom." He says: "The substance and Image of the Soul may be resembled to the Earth, having a fair Flower growing out of it, and also to the Fire and Light; as we see that Earth is a Centre, but no life; yet it is essential, and a fair flower grows out of it, which is not like Earth . . . and yet the Earth is the Mother of the Flower." The soul is a "fiery Eye, and similitude of the First Principle," a "Centre of Nature." [139]

138 The connection between tree and mother, especially in Christian tradition, is discussed at length in *Symbols of Transformation,* Part II.

139 *A Summary Appendix of the Soul,* p. 117.

593 Our mandala is indeed an "eye," the structure of which symbolizes the centre of order in the unconscious. The eye is a hollow sphere, black inside, and filled with a semi-liquid substance, the vitreous humour. Looking at it from outside, one sees a round, coloured surface, the iris, with a dark centre, from which a golden light shines. Böhme calls it a "fiery eye," in accordance with the old idea that seeing emanates from the eye. The eye may well stand for consciousness (which is in fact an organ of perception), looking into its own background. It sees its own light there, and when this is clear and pure the whole body is filled with light. Under certain conditions consciousness has a purifying effect. This is probably what is meant by Matthew 6 : 22ff., an idea expressed even more clearly in Luke 11 : 33ff.

594 The eye is also a well-known symbol for God. Hence Böhme calls his "Philosophique Globe" the "Eye of Eternity," the "Essence of all Essences," the "Eye of God." [140]

595 By accepting the darkness, the patient has not, to be sure, changed it into light, but she has kindled a light that illuminates the darkness within. By day no light is needed, and if you don't know it is night you won't light one, nor will any light be lit for you unless you have suffered the horror of darkness. This is not an edifying text but a mere statement of the psychological facts. The transition from Picture 7 to Picture 8 gives one a working idea of what I mean by "accepting the dark principle." It has sometimes been objected that nobody can form a clear conception of what this means, which is regrettable, because it is an ethical problem of the first order. Here, then, is a practical example of this "acceptance," and I must leave it to the philosophers to puzzle out the ethical aspects of the process.[141]

140 *Forty Questions,* pp. 24ff.

141 I do not feel qualified to go into the ethics of what "venerable Mother Nature" has to do in order to unfold her precious flower. Some people can, and those whose temperament makes them feel an ethical compulsion must do this in order to satisfy a need that is also felt by others. Erich Neumann has discussed these problems in a very interesting way in his *Tiefenpsychologie und Neue Ethik.* It will be objected that my respect for Nature is a very unethical attitude, and I shall be accused of shirking "decisions." People who think like this evidently know all about good and evil, and why and for what one has to decide. Unfortunately I do not know all this so precisely, but I hope for my patients and for myself that everything, light and darkness, decision and agonizing doubt, may turn to "good"—and by "good" I mean a development such as

Picture 9

596 In Picture 9 we see for the first time the blue "soul-flower," on a red background, also described as such by Miss X (naturally without knowledge of Böhme).[142] In the centre is the golden light in the form of a lamp, as she herself stated. The cortices are very pronounced, but they consist of light (at least in the upper half of the mandala) and radiate outwards.[143] The light is composed of the rainbow hues of the rising sun; it is a real *cauda pavonis*. There are six sets of sunbeams. This recalls the Buddha's Discourse on the Robe, from the Collection of the Pali Canon:

> His heart overflowing with lovingkindness . . . with compassion . . . with joyfulness . . . with equanimity, he abides, raying forth lovingkindness, compassion, joyfulness, equanimity, towards one quarter of space, then towards the second, then towards the third, then towards the fourth, and above and below, thus, all around. Everywhere, into all places the wide world over, his heart overflowing with compassion streams forth, wide, deep, illimitable, free from enmity, free from all ill-will. . . .[144]

597 But a parallel with the Buddhist East cannot be carried through here, because the mandala is divided into an upper and a lower half.[145] Above, the rings shine many-hued as a rainbow; below, they consist of brown earth. Above, there hover three white birds (*pneumata* signifying the Trinity); below, a goat

---

is here described, an unfolding which does no damage to either of them but conserves the possibilities of life.

142 *The Secret of the Golden Flower* had not been published then. Picture 9 was reproduced in it.

143 Cf. *Kabbala Denudata,* Appendix, ch. IV, sec. 2, p. 26: "The beings created by the infinite Deity through the First Adam were all spiritual beings, viz. they were simple, shining acts, being one in themselves, partaking of a being that may be thought of as the midpoint of a sphere, and partaking of a life that may be imagined as a sphere emitting rays."

144 "Parable of the Cloth," in *The First Fifty Discourses from the Collection of the Middle-Length Discourses (Majjhima Nikaya) of Gotama the Buddha,* I, pp. 39f., modified. This reference to the Buddha is not accidental, since the figure of the Tathagata in the lotus seat occurs many times in the patient's mandalas.

145 Tibetan mandalas are not so divided, but very often they are embedded between heaven and hell, i.e., between the benevolent and the wrathful deities.

is rising up, accompanied by two ravens (Wotan's birds) [146] and twining snakes. This is not the sort of picture a Buddhist holy man would make, but that of a Western person with a Christian background, whose light throws a dark shadow. What is more, the three birds float in a jet black sky, and the goat, rising out of dark clay, is shown against a field of bright orange. This, oddly enough, is the colour of the Buddhist monk's robe, which was certainly not a conscious intention of the patient. The underlying thought is clear: no white without black, and no holiness without the devil. Opposites are brothers, and the Oriental seeks to liberate himself from them by his *nirdvandva* ("free from the two") and his *neti neti* ("not this, not that"), or else he puts up with them in some mysterious fashion, as in Taoism. The connection with the East is deliberately stressed by the patient, through her painting into the mandala four hexagrams from the *I Ching*.[147]

598 The sign in the left top half is "Yü, ENTHUSIASM" (No. 16). It means "Thunder comes resounding out of the earth," i.e., a movement coming from the unconscious, and expressed by music and dancing. Confucius comments as follows:

> Firm as a rock, what need of a whole day?
> The judgment can be known.
> The superior man knows what is hidden and what is evident.
> He knows weakness, he knows strength as well.
> Hence the myriads look up to him.
> Enthusiasm can be the source of beauty, but it can also delude.

599 The second hexagram at the top is "Sun, DECREASE" (No. 41). The upper trigram means Mountain, the lower trigram means Lake. The mountain towers above the lake and "restrains" it. That is the "image" whose interpretation points to self-restraint and reserve, i.e., a seeming decrease of oneself. This is significant in the light of "ENTHUSIASM." In the top line of the hexagram, "But [one] no longer has a separate home," the homelessness of the Buddhist monk is meant. On the psychological level this does not, of course, refer to so drastic a

146 This is the lower triad that corresponds to the Trinity, just as the devil is occasionally depicted with three heads. Cf. supra, "Phenomenology of the Spirit in Fairytales," pars. 425 and 436ff.

147 Trans. by Wilhelm and Baynes (1967), pp. 67ff.

demonstration of renunciation and independence, but to the patient's irreversible insight into the conditioned quality of all relationships, into the relativity of all values, and the transience of all things.

600 The sign in the bottom half to the right is "Sheng, PUSHING UPWARD" (No. 46). "Within the earth, wood grows: The image of Pushing Upward." It also says: "One pushes upward into an empty city," and "The king offers him Mount Ch'i." So this hexagram means growth and development of the personality, like a plant pushing out of the earth—a theme already anticipated by the plant motif in an earlier mandala. This is an allusion to the important lesson which Miss X has learnt from her experience: that there is no development unless the shadow is accepted.

601 The hexagram to the left is "Ting, THE CAULDRON" (No. 50). This is a bronze sacrificial vessel equipped with handles and legs, which held the cooked viands used for festive occasions. The lower trigram means Wind and Wood, the upper one Fire. The "Cauldron" is thus made up of "fire over wood," just as the alchemical vessel consists of fire or water.[148] There is "delicious food" in it (the "fat of the pheasant"), but it is not eaten because "the handle of the *ting* is altered" and its "legs are broken," making it unusable. But, as a result of "constant self-abnegation," the personality becomes differentiated ("the *ting* has golden carrying rings" and even "rings of jade") and purified, until it acquires the "hardness and soft lustre" of precious jade.[149]

602 Though the four hexagrams were put into the mandala on purpose, they are authentic results of preoccupation with the *I Ching*. The phases and aspects of my patient's inner process of development can therefore express themselves easily in the language of the *I Ching*, because it too is based on the psychology of the individuation process that forms one of the main interests of Taoism and of Zen Buddhism.[150] Miss X's interest in Eastern philosophy was due to the deep impression which a better knowledge of her life and of herself had made upon her—an

148 *Psychology and Alchemy*, par. 338.

149 The same idea as the transformation into the *lapis*. Cf. ibid., par. 378.

150 Good examples are *The Secret of the Golden Flower* and Suzuki, *Introduction to Zen Buddhism*.

impression of the tremendous contradictions in human nature. The insoluble conflict she was faced with makes her preoccupation with Eastern therapeutic systems, which seem to get along without conflict, doubly interesting. It may be partly due to this acquaintance with the East that the opposites, irreconcilable in Christianity, were not blurred or glossed over, but were seen in all their sharpness, and in spite (or perhaps just because) of this, were brought together into the unity of the mandala. Böhme was never able to achieve this union; on the contrary, in his mandala the bright and dark semi-circles are turned back to back. The bright half is labelled "H. Ghost," the dark half "Father," i.e., *auctor rerum* [151] or "First Principle," whereas the Holy Ghost is the "Second Principle." This polarity is crossed by the paired opposites "Sonne" and "Earthly Man." The "Devills" are all on the side of the dark "Father" and constitute his "Wrath-fire," just as on the periphery of the mandala.

603 Böhme's starting-point was philosophical alchemy, and to my knowledge he was the first to try to organize the Christian cosmos, as a total reality, into a mandala.[152] The attempt failed, inasmuch as he was unable to unite the two halves in a circle. Miss X's mandala, on the other hand, comprises and contains the opposites, as a result, we may suppose, of the support afforded by the Chinese doctrine of Yang and Yin, the two metaphysical principles whose co-operation makes the world go round. The hexagrams, with their firm (yang) and yielding (yin) lines, illustrate certain phases of this process. It is therefore right that they should occupy a mediating position between above and below. Lao-tzu says: "High stands on low." This indisputable truth is secretly suggested in the mandala: the three white birds hover in a black field, but the grey-black goat

[151] Cf. the above quotation from the "Aureum vellus" of Mennens, where earth signifies the Father and his "shadow" signifies matter. Böhme's view is thoroughly consistent with the character of Yahweh, who, despite his role as the guardian of justice and morality, is amoral and unjust. Cf. Stade, *Biblische Theologie des Alten Testaments,* I, pp. 88f.

[152] I am purposely disregarding the numerous arrangements in a circle such as the *rex gloriae* with the four evangelists, Paradise with its four rivers, the heavenly hierarchies of Dionysius the Areopagite, etc. These all ignore the reality of evil, because they regard it as a mere *privatio boni* and thereby dismiss it with a euphemism.

has a bright orange-coloured background. Thus the Oriental truth insinuates itself and makes possible—at least by symbolic anticipation—a union of opposites within the irrational life process formulated by the *I Ching*. That we are really concerned here with opposite phases of one and the same process is shown by the picture that now follows.

Picture 10

604 In Picture 10, begun in Zurich but only completed when Miss X again visited her motherland, we find the same division as before into above and below. The "soul-flower" [153] in the centre is the same, but it is surrounded on all sides by a dark blue night sky, in which we see the four phases of the moon, the new moon coinciding with the world of darkness below. The three birds have become two. Their plumage has darkened, but on the other hand the goat has turned into two semi-human creatures with horns and light faces, and only two of the four snakes remain. A notable innovation is the appearance of two *crabs* in the lower, chthonic hemisphere that also represents the body. The crab has essentially the same meaning as the astrological sign Cancer.[154] Unfortunately Miss X gave no context here. In such cases it is usually worth investigating what use has been made in the past of the object in question. In earlier, prescientific ages hardly any distinction was drawn between long-tailed crabs (*Macrura,* crayfish) and short-tailed crabs (*Brachyura*). As a zodiacal sign Cancer signifies *resurrection,* because the crab sheds its shell.[155] The ancients had in mind chiefly *Pagurus bernhardus,* the hermit crab. It hides in its shell and cannot be attacked. Therefore it signifies *caution* and *foresight, knowledge of coming events.*[156] It "depends on the moon, and

[153] Cf. Rahner, "Die seelenheilende Blume."

[154] Cf. Bouché-Leclercq, *L'Astrologie grecque,* p. 136: Cancer = "crabe ou écrevisse." The constellation was usually represented as a tailless crab.

[155] "The crab is wont to change with the changing seasons; casting off its old shell, it puts on a new and fresh one." This, says Picinelli, is an "emblema" of the resurrection of the dead, and cites Ephesians 4 : 23: ". . . be renewed in the spirit of your minds" (RSV). (*Mondo simbolico,* Lib. VI, No. 45.)

[156] Foreseeing the flooding of the Nile, the crabs (like the tortoises and crocodiles) bring their eggs in safety to a higher place. "They foresee the future in their mind long before it comes." Caussin, *Polyhistor symbolicus* (1618), p. 442.

waxes with it." [157] It is worth noting that the crab appears just in the mandala in which we see the phases of the moon for the first time. Astrologically, Cancer is the house of the moon. Because of its backwards and sideways movement, it plays the role of an unlucky animal in superstition and colloquial speech ("crabbed," "catch a crab," etc.). Since ancient times cancer (καρκίνος) has been the name for a malignant tumour of the glands. Cancer is the zodiacal sign in which the sun begins to retreat, when the days grow shorter. Pseudo-Kallisthenes relates that crabs dragged Alexander's ships down into the sea.[158] "Karkinos" was the name of the crab that bit Heracles in the foot in his fight with the Lernaean monster. In gratitude, Hera set her accomplice among the stars.[159]

605 In astrology, Cancer is a feminine and watery sign,[160] and the summer solstice takes place in it. In the *melothesiae* [161] it is correlated with the *breast*. It rules over the *Western sea*. In Propertius it makes a sinister appearance: "Octipedis Cancri terga sinistra time" (Fear thou the ill-omened back of the eight-footed crab).[162] De Gubernatis says: "The crab . . . causes now the death of the solar hero and now that of the monster." [163] The *Panchatantra* (V, 2) relates how a crab, which the mother gave to her son as apotropaic magic, saved his life by killing a black snake.[164] As De Gubernatis thinks, the crab stands now for the sun and now for the moon,[165] according to whether it goes forwards or backwards.

606 Miss X was born in the first degrees of Cancer (actually about 3°). She knew her horoscope and was well aware of the significance of the moment of birth; that is, she realized that the degree of the rising sign (the ascendent) conditions the individuality of the horoscope. Since she obviously guessed the

157 Masenius, *Speculum imaginum veritatis occultae* (1714), cap. LXVII, 30, p. 768.

158 De Gubernatis, *Zoological Mythology*, II, p. 355.

159 Roscher, *Lexikon*, II, col. 959, s.v. "Karkinos." The same motif occurs in a dream described in *Two Essays on Analytical Psychology*, pars. 80ff.

160 In Egypt, the heliacal rising of Cancer indicates the beginning of the annual flooding of the Nile and hence the beginning of the year. Bouché-Leclercq, p. 137.

161 [Cf. "Psychology and Religion," p. 67, n. 5.—EDITORS.]

162 Propertius, trans. by Butler, p. 275.

163 De Gubernatis, II, p. 356.

164 *The Panchatantra Reconstructed*, ed. by Edgerton, II, pp. 403f. Cf. also Hoffmann-Krayer et al., *Handwörterbuch des Deutschen Aberglaubens*, V, col. 448, s.v. "Krebs."

165 De Gubernatis, II, p. 356.

horoscope's affinity with the mandala, she introduced her individual sign into the painting that was meant to express her psychic self.[166]

607 The essential conclusion to be drawn from Picture 10 is that the dualities which run through it are always inwardly balanced, so that they lose their sharpness and incompatibility. As Multatuli says: "Nothing is quite true, and even that is not quite true." But this loss of strength is counterbalanced by the unity of the centre, where the lamp shines, sending out coloured rays to the eight points of the compass.[167]

608 Although the attainment of inner balance through symmetrical pairs of opposites was probably the main intention of this mandala, we should not overlook the fact that the *duplication motif* also occurs when unconscious contents are about to become conscious and differentiated. They then split, as often happens in dreams, into two identical or slightly different halves corresponding to the conscious and still unconscious aspects of the nascent content. I have the impression, from this picture, that it really does represent a kind of solstice or climax, where decision and division take place. The dualities are, at bottom, Yes and No, the irreconcilable opposites, but they *have* to be held together if the balance of life is to be maintained. This can only be done by holding unswervingly to the centre, where action and suffering balance each other. It is a path "sharp as the edge of a razor." A climax like this, where universal opposites clash, is at the same time a moment when a wide perspective often opens out into the past and future. This is the psychological moment when, as the *consensus gentium* has established since ancient times, synchronistic phenomena occur—that is, when the far appears near: sixteen years later, Miss X became fatally ill with cancer of the breast.[168]

166 Her horoscope shows four earth signs but no air sign. The danger coming from the animus is reflected in ☽ □ ☿.

167 Cf. the Buddhist conception of the "eight points of the compass" in the *Amitāyur-dhyāna Sūtra;* cf. "The Psychology of Eastern Meditation," pp. 560ff.

168 I do not hesitate to take the synchronistic phenomena that underlie astrology seriously. Just as there is an eminently psychological reason for the existence of alchemy, so too in the case of astrology. Nowadays it is no longer interesting to know how far these two fields are aberrations; we should rather investigate the psychological foundations on which they rest. [Cf. Jung, "Synchronicity: An Acausal Connecting Principle," *passim.*—EDITORS.]

Picture 11

609 Here I will only mention that the coloured rays emanating from the centre have become so rarified that, in the next few pictures, they disappear altogether. Sun and moon are now outside, no longer included in the microcosm of the mandala. The sun is not golden, but has a dull, ochrous hue and in addition is clearly turning to the left: it is moving towards its own obscuration, as had to happen after the cancer picture (solstice). The moon is in the first quarter. The roundish masses near the sun are probably meant to be cumulus clouds, but with their grey-red hues they look suspiciously like bulbous swellings. The interior of the mandala now contains a quincunx of stars, the central star being silver and gold. The division of the mandala into an aerial and an earthy hemisphere has transferred itself to the outside world and can no longer be seen in the interior. The silvery rim of the aerial hemisphere in the preceding picture now runs round the entire mandala and recalls the band of quicksilver that, as *Mercurius vulgaris,* "veils the true personality." At all events, it is probable that the influence and importance of the outside world are becoming so strong in this picture as to bring about an impairment and devaluation of the mandala. It does not break down or burst (as can easily happen under similar circumstances), but is removed from the telluric influence through the symbolical constellation of stars and heavenly bodies.

Pictures 12–24

610 In Picture 12 the sun is in fact sinking below the horizon and the moon is coming out of the first quarter. The radiation of the mandala has ceased altogether, but the equivalents of sun and moon, and also of the earth, have been assimilated into it. A remarkable feature is its sudden inner animation by two human figures and various animals. The constellation character of the centre has vanished and given way to a kind of flower motif. What this animation means cannot be established, unfortunately, as we have no commentary.

611 In Picture 13 the source of radiation is no longer in the mandala but outside, in the shape of the full moon, from which

rings of rainbow-coloured light radiate in concentric circles. The mandala is laced together by four black and golden snakes, the heads of three of them pointing to the centre, while the fourth rears upwards. In between the snakes and the centre there are indications of the spermatozoon motif. This may mean an intensive penetration on the part of the outside world, but it could also mean magical protection. The breaking down of the quaternity into 3 plus 1 is in accord with the archetype.[169]

612 In Picture 14 the mandala is suspended over the lit-up ravine of Fifth Avenue, New York, whither Miss X in the meantime returned. On the blue flower in the centre the *coniunctio* of the "royal" pair is represented by the sacrificial fire burning between them. The King and Queen are assisted by two kneeling figures of a man and a woman. It is a typical marriage quaternio, and for an understanding of its psychology I must refer the reader to my account in the "Psychology of the Transference." [170] This inner bond should be thought of as a compensatory "consolidation" against disintegrating influences from without.

613 In Picture 15 the mandala floats between Manhattan and the sea. It is daylight again, and the sun is just rising. Out of the blue centre blue snakes penetrate into the red flesh of the mandala: the enantiodromia is setting in, after the introversion of feeling caused by the shock of New York had passed its climax. The blue colour of the snakes indicates that they have acquired a pneumatic nature.

614 From Picture 16 onwards, the drawing and painting technique shows a decided improvement. The mandalas gain in aesthetic value. In Picture 17 a kind of *eye motif* appears, which I have also observed in the mandalas of other persons. It seems to me to link up with the motif of *polyophthalmia* and to point to the peculiar nature of the unconscious, which can be regarded as a "multiple consciousness." I have discussed this question in detail elsewhere.[171] (See also Fig. 5.)

169 An instance of the axiom of Maria. Other well-known examples are Horus and his 4 (or 3 + 1) sons, the 4 symbolical figures in Ezekiel, the 4 evangelists and—last but not least—the 3 synoptic gospels and the 1 gospel of St. John.

170 [Ch. 2, pp. 211ff.—EDITORS.]

171 "On the Nature of the Psyche," sec. 6.

Fig. 5. Mandala by a woman patient

Aged 58, artistic and technically accomplished. In the centre is the egg encircled by the snake; outside, apotropaic wings and eyes. The mandala is exceptional in that it has a pentadic structure. (The patient also produced triadic mandalas. She was fond of playing with forms irrespective of their meaning—a consequence of her artistic gift.)

615 The enantiodromia only reached its climax the following year, in Picture 19.[172] In that picture the red substance is arranged round the golden, four-rayed star in the centre, and the blue substance is pushing everywhere to the periphery. Here the rainbow-coloured radiation of the mandala begins again for the first time, and from then on was maintained for over ten years (in mandalas not reproduced here).

616 I will not comment on the subsequent pictures, nor reproduce them all—as I say, they extend over more than ten years—because I feel I do not understand them properly. In addition, they came into my hands only recently, after the death of the patient, and unfortunately without text or commentary. Under these circumstances the work of interpretation becomes very uncertain, and is better left unattempted. Also, this case was meant only as an example of how such pictures come to be produced, what they mean, and what reflections and observations their interpretation requires. It is not intended to demonstrate how an entire lifetime expresses itself in symbolic form. The individuation process has many stages and is subject to many vicissitudes, as the fictive course of the *opus alchymicum* amply shows.

Conclusion

617 Our series of pictures illustrates the initial stages of the way of individuation. It would be desirable to know what happens afterwards. But, just as neither the philosophical gold nor the philosophers' stone was ever made in reality, so nobody has ever been able to tell the story of the whole way, at least not to mortal ears, for it is not the story-teller but death who speaks the final "consummatum est." Certainly there are many things worth knowing in the later stages of the process, but, from the point of view of teaching as well as of therapy, it is important

172 [Pictures 18–24, which were not reproduced with the earlier versions of this essay, were chosen by Professor Jung from among those painted by the patient after the termination of analytical work. The dates of the entire series of pictures were as follows: 1–6, Oct. 1928; 7–9, Nov. 1928; 10, Jan.; 11, Feb.; 12, June; 13, Aug.; 14, Sept.; 15, Oct.; 16, 17, Nov., all 1929; 18, Feb. 1930; 19, Aug. 1930; 20, March 1931; 21, July 1933; 22, Aug. 1933; 23, 1935; 24, "Night-blooming cereus, done May 1938, on last trip to Jung" (patient's notation).—EDITORS.]

not to skip too quickly over the initial stages. As these pictures are intuitive anticipations of future developments, it is worth while lingering over them for a long time, in order, with their help, to integrate so many contents of the unconscious into consciousness that the latter really does reach the stage it sees ahead. These psychic evolutions do not as a rule keep pace with the tempo of intellectual developments. Indeed, their very first goal is to bring a consciousness that has hurried too far ahead into contact again with the unconscious background with which it should be connected. This was the problem in our case too. Miss X had to turn back to her "motherland" in order to find her earth again—*vestigia retro*! It is a task that today faces not only individuals but whole civilizations. What else is the meaning of the frightful regressions of our time? The tempo of the development of consciousness through science and technology was too rapid and left the unconscious, which could no longer keep up with it, far behind, thereby forcing it into a defensive position which expresses itself in a universal will to destruction. The political and social isms of our day preach every conceivable ideal, but, under this mask, they pursue the goal of lowering the level of our culture by restricting or altogether inhibiting the possibilities of individual development. They do this partly by creating a chaos controlled by terrorism, a primitive state of affairs that affords only the barest necessities of life and surpasses in horror the worst times of the so-called "Dark" Ages. It remains to be seen whether this experience of degradation and slavery will once more raise a cry for greater spiritual freedom.

618 This problem cannot be solved collectively, because the masses are not changed unless the individual changes. At the same time, even the best-looking solution cannot be forced upon him, since it is a good solution only when it is combined with a natural process of development. It is therefore a hopeless undertaking to stake everything on collective recipes and procedures. The bettering of a general ill begins with the individual, and then only when he makes himself and not others responsible. This is naturally only possible in freedom, but not under a rule of force, whether this be exercised by a self-elected tyrant or by one thrown up by the mob.

619 The initial pictures in our series illustrate the characteristic psychic processes which set in the moment one gives a mind to that part of the personality which has remained behind, forgotten. Scarcely has the connection been established when symbols of the self appear, trying to convey a picture of the total personality. As a result of this development, the unsuspecting modern gets into paths trodden from time immemorial—the *via sancta,* whose milestones and signposts are the religions.[173] He will think and feel things that seem strange to him, not to say unpleasant. Apuleius relates that in the Isis mysteries he "approached the very gates of death and set one foot on Proserpina's threshold, yet was permitted to return, rapt through all the elements. At midnight I saw the sun shining as if it were noon; I entered the presence of the gods of the underworld and the gods of the upper world, stood near and worshipped them."[174] Such experiences are also expressed in our mandalas; that is why we find in religious literature the best parallels to the symbols and moods of the situations they formulate. These situations are intense inner experiences which can lead to lasting psychic growth and a ripening and deepening of the personality, if the individual affected by them has the moral capacity for πίστις, loyal trust and confidence. They are the age-old psychic experiences that underlie "faith" and ought to be its unshakable foundation—and not of faith alone, but also of knowledge.

620 Our case shows with singular clarity the spontaneity of the psychic process and the transformation of a personal situation into the problem of individuation, that is, of becoming whole, which is the answer to the great question of our day: How can consciousness, our most recent acquisition, which has bounded ahead, be linked up again with the oldest, the unconscious, which has lagged behind? The oldest of all is the instinctual foundation. Anyone who overlooks the instincts will be ambuscaded by them, and anyone who does not humble himself will be humbled, losing at the same time his freedom, his most precious possession.

621 Always when science tries to describe a "simple" life-process, the matter becomes complicated and difficult. So it is no wonder

173 Isaiah 45 : 8: "And a highway shall be there, and it shall be called the Holy Way" (RSV).

174 *The Golden Ass,* trans. by Graves, p. 286.

that the details of a transformation process rendered visible through active imagination make no small demands on our understanding. In this respect they may be compared with all other biological processes. These, too, require specialized knowledge to become comprehensible. Our example also shows, however, that this process can begin and run its course without any special knowledge having to stand sponsor to it. But if one wants to understand anything of it and assimilate it into consciousness, then a certain amount of knowledge is needed. If the process is not understood at all, it has to build up an unusual intensity so as not to sink back again into the unconscious without result. But if its affects rise to an unusual pitch, they will enforce some kind of understanding. It depends on the correctness of this understanding whether the consequences turn out more pathologically or less. Psychic experiences, according to whether they are rightly or wrongly understood, have very different effects on a person's development. It is one of the duties of the psychotherapist to acquire such knowledge of these things as will enable him to help his patient to an adequate understanding. Experiences of this kind are not without their dangers, for they are also, among other things, the matrix of the psychoses. Stiffnecked and violent interpretations should under all circumstances be avoided, likewise a patient should never be forced into a development that does not come naturally and spontaneously. But once it has set in, he should not be talked out of it again, unless the possibility of a psychosis has been definitely established. Thorough psychiatric experience is needed to decide this question, and it must constantly be borne in mind that the constellation of archetypal images and fantasies is not in itself pathological. The pathological element only reveals itself in the way the individual reacts to them and how he interprets them. The characteristic feature of a pathological reaction is, above all, *identification with the archetype*. This produces a sort of inflation and possession by the emergent contents, so that they pour out in a torrent which no therapy can stop. Identification can, in favourable cases, sometimes pass off as a more or less harmless inflation. But in all cases identification with the unconscious brings a weakening of consciousness, and herein lies the danger. You do not "make" an identification, you do not "identify yourself," but you experience your identity with the archetype in an unconscious way and so are possessed by it. Hence in more difficult cases it is far more necessary to strengthen and consolidate the ego than to understand and assimilate the products of the unconscious. The decision must be left to the diagnostic and therapeutic tact of the analyst.

*

622 This paper is a groping attempt to make the inner processes of the mandala more intelligible. They are, as it were, self-delineations of dimly sensed changes going on in the background, which are perceived by the "reversed eye" and rendered visible with pencil and brush, just as they are, uncomprehended and unknown. The pictures represent a kind of ideogram of unconscious contents. I have naturally used this method on myself too and can affirm that one can paint very complicated pictures without having the least idea of their real meaning. While painting them, the picture seems to develop out of itself and often in opposition to one's conscious intentions. It is interesting to observe how the execution of the picture frequently thwarts one's expectations in the most surprising way. The same thing can be observed, sometimes even more clearly, when writing down the products of active imagination.[175]

623 The present work may also serve to fill a gap I myself have felt in my exposition of therapeutic methods. I have written very little on active imagination, but have talked about it a great deal. I have used this method since 1916, and I sketched it out for the first time in "The Relations between the Ego and the Unconscious." I first mentioned the mandala in 1929, in *The Secret of the Golden Flower*.[176] For at least thirteen years I kept quiet about the results of these methods in order to avoid any suggestion. I wanted to assure myself that these things—mandalas especially—really are produced spontaneously and were not suggested to the patient by my own fantasy. I was then

[175] Case material in Meier, "Spontanmanifestationen des kollektiven Unbewussten," 284ff.; Bänziger, "Persönliches und Archetypisches im Individuationsprozess," p. 272; Gerhard Adler, *Studies in Analytical Psychology*, pp. 90ff.

[176] Active imagination is also mentioned in "The Aims of Psychotherapy," pars. 101ff. Cf. also "The Transcendent Function." For other pictures of mandalas see the next paper in the present vol.

able to convince myself, through my own studies, that mandalas were drawn, painted, carved in stone, and built, at all times and in all parts of the world, long before my patients discovered them. I have also seen to my satisfaction that mandalas are dreamt and drawn by patients who were being treated by psychotherapists whom I had not trained. In view of the importance and significance of the mandala symbol, special precautions seemed to be necessary, seeing that this motif is one of the best examples of the universal operation of an archetype. In a seminar on children's dreams, which I held in 1939–40,[177] I mentioned the dream of a ten-year-old girl who had absolutely no possibility of ever hearing about the quaternity of God. The dream was written down by the child herself and was sent to me by an acquaintance: *"Once in a dream I saw an animal that had lots of horns. It spiked up other little animals with them. It wriggled like a snake and that was how it lived. Then a blue fog came out of all the four corners, and it stopped eating. Then God came, but there were really four Gods in the four corners. Then the animal died, and all the animals it had eaten came out alive again."*

624 This dream describes an unconscious individuation process: all the animals are eaten by the one animal. Then comes the enantiodromia: the dragon changes into pneuma, which stands for a divine quaternity. Thereupon follows the apocatastasis, a resurrection of the dead. This exceedingly "unchildish" fantasy can hardly be termed anything but archetypal. Miss X, in Picture 12, also put a whole collection of animals into her mandala —two snakes, two tortoises, two fishes, two lions, two pigs, a goat and a ram.[178] Integration gathers many into one. To the child who had this dream, and to Miss X likewise, it was certainly not known that Origen had already said (speaking of the sacrificial animals): "Seek these sacrifices within thyself, and thou wilt find them within thine own soul. Understand that thou hast within thyself flocks of cattle . . . flocks of sheep and

177 [*Psychologische Interpretation von Kinderträumen,* winter semester, 1939–40, Federal Polytechnic Institute, Zurich (mimeographed stenographic record). The same dream is discussed by Dr. Jacobi in *Complex/Archetype/Symbol,* pp. 139ff.—EDITORS.]

178 One thinks here of a Noah's Ark that crosses over the waters of death and leads to a rebirth of all life.

flocks of goats. . . . Understand that the birds of the sky are also within thee. Marvel not if we say that these are within thee, but understand that thou thyself art even another little world, and hast within thee the sun and the moon, and also the stars."[179]

625 The same idea occurs again in another passage, but this time it takes the form of a psychological statement: "For look upon the countenance of a man who is at one moment angry, at the next sad, a short while afterward joyful, then troubled again, and then contented. . . . See how he who thinks himself one is not one, but seems to have as many personalities as he has moods, as also the Scripture says: A fool is changed as the moon. . . .[180] God, therefore, is unchangeable, and is called one for the reason that he changes not. Thus also the true imitator of God, who is made after God's image, is called one and the selfsame [*unus et ipse*] when he comes to perfection, for he also, when he is fixed on the summit of virtue, is not changed, but remains alway one. For every man, whiles he is in wickedness [*malitia*], is divided among many things and torn in many directions; and while he is in many kinds of evil he cannot be called one."[181]

626 Here the many animals are affective states to which man is prone. The individuation process, clearly alluded to in this passage, subordinates the many to the One. But the One is God, and that which corresponds to him in us is the *imago Dei,* the God-image. But the God-image, as we saw from Jakob Böhme, expresses itself in the mandala.

179 *In Leviticum Homiliae,* V, 2 (Migne, *P.G.,* vol. 12, col. 449).

180 Ecclesiasticus 27 : 11.

181 *In libros Regnorum homiliae,* I, 4 (Migne, *P.G.,* vol. 12, cols. 998–99).

CONCERNING MANDALA SYMBOLISM [1]

627 In what follows I shall try to describe a special category of symbols, the *mandala,* with the help of a wide selection of pictures. I have dealt with this theme on several occasions before, and in *Psychology and Alchemy* I gave a detailed account, with running commentary, of the mandala symbols that came up in the course of an individual analysis. I repeated the attempt in the preceding paper of the present volume, but there the mandalas did not derive from dreams but from active imagination. In this paper I shall present mandalas of the most varied provenance, on the one hand to give the reader an impression of the astonishing wealth of forms produced by individual fantasy, and on the other hand to enable him to form some idea of the regular occurrence of the basic elements.

628 As regards the interpretation, I must refer the reader to the literature. In this paper I shall content myself with hints, because a more detailed explanation would lead much too far, as the mandalas described in "Psychology and Religion" and in the preceding paper of this volume show.

629 The Sanskrit word *mandala* means 'circle.' It is the Indian term for the circles drawn in religious rituals. In the great temple of Madura, in southern India, I saw how a picture of this kind was made. It was drawn by a woman on the floor of the *mandapam* (porch), in coloured chalks, and measured about ten feet across. A pandit who accompanied me said in reply to my questions that he could give me no information about it. Only the women who drew such pictures knew what they

1 [First published, as "Über Mandalasymbolik," in *Gestaltungen des Unbewussten* (Psychologische Abhandlungen, VII; Zurich, 1950). The illustrations had originally been collected for a seminar which Professor Jung gave at Berlin in 1930. Nine of them (Figs. 1, 6, 9, 25, 26, 28, 36, 37, 38) were published with brief comments as "Examples of European Mandalas" in *Das Geheimnis der goldenen Blüte,* by Jung and Richard Wilhelm (Munich, 1929; 2nd edn., Zurich, 1938), translated by C. F. Baynes as *The Secret of the Golden Flower* (London and New York, 1931; rev. edn., 1962); subsequently published in *Coll. Works,* vol. 13. In his *Memories, Dreams, Reflections* Jung acknowledged having painted the mandalas in Figs. 6 and 36 (thus also those in Figs. 28 and 29) and the frontispiece; see U.S. edn., pp. 197, 195; Brit. edn., pp. 188ff., 187.—EDITORS.]

meant. The woman herself was non-committal; she evidently did not want to be disturbed in her work. Elaborate mandalas, executed in red chalk, can also be found on the whitewashed walls of many huts. The best and most significant mandalas are found in the sphere of Tibetan Buddhism.[2] I shall use as an example a Tibetan mandala, to which my attention was drawn by Richard Wilhelm.

Figure 1

630 A mandala of this sort is known in ritual usage as a *yantra,* an instrument of contemplation. It is meant to aid concentration by narrowing down the psychic field of vision and restricting it to the centre. Usually the mandala contains three circles, painted in black or dark blue. They are meant to shut out the outside and hold the inside together. Almost regularly the outer rim consists of fire, the fire of *concupiscentia,* 'desire,' from which proceed the torments of hell. The horrors of the burial ground are generally depicted on the outer rim. Inside this is a garland of lotus leaves, characterizing the whole mandala as a *padma,* 'lotus-flower.' Then comes a kind of monastery courtyard with four gates. It signifies sacred seclusion and concentration. Inside this courtyard there are as a rule the four basic colours, red, green, white, and yellow, which represent the four directions and also the psychic functions, as the Tibetan Book of the Dead [3] shows. Then, usually marked off by another magic circle, comes the centre as the essential object or goal of contemplation.

631 This centre is treated in very different ways, depending on the requirements of the ritual, the grade of initiation of the contemplator, and the sect he belongs to. As a rule it shows Shiva in his world-creating emanations. Shiva, according to Tantric doctrine, is the One Existent, the Timeless in its perfect state. Creation begins when this unextended point—known as *Shiva-bindu*—appears in the eternal embrace of its feminine side, the Shakti. It then emerges from the state of being-in-itself and attains the state of being-for-itself, if I may use the Hegelian terminology.

2 Cf. *Psychology and Alchemy,* pars. 122ff.

3 [Cf. Jung, Psychological Commentary on the *Tibetan Book of the Dead,* par. 850.—EDITORS.]

632 In *kundalini* yoga symbolism, Shakti is represented as a snake wound three and a half times round the *lingam,* which is Shiva in the form of a phallus. This image shows the *possibility* of manifestation in space. From Shakti comes Maya, the building material of all individual things; she is, in consequence, the creatrix of the real world. This is thought of as illusion, as being and not-being. It *is,* and yet remains dissolved in Shiva. Creation therefore begins with an act of division of the opposites that are united in the deity. From their splitting arises, in a gigantic explosion of energy, the multiplicity of the world.

633 The goal of contemplating the processes depicted in the mandala is that the yogi shall become inwardly aware of the deity. Through contemplation, he recognizes himself as God again, and thus returns from the illusion of individual existence into the universal totality of the divine state.

634 As I have said, mandala means 'circle.' There are innumerable variants of the motif shown here, but they are all based on the squaring of a circle. Their basic motif is the premonition of a centre of personality, a kind of central point within the psyche, to which everything is related, by which everything is arranged, and which is itself a source of energy. The energy of the central point is manifested in the almost irresistible compulsion and urge to *become what one is,* just as every organism is driven to assume the form that is characteristic of its nature, no matter what the circumstances. This centre is not felt or thought of as the ego but, if one may so express it, as the *self.* Although the centre is represented by an innermost point, it is surrounded by a periphery containing everything that belongs to the self—the paired opposites that make up the total personality. This totality comprises consciousness first of all, then the personal unconscious, and finally an indefinitely large segment of the collective unconscious whose archetypes are common to all mankind. A certain number of these, however, are permanently or temporarily included within the scope of the personality and, through this contact, acquire an individual stamp as the shadow, anima, and animus, to mention only the best-known figures. The self, though on the one hand simple, is on the other hand an extremely composite thing, a "conglomerate soul," to use the Indian expression.

635 Lamaic literature gives very detailed instructions as to how such a circle must be painted and how it should be used. Form and colour are laid down by tradition, so the variants move within fairly narrow limits. The ritual use of the mandala is actually non-Buddhist; at any rate it is alien to the original Hīnayāna Buddhism and appears first in Mahāyāna Buddhism.

636 The mandala shown here depicts the state of one who has emerged from contemplation into the absolute state. That is why representation of hell and the horrors of the burial ground are missing. The diamond thunderbolt, the *dorje* in the centre, symbolizes the perfect state where masculine and feminine are united. The world of illusions has finally vanished. All energy has gathered together in the initial state.

637 The four *dorjes* in the gates of the inner courtyard are meant to indicate that life's energy is streaming inwards; it has detached itself from objects and now returns to the centre. When the perfect union of all energies in the four aspects of wholeness is attained, there arises a static state subject to no more change. In Chinese alchemy this state is called the "Diamond Body," corresponding to the *corpus incorruptibile* of medieval alchemy, which is identical with the *corpus glorificationis* of Christian tradition, the incorruptible body of resurrection. This mandala shows, then, the union of all opposites, and is embedded between *yang* and *yin,* heaven and earth; the state of everlasting balance and immutable duration.

638 For our more modest psychological purposes we must abandon the colourful metaphysical language of the East. What yoga aims at in this exercise is undoubtedly a psychic change in the adept. The ego is the expression of individual existence. The yogin exchanges his ego for Shiva or the Buddha; in this way he induces a shifting of the psychological centre of personality from the personal ego to the impersonal non-ego, which is now experienced as the real "Ground" of the personality.

639 In this connection I would like to mention a similar Chinese conception, namely the system on which the *I Ching* is based.

Figure 2

640 In the centre is *ch'ien,* 'heaven,' from which the four emanations go forth, like the heavenly forces extending through space. Thus we have:

ch'ien: self-generated creative energy, corresponding to Shiva.
heng: all-pervading power.
yuen: generative power.
li: beneficent power.
ching: unchangeable, determinative power.

641 Round this masculine power-centre lies the earth with its formed elements. It is the same conception as the Shiva-Shakti union in *kundalini* yoga, but here represented as the earth receiving into itself the creative power of heaven. The union of heaven with *kun,* the feminine and receptive, produces the *tetraktys,* which, as in Pythagoras, underlies all existence.

642 The "River Map" is one of the legendary foundations of the *I Ching,* which in its present form derives partly from the twelfth century B.C. According to the legend, a dragon dredged the magical signs of the "River Map" from a river. On it the sages discovered the drawing, and in the drawing the laws of the world-order. This drawing, in accordance with its extreme age, shows the knotted cords that signify numbers. These numbers have the usual primitive character of qualities, chiefly masculine and feminine. All uneven numbers are masculine, even numbers feminine.

643 Unfortunately I do not know whether this primitive conception influenced the formation of the much younger Tantric mandala. But the parallels are so striking that the European investigator has to ask himself: Which view influenced the other? Did the Chinese develop from the Indian, or the Indian from the Chinese? An Indian whom I asked answered: "Naturally the Chinese developed from the Indian." But he did not know how old the Chinese conceptions are. The bases of the *I Ching* go back to the third millennium B.C. My late friend Richard Wilhelm, the eminent expert on classical Chinese philosophy, was of the opinion that no direct connections could be assumed. Nor, despite the fundamental similarity of the symbolic ideas, does there need to be any direct influence, since the ideas, as experience shows and as I think I have demonstrated, arise autochthonously again and again, independently of one another, out of a psychic matrix that seems to be ubiquitous.

Figure 3

644 As a counterpart to the Lamaic mandala, I now reproduce the Tibetan "World Wheel," which should be sharply distinguished from the former, since it represents the world. In the centre are the three principles: cock, snake, and pig, symbolizing lust, envy, and unconsciousness. The wheel has, near the centre, six spokes, and twelve spokes round the edge. It is based on a triadic system. The wheel is held by the god of death, Yama. (Later we shall meet other "shield-holders": Figs. 34 and 47.) It is understandable that the sorrowful world of old age, sickness, and death should be held in the claws of the death-demon. The incomplete state of existence is, remarkably enough, expressed by a triadic system, and the complete (spiritual) state by a tetradic system. The relation between the incomplete and the complete state therefore corresponds to the "sesquitertian proportion" of 3 : 4. This relation is known in Western alchemical tradition as the axiom of Maria. It also plays a not inconsiderable role in dream symbolism.[4]

*

645 We shall now pass on to individual mandalas spontaneously produced by patients in the course of an analysis of the unconscious. Unlike the mandalas so far discussed, these are not based on any tradition or model, seeming to be free creations of fantasy, but determined by certain archetypal ideas unknown to their creators. For this reason the fundamental motifs are repeated so often that marked similarities occur in drawings done by the most diverse patients. The pictures come as a rule from educated persons who were unacquainted with the ethnic parallels. The pictures differ widely, according to the stage of the therapeutic process; but certain important stages correspond to definite motifs. Without going into therapeutic details, I would only like to say that a rearranging of the personality is involved, a kind of new centring. That is why mandalas mostly appear in connection with chaotic psychic states of disorientation or panic. They then have the purpose of reducing the confusion to order, though this is never the conscious intention

[4] Cf. the preceding paper, par. 552.

of the patient. At all events they express order, balance, and wholeness. Patients themselves often emphasize the beneficial or soothing effect of such pictures. Usually the mandalas express religious, i.e., numinous, thoughts and ideas, or, in their stead, philosophical ones. Most mandalas have an intuitive, irrational character and, through their symbolical content, exert a retroactive influence on the unconscious. They therefore possess a "magical" significance, like icons, whose possible efficacy was never consciously felt by the patient. In fact, it is from the effect of their own pictures that patients discover what icons can mean. Their pictures work not because they spring from the patients' own fantasy but because they are impressed by the fact that their subjective imagination produces motifs and symbols of the most unexpected kind that conform to law and express an idea or situation which their conscious mind can grasp only with difficulty. Confronted with these pictures, many patients suddenly realize for the first time the reality of the collective unconscious as an autonomous entity. I will not labour the point here; the strength of the impression and its effect on the patient are obvious enough from some of the pictures.

646 I must preface the pictures that now follow with a few remarks on the formal elements of mandala symbolism. These are primarily:

1. *Circular, spherical,* or *egg-shaped* formation.

2. The circle is elaborated into a *flower* (rose, lotus) or a *wheel.*

3. A centre expressed by a *sun, star,* or *cross,* usually with four, eight, or twelve rays.

4. The circles, spheres, and cruciform figures are often represented in *rotation* (swastika).

5. The circle is represented by a *snake* coiled about a centre, either ring-shaped (uroboros) or spiral (Orphic egg).

6. *Squaring of the circle,* taking the form of a circle in a square or vice versa.

7. *Castle, city,* and *courtyard* (*temenos*) motifs, quadratic or circular.

8. *Eye* (pupil and iris).

9. Besides the tetradic figures (and multiples of four), there are also triadic and pentadic ones, though these are much rarer.

They should be regarded as "disturbed" totality pictures, as we shall see below.

Figure 4

647 This mandala was done by a woman patient in her middle years, who first saw it in a dream. Here we see at once the difference from the Eastern mandala. It is poor in form, poor in ideas, but nevertheless expresses the individual attitude of the patient far more clearly than the Eastern pictures, which have been subjected to a collective and traditional configuration. Her dream ran: *"I was trying to decipher an embroidery pattern. My sister knew how. I asked her if she had made an elaborate hemstitched handkerchief. She said, "No, but I know how it was done." Then I saw it with the threads drawn, but the work not yet done. One must go around and around the square until near the centre, then go in circles."*

648 The spiral is painted in the typical colours red, green, yellow, and blue. According to the patient, the square in the centre represents a *stone,* its four facets showing the four basic colours. The inner spiral represents the snake that, like Kundalini, winds three and a half times [5] round the centre.

649 The dreamer herself had no notion of what was going on in her, namely the beginning of a new orientation, nor would she have understood it consciously. Also, the parallels from Eastern symbolism were completely unknown to her, so that any influence is out of the question. The symbolic picture came to her spontaneously, when she had reached a certain point in her development.

650 It is, unfortunately, not possible for me to say exactly under what circumstances each of these pictures arose. That would lead us too far. The sole aim of this paper is to give a survey of the formal parallels to the individual and collective mandala. I regret also that for the same reason no single picture can be interpreted circumstantially and in detail, as that would inevitably require a comprehensive account of the analytical situation of the patient. Wherever it is possible to shed light on the origins of the picture by a passing hint, as in the present case, I shall do so.

[5] The motif of 3½ (the Apocalyptic number of days of affliction; cf. Rev. 11 : 9 and 11) refers to the alchemical dilemma "3 or 4?" or to the sesquitertian proportion (3 : 4). The *sesquitertius* is 3 + ⅓.

651 As to the interpretation of the picture, it must be emphasized that the snake, arranged in angles and then in circles round the square, signifies the circumambulation of, and way to, the centre. The snake, as a chthonic and at the same time spiritual being, symbolizes the unconscious. The stone in the centre, presumably a cube, is the quaternary form of the *lapis philosophorum*. The four colours also point in this direction.[6] It is evident that the stone in this case signifies the new centre of personality, the self, which is also symbolized by a vessel.

Figure 5

652 The painter was a middle-aged woman of schizoid disposition. She had several times drawn mandalas spontaneously, because they always had an ordering effect on her chaotic psychic states. The picture shows a rose, the Western equivalent of the lotus. In India the lotus-flower (*padma*) is interpreted by the Tantrists as the womb. We know this symbol from the numerous pictures of the Buddha (and other Indian deities) in the lotus-flower.[7] It corresponds to the "Golden Flower" of Chinese alchemy, the rose of the Rosicrucians, and the mystic rose in Dante's *Paradiso*. Rose and lotus are usually arranged in groups of four petals, indicating the squaring of the circle or the united opposites. The significance of the rose as the maternal womb was nothing strange to our Western mystics, for we read in a prayer inspired by the Litany of Loreto:

> O Rose-wreath, thy blossoming makes men weep for joy.
> O rosy sun, thy burning makes men to love.
> O son of the sun,
> Rose-child,
> Sun-beam.
> Flower of the Cross, pure Womb that blossoms
> Over all blooming and burning,
> Sacred Rose,
> Mary.

6 There is a very interesting American Indian parallel to this mandala: a white snake coiled round a centre shaped like a cross in four colours. Cf. Newcomb and Reichard, *Sandpaintings of the Navajo Shooting Chant*, Pl. XIII, pp. 13 and 78. The book contains a large number of interesting mandalas in colour.
7 The Egyptian Horus-child is likewise shown sitting in the lotus.

653 At the same time, the vessel motif is an expression of the content, just as Shakti represents the actualization of Shiva. As alchemy shows, the self is androgynous and consists of a masculine and a feminine principle. Conrad of Würzburg speaks of Mary, the flower of the sea in which Christ lies hidden. And in an old hymn we read:

> O'er all the heavens a rose appears
> And a bright dress of blossom wears.
> Its light glows in the Three-in-One
> For God himself has put it on.

Figure 6

654 The rose in the centre is depicted as a ruby, its outer ring being conceived as a wheel or a wall with gates (so that nothing can come out from inside or go in from outside). The mandala was a spontaneous product from the analysis of a male patient. It was based on a dream: *The dreamer found himself with three younger travelling companions in Liverpool.*[8] *It was night, and raining. The air was full of smoke and soot. They climbed up from the harbour to the "upper city."* The dreamer said: *"It was terribly dark and disagreeable, and we could not understand how anyone could stick it here. We talked about this, and one of my companions said that, remarkably enough, a friend of his had settled here, which astonished everybody. During this conversation we reached a sort of public garden in the middle of the city. The park was square, and in the centre was a lake or large pool. A few street lamps just lit up the pitch darkness, and I could see a little island in the pool. On it there was a single tree, a red-flowering magnolia, which miraculously stood in everlasting sunshine. I noticed that my companions had not seen this miracle, whereas I was beginning to understand why the man had settled here."*

655 The dreamer went on: "I tried to paint this dream. But as so often happens, it came out rather different. The magnolia turned into a sort of rose made of ruby-coloured glass. It shone like a four-rayed star. The square represents the wall of the park and at the same time a street leading round the park in a square. From it there radiate eight main streets, and from each

[8] Note the allusion in the name "Liver-pool." The liver is that which causes to live, the seat of life. [Cf. *Memories, Dreams, Reflections*, pp. 197f./195f.]

of these eight side-streets, which meet in a shining red central point, rather like the Étoile in Paris. The acquaintance mentioned in the dream lived in a house at the corner of one of these stars." The mandala thus combines the classic motifs of flower, star, circle, precinct (*temenos*), and plan of city divided into quarters with citadel. "The whole thing seemed like a window opening on to eternity," wrote the dreamer.

Figure 7

656 Flower motif with cross in the centre. The square, too, is arranged like a flower. The four faces at the corners correspond to the four cardinal points, which are often depicted as four deities. Here they have a demonic character. This may be connected with the fact that the patient was born in the Dutch East Indies, where she sucked up the peculiar local demonology with the mother's milk of her native ayah. Her numerous drawings all had a distinctly Eastern character, and thereby helped her to assimilate influences that at first could not be reconciled with her Western mentality.[9]

657 In the picture that followed, the demon faces were ornamentally elaborated in eight directions. For the superficial observer the flowerlike character of the whole may disguise the demonic element the mandala is meant to ward off. The patient felt that the "demonic" effect came from the European influence with its moralism and rationalism. Brought up in the East Indies until her sixth year, she came later into a conventional European milieu, and this had a devastating effect on the flowerlike quality of her Eastern spirit and caused a prolonged psychic trauma. Under treatment her native world, long submerged, came up again in these drawings, bringing with it psychic recovery.

Figure 8

658 The flowerlike development has got stronger and is beginning to overgrow the "demonishness" of the faces.

Figure 9

659 A later stage is shown here. Minute care in the draughtsmanship vies with richness of colour and form. From this we

9 [Cf. *The Practice of Psychotherapy*, 2nd edn., appendix, esp. par. 557.—EDITORS.]

can discern not only the extraordinary concentration of the patient but the triumph of Eastern "flowerlikeness" over the demon of Western intellectualism, rationalism, and moralism. At the same time the new centring of the personality becomes visible.

Figure 10

660 In this painting, done by another young woman patient, we see at the cardinal points four creatures: a bird, a sheep, a snake, and a lion with a human face. Together with the four colours in which the four regions are painted, they embody four principles. The interior of the mandala is empty. Or rather, it contains a "Nothing" that is expressed by a quaternity. This is in accord with the overwhelming majority of individual mandalas: as a rule the centre contains the motif of the *rotundum,* known to us from alchemy, or the four-fold emanation or the squaring of the circle, or—more rarely—the figure of the patient in a universal human sense, representing the Anthropos.[10] We find this motif, too, in alchemy. The four animals remind us of the cherubim in Ezekiel's vision, and also of the four symbols of the evangelists and the four sons of Horus, which are sometimes depicted in the same way, three with animal heads and one with a human head. Animals generally signify the instinctive forces of the unconscious, which are brought into unity within the mandala. This integration of the instincts is a prerequisite for individuation.

Figure 11

661 Painting by an older patient. Here the flower is seen not in the basic pattern of the mandala, but in elevation. The circular form has been preserved inside the square, so that despite its different execution this picture can still be regarded as a mandala. The plant stands for growth and development, like the green shoot in the diaphragm *chakra* of the *kundalini* yoga system. The shoot symbolizes Shiva and represents the centre and the male, whereas the calyx represents the female, the place of germination and birth.[11] Thus the Buddha sitting in the lotus is shown as the germinating god. It is the god in his rising,

10 [Cf. "Psychology and Religion," pars. 136f., 156f.]

11 [Cf. "The Philosophical Tree," par. 336 and fig. 27.—EDITORS.]

the same symbol as Ra the falcon, or the phoenix rising from the nest, or Mithras in the tree-top, or the Horus-child in the lotus. They are all symbolizations of the *status nascendi* in the seeding-place of the matrix. In medieval hymns Mary too is praised as the cup of the flower in which Christ, coming down as a bird, makes his nest. Psychologically Christ means unity, which clothes itself in the *corpus mysticum* of the Church or in the body of the Mother of God ("mystic rose"), surrounded as with flower-petals, and thus reveals itself in reality. Christ as an image is a symbol of the self.[12] Just as the plant stands for growth, so the flower depicts the unfolding from a centre.

Figure 12

662 Here the four rays emanating from the centre spread across the whole picture. This gives the centre a dynamic character. The structure of the flower is a multiple of four. The picture is typical of the marked personality of the patient, who had some artistic talent. (She also painted Fig. 5.) Besides that she had a strong feeling for Christian mysticism, which played a great role in her life. It was important for her to experience the archetypal background of Christian symbolism.

Figure 13

663 Photograph of a rug woven by a middle-aged woman, Penelope-like, at a time of great inner and outer distress. She was a doctor and she wove this magic circle round herself, working at it every day for months, as a counterbalance to the difficulties of her life. She was not my patient and could not have been influenced by me. The rug contains an eight-petalled flower. A special feature of the rug is that it has a real "above and below." Above is light; below, relative darkness. In it, there is a creature like a beetle, representing an unconscious content, and comparable with the sun in the form of Khepera. Occasionally the "above and below" are outside the protective circle, instead of inside. In that case the mandala affords protection against extreme opposites; that is, the sharpness of the conflict is not yet realized or else is felt as intolerable. The protective circle then guards against possible disruption due to the tension of opposites.

12 Cf. *Aion* (Part II of this volume), ch. 5.

Figure 14

664 An Indian picture of *Shiva-bindu,* the unextended point. It shows the divine power before the creation: the opposites are still united. The god rests in the point. Hence the snake signifies extension, the mother of Becoming, the creation of the world of forms. In India this point is also called Hiranyagarbha, 'golden germ' or 'golden egg.' We read in the Sanatsugatiya: "That pure great light which is radiant, that great glory which the gods worship, which makes the sun shine forth, that divine, eternal Being is perceived by the faithful." [13]

Figure 15

665 This picture, also by a middle-aged woman patient, shows the squaring of the circle. The plants again denote germination and growth. In the centre is a sun. As the snake-and-tree motif shows, we have here a conception of Paradise. A parallel is the Gnostic conception of Edem with the four rivers of Paradise in the Naassene gnosis. For the functional significance of the snake in relation to the mandala, see the preceding paper (comments on pictures 3, 4, and 5).

Figure 16

666 This picture was painted by a neurotic young woman. The snake is somewhat unusual in that it lies in the centre itself, its head coinciding with this. Usually it is outside the inner circle, or at least coiled round the central point. One suspects (rightly, as it turned out) that the inner darkness does not conceal the longed-for unity, the self, but rather the chthonic, feminine nature of the patient. In a later picture the mandala bursts and the snake comes out.

Figure 17

667 The picture was done by a young woman This mandala is "legitimate" in so far as the snake is coiled round the four-rayed middle point. It is trying to get out: it is the awakening of Kundalini, meaning that the patient's chthonic nature is becoming active. This is also indicated by the arrows pointing

[13] *Sacred Books of the East,* VIII, p. 186, modified.

outwards. In practice it means becoming conscious of one's instinctual nature. The snake in ancient times personified the spinal ganglia and the spinal cord. Arrows pointing outwards may in other cases mean the opposite: protection of the inside from danger.

Figure 18

668 Drawn by an older patient. Unlike the previous picture, this one is "introverted." The snake is coiled round the four-rayed centre and has laid its head on the white, central point (*Shiva-bindu*), so that it looks as if it were wearing a halo. There seems to be a kind of incubation of the middle point—the motif of the snake guarding the treasure. The centre is often characterized as the "treasure hard to attain." [14]

Figure 19

669 Done by a middle-aged woman. The concentric circles express concentration. This is further emphasized by the fishes circumnavigating the centre. The number 4 has the meaning of total concentration. The movement to the left presumably indicates movement towards the unconscious, i.e., immersion in it.

Figure 20

670 This is a parallel to Figure 19: sketch of a fish-motif which I saw on the ceiling of the Maharajah's pavilion in Benares.

Figure 21

671 A fish instead of a snake. Fish and snake are simultaneously attributes of both Christ and the devil. The fish is making a whirlpool in the sea of the unconscious, and in its midst the precious pearl is being formed. A Rig-Veda hymn says:

> Darkness there was, concealed in darkness,
> A lightless ocean lost in night.
> Then the One, that was hidden in the shell,
> Was born through the power of fiery torment.
> From it arose in the beginning love,
> Which is the germ and the seed of knowledge.[15]

[14] Cf. *Symbols of Transformation,* Part II, ch. 7.

[15] Rig-Veda, X, 129, from Deussen trans., I, p. 123.

672 As a rule the snake personifies the unconscious, whereas the fish usually represents one of its contents. These subtle distinctions must be borne in mind when interpreting a mandala, because the two symbols very probably correspond to two different stages of development, the snake representing a more primitive and more instinctual state than the fish, which in history as well was endowed with higher authority than the snake (cf. the Ichthys-symbol).

Figure 22

673 In this picture by a young woman the fish has produced a differentiated centre by circumnavigation, and in it a mother and child stand before a stylized Tree of Life or of Knowledge. Here the fish has a dragonlike nature; it is a monster, a sort of Leviathan, which, as the texts from Ras Shamra show, was originally a snake.[16] Once more the movement is to the left.

Figure 23

674 The golden ball corresponds to the golden germ (Hiranyagarbha). It is rotating, and the Kundalini winding round it has doubled. This indicates conscious realization, since a content rising out of the unconscious splits at a certain moment into two halves, a conscious and an unconscious one. The doubling is not made by the conscious mind, but appears spontaneously in the products of the unconscious. The rightwards rotation, expressed by the wings (swastika-motif), likewise indicates conscious realization. The stars show that the centre has a cosmic structure. It has four rays, and thus behaves like a heavenly body. The Shatapatha-Brahmana says:

> Then he looks up to the sun, for that is the final goal, that the safe resort. To that final goal, to that resort he goes; for this reason he looks up to the sun.
>
> He looks up, saying, "Self-existent art thou, the best ray of light!" The sun is indeed the best ray of light, and therefore he says, "Self-existent art thou, the best ray of light!" "Light-bestowing art thou: give me light (*varkas*)!" "So say I," said Yajñavalkya, "and for this indeed the Brahmin should strive, if he would be *brahmavarkasin,* illumined by brahma."
>
> He then turns from left to right, saying, "I move along the course

16 [Cf. *Aion,* pars. 181f.—EDITORS.]

of the sun." Having reached that final goal, that safe resort, he now moves along the course of yonder sun.[17]

675 This sun has seven rays. A commentator remarks that four of them point to the four quarters; one points upwards, another downwards, but the seventh and "best" points inwards. It is at the same time the sun's disc, named Hiranyagarbha. This, according to Ramanuja's commentary on the Vedanta Sutras,[18] is the highest self, the "collective aggregate of all individual souls." It is the body of the highest Brahma and represents the collective psyche. For the idea of the self as compounded of many, compare Origen's "Each of us is not one, but many" and "All are righteous, but one receiveth the crown." [19]

676 The patient was a woman of sixty, artistically gifted. The individuation process, long blocked but released by the treatment, stimulated her creative activity (Fig. 21 derives from the same source) and gave rise to a series of happily coloured pictures which eloquently express the intensity of her experience.

Figure 24

677 Done by the same patient. She herself is shown practising contemplation or concentration on the centre: she has taken the place of the fish and the snakes. An ideal image of herself is laid round the precious egg. The legs are flexible, like a nixie's. The psychology of such a picture reappears in ecclesiastical tradition. The Shiva-Shakti of the East is known in the West as the "man encompassed by a woman," Christ and his bride the Church. Compare the Maitrayana-Brahmana Upanishad:

> He [the Self] is also he who warms, the Sun, hidden by the thousand-eyed golden egg, as one fire by another. He is to be thought after, he is to be sought after. Having said farewell to all living things, having gone to the forest, and having renounced all sensuous objects, let a man perceive the Self from his own body.[20]

678 Here too the radiation from the centre spreads out beyond the protective circle into the distance. This expresses the idea of the far-reaching effect of the introverted state of conscious-

17 I, 9, 3, 15ff. Trans. from *Sacred Books of the East,* XII, pp. 271f., modified.

18 Trans. from *Sacred Books of the East,* XLVIII, p. 578.

19 *In libros Regnorum homiliae,* I, 4 (Migne, *P.G.,* vol. 12, cols. 998, 999).

20 VI, 8. Trans. from *Sacred Books of the East,* XV, p. 311.

ness. It could also be described as an *unconscious* connection with the world.

Figure 25

679 This picture was done by another middle-aged patient. It shows various phases of the individuation process. Down below she is caught in a chthonic tangle of roots (the *mūlādhāra* of *kundalini* yoga). In the middle she studies a book, cultivating her mind and augmenting her knowledge and consciousness. At the top, reborn, she receives illumination in the form of a heavenly sphere that widens and frees the personality, its round shape again representing the mandala in its "Kingdom of God" aspect, whereas the lower, wheel-shaped mandala is chthonic. There is a confrontation of the natural and spiritual totalities. The mandala is unusual on account of its six rays, six mountain peaks, six birds, three human figures. In addition, it is located between a distinct Above and Below, also repeated in the mandala itself. The upper, bright sphere is in the act of descending into the hexad or triad and has already passed the rim of the wheel. According to old tradition the number 6 means creation and evolution, since it is a *coniunctio* of 2 and 3 (even and odd = female and male). Philo Judaeus therefore calls the *senarius* (6) the "number most suited to generation." [21] The number 3, he says, denotes the surface or flatness, whereas 4 means height or depth. The *quaternarius* "shows the nature of solids," whereas the three first numbers characterize or produce incorporeal intelligences. The number 4 appears as a three-sided pyramid.[22] The hexad shows that the mandala consists of two triads, and the upper one is making itself into a quaternity, the state of "equability and justice," as Philo says. Down below lurk unintegrated dark clouds. This picture demonstrates the not uncommon fact that the personality needs to be extended both upwards and downwards.

Figures 26 and 27

680 These mandalas are in part atypical. Both were done by the same young woman. In the centre, as in the previous mandala, is a female figure, as if enclosed in a glass sphere or transparent

21 *De opificio mundi.* Cf. Colson trans., I, p. 13.

22 Ibid., p. 79.

Figure 1

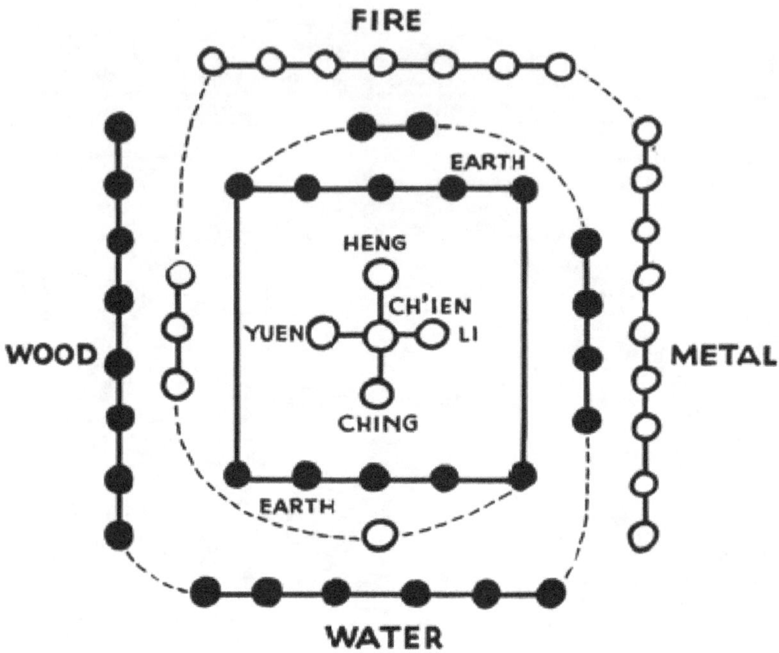

Figure 2

Figure 3

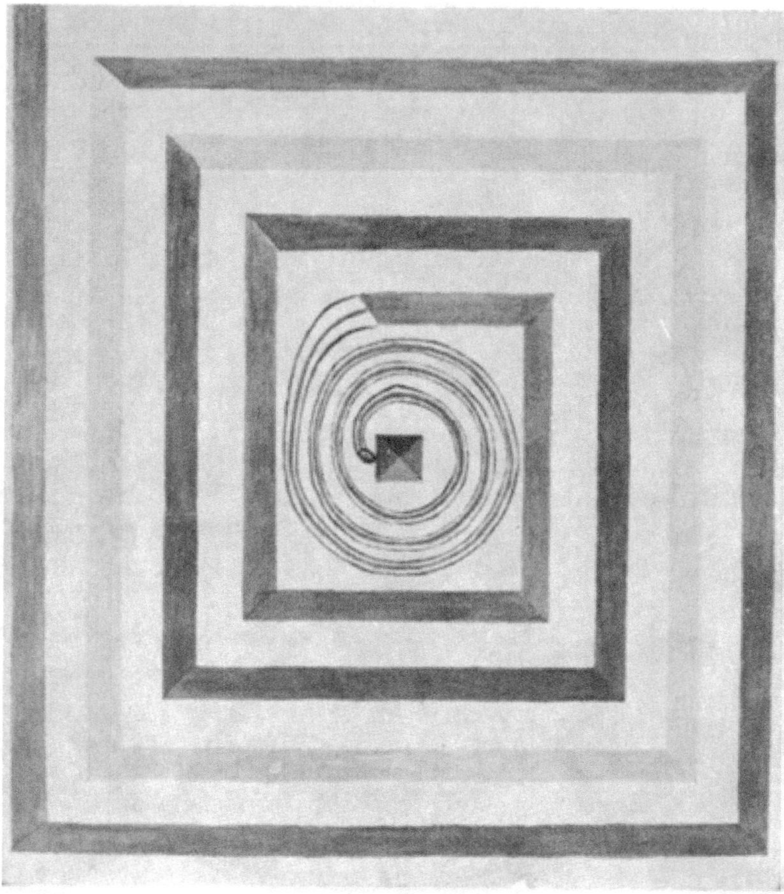

Figure 4

Figure 5

Figure 6

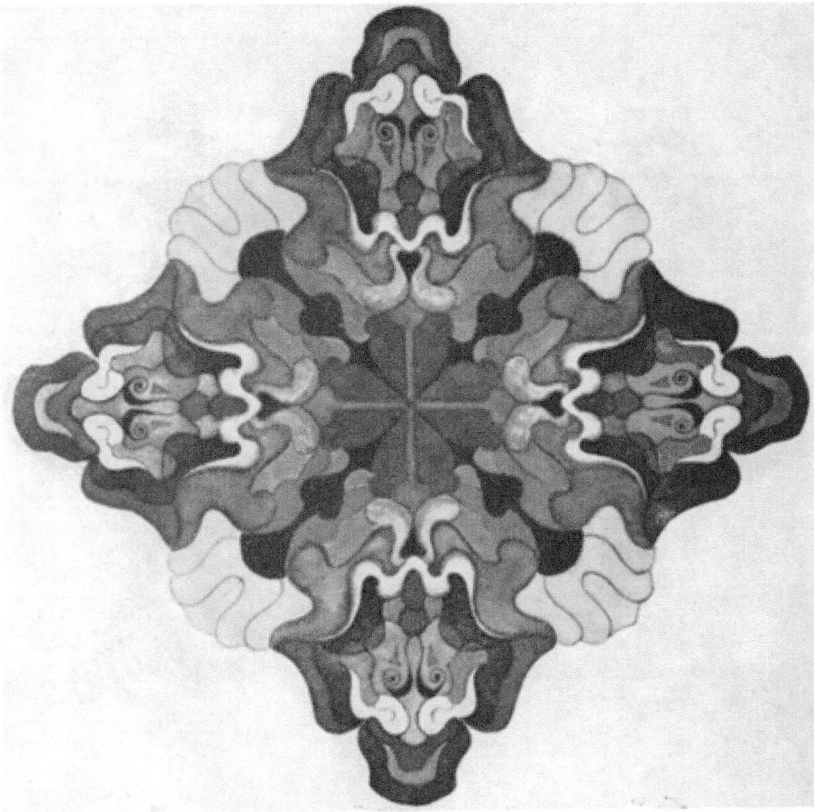

Figure 7

Figure 8

Figure 9

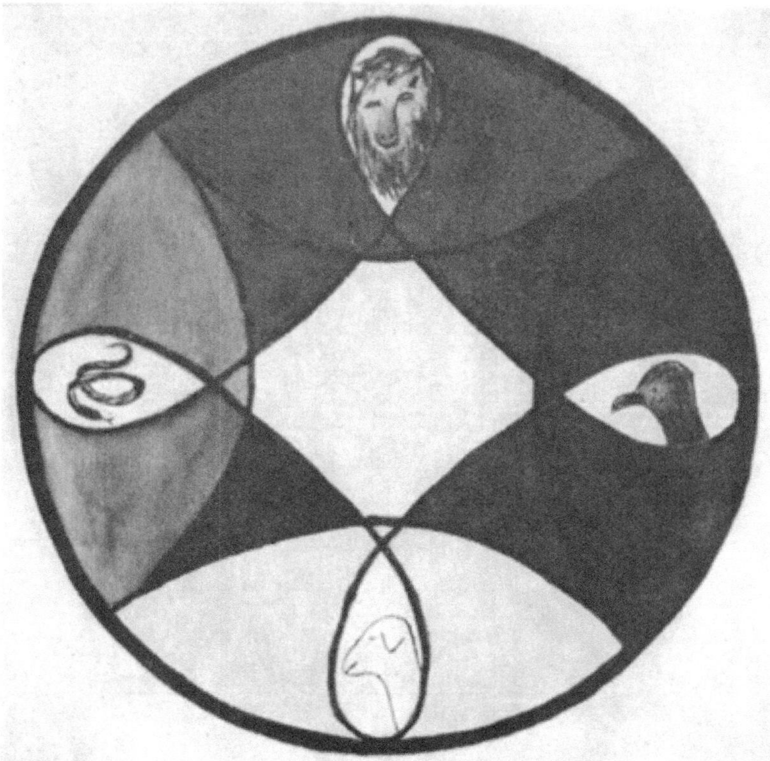

Figure 10

Figure 11

Figure 12

Figure 13

Figure 14

Figure 15

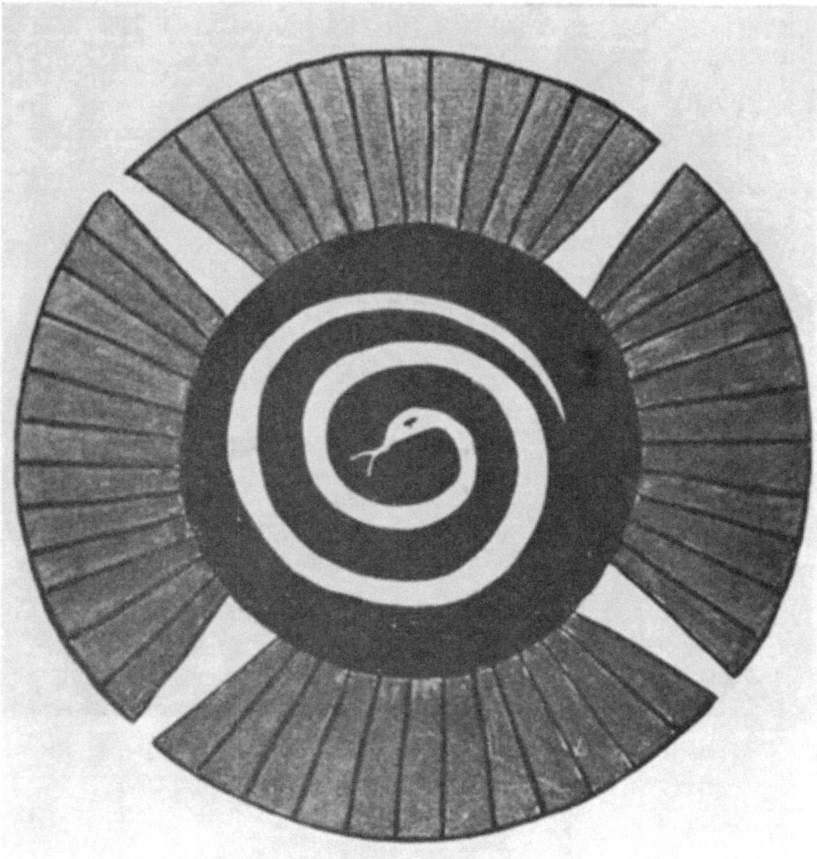

Figure 16

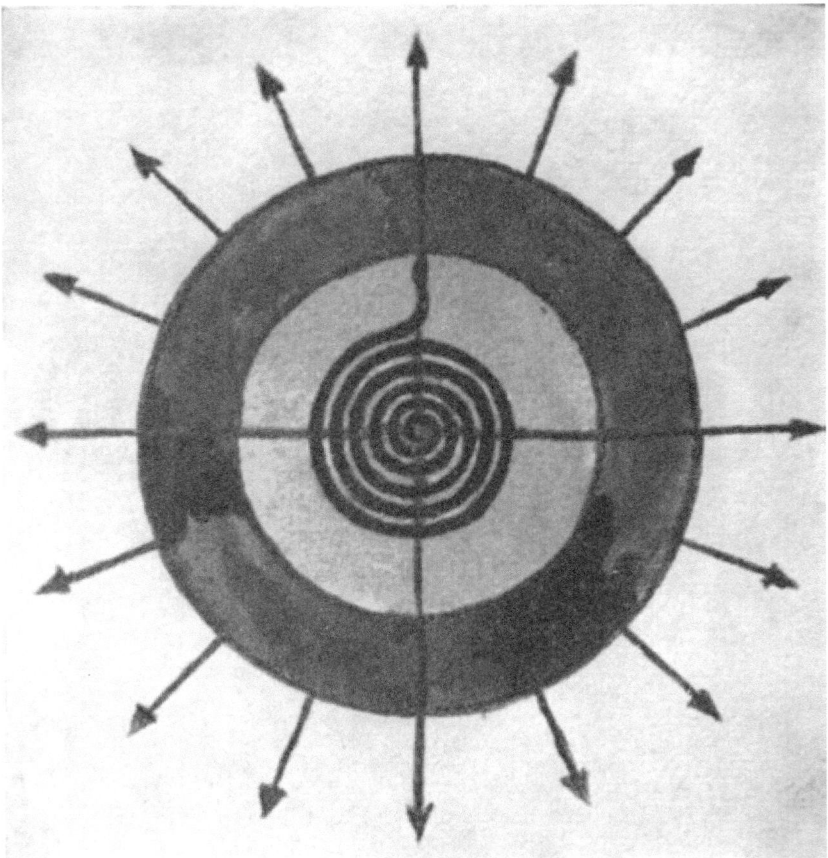

Figure 17

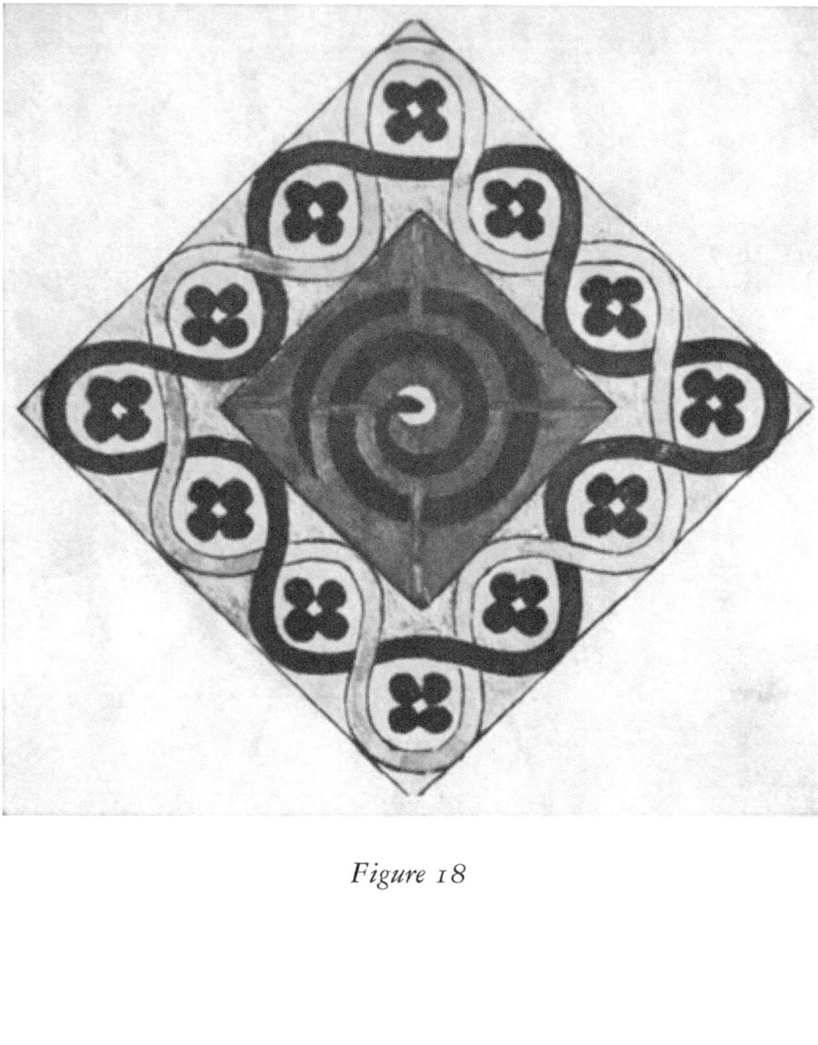

Figure 18

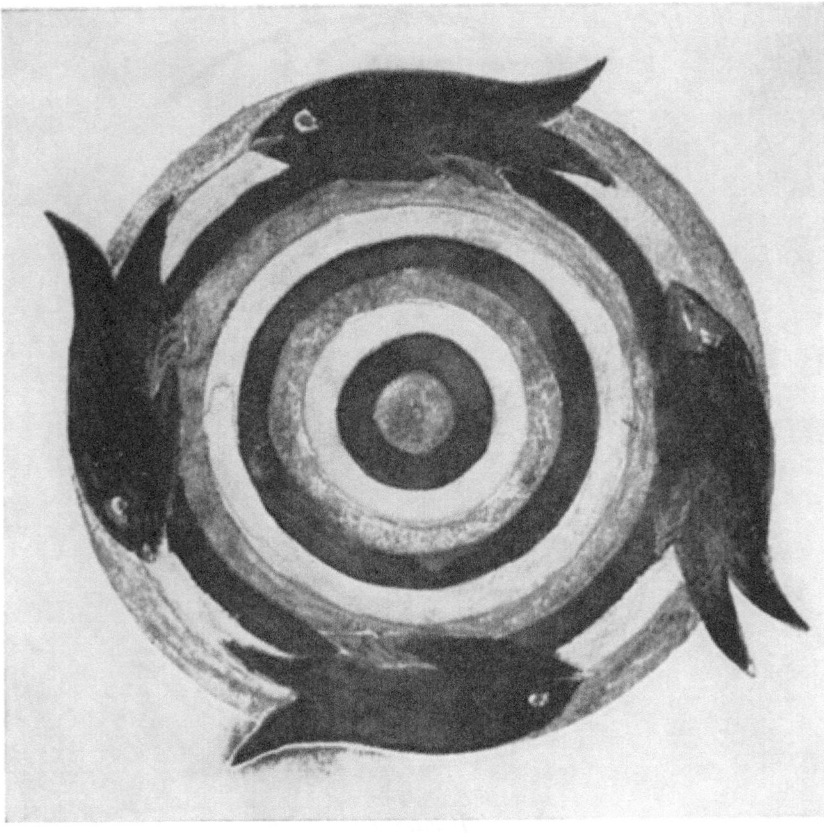

Figure 19

Figure 20

Figure 21

Figure 22

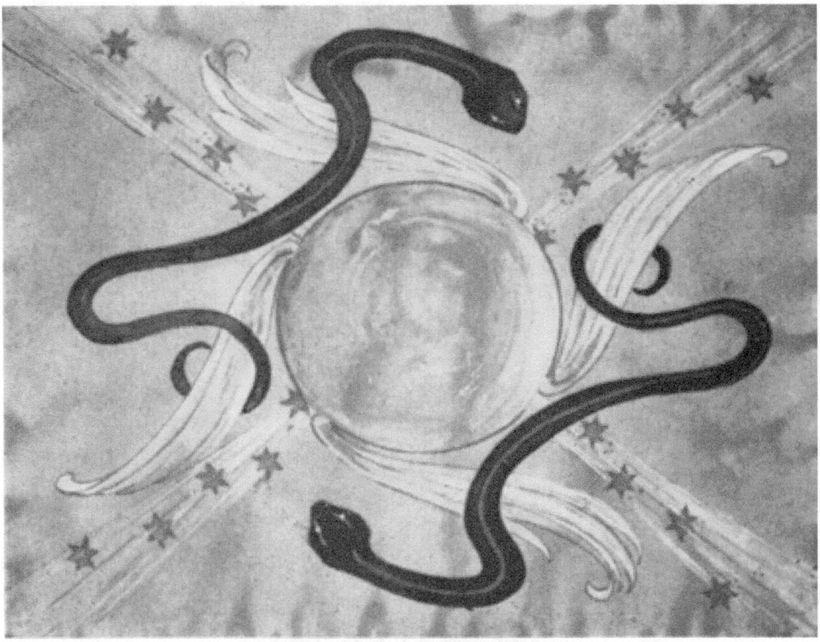

Figure 23

Figure 24

Figure 25

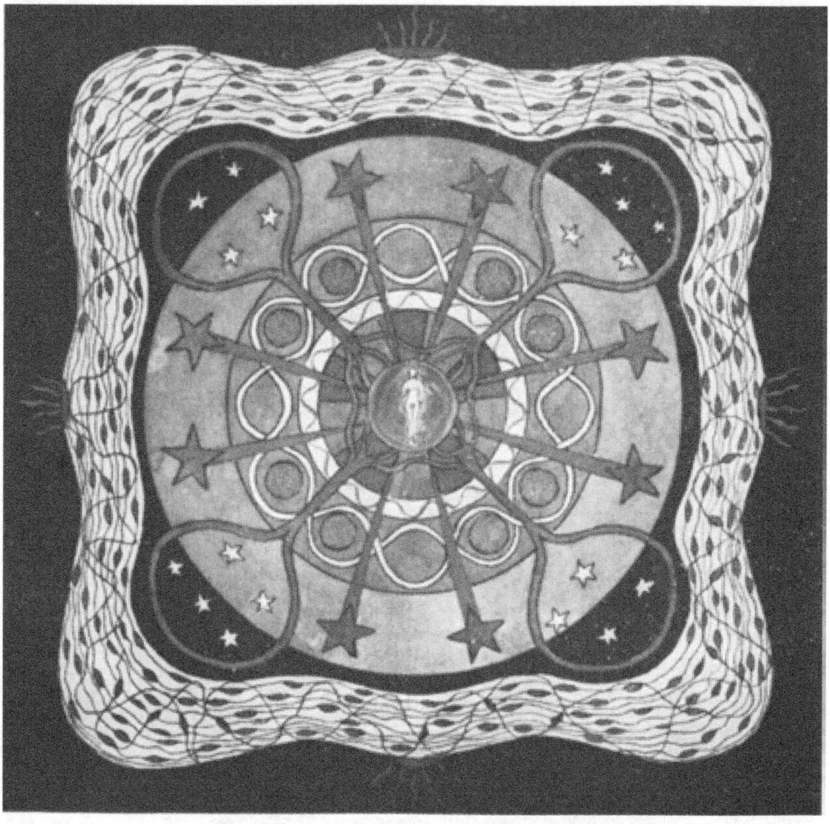

Figure 26

Figure 27

Figure 28

Figure 29

Figure 30

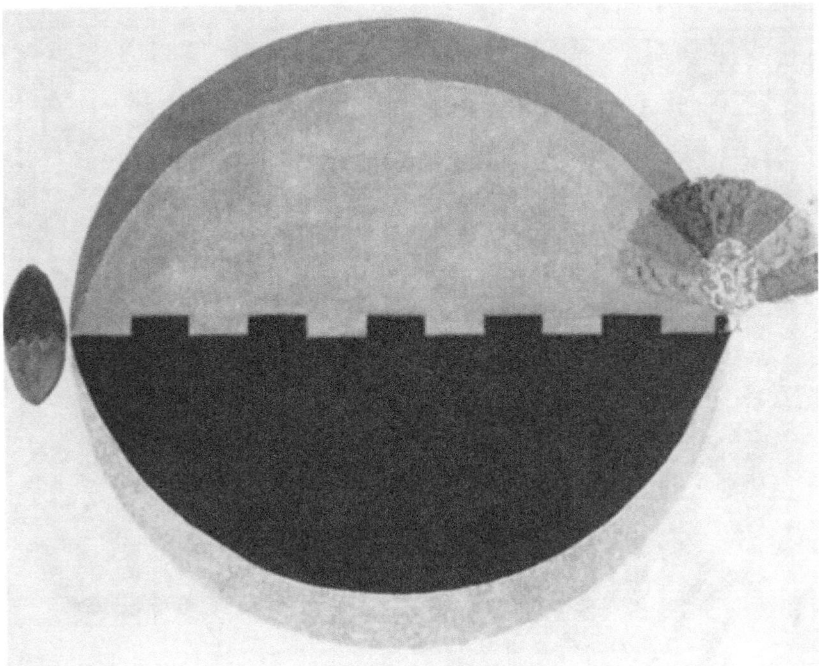

Figure 31

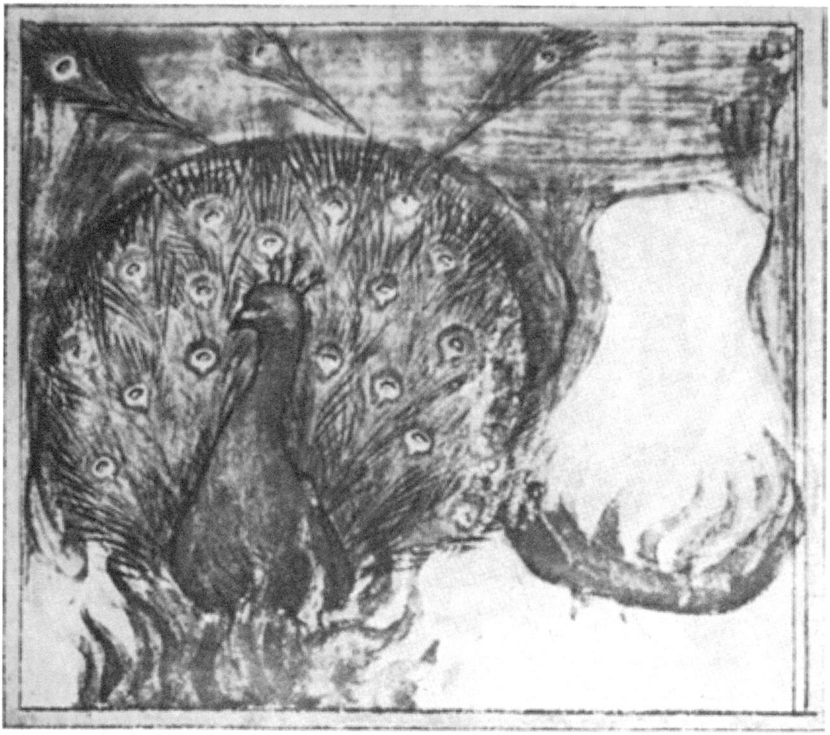

Figure 32

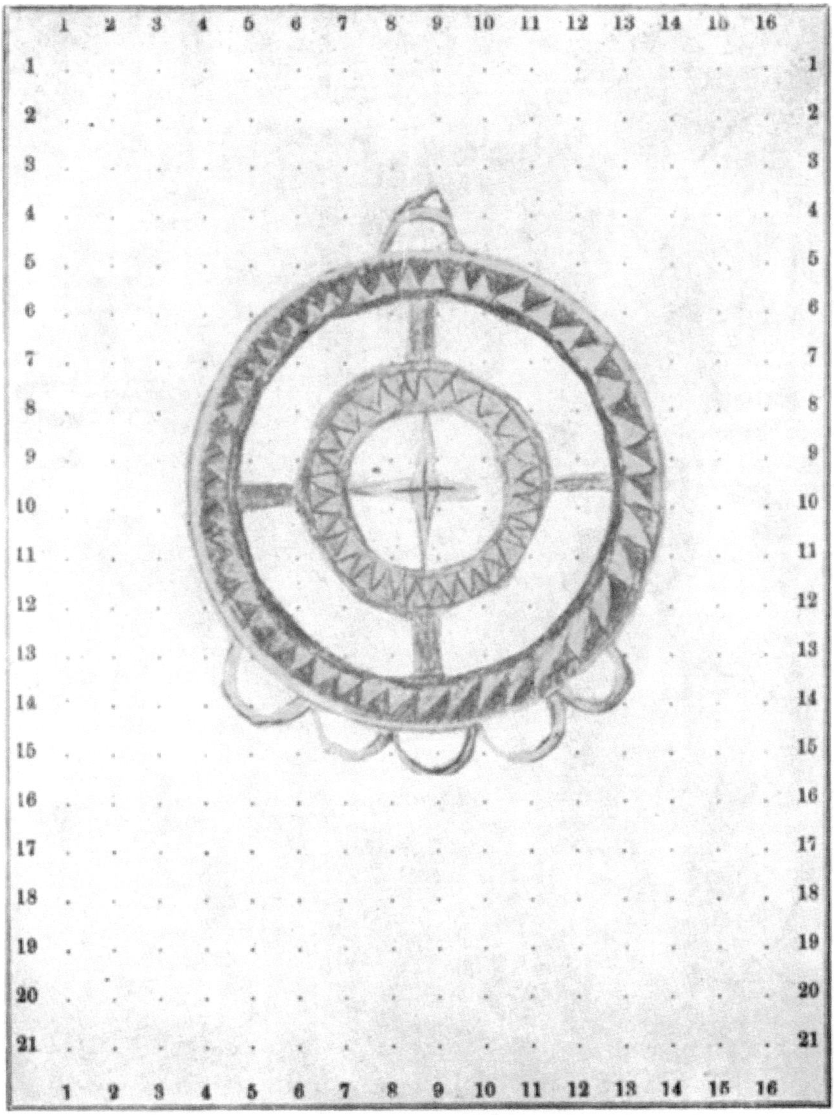

Figure 33

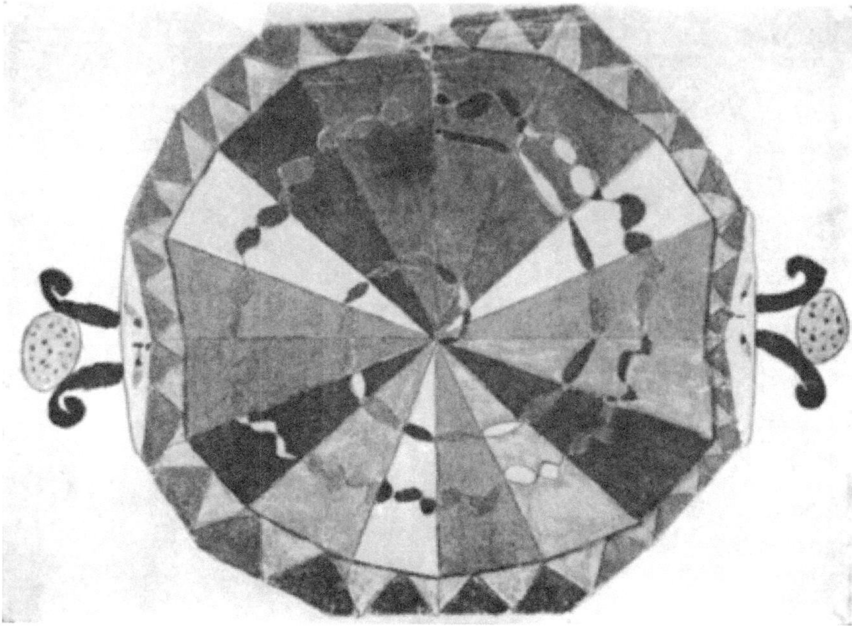

Figure 34

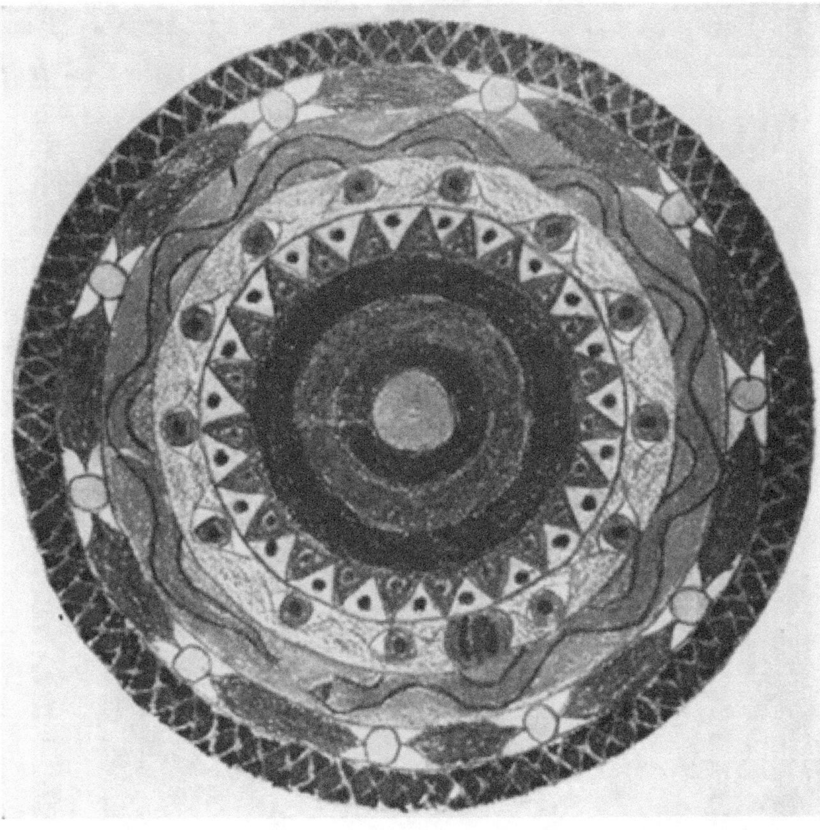

Figure 35

Figure 36

Figure 37

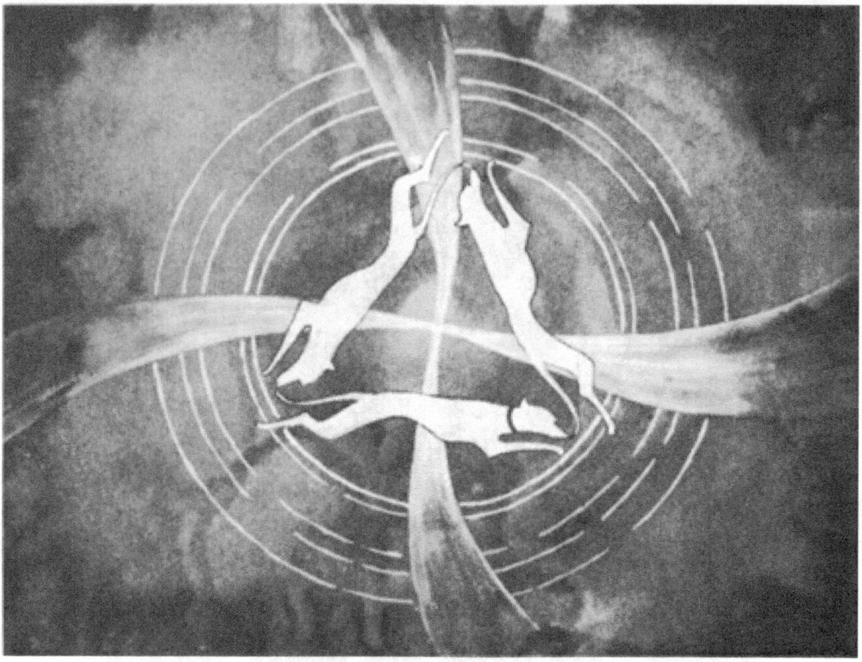

Figure 38

Figure 39

Figure 40

Figure 41

Figure 42

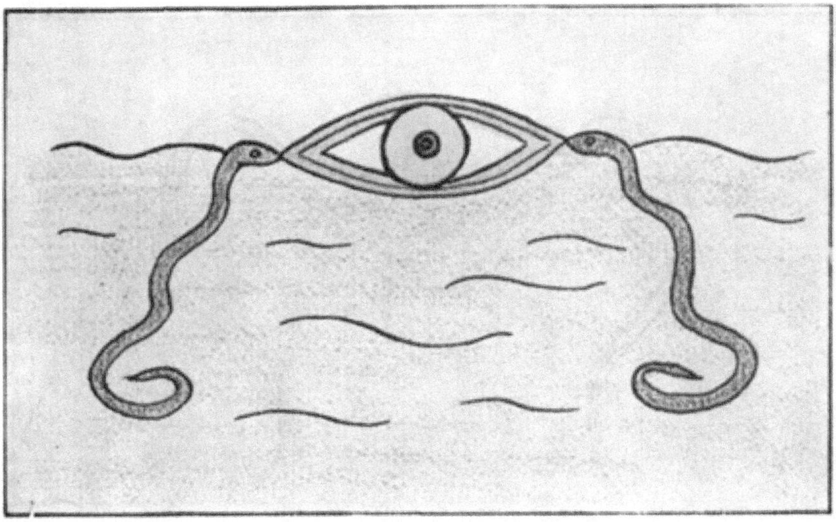

Figure 43

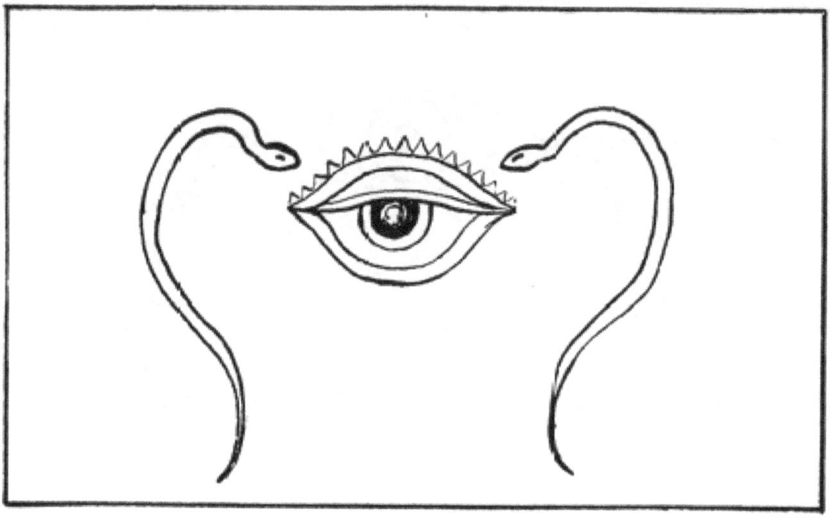

Figure 44

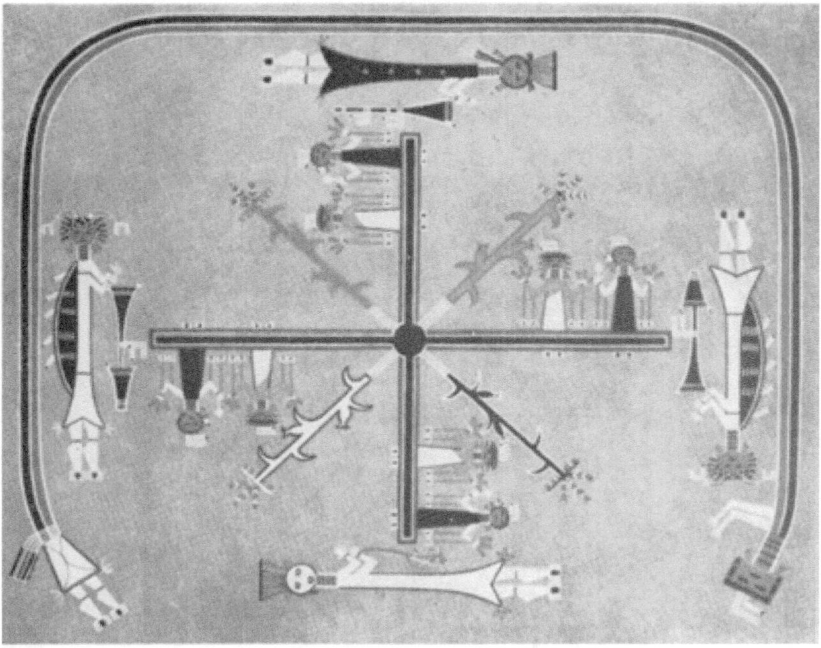

Figure 45

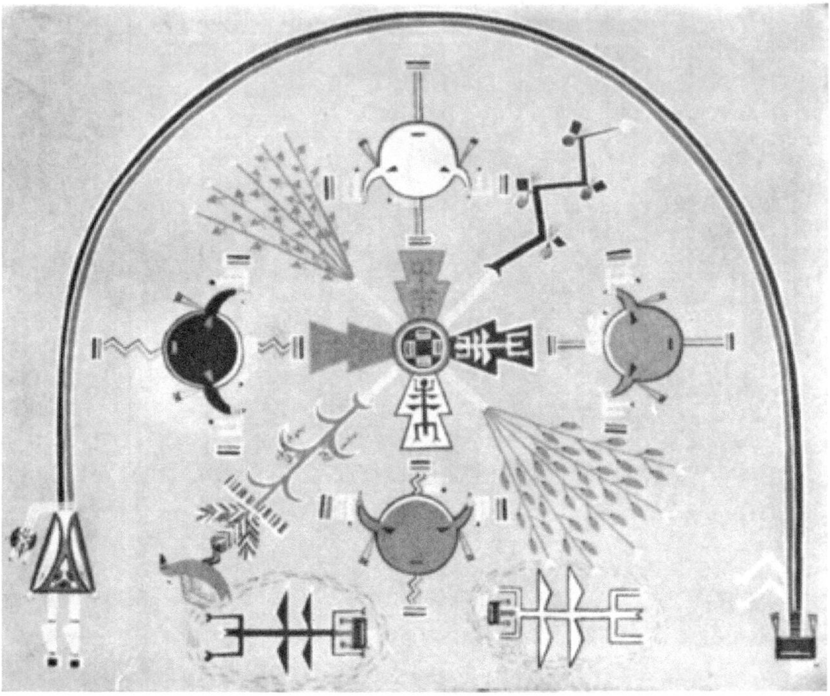

Figure 46

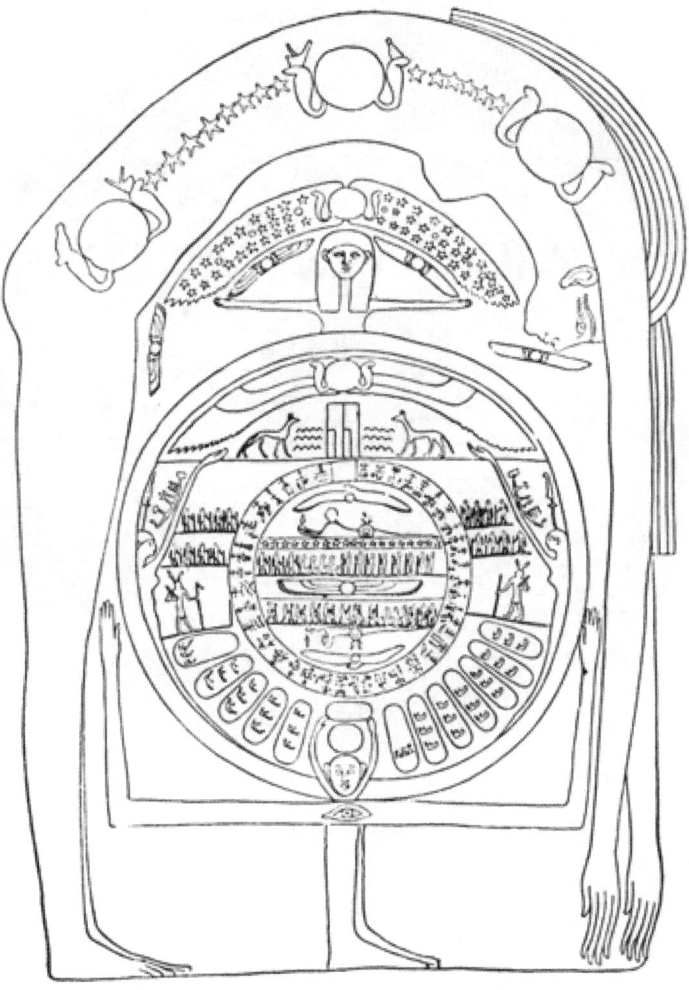

Figure 47

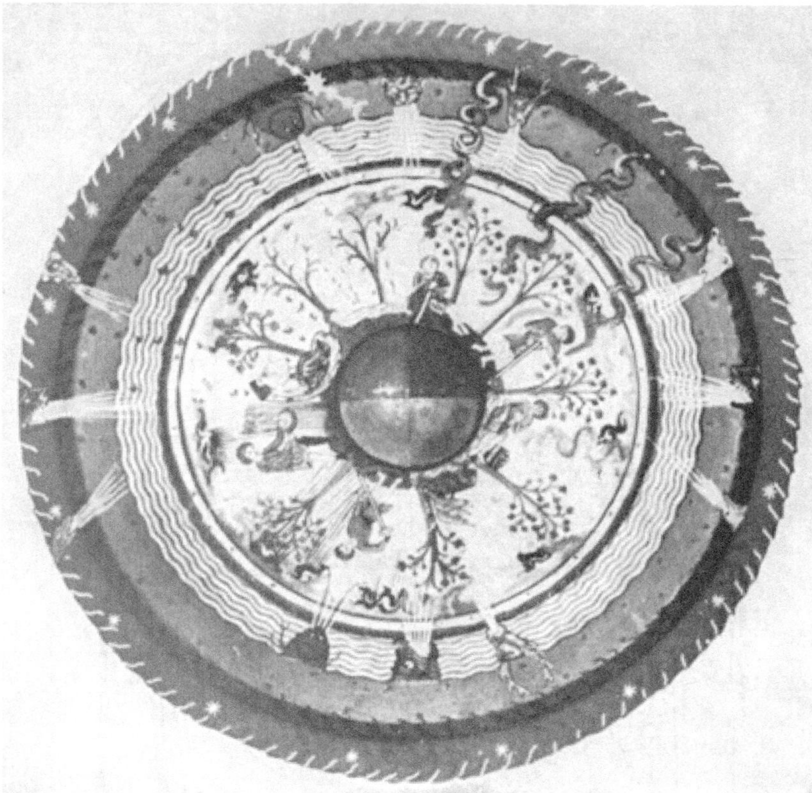

Figure 48

Figure 49

Figure 50

Figure 51

Figure 52

Figure 53

Figure 54

bubble. It looks almost as if an homunculus were in the making. In addition to the usual four or eight rays, both mandalas show a pentadic element. There is thus a dilemma between four and five. Five is the number assigned to the "natural" man, in so far as he consists of a trunk with five appendages. Four, on the other hand, signifies a *conscious* totality. It describes the ideal, "spiritual" man and formulates him as a totality in contrast to the pentad, which describes the corporeal man. It is significant that the swastika symbolizes the "ideal" man,[23] whereas the five-pointed star symbolizes the material and bodily man.[24] The dilemma of four and five corresponds to the conflict between "culture" and "nature." That was the problem of the patient. In Figure 26 the dilemma is indicated by the four groups of stars: two of them contain four stars and two of them five stars. On the rims of both mandalas we see the "fire of desire." In Figure 27 the rim is made of something that looks like lighted tissue. In characteristic contrast to the "shining" mandala, both these (especially the second one) are "burning." It is flaming desire, comparable to the longing of the homunculus in the retort (*Faust,* Part II), which was finally shattered against the throne of Galatea. The fire represents an erotic demand but at the same time an *amor fati* that burns in the innermost self, trying to shape the patient's fate and thus help the self into reality. Like the homunculus in *Faust,* the figure shut up in the vessel wants to "become."

681 The patient was herself aware of the conflict, for she told me she had no peace after painting the second picture. She had reached the afternoon of her life, and was in her thirty-fifth year. She was in doubt as to whether she ought to have another child. She decided for a child, but fate did not let her, because the development of her personality was evidently pursuing a different goal, not a biological but a cultural one. The conflict was resolved in the interests of the latter.

23 It depends very much on whether the swastika revolves to the right or to the left. In Tibet, the one that revolves to the left is supposed to symbolize the Bön religion of black magic as opposed to Buddhism.

24 The symbol of the star is favoured both by Russia and America. The one is red, the other white. For the significance of these colours see *Psychology and Alchemy,* index, s.v. "colours."

Figure 28

682 Picture by a middle-aged man. In the centre is a star. The blue sky contains golden clouds. At the four cardinal points we see human figures: at the top, an old man in the attitude of contemplation; at the bottom, Loki or Hephaestus with red, flaming hair, holding in his hands a temple. To the right and left are a light and a dark female figure. Together they indicate four aspects of the personality, or four archetypal figures belonging, as it were, to the periphery of the self. The two female figures can be recognized without difficulty as the two aspects of the anima. The old man corresponds to the archetype of meaning, or of the spirit, and the dark chthonic figure to the opposite of the Wise Old Man, namely the magical (and sometimes destructive) Luciferian element. In alchemy it is Hermes Trismegistus versus Mercurius, the evasive "trickster." [25] The circle enclosing the sky contains structures or organisms that look like protozoa. The sixteen globes painted in four colours just outside this circle derived originally from an eye motif and therefore stand for the observing and discriminating consciousness. Similarly, the ornaments in the next circle, all opening inwards, are rather like vessels pouring out their content towards the centre.[26] On the other hand the ornaments along the rim open outwards, as if to receive something from outside. That is, in the individuation process what were originally projections stream back "inside" and are integrated into the personality again. Here, in contrast to Figure 25, "Above" and "Below," male and female, are integrated, as in the alchemical hermaphrodite.

Figure 29

683 Once again the centre is symbolized by a star. This very common image is consistent with the previous pictures, where the sun represents the centre. The sun, too, is a star, a radiant cell in the ocean of the sky. The picture shows the self appear-

25 Cf. the eighth and the ninth papers in this volume; and "The Spirit Mercurius."

26 There is a similar conception in alchemy, in the Ripley Scrowle and its variants (*Psychology and Alchemy*, fig. 257). There it is the planetary gods who are pouring their qualities into the bath of rebirth.

ing as a star out of chaos. The four-rayed structure is emphasized by the use of four colours. This picture is significant in that it sets the structure of the self as a principle of order against chaos.[27] It was painted by the same man who did Figure 28.

Figure 30

684 This mandala, by an older woman patient, is again split into Above and Below: heaven above, the sea below, as indicated by the golden waves on a green ground. Four wings revolve leftwards about the centre, which is marked only by an orange-red spot. Here too the opposites are integrated and are presumably the cause of the centre's rotation.

Figure 31

685 An atypical mandala, based on a dyad. A golden moon and a silver moon form the upper and lower edges. The inside is blue sky above and something like a black crenellated wall below. On it there sits a peacock, fanning out its tail, and to the left there is an egg, presumably the peacock's. In view of the important role which the peacock and the peacock's egg together play in alchemy and also in Gnosticism, we may expect the miracle of the *cauda pavonis,* the appearance of "all Colours" (Böhme), the unfolding and realization of wholeness, once the dark dividing wall has broken down. (See Fig. 32.) The patient thought the egg might split and produce something new, maybe a snake. In alchemy the peacock is synonymous with the Phoenix. A variant of the Phoenix legend relates that the Semenda Bird consumes itself, a worm forms from the ashes, and from the worm the bird rises anew.

Figure 32

686 This picture is reproduced from the Codex Alchemicus Rhenoviensis, Central Library, Zurich. Here the peacock represents the Phoenix rising newborn from the fire. There is a similar picture in a manuscript in the British Museum, only there the peacock is enclosed in a flask, the *vas hermeticum,* like the homunculus.[28] The peacock is an old emblem of rebirth and resurrection, quite frequently found on Christian

[27] Cf. "The Psychology of Eastern Meditation," par. 942.

[28] Cf. John Read, *Prelude to Chemistry,* frontispiece.

sarcophagi. In the vessel standing beside the peacock the colours of the *cauda pavonis* appear, as a sign that the transformation process is nearing its goal. In the alchemical process the *serpens mercurialis,* the dragon, is changed into the eagle, the peacock, the goose of Hermes, or the Phoenix.[29]

Figure 33

687 This picture was done by a seven-year-old boy, offspring of a problem marriage. He had done a whole series of these drawings of circles and hung them up round his bed. He called them his "loves" and would not go to sleep without them. This shows that the "magical" pictures still functioned for him in their original sense, as a protective magic circle.

Figure 34

688 An eleven-year-old girl, whose parents were divorced, had, at a time of great difficulties and upsets, drawn a number of pictures which clearly reveal a mandala structure. Here too they were magic circles intended to stop the difficulties and adversities of the outside world from entering into the inner psychic space. They represent a kind of self-protection.

689 As on the *kilkhor,* the Tibetan World Wheel (Fig. 3), you can see at either side of this picture something that looks like horns, which as we know belong to the devil or to one of his theriomorphic symbols. The slanting eye-slits underneath them, and the two strokes for nose and mouth, are also the devil's. This amounts to saying: Behind the mandala lurks the devil. Either the "demons" are covered up by the magically powerful picture, and thereby eliminated—which would be the purpose of the mandala—or, as in the case of the Tibetan World Wheel, the world is caught in the claws of the demon of death. In this picture the devils merely peek out over the edge. I have seen what this means from another case: An artistically gifted patient produced a typical tetradic mandala and stuck it on a sheet of thick paper. On the back there was a circle to match, filled with drawings of sexual perversions. This shadow aspect of the mandala represented the disorderly, disruptive tendencies, the "chaos" that hides behind the self and bursts out in a dan-

29 Cf. *Psychology and Alchemy,* pars. 334 and 404.

gerous way as soon as the individuation process comes to a standstill, or when the self is not realized and so remains unconscious. This piece of psychology was expressed by the alchemists in their Mercurius duplex, who on the one hand is Hermes the mystagogue and psychopomp, and on the other hand is the poisonous dragon, the evil spirit and "trickster."

Figure 35

690 Drawing by the same girl. Round the sun is a circle with eyes, and round this an uroboros. The motif of polyophthalmia frequently occurs in individual mandalas. (See Picture 17 and Fig. 5 in the preceding paper.) In the Maitrayana-Brahmana Upanishad VI, 8 the egg (Hiranyagarbha) is described as "thousand-eyed." The eyes in the mandala no doubt signify the observing consciousness, but it must also be borne in mind that the texts as well as the pictures both attribute the eyes to a mythic figure, e.g., an Anthropos, who does the seeing. This seems to me to point to the fascination which, through a kind of magical stare, attracts the attention of the conscious mind. (Cf. Figs. 38 and 39.)

Figure 36

691 Painting of a medieval city with walls and moats, streets and churches, arranged quadratically. The inner city is again surrounded by walls and moats, like the Imperial City in Peking. The buildings all open inwards, towards the centre, represented by a castle with a golden roof. It too is surrounded by a moat. The ground round the castle is laid with black and white tiles, representing the united opposites. This mandala was done by a middle-aged man (cf. Figs. 6, 28, 29). A picture like this is not unknown in Christian symbolism. The Heavenly Jerusalem of Revelation is known to everybody. Coming to the Indian world of ideas, we find the city of Brahma on the world mountain, Meru. We read in the *Golden Flower:* "The *Book of the Yellow Castle* says: 'In the square inch field of the square foot house, life can be regulated.' The square foot house is the face. The square inch field in the face: what could that be other than the heavenly heart? In the middle of the square inch dwells the splendour. In the purple hall of

the city of jade dwells the God of Utmost Emptiness and Life."[30]

Figure 37

692 Painted by the same patient who did Figures 11 and 30. Here the "seeding-place" is depicted as a child enclosed in a revolving sphere. The four "wings" are painted in the four basic colours. The child corresponds to Hiranyagarbha and to the homunculus of the alchemists. The mythologem of the "Divine Child" is based on ideas of this sort.[31]

Figure 38

693 Mandala in rotation, by the same patient who did Figures 21 and 23. A notable feature is the quaternary structure of the golden wings in combination with the triad of three dogs running round the centre. They have their backs to it, indicating that for them the centre is in the unconscious. The mandala contains—another unusual feature—a triadic motif turning to the left, while the wings turn to the right. This is not accidental. The dogs represent consciousness "scenting" or "intuiting" the unconscious; the wings show the movement of the unconscious towards consciousness, as corresponded to the patient's situation at the time. It is as if the dogs were fascinated by the centre although they cannot see it. They seem to represent the fascination felt by the conscious mind. The picture embodies the above-mentioned sesquitertian proportion (3 : 4).

Figure 39

694 The same motif as before, but represented by hares. From a Gothic window in the cathedral at Paderborn. There is no recognizable centre though the rotation presupposes one.

Figure 40

695 Picture by a young woman patient. It too exhibits the sesquitertian proportion and hence the dilemma with which Plato's *Timaeus* begins, and which as I said plays a considerable role in alchemy, as the axiom of Maria.[32]

30 *The Secret of the Golden Flower* (1962), p. 22.

31 Cf. the sixth and seventh papers in this volume.

32 Cf. "A Psychological Approach to the Dogma of the Trinity," par. 184.

Figure 41

696 This picture was done by a young woman patient with a schizoid disposition. The pathological element is revealed in the "breaking lines" that split up the centre. The sharp, pointed forms of these breaking lines indicate evil, hurtful, and destructive impulses which might hinder the desired synthesis of personality. But it seems as if the regular structure of the surrounding mandala might be able to restrain the dangerous tendencies to dissociation. And this proved to be the case in the further course of the treatment and subsequent development of the patient.

Figure 42

697 A neurotically disturbed mandala. It was drawn by a young, unmarried woman patient at a time that was full of conflict: she was in a dilemma between two men. The outer rim shows four different colours. The centre is doubled in a curious way: fire breaks out from behind the blue star in the black field, while to the right a sun appears, with blood vessels running through it. The five-pointed star suggests a pentagram symbolizing man, the arms, legs, and head all having the same value. As I have said, it signifies the purely instinctual, chthonic, unconscious man. (Cf. Figs. 26 and 27.) The colour of the star is blue—of a cool nature, therefore. But the nascent sun is yellow and red—a warm colour. The sun itself (looking rather like the yolk of an incubated egg) usually denotes consciousness, illumination, understanding. Hence we could say of this mandala: a light is gradually dawning on the patient, she is waking out of her formerly unconscious state, which corresponded to a purely biological and rational existence. (Rationalism is no guarantee of higher consciousness, but merely of a one-sided one!) The new state is characterized by red (feeling) and yellow or gold (intuition). There is thus a shifting of the centre of personality into the warmer region of heart and feeling, while the inclusion of intuition suggests a groping, irrational apprehension of wholeness.

Figure 43

698 This picture was done by a middle-aged woman who, without being neurotic, was struggling for spiritual development and used for this purpose the method of active imagination. These efforts induced her to make a drawing of the birth of a new insight or conscious awareness (eye) from the depths of the unconscious (sea). Here the eye signifies the self.

Figure 44

699 Drawing of motif from a Roman mosaic on the floor of a house in Moknine, Tunis, which I photographed. It represents an apotropaism against the evil eye.

Figure 45

700 Mandala from the Navaho Indians, who with great toil prepare such mandalas from coloured sand for curative purposes. It is part of the Mountain Chant Rite performed for the sick. Around the centre there runs, in a wide arc, the body of the Rainbow Goddess. A square head denotes a female deity, a round one a male deity. The arrangement of the four pairs of deities on the arms of the cross suggests a swastika wheeling to the right. The four male deities who surround the swastika are making the same movement.

Figure 46

701 Another sand-painting by the Navahos, from the Male Shooting Chant. The four horned heads are painted in the four colours that correspond to the four directions.[33]

Figure 47

702 Here, for comparison, is a painting of the Egyptian Sky Mother, bending, like the Rainbow Goddess, over the "Land" with its round horizon. Behind the mandala stands—presumably—the Air God, like the demon in Figures 3 and 34. Underneath, the arms of the *ka,* raised in adoration and decked with

[33] I am indebted to Mrs. Margaret Schevill for both these pictures. Figure 45 is a variant of the sand-painting reproduced in *Psychology and Alchemy,* fig. 110.

the eye motif, hold the mandala, which probably signifies the wholeness of the "Two Lands." [34]

Figure 48

703 This picture, from a manuscript of Hildegard of Bingen, shows the earth surrounded by the ocean, realm of air, and starry heaven. The actual globe of the earth in the centre is divided into four.[35]

704 Böhme has a mandala in his book *XL Questions concerning the Soule* (see Fig. 1 of preceding paper). The periphery contains a bright and a dark hemisphere turning their backs to one another. They represent un-united opposites, which presumably should be bound together by the heart standing between them. This drawing is most unusual, but aptly expresses the insoluble moral conflict underlying the Christian view of the world. "The Soul," Böhme says, "is an Eye in the Eternal Abyss, a similitude of Eternity, a perfect Figure and Image of the first Principle, and resembles God the Father in his Person, as to the eternal Nature. The Essence and Substance of it, merely as to what it is purely in itself, is first the wheel of Nature, with the first four Forms." In the same treatise Böhme says: "The substance and Image of the soul may be resembled to the Earth, having a fair flower growing out of it . . ." "The Soul is a fiery Eye . . . from the eternal Centre of Nature . . . a similitude of the First Principle." [36] As an eye, the soul "receives the Light, as the Moon does the glance of the Sun . . . for the life of the soul has its original in the Fire." [37]

Figures 49 and 50

705 Figure 49 is especially interesting because it shows us very clearly in what relationship the picture stands to the painter. The patient (the same as did Fig. 42) has a shadow problem. The female figure in the picture represents her dark, chthonic side. She is standing in front of a wheel with four spokes, the two together forming an eight-rayed mandala. From her head

[34] The drawing was sent to me from the British Museum, London. The original painting appears to be in New York.

[35] Lucca, Bibliotheca governativa, Cod. 1942, fol. 37ʳ.

[36] *A Summary Appendix of the Soul,* p. 117.

[37] Ibid., p. 118.

spring four snakes,[38] expressing the tetradic nature of consciousness, but—in accordance with the demonic character of the picture—they do this in an evil and nefarious way, since they represent evil and destructive thoughts. The entire figure is wrapped in flames, emitting a dazzling light. She is like a fiery demon, a salamander, the medieval conception of a fire sprite. Fire expresses an intense transformation process. Hence the *prima materia* in alchemy was symbolized by the salamander in the fire, as the next picture shows.[39] The spear- or arrow-head expresses "direction": it is pointing upwards from the middle of the head. Everything that the fire consumes rises up to the seat of the gods. The dragon glowing in the fire becomes volatilized; illumination comes through the fiery torment. Figure 49 tells us something about the background of the transformation process. It depicts a state of suffering, reminiscent on the one hand of crucifixion and on the other of Ixion bound to the wheel. From this it is evident that individuation, or becoming whole, is neither a *summum bonum* nor a *summum desideratum,* but the painful experience of the union of opposites. That is the real meaning of the cross in the circle, and that is why the cross has an apotropaic effect, because, pointed at evil, it shows evil that it is already included and has therefore lost its destructive power.

Figure 51

706 This picture was done by a sixty-year-old woman patient with a similar problem: A fiery demon mounts through the night towards a star. There he passes over from a chaotic into an ordered and fixed state. The star stands for the transcendent totality, the demon for the animus, who, like the anima, is the connecting link between conscious and unconscious. The picture recalls the antique symbolism found, for instance, in Plutarch: [40] The soul is only partly in the body, the other part is outside it and soars above man like a star symbolizing his "genius." The same conception can be found among the alchemists.

[38] Cf. the four snakes in the chthonic, shadow-half of Picture 9 in the preceding paper.

[39] Figure X from Lambspringk's Symbols in the *Musaeum hermeticum* (Waite trans., I, p. 295).

[40] *De genio Socratis,* cap. XXII.

Figure 52

707 Picture by the same patient as before, showing flames with a soul rising up from them, as if swimming. The motif is repeated in Figure 53. Exactly the same thing—and with the same meaning—can be found in the Codex Rhenoviensis (fifteenth century), Zurich (Fig. 54). The souls of the calcined *prima materia* escape as vapours, in the form of human figures looking like children (homunculi). In the fire is the dragon, the chthonic form of the *anima mundi,* which is being transmuted.

Figures 53 and 54

708 Here I must remark that not only did the patient have no knowledge of alchemy but that I myself knew nothing at that time of the alchemical picture material. The resemblance between these two pictures, striking as it is, is nothing extraordinary, since the great problem and concern of philosophical alchemy was the same as underlies the psychology of the unconscious, namely individuation, the integration of the self. Similar causes (other things being equal) have similar effects, and similar psychological situations make use of the same symbols, which on their side rest on archetypal foundations, as I have shown in the case of alchemy.

Conclusion

709 I hope I have succeeded in giving the reader some idea of mandala symbolism with the help of these pictures. Naturally my exposition aims at nothing more than a superficial survey of the empirical material on which comparative research is based. I have indicated a few parallels that may point the way to further historical and ethnic comparisons, but have refrained from a more complete and more thorough exposition because it would have taken me too far.

710 I need say only a few words about the functional significance of the mandala, as I have discussed this theme several times before. Moreover, if we have a little feeling in our fingertips we can guess from these pictures, painted with the greatest devotion but with unskilful hands, what is the deeper meaning that the patients tried to put into them and express through them. They are *yantras* in the Indian sense, instruments of meditation,

concentration, and self-immersion, for the purpose of realizing inner experience, as I have explained in the commentary to the *Golden Flower.* At the same time they serve to produce an inner order—which is why, when they appear in a series, they often follow chaotic, disordered states marked by conflict and anxiety. They express the idea of a safe refuge, of inner reconciliation and wholeness.

711 I could produce many more pictures from all parts of the world, and one would be astonished to see how these symbols are governed by the same fundamental laws that can be observed in individual mandalas. In view of the fact that all the mandalas shown here were new and uninfluenced products, we are driven to the conclusion that there must be a transconscious disposition in every individual which is able to produce the same or very similar symbols at all times and in all places. Since this disposition is usually not a conscious possession of the individual I have called it the *collective unconscious,* and, as the bases of its symbolical products, I postulate the existence of primordial images, the *archetypes.* I need hardly add that the identity of unconscious individual contents with their ethnic parallels is expressed not merely in their form but in their meaning.

712 Knowledge of the common origin of these unconsciously preformed symbols has been totally lost to us. In order to recover it, we have to read old texts and investigate old cultures, so as to gain an understanding of the things our patients bring us today in explanation of their psychic development. And when we penetrate a little more deeply below the surface of the psyche, we come upon historical layers which are not just dead dust, but alive and continuously active in everyone—maybe to a degree that we cannot imagine in the present state of our knowledge.

APPENDIX

MANDALAS [1]

713 The Sanskrit word *mandala* means "circle" in the ordinary sense of the word. In the sphere of religious practices and in psychology it denotes circular images, which are drawn, painted, modelled, or danced. Plastic structures of this kind are to be found, for instance, in Tibetan Buddhism, and as dance figures these circular patterns occur also in Dervish monasteries. As psychological phenomena they appear spontaneously in dreams, in certain states of conflict, and in cases of schizophrenia. Very frequently they contain a quaternity or a multiple of four, in the form of a cross, a star, a square, an octagon, etc. In alchemy we encounter this motif in the form of *quadratura circuli.*

714 In Tibetan Buddhism the figure has the significance of a ritual instrument (*yantra*), whose purpose is to assist meditation and concentration. Its meaning in alchemy is somewhat similar, inasmuch as it represents the synthesis of the four elements which are forever tending to fall apart. Its spontaneous occurrence in modern individuals enables psychological research to make a closer investigation into its functional meaning. As a rule a mandala occurs in conditions of psychic dissociation or disorientation, for instance in the case of children between the ages of eight and eleven whose parents are about to be divorced, or in adults who, as the result of a neurosis and its treatment, are confronted with the problem of opposites in human nature and are consequently disoriented; or again in schizophrenics

1 [Written especially for *Du: Schweizerische Monatsschrift* (Zurich), XV:4 (April 1955), 16, 21, and subscribed "January 1955." The issue was devoted to the Eranos conferences at Ascona, Switzerland, and the work of C. G. Jung. (An anonymous translation into English accompanying the article has been consulted.) With Dr. Jung's article also were several examples of mandalas, including the frontispiece of this volume and fig. 1, p. 297. While this brief article duplicates some material given elsewhere in this volume, it is presented here as a concise popular statement on the subject.—EDITORS.]

whose view of the world has become confused, owing to the invasion of incomprehensible contents from the unconscious. In such cases it is easy to see how the severe pattern imposed by a circular image of this kind compensates the disorder and confusion of the psychic state—namely, through the construction of a central point to which everything is related, or by a concentric arrangement of the disordered multiplicity and of contradictory and irreconcilable elements. This is evidently an *attempt at self-healing* on the part of Nature, which does not spring from conscious reflection but from an instinctive impulse. Here, as comparative research has shown, a fundamental schema is made use of, an archetype which, so to speak, occurs everywhere and by no means owes its individual existence to tradition, any more than the instincts would need to be transmitted in that way. Instincts are given in the case of every newborn individual and belong to the inalienable stock of those qualities which characterize a species. What psychology designates as archetype is really a particular, frequently occurring, formal aspect of instinct, and is just as much an *a priori* factor as the latter. Therefore, despite external differences, we find a fundamental conformity in mandalas regardless of their origin in time and space.

715 The "squaring of the circle" is one of the many archetypal motifs which form the basic patterns of our dreams and fantasies. But it is distinguished by the fact that it is one of the most important of them from the functional point of view. Indeed, it could even be called the *archetype of wholeness*. Because of this significance, the "quaternity of the One" is the schema for all images of God, as depicted in the visions of Ezekiel, Daniel, and Enoch, and as the representation of Horus with his four sons also shows. The latter suggests an interesting differentiation, inasmuch as there are occasionally representations in which three of the sons have animals' heads and only one a human head, in keeping with the Old Testament visions as well as with the emblems of the seraphim which were transferred to the evangelists, and—last but not least—with the nature of the Gospels themselves: three of which are synoptic and one "Gnostic." Here I must add that, ever since the opening of Plato's *Timaeus* ("One, two, three . . . but where, my dear Socrates, is the fourth?") and right up to the Cabiri scene in *Faust*, the motif of four as three and one was the ever-recurring preoccupation of alchemy.

716 The profound significance of the quaternity with its singular process of differentiation extending over the centuries, and now manifest in the latest development of the Christian symbol,[2] may exp'ain why *Du* chose just the archetype of wholeness as an example of symbol formation. For, just as this symbol claims a central position in the historical documents, individually too it has an outstanding significance. As is to be expected, individual mandalas display an enormous variety. The overwhelming majority are characterized by the circle and the quaternity. In a few, however, the three or the five predominates, for which there are usually special reasons.

717 Whereas ritual mandalas always display a definite style and a limited number of typical motifs as their content, individual mandalas make use of a well-nigh unlimited wealth of motifs and symbolic allusions, from which it can easily be seen that they are endeavouring to express either the totality of the individual in his inner or outer experience of the world, or its essential point of reference. Their object is the *self* in contradistinction to the *ego,* which is only the point of reference for consciousness, whereas the self comprises the totality of the psyche altogether, i.e., conscious *and* unconscious. It is therefore not unusual for individual mandalas to display a division into a light and a dark half, together with their typical symbols. An historical example of this kind is Jakob Böhme's mandala, in his treatise *XL Questions concerning the Soule.* It is at the same time an image of God and is designated as such. This is not a matter of chance, for Indian philosophy, which developed the idea of the self, Atman or Purusha, to the highest degree, makes no distinction in principle between the human essence and the divine. Correspondingly, in the Western mandala, the *scintilla* or soul-spark, the innermost divine essence of man, is characterized by symbols which can just as well express a God-image, namely the image of Deity unfolding in the world, in nature, and in man.

718 The fact that images of this kind have under certain circumstances a considerable therapeutic effect on their authors is empirically proved and also readily understandable, in that they often represent very bold attempts to see and put together

2 [Proclamation of the dogma of the Assumption of the Virgin, in 1950. Cf. *Psychology and Religion: West and East,* pars. 119ff., 251f., 748ff.—EDITORS.]

apparently irreconcilable opposites and bridge over apparently hopeless splits. Even the mere attempt in this direction usually has a healing effect, but only when it is done spontaneously. Nothing can be expected from an artificial repetition or a deliberate imitation of such images.

BIBLIOGRAPHY

BIBLIOGRAPHY

The items of the bibliography are arranged alphabetically under two headings: *A*. Ancient volumes containing collections of alchemical tracts by various authors; *B*. General bibliography, including cross-references to the material in section *A*. Short titles of the ancient volumes are printed in capital letters.

A. ANCIENT VOLUMES CONTAINING COLLECTIONS OF ALCHEMICAL TRACTS BY VARIOUS AUTHORS

ARS CHEMICA, quod sit licita recte exercentibus, probationes doctissimorum iurisconsultorum. . . . Argentorati [Strasbourg], 1566.

Contents quoted in this volume:

Septem tractatus seu capitula Hermetis Trismegisti aurei [pp. 7–31; usually referred to as "Tractatus aureus"]

ARTIS AURIFERAE quam chemiam vocant. . . . Basileae [Basel], [1593]. 2 vols.

Contents quoted in this volume:

VOLUME I

i Allegoriae super librum Turbae [pp. 139–45]

ii Aurora consurgens, quae dicitur Aurea hora [pp. 185–246]

iii [Zosimus:] Rosinus ad Sarratantam episcopum [pp. 277–319]

iv [Kallid:] Calidis Liber secretorum [pp. 325–51]

v Tractatulus Aristotelis de practica lapidis philosophici [pp. 361–73]

vi Rachaidibus: De materia philosophici lapidis [pp. 397–404]

vii Liber de arte chymica [pp. 575–631]

VOLUME II

viii Rosarium philosophorum [pp. 204–384]; contains a version of the "Visio Arislei," pp. 246ff. Another edition of the

Artis auriferae, occasionally quoted in this volume, appeared in 1572 at Basel; contains the "Tractatus aureus," pp. 641ff.

MANGETUS, JOANNES JACOBUS (ed.). *BIBLIOTHECA CHEMICA CURIOSA, seu Rerum ad alchemiam pertinentium thesaurus instructissimus* . . . Coloniae Allobrogum [Geneva], 1702, 2 vols.

Contents quoted in this volume:

VOLUME I

i Hermes Trismegistus: Tractatus aureus de lapidis physici secreto [pp. 400–45]

ii Morienus: Liber de compositione alchemiae [pp. 509–19]

VOLUME II

iii Sendivogius: Epistola XIII [p. 496]

THEATRUM CHEMICUM, praecipuos selectorum auctorum tractatus . . . continens. Ursellis [Ursel] and Argentorati [Strasbourg], 1602–61. 6 vols. (Vols. I–III, Ursel, 1602; Vols. IV–VI, Strasbourg, 1613, 1622, 1661 respectively.)

Contents quoted in this volume:

VOLUME I

i Dorn: Speculativae philosophiae, gradus septem vel decem continens [pp. 255–310]

ii Dorn: De tenebris contra Naturam et vita brevi [pp. 518–35]

iii Dorn: De transmutatione metallorum [pp. 563–646]

VOLUME II

iv Dee: Monas hieroglyphica [pp. 218–43]

VOLUME IV

v Hermetis Trismegisti Tractatus vere aureus de lapide philosophici secreto [pp. 672–797; usually referred to as "Tractatus aureus"]

vi David Lagneus: Harmonia seu Consensus philosophorum chemicorum (frequently called Harmonia chemica) [pp. 813–903]

VOLUME V

vii Mennens: De aureo vellere . . . libri tres [pp. 267–470]

VOLUME VI

viii Vigenerus (Blaise de Vigenère): Tractatus de igne et sale [pp. 1–139]

B. GENERAL BIBLIOGRAPHY

ABRAHAM, KARL. *Dreams and Myths*. Translated by William A. White. (Nervous and Mental Disease Monograph Series, 15.) New York, 1913. (Original: *Traum und Mythus*. Schriften zur angewandten Seelenkunde, 4. Vienna, 1909.)

ADLER, GERHARD. *Studies in Analytical Psychology*. London, 1948; 2nd edn., London, 1966, New York, 1967.

AELIAN. *De natura animalium*, etc. Edited by Rudolf Hercher. Paris, 1858.

AETIUS. *De placitis philosophorum reliquiae*. In: HERMANN DIELS (ed.). *Doxographi Graeci*. Berlin, 1879.

AFANAS'EV, E. N. *Russian Fairy Tales*. Translated by Norbert Guterman. New York, [1946].

AGRICOLA, GEORG. *De animantibus subterraneis*. Basel, 1549.

ALDROVANDUS, ULYSSES [Ulisse Aldrovandi]. *Dendrologiae libri duo*. Bologna, 1668; another edn., 1671.

"Allegoriae sapientum supra librum Turbae." See (*A*) *Artis auriferae*, i.

Amitāyur-dhyāna Sūtra. In: *Buddhist Mahāyāna Sūtras*, Part II. Translated by F. Max Müller and Junjiro Takakusu. (Sacred Books of the East, 49.) Oxford, 1894.

APTOWITZER, VICTOR. "Arabisch-Jüdische Schöpfungstheorien," *Hebrew Union College Annual* (Cincinnati), VI (1929).

APULEIUS, LUCIUS. *The Golden Ass*. Translated by Robert Graves. (Penguin Classics.) Harmondsworth, 1954.

ARISLEUS. "Visio Arislei." See (*A*) *Artis auriferae*, viii.

AUGUSTINE, SAINT. *The Confessions: Books I–X*. Translated by F. J. Sheed. London and New York, 1942. See also *Confessiones*, in MIGNE, *P.L.*, vol. 32.

———. *De diversis quaestionibus LXXXIII*. See MIGNE, *P.L.*, vol. 40, cols. 11–100.

"Aurea hora." See "Aurora consurgens."

"Aurora consurgens." See (*A*) *Artis auriferae*, ii.

AVALON, ARTHUR, pseud. (Sir John Woodroffe) (ed. and trans.) *The Serpent Power (Shat-chakra-nirupana and Paduka-panchaka)*. (Tantrik Texts.) London, 1919.

——— (ed.) *Shrī-chakra-sambhāra Tantra*. Translated by Kazi Dawa-Samdup. (Tantrik Texts, 7.) London and Calcutta, 1919.

———. See also WOODROFFE.

BACON, JOSEPHINE DASKAM. *In the Border Country*. New York, 1919.

BANDELIER, ADOLPH FRANCIS ALPHONSE. *The Delight Makers*. New York, 1890; 2nd edn., 1918.

BÄNZIGER, HANS. "Persönliches und Archetypisches in Individuationsprozess," *Schweizerische Zeitschrift für Psychologie und ihre Anwendungen* (Bern), VI (1947), 272–83.

BARLACH, ERNST. *Der tote Tag*. Berlin, 1912; 2nd edn., 1918.

Baruch, Syrian Apocalypse of. See CHARLES, vol. 2, pp. 470–526.

BASTIAN, ADOLF. *Der Mensch in der Geschichte*. Leipzig, 1860. 3 vols.

BAUMGARTNER, MATHIAS. *Die Philosophie des Alanus de Insulis*. (Beiträge zur Geschichte der Philosophie des Mittelalters, 2:4.) Munster, 1896.

BAYNES, H. G. *Mythology of the Soul*. London, 1940.

BELLOWS, HENRY ADAMS (trans.). *The Poetic Edda*. New York, 1923.

BENOÎT, PIERRE. *Atlantida*. Translated by Mary C. Tongue and Mary Ross. New York, 1920. (Original: *L'Atlantide*. Paris, 1920.)

BERNOULLI, RUDOLF. "Zur Symbolik geometrischer Figuren und Zahlen," *Eranos Jahrbuch 1934* (Zurich, 1935), 369–415.

BERTHELOT, MARCELLIN. *La Chimie au moyen âge*. Paris, 1893. 3 vols.

———. *Collection des anciens alchimistes grecs*. Paris, 1887–88. 3 vols.

BIN GORION, MICHA JOSEPH (pseud. of Micah Joseph Berdyczewski). *Der Born Judas*. Leipzig, 1916–23. 6 vols.

BLANKE, FRITZ. *Bruder Klaus von Flüe*. Zurich, 1948.

BLOCK, RAYMOND DE. *Euhémère, son livre et sa doctrine*. (Liège University dissertation.) Mons, 1876.

[BÖHME, JAKOB.] *XL Questions concerning the Soule, propounded by Dr. Balthasar Walter and answered by Jacob Behmen*. London, 1647.

——. *Des gottseligen hocherleuchteten Jacob Böhmen Teutonici Philosophi Alle Theosophische Schrifften*. Amsterdam, 1682. (This edition of Böhme's works consists of a number of parts, each separately paginated and variously bound up. The parts are not numbered. It includes, *inter alia*, the following works referred to in the present volume. The bracketed English titles and volume references following the German title of each work refer to the 1764–81 London translation cited below.)

Aurora. Morgenröte im Ausgang . . . [*Aurora:* Vol. I.]

[*Drey principia.*] *Beschreibung der drey Principien Göttliches Wesens.* [*Three Principles of the Divine Essence:* Vol. I.]

Hohe und tiefe Gründe von dem dreyfachen Leben des Menschen. [*The High and Deep Searching of the Threefold Life of Man:* Vol. II.]

Signatura rerum. [*Signatura rerum:* Vol. IV.]

Tabulae principiorum. [*Four Tables of Divine Revelation:* Vol. III.]

[*Quaestiones Theosophicae.*] *Theosophische Fragen in Betrachtung Göttliche Offenbharung* . . . [Not included in English collection.]

Vierzig Fragen von der Seelen Urstand . . . verfasset von Dr. Balthasar Walter und beantwortet durch Jacob Böhme. [*Forty Questions concerning the Soul:* Vol. II.]

Die Umgewandte Auge. [*A Summary Appendix of the Soul:* Vol. II.]

——. *Mysterium pansophicum, oder Gründliche Bericht vom irdischen und himmlischen Mysterio.* In: *Jakob Böhme's sämtliche Werke.* Edited by K. W. Schiebler. Leipzig, 1831–46. 6 vols. (Vol. 6, pp. 411–24.)

——. *The Works of Jacob Behmen.* [Edited by G. Ward and T. Langcake.] London, 1764–81. 4 vols.

Bouché-Leclercq, Auguste. *L'Astrologie grecque*. Paris, 1899.

Bousett, Wilhelm. *Hauptprobleme der Gnosis*. (Forschugen zur Religion und Literatur des Alten und Neuen Testaments, 10.) Göttingen, 1907.

Bovillus, Karl (Charles de Bouelles). *Ein gesichte Bruder Clausen ynn Schweytz und seine deutunge*. Wittemberg, 1528.

Bozzano, Ernesto. *Popoli primitivi e Manifestazioni supernormali*. Verona, 1941.

Budge, E. A. Wallis. *The Gods of the Egyptians*. London, 1904. 2 vols.

Buri, F. "Theologie und Philosophie," *Theologische Zeitschrift* (Basel), VIII (1952), 116–34.

Caesarius of Heisterbach. *The Dialogue on Miracles*. Translated by H. von E. Scott and C. C. Swinton Bland. London, 1929. 2 vols. (Original: *Dialogus Miraculorum*. Edited by J. Strange, 1851.)

Calidis Liber Secretorum. See Kallid.

Cantril, Hadley. *The Invasion from Mars*. Princeton, 1940.

Carus, Carl Gustav. *Psyche*. Pförzheim, 1846.

Caussin, Nicholas. *De symbolica Aegyptiorum sapientia. Polyhistor symbolicus, Electorum symbolorum, & Parabolarum historicarum stromata*. Paris, [1618 and] 1631.

Cellini, Benvenuto. *Autobiography*. Translated by John Addington Symonds. London, 1887.

Chantepie de la Saussaye, P. D. *Lehrbuch der Religionsgeschichte*. Tübingen, 1905. 2 vols.

Charles, Robert Henry (ed.). *The Apocrypha and Pseudepigrapha of the Old Testament in English*. Oxford, 1913. 2 vols.

Cicero, Marcus Tullius. *De natura deorum: Academica*. With an English text by H. Rackham. (Loeb Classical Library.) London and New York, 1933.

Clement of Alexandria. *Stromata*. In: Clemens Alexandrinus. *Werke*, Vol. II. Edited by Otto Stählin. (Griechische christliche

Schriftsteller.) Leipzig, 1906. For translation see: *The Writings of Clement of Alexandria.* Translated by William Wilson. (Ante-Nicene Christian Library, 4, 12.) Edinburgh, 1867, 1869. 2 vols.

CRAWLEY, ALFRED ERNEST. *The Idea of the Soul.* London, 1909.

CUMONT, FRANZ. *Textes et monuments figurés relatifs aux mystères de Mithra.* Brussels, 1894–99. 2 vols.

CUSTANCE, JOHN. *Wisdom, Madness and Folly.* New York and London, 1951.

DAUDET, LÉON. *L'Hérédo.* Paris, 1916.

"De arte chymica." See (*A*) *Artis auriferae,* **vii.**

DEE, JOHN. "Monas hieroglyphica." See (*A*) *Theatrum chemicum,* **iv.**

DE GUBERNATIS, ANGELO. *Zoological Mythology.* London, 1872. 2 vols.

DELACOTTE, JOSEPH. *Guillaume de Digulleville. . . . Trois romans-poèmes du XIVe siècle.* Paris, 1932.

DELATTE, LOUIS (ed.). *Textes latins et vieux français relatifs aux Cyranides.* (Bibliothèque de la Faculté de Philosophie et Lettres de l'Université de Liège, fasc. 93.) Liège and Paris, 1942.

DEUSSEN, PAUL. *Allgemeine Geschichte der Philosophie.* Leipzig, 1894–1917. 2 vols.

DIELS, HERMANN. *Fragmente der Vorsokratiker.* 5th edn., Berlin, 1934–37. 3 vols.

DIETERICH, ALBRECHT. *Eine Mithrasliturgie.* Leipzig, 1903; 2nd edn., 1910.

DIONYSIUS THE AREOPAGITE, pseud. *De divinis nominibus.* See MIGNE, *P.G.,* vol. 3, cols. 585–996. For translation, see: *On the Divine Names and the Mystical Theology.* Translated by C. E. Rolt. London, 1920.

——. *De caelesti hierarchia* [*De caelestibus hierarchiis*]. See MIGNE, *P.G.,* vol. 3, cols. 119–30. For translation, see: *The Celestial Hierarchies.* Translated by the Editors of the Shrine of Wisdom. London, 1935.

DORN, GERHARD (Gerardus Dorneus) . See (*A*) *Theatrum chemicum,* **i–iii.**

Du Cange, Charles. *Glossarium ad scriptores mediae et infirmae latinitatis.* Paris, 1733–36. 6 vols. New edn., Graz, 1954. 5 vols.

Duchesne, Louis. *Christian Worship: Its Origin and Evolution.* Translated by M. L. McClure. 5th edn., London, 1919. (Original: *Origines du culte chrétien.* 3rd edn., revised, Paris, 1903.)

[Eckhart, Meister.] *Meister Eckhart.* By Franz Pfeiffer. Translated by C. de B. Evans. London, 1924–52. 2 vols.

Eisler, Robert. *Weltenmantel und Himmelszelt.* Munich, 1910. 2 vols.

Eleazar, R. Abraham. *Uraltes Chymisches Werk.* Leipzig, 1760.

Eliade, Mircea. *Shamanism: Archaic Techniques of Ecstasy.* Translated by Willard R. Trask. New York (Bollingen Series) and London, 1964.

Erman, Adolf. *Handbook of Egyptian Religion.* London, 1907.

——. *Die Religion der Agypter.* Berlin and Leipzig, 1934.

Erskine, John. *Private Life of Helen of Troy.* New York, 1925; London, 1926.

Fechner, Gustav Theodor. *Elemente der Psychophysik.* Leipzig, 1860.

Fendt, Leonhard. *Gnostische Mysterien.* Munich, 1922.

Ficino, Marsilio. *Commentary on Plato's Symposium.* Text and translation with introduction by Sears Reynolds Jayne. (University of Missouri Studies, 19: 1.) Columbia, Mo., 1944.

[Fierz-David, Linda.] *The Dream of Poliphilo.* Related and interpreted by Linda Fierz-David. Translated by Mary Hottinger. (Bollingen Series XXV.) New York, 1950.

Flamel, Nicholas. *Exposition of the Hieroglyphicall Figures . . .* Translated by Eirenaeus Orandus. London, 1624.

Flournoy, Théodore. *From India to the Planet Mars.* Translated by D. B. Vermilye. New York and London, 1900. (Original: *Des Indes à la Planète Mars.* Paris and Geneva, 3rd edn., 1900.)

——. "Nouvelles Observations sur un cas de somnambulisme avec glossolalie," *Archives de psychologie* (Neuchâtel), I (1901): 2.

Folktales. (The following volumes are all from the series Die Märchen der Weltliteratur, edited by Friedrich von der Leyen and Paul Zaunert, Jena.)

Balkanmärchen aus Albanien, Bulgarien, Serbien und Kroatien. Edited by A. Laskien. 1915.

Chinesische Volksmärchen. Edited by R. Wilhelm. 1913.

Deutsche Märchen seit Grimm. Edited by Paul Zaunert. 1912.

Finnische und Estnische Volksmärchen. Edited by August von Löwis of Menar. 1922.

Indianermärchen aus Nordamerika. Edited by Walter Krickeberg. 1924.

Indianermärchen aus Südamerika. Edited by T. Koch-Grünberg. 1920.

Kaukasische Märchen. Edited by A. Dirr. 1919.

Märchen aus Iran. 1939.

Märchen aus Sibirien. 2nd edn., 1940.

Nordische Volksmärchen. Edited by K. Stroebe. 1915–22. 2 vols.

Russische Volksmärchen. Edited by August von Löwis of Menar. 1914.

Spanische und Portugiesische Märchen. Edited by Harri Meier. 1940.

See also AFANAS'EV; GRIMM.

FORDHAM, MICHAEL. *The Life of Childhood.* London, 1944.

FOUCART, PAUL FRANÇOIS. *Les Mystères d'Eleusis.* Paris, 1914.

FREEMAN, KATHLEEN. *Ancilla to the Pre-Socratic Philosophers.* Oxford, 1948.

FREUD, SIGMUND. *The Interpretation of Dreams.* Translated by James Strachey et al. In: Standard Edition of the Complete Psychological Works, 4–5. London, 1953. 2 vols.

——. "Psycho-Analytic Notes on an Autobiographical Account of a Case of Paranoia." [Translated by Alix and James Strachey.] In: Standard Edition of the Complete Psychological Works, 12. London, 1958.

——. "Leonardo da Vinci and a Memory of His Childhood." Translated by Alan Tyson. In: Standard Edition of the Complete Psychological Works, 11. London, 1957.

FROBENIUS, LEO. *Schicksalskunde.* (Schriften zur Schicksalskunde, 5.) Weimar, 1938.

GARBE, RICHARD. *Die Samkhya Philosophie.* Leipzig, 1894.

GESSMANN, GUSTAV WILHELM. *Die Geheimsymbole der Alchymie, Arzneikunde und Astrologie des Mittelalters.* 2nd edn., Berlin, 1922.

GLAUBER, JOHANN RUDOLPH. *Tractatus de natura salium.* Amsterdam, 1658. 2 parts.

GOETHE, JOHANN WOLFGANG VON. "Die neue Melusine." See *Wilhelm Meisters Wanderjahre,* in *Werke,* q.v., VIII, pp. 380ff.

———. *Faust, Part One.* Translated by Philip Wayne. (Penguin Classics.) Harmondsworth, 1949.

———. *Werke.* (Gedankausgabe.) Edited by Ernst Beutler. Zurich, 1948–54. 24 vols. (Vols. I–II: *Sämtliche Gedichte.*)

GOETZ, BRUNO. *Das Reich ohne Raum.* Potsdam, 1919. 2nd enl. edn., Constance, 1925.

GRIMM, THE BROTHERS. *Fairy Tales.* Translated by Margaret Hunt. Revised by James Stern. New York, 1944.

HAGGARD, H. RIDER. *Ayesha: the Return of She.* London, 1905.

——. *She.* London, 1887.

——. *Wisdom's Daughter.* London, 1923.

HARDING, M. ESTHER. *Psychic Energy: Its Source and Goal.* (Bollingen Series X.) New York, 1948; 2nd edn., 1963: *Psychic Energy: Its Source and Its Transformation.*

HAUCK, ALBERT (ed.). *Real-encyclopädie für protestantische Theologie und Kirche.* Leipzig, 1896–1913. 24 vols.

HERMES TRISMEGISTUS. See "Septem tractatus."

———. *Tractatus vere aureus de Lapidis Philosophici secreto.* Opere et studio Dominici Gnosii . . . in lucem editus. Leipzig, 1610. See also (*A*) *Ars chemica; Theatrum chemicum,* v.

HILDEGARDE OF BINGEN, SAINT. "Liber divinorum operum." Biblioteca governativa, Lucca, Codex 1942.

HIPPOLYTUS. *Elenchos* (*Refutatio omnium haeresium*). In: *Hippolytus' Werke*. Edited by Paul Wendland. (Griechische christliche Schriftsteller.) Vol. III. Leipzig, 1916. For translation, see: *Philosophumena: or, The Refutation of all Heresies*. Translated by Francis Legge. London and New York, 1921. 2 vols.

HOFFMANN, ERNST THEODORE WILHELM [AMADEUS]. *The Devil's Elixir*. Edinburgh, 1824. 2 vols.

HOFFMANN-KRAYER, E., and BÄCHTOLD-STÄUBLI, HANNS. *Handwörterbuch des deutschen Aberglaubens*. (Handwörterbucher für deutschen Volkskünde, Abt. I.) Berlin and Leipzig, 1927–37. 8 vols.

HÖLDERLIN, JOHANN CHRISTIAN FRIEDRICH. *Gedichte*. Edited by Franz Zinkernagel. Leipzig, 1922.

HOLLANDUS, JOANNES ISAACS. *Opera mineralia*. Middelburg, 1600.

HOMER. *The Odyssey*. Translated by E. V. Rieu. (Penguin Classics.) Harmondsworth, 1958.

Homeric Hymns. See: *Hesiod, the Homeric Hymns, and Homerica*. With an English translation by Hugh G. Evelyn-White. (Loeb Classical Library.) London and New York, 1914.

HONORIUS OF AUTUN. *Expositio in Cantica canticorum*. See MIGNE, *P.L.*, vol. 172, cols. 347–496.

HORAPOLLO NILIACUS. *Hieroglyphica*. See: *The Hieroglyphics of Horapollo*. Translated by George Boas. (Bollingen Series XXIII.) New York, 1950. (Original: *Selecta Hieroglyphica*. Rome, 1597.)

HORNEFFER, ERNST. *Nietzsches Lehre von der ewigen Wiederkunft*. Leipzig, 1900.

Hovamol. See BELLOWS.

HUBERT, HENRI, and MAUSS, MARCEL. *Mélanges d'histoire des religions*. Paris, 1909.

HUME, ROBERT ERNEST (trans.). *The Thirteen Principal Upanishads*. Oxford, 1921. (Shvetashvatara Upanishad, pp. 394–411.)

I Ching, or Book of Changes. The German translation by Richard Wilhelm, rendered into English by Cary F. Baynes. New York (Bollingen Series XIX) and London, 1950; 3rd edn., 1967.

INGRAM, JOHN H. *The Haunted Homes and Family Traditions of Great Britain.* London, 1890.

IRENAEUS, SAINT. *Adversus* [or *Contra*] *haereses libri quinque.* See MIGNE, *P.G.*, vol. 7, cols. 433–1224. For translation, see: *The Writings of Irenaeus.* Translated by Alexander Roberts and W. H. Rambaut. (Ante-Nicene Christian Library, 5, 9.) Edinburgh, 1868. 2 vols.

IZQUIERDO, SEBASTIAN. *Pratica di alcuni Esercitij Spirituali di S. Ignatio.* Rome, 1686.

JACOBI, JOLANDE. *Complex/Archetype/Symbol.* Translated by Ralph Manheim. New York (Bollingen Series) and London, 1959.

JACOBSOHN, HELMUTH. "Die dogmatische Stellung des Königs in der Theologie der alten Aegypter," *Aegyptologische Forschungen* (Glückstadt), no. 8 (1939).

JAFFÉ, ANIELA. "Bilder und Symbole aus E. T. A. Hoffmanns Märchen 'Der Goldne Topf,'" in: C. G. JUNG. *Gestaltungen des Unbewussten.* Zurich, 1950.

JAMES, M. R. (trans.) *The Apocryphal New Testament.* Oxford, 1924.

JAMES, WILLIAM. *The Varieties of Religious Experience.* London, 1902.

JANET, PIERRE. *L'Automatisme psychologique.* Paris, 1889.

———. *L'État mental des hystériques.* Paris [1893]. For translation, see: *The Mental State of Hystericals.* Translated by Caroline Rollin Corson. New York and London, 1901.

———. *Les Névroses.* Paris, 1909.

———. *Névroses et idées fixes.* Paris, 1898. 2 vols.

JEROME, SAINT. *Epistola II ad Theodosium et ceteros Anachoretas.* In: *Hieronymi Epistularum Pars I.* (Corpus Scriptorum Ecclesiasticorum Latinorum, 54.) Vienna and Leipzig, 1910.

JUNG, CARL GUSTAV. "The Aims of Psychotherapy." In: *The Practice of Psychotherapy. Collected Works,** Vol. 16. New York and London, 2nd edn., 1966.

* For details of the *Collected Works of C. G. Jung,* see end of this volume.

——. *Aion: Researches into the Phenomenology of the Self. Collected Works,** Vol. 9, Part II. New York and London, 2nd edn., 1968.

——. *Alchemical Studies. Collected Works,** Vol. 13. New York and London, 1968.

——. "Answer to Job." In: *Psychology and Religion: West and East,* q.v.

——. "Brother Klaus." In: *Psychology and Religion: West and East,* q.v.

——. *Civilization in Transition. Collected Works,** Vol. 10. New York and London, 1964.

——. *Collected Papers on Analytical Psychology.* Edited by Constance Long. 2nd edn., London, 1917; New York, 1920.

——. Commentary on "The Secret of the Golden Flower." In: *Alchemical Studies.* (See also WILHELM and JUNG, *The Secret of the Golden Flower.*)

——. "The Enigma of Bologna." In: *Mysterium Coniunctionis,* q.v., pars. 51ff.

——. "Instinct and the Unconscious." In: *The Structure and Dynamics of the Psyche,* q.v.

——. *The Integration of the Personality.* Translated by Stanley Dell. New York, 1939; London, 1940.

——. *Memories, Dreams, Reflections.* Recorded and edited by Aniela Jaffé. Translated by Richard and Clara Winston. New York and London, 1963. (U.S. and Brit. edns. separately paginated.)

——. *Mysterium Coniunctionis. Collected Works,** Vol. 14. New York and London, 1963.

——. "On the Nature of the Psyche." In: *The Structure and Dynamics of the Psyche,* q.v.

——. "On the Psychology and Pathology of So-called Occult Phenomena." In: *Psychiatric Studies,* q.v.

——. "Paracelsus as a Spiritual Phenomenon." In: *Alchemical Studies,* q.v.

——. "The Philosophical Tree." In: *Alchemical Studies,* q.v.

——. *The Practice of Psychotherapy. Collected Works,** Vol. 16. New York and London, 2nd edn., 1966.

——. *Psychiatric Studies. Collected Works,** Vol. 1. New York and London, 1957.

——. "A Psychological Approach to the Dogma of the Trinity." In: *Psychology and Religion: West and East,* q.v.

——. Psychological Commentary on "The Tibetan Book of the Dead." In: ibid.

——. *Psychological Types. Collected Works,** Vol. 6. (Alternative source: translation by H. G. Baynes, London and New York, 1923.)

——. *Psychology and Alchemy. Collected Works,** Vol. 12. New York and London, 2nd edn., 1968.

——. "The Psychology of Eastern Meditation." In: *Psychology and Religion: West and East,* q.v.

——. "Psychology and Education." In: *The Development of Personality. Collected Works,** Vol. 17. New York and London, 1954.

——. "Psychology and Religion" (The Terry Lectures). In: *Psychology and Religion: West and East,* q.v.

——. *Psychology and Religion: West and East. Collected Works,** Vol. 11. New York and London, 1958.

——. "The Psychology of the Transference." In: *The Practice of Psychotherapy,* q.v.

——. *Psychology of the Unconscious.* Translated by Beatrice M. Hinkle. New York, 1916; London, 1917. (Superseded by *Symbols of Transformation,* q.v.)

——. "The Relations between the Ego and the Unconscious." In: *Two Essays on Analytical Psychology,* q.v.

——. "Spirit and Life." In: *The Structure and Dynamics of the Psyche,* q.v.

* For details of the *Collected Works of C. G. Jung,* see end of this volume.

——. "The Spirit Mercurius." In: *Alchemical Studies,* q.v.

——. *The Structure and Dynamics of the Psyche, Collected Works,** Vol. 8. New York and London, 1960.

——. "The Structure of the Psyche." In: *The Structure and Dynamics of the Psyche,* q.v.

——. *Symbols of Transformation. Collected Works,** Vol. 5. New York and London, 2nd edn., 1967.

——. "Synchronicity: An Acausal Connecting Phenomenon." In: *The Structure and Dynamics of the Psyche,* q.v.

——. "The Transcendent Function." In: ibid.

——. "Transformation Symbolism in the Mass." In: *Psychology and Religion: West and East,* q.v.

——. *Two Essays on Analytical Psychology. Collected Works,** Vol. 7. New York and London, 2nd edn., 1966.

——. "The Visions of Zosimos." In: *Alchemical Studies,* q.v.

——. *Von den Wurzeln des Bewusstseins.* Zurich, 1954.

——. *Wandlungen und Symbole der Libido.* Leipzig and Vienna, 1912.

——. "Wotan." In: *Civilization in Transition,* q.v.

JUNG, EMMA. "On the Nature of the Animus." Translated by Cary F. Baynes, in: *Animus and Anima.* (The Analytical Psychology Club of New York.) New York, 1957.

Kabbala Denudata. See KNORR VON ROSENROTH.

[KALLID (Khalid ibn-Jazid ibn-Muawiyah).] "Liber secretorum." See (*A*) *Artis auriferae,* iv.

KERÉNYI, KARL. "Hermes der Seelenführer," *Eranos Jahrbuch 1942* (Zurich, 1943), 9–107.

——. "Kore" and "The Primordial Child in Primordial Times." In: KERÉNYI and C. G. JUNG. *Essays on a Science of Mythology.* (Bollingen Series XXII.) New York, 1949. (Also pub. as *Introduction to a Science of Mythology,* London, 1950.) See also Torchbooks edn., rev., 1963.

KERNER, JUSTINUS. *Die Seherin von Prevorst.* Stuttgart and Tübingen, 1829. 2 vols. For translation, see: *The Seeress of Prevorst.* Translated by Mrs. [Catherine] Crowe. New York, 1859.

KEYSERLING, HERMANN COUNT VON. *South-American Meditations.* Translated by Therese Duerr. New York and London, 1932. (Original: *Südamerikanische Meditationen.* Stuttgart, 1932.)

KHUNRATH, HENRICUS. *Von hylealischen, das ist, pri-materialischen . . . Chaos.* Magdeburg, 1597.

KIRCHER, ATHANASIUS. *Mundus subterraneus.* Amsterdam, 1678.

KLAGES, LUDWIG. *Der Geist als Widersacher der Seele.* Leipzig, 1929–32. 3 vols.

KNORR VON ROSENROTH, CHRISTIAN. *Kabbala Denudata.* Sulzbach, 1677–78 (Vol. I); Frankfurt a. M., 1684 (Vol. II). 2 vols. (*Adumbratio Kabbalae Christianae* is an appendix to Vol. II.) For partial translation, see: S. LIDELL MACGREGOR MATHERS. *The Kabbalah Unveiled.* London, 1887.

KOEPGEN, GEORG. *Die Gnosis des Christentums.* Salzburg, 1939.

KÖHLER, REINHOLD. *Kleinere Schriften zur Märchenforschung.* Weimar, 1898.

Koran, The. Translated by N. J. Dawood. (Penguin Classics.) Harmondsworth, 1956.

LACTANTIUS FIRMIANUS. *Divinae institutiones.* In: *Opera omnia.* Edited by Samuel Brandt and Georg Laubmann. (Corpus scriptorum ecclesiasticorum Latinorum.) Vienna, 1890–97. 3 vols. Vol. I. For translation, see: *The Works of Lactantius.* Translated by William Fletcher. (Ante-Nicene Christian Library, 21, 22.) Edinburgh, 1871. 2 vols.

LAGNEUS, DAVID. "Harmonia seu Consensus philosophorum chemicorum" (Harmonia chemica). See (*A*) *Theatrum chemicum,* vi.

LAMBSPRINGK. See WAITE.

LA ROCHEFOUCAULD, FRANÇOIS DE. *The Moral Maxims and Reflections of the Duke de la Rochefoucauld.* Translated by George H. Powell. London, 1903.

LAVAUD, BENOÎT. *Vie Profonde de Nicolas de Flue.* Fribourg, 1942.

LE BON, GUSTAVE. *The Crowd.* 19th impr., London, 1947. (English version first published 1896.)

LEISEGANG, HANS. *Die Gnosis.* Leipzig, 1924.

LENGLET DU FRESNOY, PIERRE NICOLAS. *Histoire de la philosophie hermétique.* 1742. 3 vols.

LEONE EBREO (Leo Hebraeus) (Don Judah Abarbanel). *The Philosophy of Love.* Translated by F. Friedeberg-Seeley and Jean H. Barnes. London, 1937.

LÉVY-BRUHL, LUCIEN. *La Mythologie primitive.* Paris, 1935.

[*Liber mutus.*] *Mutus liber, in quo tamen tota Philosophia hermetica figuris hieroglyphicis depingitur.* La Rochelle, 1677.

LONGFELLOW, HENRY WADSWORTH. *The Song of Hiawatha.* Boston, 1855.

LÜDY, F. *Alchemistische und Chemische Zeichen.* Berlin, 1929.

MCGLASHAN, ALAN. "Daily Paper Pantheon," *The Lancet* (London), vol. 264(i) (1953), 238–39.

MACROBIUS. *Commentary on the Dream of Scipio.* Translated by William Harris Stahl. (Records of Civilization, Sources and Studies, 48.) New York, 1952.

MAEDER, A. "Essai d'interprétation de quelques rêves," *Archives de psychologie* (Geneva), VI (1907), 354–75.

——. "Die Symbolik in den Legenden, Märchen, Gebrauchen, und Traumen," *Psychologisch-neurologische Wochenschrift* (Halle), X (1908–9), 45–55.

MAIER, MICHAEL. *De circulo physico quadrato.* Oppenheim, 1616.

——. *Symbola aureae mensae duodecim nationum.* Frankfurt a. M., 1617.

MAITLAND, EDWARD. *Anna Kingsford: Her Life, Letters, Diary, and Work.* London, 1896. 2 vols.

Maitrayana-Brahmana Upanishad. In: *The Upanishads, Part II.* Translated by F. Max Müller. (Sacred Books of the East, 15.) Oxford, 1900.

Majjhima-Nikaya. See BHIKKHU SILACARA (ed. and trans.). *The First Fifty Discourses from the Collection of the Middle-Length Discourses (Majjhima Nikaya) of Gotama the Buddha*. Breslau and Leipzig, 1912–13. 2 vols.

MANGETUS, JOANNES JACOBUS. See under (*A*).

MASENIUS, JACOBUS. *Speculum imaginum veritatis occultae*. Cologne, 1714. 2 vols.

MATTHEWS, WASHINGTON. "The Mountain Chant." In: *Fifth Annual Report of the U. S. Bureau of American Ethnology*. Washington, 1887. (Pp. 379–467.)

MECHTHILD, SAINT. *The Revelations of Mechthild of Magdeburg (1210–1297), or The Flowing Light of the Godhead*. Translated by Lucy Menzies. London, 1953.

MEIER, C. A. *Antike Inkubation und Moderne Psychotherapie*. Zurich, 1949.

———. "Spontanmanifestationen des kollektiven Unbewussten," *Zentralblatt für Psychotherapie* (Leipzig), XI (1939), 284ff.

MENNENS, GULIELMUS. *Aurei velleris, sive sacrae philosophiae, naturae et artis admirabilium libri tres*. Antwerp, 1604. See also "De aureo vellere" in (*A*) *Theatrum chemicum*, vii.

MEYRINK, GUSTAV. *Der weisse Dominikaner*. Vienna, 1921.

MIGNE, JACQUES PAUL (ed.). *Patrologiae cursus completus*.
[*P.L.*] Latin series. Paris, 1844–64. 221 vols.
[*P.G.*] Greek series, Paris, 1857–66. 166 vols.
(These works are referred to in the text as "Migne, *P.L.*," and "Migne, *P.G.*," respectively.)

MORIENUS ROMANUS. "De compositione Alchemiae." See (*A*) MANGETUS, *Bibliotheca chemica curiosa*, ii.

Musaeum hermeticum. See WAITE.

MYLIUS, JOHANN DANIEL. *Philosophia reformata*. Frankfurt a. M., 1622.

Mythographus Vaticanus III. See: *Classicorum Auctorum e Vaticanis Codicibus Editorum*, Vol. 6: *Complectens Mythographi tres*. Edited by Angelo Mai. Rome, 1831.

NEEDHAM, JOSEPH. *Science and Civilization in China.* Cambridge, 1954– . (Vols. I and II published.)

NELKEN, JAN. "Analytische Beobachtungen über Phantasien eines Schizophrenen," *Jahrbuch für psychoanalytische und psychopathologische Forschungen* (Leipzig), IV (1912), 504ff.

NEUMANN, ERICH. *The Great Mother.* Translated by Ralph Manheim. New York (Bollingen Series XLVII) and London, 1955.

——. *The Origins and History of Consciousness.* New York (Bollingen Series XLII) and London, 1954.

——. *Tiefenpsychologie und neue Ethik.* Zurich, 1949.

NEWCOMB, FRANC JOHNSON, and REICHARD, GLADYS A. *Sand-paintings of the Navajo Shooting Chant.* New York, 1938.

NIETZSCHE, FRIEDRICH. *Beyond Good and Evil.* (Collected Works, 12.) Translated by Helen Zimmern. 2nd edn., London, 1909.

——. *Thus Spake Zarathustra.* Translated by Thomas Common, revised by Oscar Levy and John L. Beevers. London, 1932.

——. *Gedichte und Sprüche.* Leipzig, 1898.

NIKLAUS VON DER FLÜE (Brother Klaus). *Ein nützlicher und loblicher Tractat von Bruder Claus und einem Bilger.* Nuremberg, 1488.

NINCK, MARTIN. *Wodan und germanischer Schicksalsglaube.* Jena, 1935.

ORANDUS, EIRENAEUS. See FLAMEL.

ORIGEN. *In Jeremiam homiliae.* In MIGNE, *P.G.,* vol. 13, cols. 255–544.

——. *In Leviticum homiliae.* In MIGNE, *P.G.,* vol. 12, cols. 405–574.

——. *In libros Regnorum homiliae.* In MIGNE, *P.G.,* vol. 12.

[Panchatantra.] *The Panchatantra Reconstructed.* By Franklin Edgerton. (American Oriental Series, 2, 3.) New Haven, 1924. 2 vols.

PARACELSUS (Theophrastus Bombastes of Hohenheim). *De vita longa.* Edited by Adam von Bodenstein. Basel, 1562. Also see: KARL SÜDHOFF (ed.). *Theophrast von Hohenheim genannt Paracelsus sämtliche Werke.* Munich and Berlin, 1922–35. 15 vols. (Vol. III, pp. 247ff.)

PHILALETHES, EIRENAEUS. *Ripley Reviv'd: or, An Exposition upon Sir George Ripley's Hermetico-Poetical Works.* London, 1678.

PHILO JUDAEUS. *De opificio mundi.* In: *Philo.* With an English translation by Francis Henry Colson and George Herbert Whitaker. (Loeb Classical Library.) London and New York, 1929– . 12 vols. published. (Vol. I.)

PICINELLI, FILIPPO. *Mondo simbolico.* Milan, 1669. Translated into Latin as: *Mundus symbolicus.* Cologne, 1680–81.

PLATO. *The Symposium.* Translated by W. Hamilton. (Penguin Classics.) Harmondsworth, 1959.

———. *The Timaeus and the Critias.* The Thomas Taylor translation. (Bollingen Series III.) New York, 1944.

PLINY. [*Historia naturalis.*] *Natural History.* With an English translation by H. Rackham. (Loeb Classical Library.) London and New York, 1938– . 10 vols. published.

PLUTARCH. *De genio Socratis.* In: *Moralia.* Edited by C. Hubert et al. Leipzig, 1892–1935. 7 vols (Vol. III, pp. 460–511.)

PREISENDANZ, KARL. *Papyri Graecae magicae.* Leipzig and Berlin, 1928–31. 2 vols.

[PROPERTIUS, SEXTUS.] *Propertius.* With an English translation by H. E. Butler. (Loeb Classical Library.) London and New York, 1912.

PRUDENTIUS. *Contra Symmachum.* In: [*Works.*] With an English translation by H. J. Thomson. (Loeb Classical Library.) London and Cambridge, Mass., 1949–53. (Vol. I, p. 344 – Vol. II, p. 97.)

RACHAIDIBUS. "De materia philosophici lapidis." See (*A*) *Artis auriferae,* vi.

RADIN, PAUL. *The World of Primitive Man.* New York, 1953.

RAHNER, HUGO. "Antenna Crucis II: Das Meer der Welt," *Zeitschrift für Katholische Theologie* (Innsbruck), LXVI (1942), 89ff.

———. "Earth Spirit aud Divine Spirit in Patristic Theology." In: *Spirit and Nature.* (Papers from the Eranos Yearbooks, 1.) Translated by Ralph Manheim. New York (Bollingen Series XXX), 1954; London, 1955.

———. "Die seelenheilende Blume," *Eranos Jahrbuch* (Zurich), XII (C.G. Jung Festgabe, 1945), 117–239.

RANK, OTTO. *The Myth of the Birth of the Hero.* Translated by F. Robbins and Smith Ely Jelliffe. New York, 1952. (Original: *Der Mythus von der Geburt des Helden.* Leipzig and Vienna, 1922.)

READ, JOHN. *Prelude to Chemistry.* London, 1939.

REITZENSTEIN, RICHARD. *Poimandres.* Leipzig, 1904.

REUSNER, HIERONYMUS. *Pandora: das ist, die edelst Gab Gottes, oder der Werde und heilsame Stein der Weysen.* Basel, 1588.

RHINE, J. B. *New Frontiers of the Mind.* London, 1937.

RICHARD OF ST. VICTOR. *Benjamin minor.* In MIGNE, *P.L.*, vol. 196, cols. 1–64.

Rig-Veda. See: *Hindu Scriptures.* Edited by Nicol MacNicol. (Everyman's Library.) London and New York, 1938. See also DEUSSEN.

RIKLIN, F. "Über Gefängnispsychosen," *Psychologisch-neurologische Wochenschrift* (Halle), IX (1907), 269–72.

———. *Wishfulfilment and Symbolism in Fairy Tales.* Translated by William A. White. (Nervous and Mental Disease Monograph Series, 21.) New York, 1915. (Original: *Wunscherfüllung und Symbolik in Märchen.* Leipzig and Vienna, 1908.)

RIPLEY, SIR GEORGE. "Cantilena." In: *Opera omnia chemica.* Kassel, 1649.

Rosarium philosophorum. Secunda pars alchimiae de lapide philosophico. Frankfurt a. M., 1550. See also (*A*) *Artis auriferae*, viii.

ROSCHER, WILHELM HEINRICH. *Ausführliches Lexikon der Griechische und Römische Mythologie.* Leipzig, 1884–1937. 6 vols.

ROSENCREUTZ, CHRISTIAN. *Chymische Hochzeit.* Strasbourg, 1616. For translation, see: *The Hermetick Romance; or, The Chemical Wedding.* Translated by E. Foxcroft. London, 1690.

ROSINUS. See ZOSIMUS.

ROUSSELLE, ERWIN. "Spiritual Guidance in Contemporary Taoism." In: *Spiritual Disciplines.* (Papers from the Eranos Yearbooks, 4).

Translated by Ralph Manheim. New York (Bollingen Series XXX) and London, in press.

RULAND, MARTIN. *A Lexicon of Alchemy.* [London, 1893.] (Original: *Lexicon alchemiae.* Frankfurt a. M., 1612.)

RUSKA, JULIUS FERDINAND. "Die Vision des Arisleus." In: [KARL SUDHOFF, ed.] *Historische Studien und Skizzen zur Natur- und Heilwissenschaft.* (Memorial volume presented to Georg Sticker on his seventieth birthday.) Berlin, 1930.

SALOMON, RICHARD. *Opicinus de Canistris.* (Studies of the Warburg Institute, I a and b.) London, 1936. 2 parts.

Samyutta-Nikaya. See: *The Book of the Kindred Sayings (Sangyutta-Nikaya).* Part II: *The Nidana Book (Nidana-Vagga).* Translated by Mrs. C. A. F. Rhys Davids. London, [1922]. Also: *Dialogues of the Buddha.* Part II. Translated by T. W. and C. A. F. Rhys Davids. (Sacred Books of the Buddhists, 3.) London, 1951.

Sanatsugatiya. See: *The Bhagavadgita, with the Sanatsugatiya and the Anugita.* Translated by Kashinath Trimbak Telang. (Sacred Books of the East, 8.) Oxford, 1882.

[SAND, GEORGE.] *Intimate Journal of George Sand.* Translated and edited by Marie Jenney Howe. New York, 1929.

SCHELER, MAX FERDINAND. *Die Stellung des Menschen im Kosmos.* Darmstadt, 1928.

SCHILLER, FRIEDRICH. *Die Piccolomini.* In: *Schillers Werke.* Edited by Paul Brandt. Leipzig, [1923]. 5 vols. (Vol. III, pp. 59–174.)

SCHMALTZ, GUSTAV. *Östliche Weisheit und Westliche Psychotherapie.* Stuttgart, 1951.

SCHMITZ, OSKAR A. H. *Märchen aus dem Unbewussten.* Munich, 1932.

SCHOPENHAUER, ARTHUR. *Aphorismen zur Lebensweisheit.* Translated in: *Essays from the Parerga and Paralipomena.* Translated by T. Bailey Saunders. London, 1951. ("The Wisdom of Life," in section "The Art of Controversy," pp. 56–71.) (Original in: *Sämmtliche Werke.* Edited by Julius Frauenstädt. Vol. V: *Parerga und Paralipomena,* 1. Leipzig, 1877.)

SCHREBER, DANIEL PAUL. *Memoirs of My Nervous Illness*. Translated by Ida Macalpine and Richard A. Hunter. London, 1955. (Original: *Denkwürdigkeiten eines Nervenkranken*. Leipzig, 1903.)

SCHUBERT, GOTTHILF HEINRICH VON. *Altes und Neues aus dem Gebiet der inneren Seelenkunde*. Leipzig, 1825–44. 5 vols.

SCHULTZ, WOLFGANG. *Dokumente der Gnosis*. Jena, 1910.

SCOTT, WALTER (ed.). *Hermetica*. Oxford, 1924–36. 4 vols.

SENDIVOGIUS, MICHAEL (Micha Sedziwoj). "Epistola XIII." See (*A*) MANGETUS, *Bibliotheca chemica curiosa*, iii.

"Septem tractatus seu capitula Hermetis Trismegisti." See (*A*) *Ars chemica*.

Shatapatha-Brahmana. Translated by Julius Eggeling. (Sacred Books of the East, 12.) Oxford, 1882.

Shvetashvatara Upanishad. See HUME.

SILBERER, HERBERT. *Problems of Mysticism and Its Symbolism*. New York, 1917.

SLOANE, WILLIAM M. *To Walk the Night*. New York, 1937.

SPAMER, ADOLF (ed.). *Texte aus der deutschen Mystik des 14. und 15. Jahrhunderts*. Jena, 1912.

SPENCER, SIR WALTER B., and GILLEN, FRANCIS JAMES. *The Northern Tribes of Central Australia*. London, 1904.

SPITTELER, CARL. *Prometheus and Epimetheus*. Translated by James Fullarton Muirhead. London, 1931. (Original: Jena, 1920.)

——. *Imago*. Jena, 1919.

STADE, BERNHARD. *Biblische Theologie des Alten Testaments*. Vol. I (no more published). Tübingen, 1905.

STEVENSON, JAMES. "Ceremonial of Hasjelti Dailjis and Mythical Sand Painting of the Navaho Indians." In: *Eighth Annual Report of the U. S. Bureau of American Ethnology, 1886–87*. Washington, 1891. (Pp. 229–85.)

STOECKLI, ALBAN. *Die Visionen des seligen Bruder Klaus*. Einsiedeln, 1933.

SUSO, HENRY. *Little Book of Eternal Wisdom and Little Book of Truth.* Translated by James M. Clark. London, [1953].

SUZUKI, DAISETZ TEITARO. *An Introduction to Zen Buddhism.* London, [1948].

TERTULLIAN. *Apologeticus adversus gentes.* See MIGNE, *P.L.*, vol. 1, cols. 257–536.

TONQUÉDEC, JOSEPH DE. *Les Maladies nerveuses ou mentales et les manifestations diaboliques.* Paris, 1938.

"Tractatulus Aristotelis." See (*A*) *Artis auriferae,* v.

Tractatus aureus. See (*A*) *Artis auriferae;* MANGETUS, *Bibliotheca chemica curiosa,* i; *Ars chemica,* i.

"Turba philosophorum." See: JULIUS FERDINAND RUSKA. *Turba Philosophorum.* Berlin, 1931.

Upanishads. See HUME; Maitrayana-Brahmana Upanishad.

USENER, HERMANN. *Das Weihnachtsfest.* 2nd edn., Bonn, 1911.

Vedanta-Sutras, with the Commentary of Ramanuga (*Ramanuja*). Translated by George Thibaut. Part III. (Sacred Books of the East, 48.) Oxford, 1904.

VIGENERUS (Blaise de Vigenère). "Tractatus de igne et sale." See (*A*) *Theatrum chemicum,* viii.

"Visio Arislei." See *Rosarium philosophorum,* which contains it.

VITUS, RICHARDUS (Richard White of Basingstoke). *Aelia Laelia Crispis.* Padua, 1568.

VOLLERS, K. "Chidher," *Archiv für Religionswissenschaft* (Leipzig), XII (1909), 234–384.

WAITE, ARTHUR EDWARD (ed. and trans.). *The Hermetic Museum Restored and Enlarged.* London, 1953. 2 vols. (The Book of Lambspring, I, pp. 271–306.)

WARNECKE, JOHANNES. *Die Religion der Batak.* Leipzig, 1909.

WECKERLING, ADOLF (trans.). *Ananda-raya-makhi. Das Glück des Lebens.* (Arbeiten der deutsch-nordischen Gesellschaft für Geschichte der Medizin, der Zahnheilkunde und der Nervenwissenschaften, 13.) Greifswald, 1937.

[WEI PO-YANG.] "An Ancient Chinese Treatise on Alchemy entitled Ts'an T'ung Ch'i, written by Wei Po-yang about 142 A.D." Translated by Lu-ch'iang Wu and Tenney L. Davis. In: *Isis* (Bruges), XVIII (1932), 210–89.

WELLS, HERBERT GEORGE. *The War of the Worlds*. London, 1898.

WILHELM, RICHARD, and JUNG, CARL GUSTAV. *The Secret of the Golden Flower*. Translated by Cary F. Baynes. London and New York, 1931; revised edition, 1962.

——. See also *I Ching*.

WILLIAMS, MENTOR L. (ed.). *Schoolcraft's Indian Legends*. East Lansing, Michigan, 1956.

WINTHUIS, JOSEF. *Das Zweigeschlechterwesen bei den Zentralaustraliern und andern Völkern*. Leipzig, 1928.

WOLFF, TONI. "Einführung in die Grundlagen der komplexen Psychologie." In: *Die kulturelle Bedeutung der komplexen Psychologie*. Berlin, 1935. (Pp. 1–168.)

WOODROFFE, SIR JOHN. *Shakti and Shakta*. Madras, 1920.

——. See also AVALON.

WUNDT, WILHELM. *Principles of Physiological Psychology*. Translated from 5th German edition. London, 1904. (Original: *Grundzüge der physiologischen Psychologie*. Leipzig, 1874.)

——. *Völkerpsychologie*. Leipzig, 1911–20. 10 vols.

WYLIE, PHILIP. *Generation of Vipers*. New York, 1942.

ZIMMER, HEINRICH. *Philosophies of India*. Edited by Joseph Campbell. New York (Bollingen Series XXVI) and London, 1952.

[ZOSIMUS.] "Rosinus ad Sarratantam Episcopum." See (*A*) *Artis auriferae*, iii.

INDEX

INDEX

C

E

F

I

K

N

O

P

T

X/Y/Z

THE COLLECTED WORKS OF

C. G. JUNG

THE PUBLICATION of the first complete edition, in English, of the works of C. G. Jung was undertaken by Routledge and Kegan Paul, Ltd., in England and by Bollingen Foundation in the United States. The American edition is number XX in Bollingen Series, which since 1967 has been published by Princeton University Press. The edition contains revised versions of works previously published, such as *Psychology of the Unconscious*, which is now entitled *Symbols of Transformation*; works originally written in English, such as *Psychology and Religion*; works not previously translated, such as *Aion*; and, in general, new translations of virtually all of Professor Jung's writings. Prior to his death, in 1961, the author supervised the textual revision, which in some cases is extensive. Sir Herbert Read (d. 1968), Dr. Michael Fordham, and Dr. Gerhard Adler compose the Editorial Committee; the translator is R. F. C. Hull (except for Volume 2) and William McGuire is executive editor.

The price of the volumes varies according to size; they are sold separately, and may also be obtained on standing order. Several of the volumes are extensively illustrated. Each volume contains an index and in most a bibliography; the final volumes will contain a complete bibliography of Professor Jung's writings and a general index to the entire edition.

In the following list, dates of original publication are given in parentheses (of original composition, in brackets). Multiple dates indicate revisions.

*1. PSYCHIATRIC STUDIES

On the Psychology and Pathology of So-Called Occult Phenomena (1902)
On Hysterical Misreading (1904)
Cryptomnesia (1905)
On Manic Mood Disorder (1903)
A Case of Hysterical Stupor in a Prisoner in Detention (1902)
On Simulated Insanity (1903)
A Medical Opinion on a Case of Simulated Insanity (1904)
A Third and Final Opinion on Two Contradictory Psychiatric Diagnoses (1906)
On the Psychological Diagnosis of Facts (1905)

†2. EXPERIMENTAL RESEARCHES

Translated by Leopold Stein in collaboration with Diana Riviere

STUDIES IN WORD ASSOCIATION (1904–7, 1910)
The Associations of Normal Subjects (by Jung and F. Riklin)
An Analysis of the Associations of an Epileptic
The Reaction-Time Ratio in the Association Experiment
Experimental Observations on the Faculty of Memory
Psychoanalysis and Association Experiments
The Psychological Diagnosis of Evidence
Association, Dream, and Hysterical Symptom
The Psychopathological Significance of the Association Experiment
Disturbances in Reproduction in the Association Experiment
The Association Method
The Family Constellation

PSYCHOPHYSICAL RESEARCHES (1907–8)
On the Psychophysical Relations of the Association Experiment
Psychophysical Investigations with the Galvanometer and Pneumograph in Normal and Insane Individuals (by F. Peterson and Jung)
Further Investigations on the Galvanic Phenomenon and Respiration in Normal and Insane Individuals (by C. Ricksher and Jung)
Appendix: Statistical Details of Enlistment (1906); New Aspects of Criminal Psychology (1908); The Psychological Methods of Investigation Used in the Psychiatric Clinic of the University of Zurich (1910); On the Doctrine of Complexes ([1911] 1913); On the Psychological Diagnosis of Evidence (1937)

* Published 1957; 2nd edn., 1970. † Published 1973.

*3. THE PSYCHOGENESIS OF MENTAL DISEASE
The Psychology of Dementia Praecox (1907)
The Content of the Psychoses (1908/1914)
On Psychological Understanding (1914)
A Criticism of Bleuler's Theory of Schizophrenic Negativism (1911)
On the Importance of the Unconscious in Psychopathology (1914)
On the Problem of Psychogenesis in Mental Disease (1919)
Mental Disease and the Psyche (1928)
On the Psychogenesis of Schizophrenia (1939)
Recent Thoughts on Schizophrenia (1957)
Schizophrenia (1958)

†4. FREUD AND PSYCHOANALYSIS
Freud's Theory of Hysteria: A Reply to Aschaffenburg (1906)
The Freudian Theory of Hysteria (1908)
The Analysis of Dreams (1909)
A Contribution to the Psychology of Rumour (1910–11)
On the Significance of Number Dreams (1910–11)
Morton Prince, "The Mechanism and Interpretation of Dreams": A Critical Review (1911)
On the Criticism of Psychoanalysis (1910)
Concerning Psychoanalysis (1912)
The Theory of Psychoanalysis (1913)
General Aspects of Psychoanalysis (1913)
Psychoanalysis and Neurosis (1916)
Some Crucial Points in Psychoanalysis: A Correspondence between Dr. Jung and Dr. Loÿ (1914)
Prefaces to "Collected Papers on Analytical Psychology" (1916, 1917)
The Significance of the Father in the Destiny of the Individual (1909/1949)
Introduction to Kranefeldt's "Secret Ways of the Mind" (1930)
Freud and Jung: Contrasts (1929)

‡5. SYMBOLS OF TRANSFORMATION (1911–12/1952)
PART I
Introduction
Two Kinds of Thinking
The Miller Fantasies: Anamnesis
The Hymn of Creation
The Song of the Moth

(*continued*)

* Published 1960. † Published 1961.
‡ Published 1956; 2nd edn., 1967. (65 plates, 43 text figures.)

5. *(continued)*

PART II

Introduction

The Concept of Libido

The Transformation of Libido

The Origin of the Hero

Symbols of the Mother and of Rebirth

The Battle for Deliverance from the Mother

The Dual Mother

The Sacrifice

Epilogue

Appendix: The Miller Fantasies

*6. PSYCHOLOGICAL TYPES (1921)

Introduction

The Problem of Types in the History of Classical and Medieval Thought

Schiller's Ideas on the Type Problem

The Apollinian and the Dionysian

The Type Problem in Human Character

The Type Problem in Poetry

The Type Problem in Psychopathology

The Type Problem in Aesthetics

The Type Problem in Modern Philosophy

The Type Problem in Biography

General Description of the Types

Definitions

Epilogue

Four Papers on Psychological Typology (1913, 1925, 1931, 1936)

†7. TWO ESSAYS ON ANALYTICAL PSYCHOLOGY

On the Psychology of the Unconscious (1917/1926/1943)

The Relations between the Ego and the Unconscious (1928)

Appendix: New Paths in Psychology (1912); The Structure of the Unconscious (1916) (new versions, with variants, 1966)

‡8. THE STRUCTURE AND DYNAMICS OF THE PSYCHE

On Psychic Energy (1928)

The Transcendent Function ([1916]/1957)

A Review of the Complex Theory (1934)

The Significance of Constitution and Heredity in Psychology (1929)

* Published 1971.

† Published 1953; 2nd edn., 1966.

‡ Published 1960; 2nd edn., 1969.

 (*continued*)

* Published 1959; 2nd edn., 1968. (Part I: 79 plates, with 29 in colour.)

9\. (*continued*)

The Prophecies of Nostradamus
The Historical Significance of the Fish
The Ambivalence of the Fish Symbol
The Fish in Alchemy
The Alchemical Interpretation of the Fish
Background to the Psychology of Christian Alchemical Symbolism
Gnostic Symbols of the Self
The Structure and Dynamics of the Self
Conclusion

*10. CIVILIZATION IN TRANSITION

The Role of the Unconscious (1918)
Mind and Earth (1927/1931)
Archaic Man (1931)
The Spiritual Problem of Modern Man (1928/1931)
The Love Problem of a Student (1928)
Woman in Europe (1927)
The Meaning of Psychology for Modern Man (1933/1934)
The State of Psychotherapy Today (1934)
Preface and Epilogue to "Essays on Contemporary Events" (1946)
Wotan (1936)
After the Catastrophe (1945)
The Fight with the Shadow (1946)
The Undiscovered Self (Present and Future) (1957)
Flying Saucers: A Modern Myth (1958)
A Psychological View of Conscience (1958)
Good and Evil in Analytical Psychology (1959)
Introduction to Wolff's "Studies in Jungian Psychology" (1959)
The Swiss Line in the European Spectrum (1928)
Reviews of Keyserling's "America Set Free" (1930) and "La Révolution Mondiale" (1934)
The Complications of American Psychology (1930)
The Dreamlike World of India (1939)
What India Can Teach Us (1939)
Appendix: Documents (1933–1938)

†11. PSYCHOLOGY AND RELIGION: WEST AND EAST

WESTERN RELIGION

Psychology and Religion (The Terry Lectures) (1938/1940)

* Published 1964; 2nd edn., 1970. (8 plates.)
† Published 1958; 2nd edn., 1969.

A Psychological Approach to the Dogma of the Trinity (1942/1948)
Transformation Symbolism in the Mass (1942/1954)
Forewords to White's "God and the Unconscious" and Werblowsky's "Lucifer and Prometheus" (1952)
Brother Klaus (1933)
Psychotherapists or the Clergy (1932)
Psychoanalysis and the Cure of Souls (1928)
Answer to Job (1952)

EASTERN RELIGION

Psychological Commentaries on "The Tibetan Book of the Great Liberation" (1939/1954) and "The Tibetan Book of the Dead" (1935/1953)
Yoga and the West (1936)
Foreword to Suzuki's "Introduction to Zen Buddhism" (1939)
The Psychology of Eastern Meditation (1943)
The Holy Men of India: Introduction to Zimmer's "Der Weg zum Selbst" (1944)
Foreword to the "I Ching" (1950)

*12. PSYCHOLOGY AND ALCHEMY (1944)
Prefatory note to the English Edition ([1951?] added 1967)
Introduction to the Religious and Psychological Problems of Alchemy
Individual Dream Symbolism in Relation to Alchemy (1936)
Religious Ideas in Alchemy (1937)
Epilogue

†13. ALCHEMICAL STUDIES
Commentary on "The Secret of the Golden Flower" (1929)
The Visions of Zosimos (1938/1954)
Paracelsus as a Spiritual Phenomenon (1942)
The Spirit Mercurius (1943/1948)
The Philosophical Tree (1945/1954)

‡14. MYSTERIUM CONIUNCTIONIS (1955-56)

AN INQUIRY INTO THE SEPARATION AND SYNTHESIS OF PSYCHIC OPPOSITES IN ALCHEMY

The Components of the Coniunctio
The Paradoxa
The Personification of the Opposites
Rex and Regina

(continued)

* Published 1953; 2nd edn., completely revised, 1968. (270 illustrations.)
† Published 1968. (50 plates, 4 text figures.)
‡ Published 1963; 2nd edn., 1970. (10 plates.)

14. *(continued)*
Adam and Eve
The Conjunction

*15. THE SPIRIT IN MAN, ART, AND LITERATURE
Paracelsus (1929)
Paracelsus the Physician (1941)
Sigmund Freud in His Historical Setting (1932)
In Memory of Sigmund Freud (1939)
Richard Wilhelm: In Memoriam (1930)
On the Relation of Analytical Psychology to Poetry (1922)
Psychology and Literature (1930/1950)
"Ulysses": A Monologue (1932)
Picasso (1932)

†16. THE PRACTICE OF PSYCHOTHERAPY
GENERAL PROBLEMS OF PSYCHOTHERAPY
Principles of Practical Psychotherapy (1935)
What Is Psychotherapy? (1935)
Some Aspects of Modern Psychotherapy (1930)
The Aims of Psychotherapy (1931)
Problems of Modern Psychotherapy (1929)
Psychotherapy and a Philosophy of Life (1943)
Medicine and Psychotherapy (1945)
Psychotherapy Today (1945)
Fundamental Questions of Psychotherapy (1951)
SPECIFIC PROBLEMS OF PSYCHOTHERAPY
The Therapeutic Value of Abreaction (1921/1928)
The Practical Use of Dream-Analysis (1934)
The Psychology of the Transference (1946)
Appendix: The Realities of Practical Psychotherapy ([1937] added, 1966)

‡17. THE DEVELOPMENT OF PERSONALITY
Psychic Conflicts in a Child (1910/1946)
Introduction to Wickes's "Analyses der Kinderseele" (1927/1931)
Child Development and Education (1928)
Analytical Psychology and Education: Three Lectures (1926/1946)
The Gifted Child (1943)
The Significance of the Unconscious in Individual Education (1928)

* Published 1966.
† Published 1954; 2nd edn., revised and augmented, 1966. (13 illustrations.)
‡ Published 1954.

The Development of Personality (1934)
Marriage as a Psychological Relationship (1925)

*18. THE SYMBOLIC LIFE
Miscellaneous Writings

†19. GENERAL BIBLIOGRAPHY OF C. G. JUNG'S WRITINGS

†20. GENERAL INDEX TO THE COLLECTED WORKS

See also:

C. G. JUNG: LETTERS
Selected and edited by Gerhard Adler, in collaboration with Aniela Jaffé. Translations from the German by R.F.C. Hull.
VOL. 1: 1906–1950
VOL. 2: 1951–1961

THE FREUD/JUNG LETTERS
Edited by William McGuire, translated by Ralph Manheim and R.F.C. Hull

C. G. JUNG SPEAKING: Interviews and Encounters
Edited by William McGuire and R.F.C. Hull

C. G. JUNG: Word and Image
Edited by Aniela Jaffé

* Published 1976.
† Published 1979.

For Product Safety Concerns and Information please contact our
EU representative GPSR@taylorandfrancis.com Taylor & Francis
Verlag GmbH, Kaufingerstraße 24, 80331 München, Germany